THE WRITER AND THE TRAITOR

Also by Robert Verkaik:

The Traitor of Colditz
The Traitor of Arnhem

THE WRITER AND THE TRAITOR

Graham Greene, Kim Philby and the Great Betrayal

ROBERT VERKAIK

WELBECK

Copyright © Robert Verkaik 2026

The right of Robert Verkaik to be identified as the Author of the Work has been asserted by him in accordance with the Copyright, Designs and Patents Act 1988.

Material from Graham Greene's *Collected Essays*; *A Sort of Life*; *Ways of Escape*; *The Third Man* (all Vintage Classics); and *The Life of Graham Greene, Vol. 2* by Norman Sherry (Jonathan Cape) © Verdant Sàrl

First published in 2026 by Headline Welbeck Non-Fiction
An imprint of Headline Publishing Group Limited

1

Apart from any use permitted under UK copyright law, this publication may only be reproduced, stored, or transmitted, in any form, or by any means, with prior permission in writing of the publishers or, in the case of reprographic production, in accordance with the terms of licences issued by the Copyright Licensing Agency.

Cataloguing in Publication Data is available from the British Library

Hardback ISBN 978 1 0354 1817 6
Trade Paperback ISBN 978 1 0354 1855 8

Typeset in 11/16pt ITC Galliard Pro by Six Red Marbles UK, Thetford, Norfolk

Printed and bound in Great Britain by Clays Ltd, Elcograf S.p.A.

Headline's policy is to use papers that are natural, renewable and recyclable products and made from wood grown in well-managed forests and other controlled sources. The logging and manufacturing processes are expected to conform to the environmental regulations of the country of origin.

Headline Publishing Group Limited
An Hachette UK Company
Carmelite House
50 Victoria Embankment
London EC4Y 0DZ

The authorised representative in the EEA is Hachette Ireland,
8 Castlecourt Centre, Dublin 15, D15 XTP3, Ireland (email: info@hbgi.ie)

www.headline.co.uk
www.hachette.co.uk

For Max.

'If anybody ever tries to write a biography of me, how complicated they are going to find it and how misled they are going to be.'
Graham Greene[1]

'Some writers have recently spoken of me as a double agent, or even as a triple agent. If this is taken to mean that I was working with equal zeal for two or more sides at once, it is seriously misleading.'
Kim Philby[2]

'One's file, you know, is never quite complete: a case is never really closed, even after a century when all the participants are dead.'
From the screenplay of *The Third Man*.

Contents

	Introduction	ix
1.	The Great Betrayal	1
2.	The First Man	12
3.	The Confidential Agent	25
4.	The Vienna Circle	36
5.	War of Words	52
6.	Ace of Spies	59
7.	Ways of Escape	70
8.	Station Chief	82
9.	Philby's War	102
10.	The Heart of the Matter	114
11.	Mole Hunt	127
12.	Our Man in Greeneland	136
13.	Josef K and the Canaries	145
14.	Betrayal of Trust	153
15.	Island Agents	167
16.	Dramatic Pause	184
17.	Moscow Calling	202
18.	The Start of the Affair	218
19.	The Third Man	237
20.	Secrets in the Sewer	256
21.	The End of the Affair	265
	Epilogue: Final Curtain	307

Appendix: The Numbered Men	314
Acknowledgements	318
Bibliography	320
Notes	326
Index	357

Introduction

Desertion of Duty

As the clock ticked down to D-Day, the biggest amphibious invasion in military history, the atmosphere in the Central London offices of Britain's Secret Intelligence Service, MI6, reached feverish anticipation. Years of carefully calibrated deception, casting spells over the German generals defending the beaches and landing grounds earmarked for Operation Overlord, was to be finally put to the test. For the men and women of British intelligence it was the culmination of everything they had been working towards.

Failure was unimaginable. If the Germans discovered the destination of the Allied armada, tens of thousands of British, American and Commonwealth troops would be slaughtered on the Normandy beaches and the war would drag on for years. The difference between defeat or victory depended on Hitler believing the Allies' intended target was the Pas de Calais, 200 miles further down the coast.

Given such high stakes and high drama, it seems incredible that one British intelligence officer, someone who had been involved in the Double Cross campaign crucial to Operation Overlord, would walk out on the service before a single ship had set sail for France. Before a single bullet had been fired. And before victory had been assured.

On 2 June 1944, three MI6 counter-intelligence officers arranged to have lunch at the Café Royal, a short ten-minute walk across St James's Park from Ryder Street where MI6's formidable counter-intelligence department was based for the final years of the war.¹

Two of them were old Westminster School friends. Kim Philby, 32, swept-back brown hair and crooked teeth, deputy head of Section V. His charm was legendary – as one wife of a serving MI6 officer put it: 'It was impossible not to like Kim.'² When in a tight spot, his stammer was pronounced and he rolled his tongue around the inside of his cheeks. Tim Milne, 32, the sandy-haired nephew of *Winnie-the-Pooh* author A.A. Milne, had been a copywriter at a London advertising agency before the war.³ Philby had recruited Milne to MI6 to cultivate him as his loyal number two.⁴

The third officer was the oldest and much the tallest of the three. He had served as a head of station in West Africa and returned to be placed in charge of MI6's Portuguese desk in the months before D-Day. His name was Graham Greene, 39, known to the outside world as the author of thrillers and complex psychological studies of the human condition.

The three, by now seasoned spies, made a good team. Greene remembered fondly 'those long Sunday lunches at St Albans [where MI6's counter-intelligence section had been based before moving back to London in 1943] when the whole subsection relaxed under his [Kim Philby's] leadership for a few hours of heavy drinking and later the meetings over a pint on fire watching nights at the pub behind St James' Street [Red Lion in Crown Passage].'⁵

Philby and Milne were proud and protective of their most famous recruit. In turn, Greene was grateful to Philby and Milne for their loyal support during his troubled tour of duty in Sierra Leone and a damaging row with MI5 over an intelligence operation in the Portuguese-held islands of the Azores. MI6 (the Secret Intelligence Service) was concerned with intelligence gathering and counter-espionage abroad while MI5 had responsibility for home security. Philby had also recently bailed out Greene after he had

INTRODUCTION

been caught playing a prank on American intelligence officers who shared the MI6 offices in Ryder Street. Greene and Philby instinctively disliked their American colleagues, but the incident served as an early indicator of which country's intelligence agency would emerge after the war as the senior partner.

The three British intelligence officers gathered at the bar in the Café Royal, a temple of Bohemian dining in the interwar years. Greene told his MI6 colleagues that the lunch was his treat. Perhaps he hoped this act of generosity would help sweeten the bitter news he was about to deliver.

While they tucked into their food, Greene let his two friends into his secret – he intended to leave MI6 immediately. Greene made it plain his mind was made up and there was no budging him.[6] Philby and Milne were mystified and tried to persuade Greene to delay his decision until after D-Day.[7] Greene still refused to change his mind.

Greene's subsequent explanation for leaving MI6 on the eve of its greatest triumph, and with many agents run by him still in play in Portugal and the Azores, is not altogether convincing. He claims that he told Philby and Milne that he was not happy with his new responsibilities and that, although he didn't mind 'chivvying Portuguese on orders from above', he had no intention of personally doing so.[8] In 1967, Greene clarified this explanation, saying that his resignation was 'over a piece of office jobbery [office politics]'.[9]

A year later, when Greene wrote a contentious foreword to Philby's memoir *My Silent War*, he attempted to add substance but succeeded only in further muddying the waters:

'I moved out of MI6,' he explained, 'because Philby wanted to promote me and I didn't wish to be promoted and I also wished to get abroad if I could. I quite unjustly thought it was personal ambition on his part. He was moving up and I thought he was thinking of moving up his friends to guard his flanks, as it were, for personal reasons.'

Greene said he had not wanted to 'accept the promotion' because he regarded it as 'one tiny cog in the machinery of his [Philby's] intrigue', adding: 'I attributed it then to a personal drive for power, which I thought disagreeable. I am glad now that I was wrong. He was serving a cause and not himself . . .'[10]

The only trouble with Greene's explanation is that it cannot be true.

Tim Milne knew it and had been so disturbed by Greene's account that he finally took it up with him in 1977 when he was planning to write his own book of his time in the service. Milne said that as far as he could recall there were no office promotions at that time and certainly none concerning Philby. He wrote to Greene: 'I couldn't make sense of this – for one thing I had been head of VD [Iberian section] as early as September 1943 when Philby became VK [German section (K was for Kim)], after two years in which neither of us had any promotion.'[11] Milne was sure that in April, May and June 1944 there was no powerplay on Philby's part, while the previous year's office promotions had been a natural consequence of time served. Milne did recall the lunch at the Café Royal, but told Greene 'I don't remember any intrigue on behalf of Kim'.

Philby would soon begin scheming to take control of MI6's counter-communism section, perhaps the greatest Soviet intelligence coup of the Second World War. But that was all to come.

Replying to Milne's letter in 1977 Greene was unable to 'put his finger on any specific piece of evidence' to back up his insight into Philby's intrigues.[12] Milne archly concluded: 'Evidently he [Greene] saw more at that time with his novelist's eye than I did.'[13]

*

INTRODUCTION

Over the years, Greene variously attempted to justify his departure from MI6 at such a crucial juncture in the war, saying once that he really wanted to 'get abroad' before the end of the fighting.[14] This too is unconvincing as he elected to move from MI6 to the Foreign Office's Political Intelligence Department (PID) in Whitehall, the cover name for the black propaganda unit of the Political Warfare Executive (PWE), thus swapping one Whitehall desk job for another.[15] Greene claimed that the PID had promised him a frontline posting after the invasion. No such position ever materialised, and given the efforts he took to avoid a front-line call up at the start of the war, the idea that four years later Greene wanted to get closer to the action doesn't ring true.

The offer to Greene of a gentle promotion to lead the Iberian section was not part of a bigger intrigue on the part of Philby, as he later admitted. Writing to his biographer Norman Sherry on 23 April 1981, Greene now claimed there was another candidate for the post who he thought was much more suitable, and so 'I refused the promotion and resigned'. Greene's change of reason and false modesty only added to the mystery of his rushed departure.

Yet one former MI6 officer believed Greene's behaviour was completely understandable and went out of his way after the war to offer another rationale for his resignation. Kim Philby wrote to Norman Sherry from Moscow and suggested: 'I prefer to think that the human factor in his job had been on his mind for some time. Pretty well all the Portuguese [agents] who played around with the Germans were of humble status and wretchedly poor; probably courting trouble for a new pair of shoes and who could blame them? I could not think evil of them, and I'm sure that Graham, with his greater charity and understanding, could not either. I also think that the wider futility of his occupation bore hard on Graham. The war was virtually won, nothing that he could do would hasten the end and I had given him a pretext for cutting loose from a dreary and distasteful routine.'[16] Philby was bending over backwards to attribute a rationale for a seemingly inexplicable motive.

By invoking *The Human Factor*, Greene's book about the treachery of a Soviet mole working for MI6 who many have likened to Philby, Philby's reasoning for Greene's desertion looks like playful artifice. It begs a much more intriguing question: was Philby covering up for Greene because he knew the truth about the resignation only too well?

Some of Greene's biographers, notably Michael Shelden and Norman Sherry, have argued that the writer must have felt betrayed by Philby and believe that this is the true reason for his decision to quit the service at this pivotal moment in the war.

'It is hard to believe,' says Sherry, 'that Greene would resign on the eve of D-Day, the emotional and strategic climax of a long war without having a very important reason.'[17]

Philby admitted that while working with Greene in 1944 he handed over to the Russians the MI6 'purple primers' – detailed workings of the operations and agents of the Abwehr (Germany's military intelligence), including the unredacted names of some British agents – documents that Greene had proudly and painstakingly helped to compile.[18]

More significantly Philby had given the Russians the entire D-Day plans, jeopardising Operation Overlord should Stalin have decided to double cross the British and Americans at this critical juncture of the war.[19] Hugh Trevor-Roper, one of Greene's colleagues with Section V during the run-up to D-Day, said: 'If the Russians had thought they could win the war on their own we would have been butchered on the beaches.'[20]

Philby and Greene had worked together closely for 18 months. Greene was extraordinarily intuitive, with a razor-sharp ability to dissect character and divine geopolitical moments before anyone else, which meant he could read people and countries better than any other writer. He was also blessed from an early age with what he said was a 'gift of prescience', premonitions in which he said he foresaw the sinking of the Titanic[21] and the first doodlebugs arriving in London in 1944.[22]

Had he read Philby, had he had a premonition about his treachery? Had Philby given himself away? One of Philby's MI6 colleagues Charles Arnold-Baker, born in Berlin and christened Wolfgang Charles Werner von Blumenthal before changing his name when his English mother returned to the UK in the 1920s, claimed not to have been taken in by Philby. As an outsider, Arnold-Baker, who became a successful barrister after leaving MI6, saw through the Philby charm, describing his boss as really 'very, very nasty',[23] but not enough to suspect him of being a traitor, just duplicitous in his dealings in the office.

There were further grounds for suspicion.

After the war, a number of MI6 officers testified that they had found Philby's hostile treatment of Germany's spy chief Admiral Wilhelm Canaris baffling. Canaris was a key anti-Nazi figure who wanted to depose Hitler. Why was Philby suddenly so intransigent about Canaris and other anti-Nazi Germans who were reaching out to the Allies? It didn't make sense. Greene later admitted that his own role in the harassment of Admiral Canaris in Portugal, at Philby's behest, made him wonder whether Philby was using him as a pawn in the service of the Soviets. The German spy chief had been trying to cut a separate peace deal with the Allies that would have given America and Britain control of German forces and left Russia out in the cold. Canaris used his 1943 visits to Portugal, Greene's patch, to facilitate these contacts but Kim Philby instructed Greene to pass on details of Canaris' movements to the Portuguese secret police who made the German's stay very uncomfortable indeed.

Greene wondered whether Philby 'was smiling up his sleeve' at him: 'My telegrams had to be passed by Kim and he didn't prevent it and everyone knows *now* that Admiral Canaris was on our side. He was anti-Hitler. But there was talk on the German side of a separate peace which the Russians were very much afraid of. I wonder whether Kim knew this and was letting me harass him because the Russians feared a separate peace.'[24]

So could Greene have really been on to Philby in 1944?

Philby and Greene often discussed their shared left-wing views and dislike of America's shallow capitalism, although Philby was always careful not to profess any love of communist ideology.[25] Had Greene become suspicious of Philby's fake denunciation of communism in public knowing that he privately held pro-Russian sympathies? Is it then possible that Philby approached Greene with a view to recruiting him to the Soviet cause? Moscow had given Greene the codename 'LORAN' which suggests the Russian intelligence service had at least considered him as double agent material, possibly on the recommendation of Philby.[26] After all, Philby had tried in vain to recruit his old friend Tim Milne, an idea ultimately rejected by Moscow.[27]

Or could Greene have confronted Philby, confiding in him that he knew Philby was playing a double game but that because he valued their friendship more than loyalty to his country he had decided to walk away from the Service? Or had Greene become suspicious of what he later described as Philby's 'chilling certainty'[28] and only deserted MI6 to stop himself from being able to ask any more questions – and so relieve himself from having to do something about it?

In February 1948, nearly four years after resigning, Graham Greene arrived in Vienna to research a new film venture. The film was called *The Third Man*, a film noir that set the standard for modern spy cinema. The central character was Harry Lime, a double-crossing Cold War racketeer moulded on Kim Philby who

INTRODUCTION

as Greene knew had run refugees through the sewers of Vienna in 1934.

During his stay in the bombed-out Austrian capital, Greene encountered a mysterious Soviet double agent who helped him develop his plot. The Austrian spy's name was Peter 'Harry' Smolka who had worked as a Soviet mole inside the heart of the British government during the war. Now he was considering defecting to the West. Smolka and Greene had one close friend in common – Smolka had helped in the recruitment of Kim Philby to Russian intelligence before the war.

The film was peppered with anti-Russian references and, like a stick of Brighton rock, run through with treachery. What had Greene discovered about Philby during filming in Vienna? Had Greene's suspicions about his former MI6 colleague Kim Philby been borne out by Harry Smolka? And was *The Third Man* Greene's warning to the West about the traitor in its midst? Or was it a warning to his old friend that the MI5 spy catchers were hot on his trail?

Chapter 1

The Great Betrayal

Graham Greene was born into a middle-class family who ran a private boarding school in Berkhamsted, Hertfordshire.[1] Berkhamsted School, founded towards the end of the reign of Henry VIII, still dominates the town today and it continued to have a disturbing psychological hold on Graham Greene throughout his life.

Born in 1904, the fourth of six siblings, Graham shared a room with two of his brothers in a large house that served as the term-time dormitory for 40 boarders. Graham's father, Charles Greene, a grammar-school-educated Oxford graduate, had not intended to be a schoolmaster and had high hopes of becoming a barrister, but was persuaded to take up the teaching post at Berkhamsted, where he stayed for 39 years. The Greene children's day-to-day care was delegated to a series of live-in nurses and nannies organised by their mother who, in keeping with Edwardian custom, saw the children for half an hour at teatime every day.[2] When Graham was six years old, his father was elected Berkhamsted headmaster and became a much more distant figure to his young son.

It was a time of innocence before the conflagration of the Great War that would soon empty country towns like Berkhamsted of their young men, never to return from foreign fields.

Although the Greenes were spared personal tragedy, the war still left its imprint on the family and the school. Greene's older brother, Herbert, was called up to the Honourable Artillery

Company, although the fighting ended too soon for him to see action and he had to content himself with guarding German spies in the Tower of London.

Charles Greene denounced a German master as a spy because he had been seen under the railway bridge without a hat, a very un-British thing to do in those days.[3] A Dachshund was stoned in Berkhamsted High Street and there was an invasion scare when one of the Greenes' cars was commandeered by the army following false reports of a German army column advancing on London.[4]

At the end of the war, on Armistice Day, drunken soldiers broke into the school, inciting the pupils to riot and threatening to throw its headmaster into the canal. The next day at school prayers Charles Greene delivered a withering attack on the perpetrators, denouncing the soldiers as dangerous Bolsheviks.[5]

Such incidents only helped to stir up interest in Britain's military history among Berkhamsted's young boys, including Graham. The staple reading material in the Greene household was infused with romantic stories of Empire and military adventure. Among Graham's favourites were *Ivanhoe*, *Under Drake's Flag*, *With Wolfe in Canada* and *With Clive in India*. But it was H. Rider Haggard's *King Solomon's Mines*[6] that lay the foundations for his love of travel and John Buchan's *The Thirty-Nine Steps*[7] that introduced him to the thrilling world of international espionage. Reading, he said, had become his religion.[8]

In 1918, aged thirteen, Graham entered what he described as the 'grim portal'[9] to his senior education. In many ways he was an outsider, not helped by his tall gangly physical appearance and bulbous blue eyes encased in a big, round cannonball head.

Graham Greene was already a sensitive soul who did not make friends easily, announcing to his parents that he would no longer attend children's parties.[10] He did not inherit his father's sporting prowess and stood in awe of his brother Raymond's natural talent for cricket and rugby. Graham was excused games on account of his flat feet. Neither was the Officer Training Corps (OTC), the military wing of the private school that had prepared young subalterns for the Western Front, to his liking.[11] Greene felt contempt whenever he passed the 'sweating trudging ranks of the OTC singing a gloomy military song, "we're here because we're here, because we're here".'[12]

He much preferred the solipsistic hobbies of stamp collecting, cigarette cards and, of course, reading.[13] Graham had also developed a debilitating neurosis born out of a series of childhood maladies, including epilepsy,[14] and medical operations, which manifested itself in pathological fears of drowning, blood and, bizarrely, moths.

The brutality of the senior school affected Graham badly and he could never forget witnessing his father severely caning one of his friends for a nebulous transgression that was never explained to him. Graham's sensitivity meant he was also acutely aware of the school's social inequalities whereby the 'day boys' were made to stand up in class so that the full fee-paying pupils would know which scholarship children their parents had been subsidising.[15]

Then there were the quotidian indignities of daily school life – the constant 'odour of farts'[16] and the infernal banging of lavatory doors:

'I had left civilization behind and entered a savage country of strange customs and inexplicable cruelties: a country in which I was a foreigner and the suspect, quite literally a hunted creature, known to have dubious associates.'[17]

Yet the young Graham Greene demonstrated a remarkable maturity, taking an interest in women's rights and being critically influenced by the Marjorie Bowen novel *The Viper of Milan*, a work that he credited with sparking his interest in writing.[18] This historical novel is set in Renaissance Italy during the 14th century and concerns the corrupt and immoral scheming of

Visconti, Duke of Milan.[19] The book came at a critical moment in Greene's life and offered a narrative for a damaging experience that would have a profound influence on his ability and willingness to trust people for the rest of his life. In his memoir, *A Sort of Life*, Greene called this episode the 'great betrayal'.[20]

At Berkhamsted, Graham found himself in an invidious position, the son of the headmaster seeking the trust and friendship of his fellow pupils who all viewed him with suspicion: 'I was like the son of a quisling in a country under occupation.' His situation was not helped by the fact his elder brother Raymond was a school prefect – 'in other words one of Quisling's collaborators.'

Standing with the other pupils was his cousin, Ben Greene, who cultivated friendship and popularity by working directly against Raymond while Graham was 'surrounded by the forces of the resistance and yet I couldn't join them without betraying my father.'

Into Greene's troubled world stepped a very real Viper of Milan, a boy named Lionel Carter who falsely befriended Greene before executing a campaign of mental torture just as vicious and cruel as Bowen's monster. According to one of Greene's Berkhamsted contemporaries, Carter had 'pale red hair and a snake-like skull'. At the approach of his victims, he 'curled the lip and distended the lip'.[21] Greene said: 'Carter had an adult imagination, he could conceive the conflict of loyalties, loyalties to my age group, loyalties to my father and brother. The sneering nicknames are inserted like splinters under the nails.'[22]

Later Greene wrote: 'Unhappiness in a child accumulates because he sees no end to the dark tunnel. The 13 weeks of a term might just as well be 13 years. The unexpected never happens. Unhappiness is a daily routine. I imagine that a man condemned to a long prison sentence feels much the same.'[23] Greene's schooldays exacerbated his mental illness, later identified as manic depression (now called bipolar disorder), which saw him leave school for months of psychoanalysis treatment in London.

THE GREAT BETRAYAL

What Greene doesn't say is whether he succumbed to pressure to inform on his classmates. Although Carter was the instrument of his torture, Greene retained a strange admiration for his tormentor's 'ruthlessness' and in turn believed Carter respected Greene's stoic resistance.

Instead, it was Carter's accomplice, a boy he named 'Watson', on whom Greene vented all his hatred:

'Watson was one of my friends, and he deserted me for Carter,' recalled Greene in *A Sort of Life*. 'He had none of Carter's finesse – Carter continually tempted me with offers of friendship snatched away like a sweet, but leaving the impression that somewhere sometime the torture would end, while Watson imitated him only at a blundering unimaginative level. Alone he would have had no power to hurt. Nonetheless it was on Watson that I swore revenge, for with his defection my isolation had become almost complete.'[24]

Watson was in fact Augustus Wheeler, a boy who came from a military background; his father was dead, and his mother had sent him to boarding school.[25] It was Watson/Wheeler, Greene said, who was responsible for the 'great betrayal'.[26]

The misnaming of Wheeler by Greene in his memoirs was part of a well-honed literary device where the author used a close approximation to a real name to avoid libel proceedings and throw readers off the scent of any living witnesses to his life. Lionel Carter died shortly after the war, so no such precaution was necessary in his case.

Inevitably, Carter and Watson/Wheeler became characters, or parts of characters, in Graham Greene's books, and the 'great betrayal' was a theme to which he returned again and again.

Scarred by his school days, Graham Greene arrived at Balliol College, Oxford University, for the Michaelmas Term of 1922 to read history. Tormented by his demons, caught up in his introspection and even more serious about his writing, he did not mix well.

The writer Evelyn Waugh remembered: 'Graham Greene looked down on us (and perhaps all undergraduates) as childish and ostentatious. He certainly shared in none of our revelry.'[27]

Instead, Greene sought recreation in a new obsession – a quest for romance and he became embroiled in a series of infatuations and unrequited loves. Among his intended lovers were his tennis-playing cousin, a young nurse to his sister, and a waitress in the George pub in Oxford.

Then, in the autumn of 1923, he fell for a governess to his younger siblings Hugh and Elisabeth. Her name was Gwen Howell, and she was ten years his senior. Greene recalls how one day he saw her lying on the sandy beach, her skirt pulled up to show 'a long length of naked thigh. Suddenly at that moment I fell in love, body and mind.'[28]

Gwen was engaged to another man and dismissive of Greene's infatuation, although she happily flirted with him and even exchanged furtive kisses. After six months, it was time for her to leave the service of the Greene household at Berkhamsted. Graham was bereft. The incident triggered one of his great depressions, a debilitating illness that afflicted him all his life: 'I could take no aesthetic interest in any visual thing: staring at a sight that others assured me was beautiful I felt nothing. I was fixed, like a negative in a chemical bath.'[29]

The combination of his impossible love for Gwen Howell and his mental health issues led him to distraction through binge drinking and a dangerous game that has come to symbolise Greene's flawed psyche. Greene claims that he found a revolver in the cupboard of the bedroom he shared with his brother Raymond, who had been given the gun by a cousin who later died on the Western Front.[30] He described how he first came across the gun in *A Sort of Life*: 'The revolver was a small ladylike object with six chambers like a tiny egg-stand, and there was a cardboard box full of bullets. I never mentioned the discovery to my brother because I had realised the moment I saw the revolver the use I intended to make of it.'[31]

Greene wrote that his actions were inspired by a book he had read on White Russian officers who, exhausted by the drudgery and isolation of their postings in frozen Siberia, would invent ways to literally kill time: 'One man would slip a charge into a revolver and turn the chambers at random, and his companion would put the revolver to his head and pull the trigger. The chance, of course, was five to one in favour of life.'[32] Greene took his brother's revolver and resolved to take the Russians' cue 'to escape in one way or another'.

He later explained: 'Unhappy love, I suppose, has sometimes driven boys to suicide, but this was not suicide, whatever a coroner's jury might have said: it was a gamble with five chances to one against an inquest. The discovery that it was possible to enjoy again the visual world by risking its total loss was one I was bound to make sooner or later. I put the muzzle of the revolver into my right ear and pulled the trigger. There was a minute click, and looking down at the chamber I could see that the charge had moved into the firing position. I was out by one. I remember an extraordinary sense of jubilation, as if carnival lights had been switched on in a dark drab street. My heart knocked in its cage, and life contained an infinite number of possibilities ... This experience I repeated a number of times. Slowly the effect of the drug wore off – I lost the sense of jubilation, I began to receive from the experience only the crude kick of excitement. It was the difference between love and lust.'[33]

The veracity of this story has been questioned by Greene's biographers.[34] His mother rejected the idea behind the story while Raymond, the brother who owned the revolver, said there was no box of bullets. Even Greene's own versions of events were inconsistent. He changed his mind later in life to say he believed the bullets were blanks, meaning there was actually no jeopardy in the game.

To Greene, it didn't really matter whether his Russian roulette was an embellished truth or not. His interests had switched from romance to writing, and his death-wish dabbling with loaded pistols made very good copy for an aspiring poet. Greene drew on the incident in his 1925 poem 'Sensation', published in his first book of verse, *Babbling April*.[35]

'How we make our tumorous advances to death, by pulling the trigger of a revolver, which we already know to be empty.

Even as I do now.'

Greene's poetry was not universally appreciated, one critical review dismissing his verse as 'a diary of average adolescent moods'. His initial efforts at the longer prose form were equally unsuccessful and he failed to find a publisher for his first two novels.

Greene turned his literary hand to journalism: first on the *Nottingham Journal*, and then as a sub-editor on *The Times*, although he hadn't given up all hope for a career as a novelist. Neither had he completely given up on love, and on 15 October 1927, he combined the two by marrying Vivien Dayrell-Browning, who was secretary to the owner of Blackwells publishers, still thriving in Oxford today. The marriage cost him his atheism. A condition of his betrothal to Vivien was his conversion to Catholicism, a faith that tormented him throughout life.

Greene quickly acquired a literary agent and resumed his quest to become a published novelist. His first title was *The Man Within*, a story about smuggling and betrayal and a Freudian relationship between the protagonist and his deceased father, which was published in 1929 to polite applause and poor sales.[36]

Undaunted, and with a much-reduced advance, his fourth book was the hit he had been hoping for. *Stamboul Train*, upon which the film *Orient Express* was based, was partly set in Vienna and follows the fortunes of a Catholic communist planning a revolution in Belgrade. It confirms Greene's deep interest in communist politics at this time and launched his popular writing career, although the author's habit of basing his characters on real people very nearly forced the publishers to pulp the entire print run. A review copy had been sent to the writer J.B. Priestley, who recognised the bumbling faux-working class author on the train, Q.C. Savory, as himself and threatened to sue. Greene was taking revenge on Priestley who had critically reviewed *The Man Within*, describing it as 'too mannered'. Priestley and Greene shared the same publishers, Heinemann, and Priestley was more valuable to them than Greene.[37] Heinemann edited out Priestley's give-away characteristics from 13,000 copies of the book at a cost of £400 (£35,000 today), a fee that was directly passed on to Greene, keeping him in hock to his publishers until 1938.[38]

But Greene had found his audience, and he was now set on a road to literary stardom.

The 'Long Greenes', as the Charles Greene family became known (they were all tall and Graham, not even the tallest, stood 6ft 2ins) shared a strong sense of identity. They were proud cousins of *Treasure Island* author Robert Louis Stevenson. To be a Greene was to be something in the world. Hugh became Director General of the BBC, Raymond led an expedition up Mount Everest and Herbert, the black sheep of the family, carved out a name for himself as a 'spy' and double agent working for the Russians and the Japanese.

But the most famous Greene of all was Graham.

During his long career as an author Graham Greene wrote more than 26 novels, exploring the conflicting moral and political issues of the modern world. Even before the Second World War he was regarded as one of Britain's greatest authors with critically acclaimed works such as *Brighton Rock* and *The Power and Glory*. In the aftermath of the war, his novel *The Heart of the Matter*, based on his wartime service in Sierra Leone, and a year later, the release of the film *The Third Man*, won him even wider audiences and greater acclaim.

In 1951, Greene ran into Augustus Wheeler, his schoolboy betrayer and tormentor. Greene was reporting on the 'Malaya emergency', in which British forces were successfully combating an insurgency being waged by communist guerrillas. Greene had just returned from a three-day jungle patrol with the 2/7th Gurkha Rifles in Pahang and was visiting the shop of the Cold Storage Company in Kuala Lumpur. While Greene was choosing some whiskey for Christmas, a foxy-faced man with a small moustache approached him out of the blue: 'You are Greene?'[39] To which Greene replied that he was.

'My name's Watson [Wheeler] . . . we were at school together, don't you remember? We used to go around with a chap called Carter. The three of us. Why, you used to help me and Carter with our Latin prep.'

In the intervening years, Greene had spent many hours dreaming, imagining meeting Wheeler at a cocktail party or some other event and achieving his revenge by humiliating him in public. But when the moment of retribution arrived, all he was able to do was enquire about Watson/Wheeler's line of work.

'Customs and Excise. Do you play polo?'

'No,' replied Greene.

'Come along and see me play one evening . . . what inseparables we were – you me and old Carter.'

Wheeler told Greene that Carter had joined Cable and Wireless after the war, and had then died, although Wheeler didn't explain how.

Greene would never see Wheeler again, and so would never reach a reckoning with the classroom traitor.

'I wondered all the way back to my hotel whether I would ever have written a book had it not been for Watson and the dead Carter, if those years of humiliation had not given me an excessive desire to prove that I was good at something, however long the effort might prove. Was that a reason to be grateful to Watson or the reverse?'[40]

Greene later analysed his unhappy childhood, quoting the poet George 'AE' Russell: 'In the lost boyhood of Judas, Christ was betrayed.'[41]

It was during the Second World War, between his two most profitable writing spells, that Graham Greene was to suffer another 'great betrayal', by a friend working with him in the defence of the realm when Britain faced its darkest hour, and who also pretended to be on his side. Greene had made some kind of peace with his schoolboy tormentors and the treachery they perpetuated against him. But this second 'great betrayal' by Kim Philby was not so easily to be forgiven or forgotten.

Chapter 2

The First Man

Vienna was the jewel in the crown of the Hapsburg Empire – the city of Mozart, Beethoven and Strauss, of waltzes, Gustav Klimt, Art Nouveau and Sachertorte. But it kept a shameful secret.

Deep beneath the cobbled streets and elegant tramways of old Vienna millions of gallons of water rushed along a giant sewer system half as wide as the River Thames. These foul-smelling tunnels, inhabited by colonies of oversized rats, were the subterranean home to an underclass of vagabonds and petty criminals, or 'Strotters', who scratched a living from the debris fished out of the effluence and the pilfered pockets of the rich denizens who lived above. Disease and violence made it an ungovernable space, a no-go zone beyond the reach of the police.[1]

In 1934 the sewers served another function – they had become a vital network of escape lines for the communist fighters seeking refuge from the fascist overlords who had swept to power in Austria the year before. Hundreds of political refugees were secretly couriered beneath the city under the noses of the Austrian paramilitaries who vainly sent soldiers and dogs into the sewers to try to catch them. Through the dark, damp passageways, lines of brave resistance couriers and 'passeurs' led their human cargo to the ladders that stepped up to the open sewer covers dotted across the city, bypassing the army checkpoints. Among them was a young Cambridge University graduate who had arrived in Vienna on his powerful Brough motorbike and sidecar the year before in search of adventure and a political purpose.² His name was Harry 'Kim' Philby.

Five years earlier, in 1929, the Wall Street Crash had shaken the world economic system to its foundations, just three years after the 1926 General Strike in Britain. It left a profound impression on a troubled generation of young Britons and helped to create the conditions for the birth of a new political ideology. Fascism was not just a threat to the stability of continental Europe, it was being championed by elements of the British ruling class, including Philby's own father.

1929 was also the year that Kim Philby went up to Cambridge University to study economics.

Like many young men at Cambridge who were deeply affected by the economic depression that followed the Crash, Philby was a self-declared communist, bitterly opposed to fascism and concerned about the plight of the working class. 'Everybody,' said Philby, 'was talking and reading Marx'.³

And everyone knew Philby was a communist. Much later, confronting Philby with his treachery in Beirut in 1963, his close friend Nicholas Elliott told him: 'there was never any doubt in my mind of your communist views at Cambridge, any don at Trinity would tell one about that . . .'⁴

During his time at Cambridge, from 1929 to 1933, Philby had canvassed on behalf of local Labour candidates.⁵ But a British notion of socialism could never satisfy Philby's radical instincts for confronting fascism and creating a fairer system for the redistribution of wealth and property. Although how much Philby cared for the plight of the working class is debatable. His old school friend and MI6 colleague Tim Milne said Philby had always been a 'natural elitist.'⁶

Philby joined the Cambridge University Socialist Society, a hard Marxist group set up by his tutor Maurice Dobb, which advocated a workers' revolution. In 1932, Philby was the elected treasurer and fellow Cambridge spy Donald Maclean was on its committee.⁷

After Cambridge, the young Philby decided to find answers to these questions in the conflagration of ideologies facing off in Europe. He spent the summer visiting Germany, where he witnessed at close quarters the Nazi brutalisation of the Jews and other minorities. He had even placed himself in harm's way by refusing to stand aside when the Nazis tried to ransack a Jewish shop in Berlin.

When he arrived in Vienna in the late summer of 1933, Philby's only contact, supplied to him by Dobb, was the name of a political activist working for the Organisation for Aid to Revolutionaries, a pan-Europe communist support group backed by the Kremlin.

His offer of help was readily accepted and at a secret meeting of Vienna's communist underground, Philby was introduced to Lizy (Litzi)[8] Kohlmann, a strikingly vivacious 23-year-old divorcée who worked as a secretary in a law office.[9] The daughter of a Jewish owner of a Viennese publishing house, Lizy had briefly been married to an older man, a wealthy Austrian called Karl Friedmann, whom she wed when she was 19 and divorced one year later, although she kept his name.[10]

Philby, only 21 himself, was immediately drawn to the more experienced communist firebrand who had taken the young Englishman under her political wing. It seems the Cambridge graduate had much more to offer the communist cause than the other apprentice revolutionaries. Philby's father was the Arabist Harry St John Philby, who opposed British policy in the Middle East and who counted Winston Churchill and the British general Bernard Montgomery as personal friends. His only son Harold was born on New Year's Day 1912 in Ambala, the Punjab, where his father nicknamed him 'Kim' after the character in Rudyard Kipling's novel *Kim* because his first words were spoken in Punjabi. But of course Kipling's story unfolds against the backdrop of the Great Game, the political conflict between Russia and Britain in Central

Asia, and according to Stella Rimington, a former head of MI5 writing in a foreword to Graham Greene's *A Spy's Beside Book,* Kipling's Kim was the first modern spy.[11] Harry St John Philby cast a long shadow over his son. For a great deal of his childhood, Kim was abandoned to the care of his grandparents while his father travelled the world picking fights with colonial administrators. His father's volcanic temper and Kim's abandonment badly affected the young boy who developed a debilitating stammer.[12]

Kim followed his father to Westminster School and Cambridge, where his academic record was hampered by more hedonistic pursuits.[13] He rode his motorbike and sidecar around Cambridge going from pub to party.

Philby was the least academic[14] and yet, when it came to the dark art of subterfuge, the most gifted of the so-called Cambridge Five (spies recruited at Cambridge University by the Soviet Union in the 1930s): Kim Philby, Guy Burgess, Donald Maclean, Anthony Blunt and John Cairncross.[15] Rather than follow his father's political meddling in the Middle East, Kim, who spoke good German, sought to forge his own identity in the ideological conflict being waged in Austria.

In the company of Lizy, he was able to mix idealism with romance.

Lizy had chosen a dangerous political path and her communist activism had already attracted the attention of the authorities, who imprisoned her for a short spell.[16] Yet the Viennese police had failed to discover her ties to Moscow or her communist codename, 'Mary'. Lizy's recruiters were two Hungarian communists.[17] The first was Gabor Peter, a refugee from the dictatorship of the Hungarian fascist leader Admiral Horthy.[18] Gabor was physically unappealing – a hunchback with a thin ugly face who walked with a limp. But Lizy described him as 'a real Stalinist, a tough, ruthless and professional operator'.[19] The second was Teodor Maly, a lapsed Catholic priest and soldier who had been captured by the Russians in the First World War and then converted to communism. It was Maly who first recognised Philby's potential as a Soviet spy in those tumultuous months in Red Vienna.[20]

Philby had been greatly impressed by the old socialist government of Vienna, describing it as the 'finest in the world'.[21] One socialist writer, Edward Spiro (later E.H. Cookridge), who met Philby in Vienna at this time, said he greatly admired the Englishman's 'courage' in standing up to the fascists, but became suspicious of him when it became clear he was a 'communist courier' doing Stalin's bidding.[22] Cookridge identified a particular stratagem employed by Philby for insinuating himself into the heart of political groups – Philby listened attentively to others but rarely spoke himself. 'In a sense,' said Cookridge, 'he had already become "a third man"; self-effacing, secretive and fully dedicated to the danger, leading a double life in more ways than one.'[23]

For Lizy, the arrival of Kim Philby was an exciting and welcome distraction, and she described him as 'a very good-looking man' and 'a gentleman Marxist', which she found to be a unique and attractive combination. 'He stammered, sometimes more, sometimes less,' said Lizy. 'Like many people with a handicap he was very charming. We fell in love immediately.'[24]

Lizy had no hesitation of inviting Philby to billet with her family in central Vienna, where she was the head of the local communist council.[25] But there was precious little time to nurture their mutual attraction as the fighting was about to reach the streets of Vienna.[26] The Austro-fascist chancellor Engelbert Dollfuss, fearing the hand of Stalin, moved against his revolutionary opponents by imposing a ban on the Communist Party of Austria (KPÖ) and ordering his paramilitaries to crush the resistance. In Vienna the workers prepared to defend themselves in the fortified council accommodation blocks on the city's outskirts. It was a forlorn last stand that exposed the socialists' fatal lack of leadership and resources. Philby and Lizy Friedmann were ordered to take charge of a machine gun post at a key road junction in the city. The machine gun in question never materialised.[27]

Seizing the initiative, Dollfuss ordered the shelling of the workers' homes, killing hundreds of revolutionaries. The Soviet-directed communists could do little to prevent the inevitable defeat that was achieved in just four days of fighting. The revolution had failed and now it was a case of every revolutionary for themselves. Government sentry posts were strung out across the city and communists were ruthlessly hunted down and arrested. Escape lay in the newly built giant sewers that ran under the city.

One of the Kremlin agents, a Viennese journalist called Harry Smolka, agent 'ABO' and a childhood friend of Lizy Friedmann, had mapped out the evacuation. The year before Dollfuss set his paramilitaries against the people, Smolka had befriended one of the city's 'Strotters', who showed him how they used the sewers as a base for their nefarious activities in the streets above. From this encounter Smolka saw the potential of the underground tunnels as a pathway through the city, and he carefully drew up a detailed map of nearly 2,500 kilometres of subterranean tunnels.[28]

Hundreds of communist fighters and refugees evaded Dollfuss's soldiers and secret police by escaping through the city's labyrinthine sewer network.[29] Kim Philby and Lizy Friedmann, working with a communist unit in the Floridsdorf suburb,[30] were able to guide the desperate fugitives through the tunnels while Dollfuss's men were searching for them in the streets above.[31] Philby begged for clothes from his British contacts, telling the *Daily Telegraph* journalist Eric Gedye, 'I have six wounded men in the sewers in danger of the gallows.'[32]

Soon the time came to save themselves. Philby had already used his British passport to extract himself from a number of tricky situations in Vienna. Now he deployed it to help Lizy. The couple were married in a rushed ceremony in a Vienna town hall on 24 February,[33] witnessed by Hugh Gaitskell, the future leader of the Labour Party who had got to know Philby while on a Rockefeller scholarship attached to the University of Vienna.[34] Also in attendance was Viennese Jew Teddy Kollek, the future mayor of Jerusalem, who had been fighting the fascists alongside Kim and Lizy. He would later recall Philby's communist zeal.[35]

Now a bona fide British subject, Lizy was free to leave the country and accompany her husband to Britain. On the surface it looked like a desperate measure to evade Dollfuss's paramilitaries. But the couple's emergency nuptials were part of a well-prepared Soviet contingency plan.[36] Whether Philby knew it or not, he was being drawn into the Kremlin's orbit through his wife's work. Later, in a 1987 interview with Russian journalist Genrikh Borovik, Philby chose to frame this time with Lizy in more romantic terms: 'Even though the basis of our relationship was political to some extent, I truly loved her and she loved me. I did not want to leave her. Dollfuss had nipped social democracy in the bud, the only force that could have stood up to the Nazis in Austria.' MI5 later described Lizy somewhat differently: 'a woman, although an out and out communist, who enjoys good living and is certainly not the self-sacrificing type.'[37]

On 25 July 1934, Dollfuss was assassinated by a group of pro-Hitler Austrian Nazis, presaging the Anschluss four years later, wherein Austria was annexed by Germany.

The return to England of the son of a well-known British diplomat and his Austrian bride did not go unnoticed. A report of Kim Philby's adventures in the Austrian struggle appeared in *The Times* with a description of his marriage to Lizy as being one of political convenience.[38]

Philby had left other traces of his presence in Vienna. Before the fighting had started, he had been introduced to Edith Suschitzky, another Soviet agent of Jewish extraction, who had once been deported from Britain over allegations of fomenting revolution. Suschitzky first arrived in Britain in 1931 under the cover of her work as a freelance photographer, part of an advance guard of Kremlin-trained agents mostly drawn from the Austrian communist milieu. The following year when she was kicked out of Britain, Alex Tudor-Hart, who was working as a hospital doctor in the Midlands, went to Vienna, to bring her safely back to the UK, where the authorities failed to realise she was part of a Soviet penetration network.[39] Like Philby, Tudor-Hart returned to Britain full of communist fervour, happy to aid and abet his new wife, also married in the Austrian capital, in her political endeavours.[40]

In Britain, Suschitzky, slim with blue-grey eyes, had tried to remain inconspicuous by styling her hair in a fashionable London bob and wearing colourless horn-rimmed spectacles.[41] Yet she and a number of the other Austrian émigrés residing in London were already well known to the British authorities, who had taken a careful note of their communist links. As early as 1930, a Scotland Yard detective had picked up reports of Suschitzky's involvement in anti-capitalism rallies and her connections to known communist activists. The detective was Guy Liddell, a shrewd intelligence officer recruited by Scotland Yard to counter the Russian threat.

Liddell wanted to break up the group as quickly as possible, but when he passed on his concerns about Suschitzky to MI6 and requested background checks[42] in Vienna, he was told the SIS man had given her a clean bill of health: 'nothing on record that she has communist tendencies or come to the attention of the [Vienna] police. Like her parents she is a Social Democrat.'[43]

It took Liddell four more years, and a transfer to MI5, before he could amass enough of his own intelligence against Suschitzky to have her removed from the country. By then, MI5 had a much clearer picture of Suschitzky and her associates, including Maurice Dobb and

Alex Tudor-Hart who had both bitterly protested at her treatment at the hands of the British authorities. Intelligence unearthed about Tudor-Hart portrayed him as an anti-monarchist, reported for singing a song in a pub about turning Buckingham Palace into a 'gigantic latrine for the convenience of the proletariat'.[44]

When Mr and Mrs Tudor-Hart returned from Vienna to London, they picked up where they had left off with their communist associations. A Special Branch report of 16.8.1935 noted: 'Mrs Edith Tudor-Hart nee Suschitzky is a freelance photographer, she has been known to Special Branch as an extremist and an associate of leading members of the Communist Party of Great Britain since October 1930 when she came under notice as Edith Suschitzky'.[45]

What MI5, SIS and Special Branch had failed to grasp was that Suschitzky was not merely an 'extremist' but also a highly determined and resourceful agent of the NKVD, the Russian foreign secret service and forerunner of the KGB. None of the British reports had picked up on her links to her Kremlin handler, perhaps the most important communist agent to ever work in Britain.

Arnold Deutsch was a gifted intellectual and like many of the other members of the Vienna cell, of Jewish extraction. But Deutsch was a Jew in name only, having exchanged his religion for a zealous commitment to international communism.[46] Deutsch excelled at Vienna University in chemistry, psychology and philosophy, and at the age of 24 took a PHD with a distinction. Soon afterwards he began work as courier and then recruiter for the Kremlin. Like many Vienna academics of the 1930s, he was influenced by Sigmund Freud and the new sexual politics that blended Freud's teachings with Karl Marx. For Deutsch, sexual and political repression were two sides of the same coin.[47] Following his training in Moscow, Deutsch was set up by the OGPU, a forerunner to the NKVD and KGB, as an 'illegal' station chief working from his base in Paris under the alias Stefan Lange. When the Austrian crisis took off, he hastily moved to Vienna but left in 1934 to carry out an even more important mission for the Party.

Deutsch and his wife Josephine, a trained OGPU radio operator,[48] were told to make their home in Britain, where the left-wing intelligentsia had joined forces with the communists.[49] The Great Depression had left nearly 3 million people unemployed, although Britain's economic recovery in the mid-1930s averted any serious threat of revolution.

Nevertheless, the Communist Party of Great Britain summoned 'the workers of Britain to those tasks of organisation and struggle which are necessary to the overthrow of British capitalism. It does so in the knowledge that there is no other way out for the people of Britain. There are only two alternatives: Fascism, War, and Decay, or Revolution, Peace, and Socialism.'[50] Britain was also a world power and a committed enemy of Bolshevism. Its government had tried to strangle the Soviet communist state at birth, supporting the White Russians in the civil war against the revolution. The Soviets were not sure how long it would take to bring about a British workers' revolt, so Deutsch and the other 'illegals' were told to establish a network of agents capable of infiltrating the highest echelons of the British establishment. But first Deutsch needed to establish himself and his own network of Austrians at the heart of respectable British society. In May 1933, Deutsch had sent Harry Smolka, the Austrian journalist who had mapped out the Vienna sewer system, to Britain under the cover of employment as an Austrian journalist attached to the *Neu Freie Presse*, a leftwing newspaper that also employed Deutsch. Smolka was an experienced Russian agent who had undertaken espionage missions in France, where he had been expelled when he was caught by the French security service taking photographs of Fort St Jean, Marseilles.[51] In 1930, he made his first visit to London and immediately fell under the suspicion of

Special Branch for his communist links. Like Suschitzky, he was placed under close observation.[52]

Smolka had tried to pass himself off as an author, but it soon became clear he was more interested in fomenting revolution. A Special Branch agent reported that Smolka had attended a meeting of the Friends of India Society, a group committed to the overthrow of the Raj. Smolka, a risk-taking charismatic spy, had advertised his pro-Soviet sympathies by paying regular visits to Russia and writing pro-Russian articles in *The Times*. He had also made himself known to the local constabulary by racking up three speeding fines racing around London in his sports car.[53] By the end of 1930, MI5 had built up a large file on the flamboyant Smolka, who was described as 'somewhat arrogant with communist tendencies and a most unsatisfactory individual'.[54] The authors of this report concluded: 'Will continue to have him watched.'

Eventually, Smolka was caught taking photographs of London monuments and key Whitehall buildings.[55] This made his activities impossible to ignore, and on 25 March 1931, he was forced to leave the UK for Vienna. The head of MI5's counter-intelligence division, Oswald 'Jasper' Harker closed the file saying that, although he would retain Smolka's immigration card, he considered the Austrian communist to be 'no longer of interest to us'.[56] But on 7 May 1933, Smolka slipped back into the UK on a ferry that docked at the port of Folkestone on the Kent coast. He was now the London editor of the *Neu Freie Presse* with instructions from 'comrade' Deutsch to melt into British society.

Deutsch himself arrived in London the following year soon after the Austrian crisis had been decided in favour of the fascists. He had given the port authorities his real name and his occupation as 'university lecturer'.[57] He took a flat in Lawn Road, Hampstead, a popular area for London's artists and hard-line Marxist intelligentsia. Deutsch's next-door neighbour was Britain's greatest crime writer, Agatha Christie.[58] Another was Smolka, who had marked out the Lawn Road flats, a modernist apartment block, as an ideal location for the Deutsch cell of Austrian communist agents to base itself.[59] Not far away were Dr Alexander Tudor-Hart and Edith Suschitzky. Meanwhile the Philbys, impecunious after their escape from Vienna, were forced to set up home with Kim's parents in Kensington.[60] This was far from satisfactory as Philby's mother, Dora, disapproved of her son's marriage to a foreign divorcée almost as much as his new-found passion for international communism.[61] As soon as they could, Philby and his new bride moved out to 22 Glenross, Belsize Road, NW6, much closer to the Viennese communists.[62] During this period Smolka and his wife Lotte and the Philbys became close, often socialising together and visiting each other's homes.[63]

How far Philby had been brought into the Soviet fold while he was working with the communists in Austria remains unclear. But once back in London, Deutsch and Suschitzky had identified him as a prime candidate for recruitment. The Soviet agents tried to cover their communist tracks. Smolka became a British citizen and changed his name to Peter Smollett. Suschitzky separated from Alex Tudor-Hart and broke links with the British Communist Party.

Deutsch made contact with his British millionaire cousin Oscar, who owned a chain of Odeon cinemas, and applied to the Home Office to be allowed to use his training in industrial psychology to advise his relative on the siting of 100 new cinemas across the country.[64] In May 1936, the Deutsches welcomed their first child and shortly afterwards Arnold Deutsch arranged for his mother-in-law to join them,[65] reinforcing the impression that they were refugees who had chosen Britain as their permanent home to escape Austria's anti-semitism and openly fascist government.

Meanwhile, Edith Suschitzky joined Sun Studios, a thriving London photographers' studio based in Haverstock Road and Baker Street,[66] and had her work published in *The Listener*, *Picture Post* and *Lilliput*.[67] One of her practice subjects was Kim Philby, a portrait of whom she dearly held on to all her life. It was a photograph that would cause the Soviet cell in London much anxiety in the years to come: a dangerous clue to Philby's true political loyalties that would come back to haunt both Suschitzky and Philby. Philby's Cambridge colleague Anthony Blunt told MI5 after the war that Suschitzky was the grandmother of the group, whose early recruitment of Lizy Friedmann had set the ball rolling in the formation of the Austrian circle and the Cambridge Five.[68]

Having embedded themselves in the fabric of English society, Deutsch and his agents turned to the business of penetration of the highest echelons of the British state. It was at this point that he struck upon his brilliant analysis of the British class system. Deutsch realised that the Soviet task would be made much more effective by recruiting from members of the upper strata of society. Young men and women, undergraduates at Oxford and Cambridge, were the obvious targets for Deutsch's programme since these two universities almost exclusively serviced the senior ranks of the government, judiciary, military and other national institutions. It was a waste of time recruiting from the lower tiers of society from where there was little chance of advancing people to influential posts.[69] Among these left-leaning Oxbridge students targeted by the Russians was a British communist and journalist who was also Graham Greene's closest school friend and his loyal travelling companion.

Chapter 3

The Confidential Agent

Graham Greene's political awakening took place when he was at Oxford University and became drawn to the political tumult threatening to consume Europe. Like Kim Philby nine years later, Greene's chosen destination of agitation was Germany, although in 1924 the country was gripped by the economic woes of the Weimar Republic rather than the grisly horrors of Nazism. Adolf Hitler was still in prison on charges of treason after his failed coup d'etat the year before that had become known as the Munich Beer Hall Putsch.

Five years after the end of the First World War, the German people were still extracting themselves from the harsh terms imposed on them by the Allies at the Treaty of Versailles.

Greene, with an early nose for the epicentre of geopolitical tension, wrote to the German embassy in London suggesting that he should write a series of Germany-friendly articles to be published in the Oxford University magazine. He said he was particularly interested in the fate of the German inhabitants of the Ruhr still living under the occupation of a French army. Greene's offer was welcomed by the embassy, who treated it as an application to work as a freelance German spy. A senior diplomat, Albrecht von Bernstorff, was sent to meet Greene in his college rooms. Von Bernstorff had studied at Oxford as a Rhodes Scholar and was something of an Anglophile, and later would become a prominent anti-Nazi until his assassination by the SS in 1945. He presented Greene with £25 to fund his trip (£1,300 today) as well as diplomatic letters of introduction and instructions to spend his time spying on separatist activists in the Rhineland, rather than the Ruhr. The Germans were much more concerned about the Rhineland, also occupied by the French, because of strong local support for an independent breakaway state.[1] The 19-year-old Greene, showing remarkable cunning at such a young age, secretly wrote to a pro-French publication, funded by the Duke of Northumberland, with an alternative offer – to write France-friendly articles about the occupation. However, nothing came of the second limb of his plan.

Greene's easy association with duplicity seems to have stemmed from his Berkhamsted school days, when he had found himself isolated and viewed with deep suspicion by the other boys who bullied him for his imagined and sometimes real betrayals. Playing family, teachers and pupils off against each other had become second nature to Greene in the game of adolescent survival.

In the summer of 1924, Greene took a break from his studies and set off for Germany with his old school friend Claud Cockburn, a cousin of Evelyn Waugh, and Greene's own cousin Tooter Greene, who spoke fluent German.[2] It was Cockburn who later came to the attention of Deutsch's Red Vienna circle in London.

The trio of amateur English spies, using their youth as cover, arrived in the Rhineland and dutifully reported to the German foreign office anything they thought would interest their spymasters about the French and any German 'collaborators' they were able to point a finger at.[3] When Greene got back to England, he wrote two articles decrying the behaviour of the French soldiers and upholding the German state's right to take back control of both the Ruhr and the Rhineland. Still holding out the hope of being employed as a 'double agent', Greene also contacted the French embassy to offer his propaganda services. Again, nothing came of it. In the summer of 1924, international diplomacy intervened to curtail his career as an agent of influence when the Allies agreed to negotiate a reduction in First World War reparations and, more critically, the removal of all occupying forces from the Ruhr.

Greene later remarked of his first dabbling in espionage: 'Today I would have scruples about the purpose I served, but at that age I was ready to be mercenary in any cause so long as I were paid with excitement and a little risk.'[4]

Greene demonstrated his early promise as an astute political commentator on world events by using one of the articles to write about the brewing resentments of 1920s' Germany and declaring that 'unless things change there will be another war in 20 years'.[5] This uncanny ability to be in the right place at the right time and to divine the significance of what he was witnessing lent his writing an extraordinary prophetic quality.

During his mission to Germany, Greene, like Philby a decade later, encountered the reality of communism, although he was still naive as to the authoritarianism of the ideology in practice.

The Moscow-backed Comintern had resolved at its Second Congress in 1920 to 'struggle by all available means, including armed force, for the overthrow of the international bourgeoisie and the creation of an international soviet republic as a transition stage to the complete abolition of the state'.

Germany was identified by the Soviets as the Central European country most likely to fall to revolution. The Communist Party of Germany had a military wing that had tried to seize power by violent uprising in 1921. A second attempt was made at the time of the Ruhr crisis and then again in other parts of Germany just before Greene arrived in the country on his spying mission. The Red Army was mobilised, ready to come to the aid of a planned insurrection. It was only resolute action by the German government that thwarted the coup. In Hamburg, 200 to 300 communists attacked police stations, but they were quickly defeated.

*

When Greene returned from Germany he immediately joined the Communist Party of Oxford University in 1925, telling one of his Oxford friends who challenged him about his membership: 'Well, I think it's the only future.'[6] So did Claud Cockburn, who would turn out to be a staunch supporter of the Russian state and of interest to MI5 during the Second World War. Greene later described Cockburn as 'the greatest journalist of the 20th century', while US senator Joe McCarthy said he was one of the 'world's most dangerous reds'.[7] In 1939, Cockburn was a leading British Communist Party member and was even said to be a leader of the Comintern in Western Europe.[8]

Many years later, under intense questioning by MI5 in 1951, Kim Philby tried to throw Cockburn to the wolves by claiming he was dangerously close to Guy Burgess.[9] This was half true and Cockburn's name appears in many MI5 files concerned with the Vienna Circle and the Cambridge Five.[10] But Cockburn, who was more patriotic than he was political, never signed up to Stalin's brand of communism.

How much his friend Graham Greene was committed to the ideals of the Communist International (Comintern) has been a subject of much debate and controversy. Greene's short membership of the Party caused him considerable trouble later in his life.

After securing their communist credentials, Greene and Cockburn sent themselves to the Paris headquarters of the Comintern in January 1925,[11] where they were shown and read messages from other member branches. Greene said he endured the tedium of this communist bureaucracy in the hope that the Paris group would pass them on to Moscow and into the heart of the newly founded Soviet empire, where he hoped for more excitement. But after a month his party membership was cancelled either because Greene had been rumbled as a 'double agent' or because he himself had lost interest in the idea of breaking into the citadel of international communism.[12]

Greene took his first serious steps towards mainstream left-wing politics when he joined the Independent Labour Party (ILP), a radical version of the party, whose membership included his first cousin Ben Greene.

Greene harboured a lingering sense of shame over his failure to support the General Strike when he was working as a sub-editor for *The Times* and had volunteered to get the paper out in the face of the industrial action. Now he wanted to make amends by playing a leading role in a workers' party by setting up an Oxford branch of the ILP.[13] He declared: 'The growth of fascism, the new Unemployment Bill, the police repression, all call for action.'[14] With one eye on good copy, Greene hoped his branch would bring him into contact with Oswald Mosley's fascist blackshirts who were whipping up a race hate war in London. But the ILP leadership, which had established the International Revolutionary Marxist Centre, was more concerned with fighting the mother Labour Party from which it successfully broke away in 1932, sending five ILP MPs to Parliament.

So Greene set his sights on a return to Germany, where he wanted to see for himself how fascism had taken such a tight grip of the Prussian proletariat. Arriving in Berlin in 1934, when Philby was fighting fascist forces in Vienna, Greene stayed with his brother Hugh, a journalist on the *Daily Telegraph*, and was reunited with his spy sponsor Albrecht von Bernstorff. Greene was appalled how the country he last visited ten years ago had been transformed into the Nazi state with swastikas stamped on every public building and ordinary Berliners greeting each other with Sieg Heils on street corners. This was the same abhorrence experienced by Kim Philby after he had witnessed the city's rabid descent into anti-semitism the year before.

Greene's exposure to Nazism had drawn him into the orbit of Soviet Russia, which he judged to be a counter to the threat of fascism. He had recently met a mysterious White Russian refugee, Moura Budberg, at a London cocktail party, and she had suggested to him a trip to her family estates in Estonia, which she offered as a jumping-off point for a possible visit to Moscow, the city he had tried to reach in 1925 with Cockburn. Budberg, a one-time girlfriend of H.G. Wells, was not what she seemed, and MI5 suspected her of being one of Stalin's spies as she retained unusually close ties to the Russian embassy in London.[15] Greene had also sought assistance for this part of his trip from the Cambridge University journalist Malcolm Muggeridge, who was so enthralled by communism he had moved his family to Moscow. Muggeridge was regularly commissioned by Greene to write for the magazine *Night and Day* that Greene now edited. Greene saw in Muggeridge a kindred spirit whose ambitions to be a novelist had also been initially torpedoed by libel threats until he successfully published *Winter in Moscow* (1934), in which he described his Damascene re-evaluation of Russia and the reality of life in a 'socialist utopia'.

On Greene's flight from Riga to Tallinn there was only one other passenger. Peter Leslie had been a vicar in the East End of London, an Army chaplain in the First World War and then an arms dealer. Along the way he had converted to Catholicism, joined British intelligence and was now the head of the MI6 station in Estonia, the front-line against an emboldened Soviet Union.[16]

The two men hit it off when Greene noticed Leslie reading a copy of Henry James's *The Ambassadors*. Leslie, who confided in Greene about his secret role in Tallinn, became the author's street guide to the Soviet spy machine that had taken root in the city. It was Leslie who revealed to Greene the West's muted response to the Soviet threat to the West. British intelligence kept a constant vigil but could do little to stop NKVD men hunting down White Russians who had exported their wealth to the Baltic states, from where they plotted the downfall of the Bolsheviks from its Western borders.

Greene's association with Leslie was the first of many encounters with British secret agents during his parallel careers as a spy and author. His Baltic adventure had introduced Greene to Soviet espionage long before the Cold War and directly informed his satirical spy classic *Our Man in Havana*, which he had originally set in Tallinn. The city also allowed Greene to explore one of his other fascinations – prostitution – and he spent his evenings in the Estonian capital vainly searching for a 300-year-old brothel recommended to him by Moura Budberg for its architectural splendour.[17]

In a change of tack, Greene next left Europe in search of African adventure (inspired by *King Solomon's Mines* and partly driven by his intense fear of boredom) and better material for his books. He arrived in Liberia in 1935 on an uncharted exploration of the backcountry. Greene had secured financial support for a fact-finding mission from the anti-slavery movement, as well as political interest from the Foreign Secretary Sir John Simon, who recognised the country's importance in the interwar colonial scramble for Africa. The party sailed first to neighbouring Sierra Leone, from where they set off into the African bush.

Mirroring his German adventure, Greene immediately betrayed his British sponsors by offering his services to the French Colonial Office.[18] His proposal to write a separate report in line with French colonial policy was not taken up, but it is further evidence of a love for duplicity.

The resulting book, *Journey Without Maps*, was a critical success although once again Greene had been unable to resist the urge to write real people into his story. In describing a 'loudmouth drunk' official he encountered in Sierra Leone, Greene hadn't even bothered to change his name. The official, a medical doctor called P.D. Oakley, recognised himself and instigated legal action, although Greene unconvincingly argued the name, P.A. Oakley, was completely invented. Fortunately, only 200 copies had been printed and Greene agreed to rewrite the character before the full print run. Greene's creative process relied on basing characters on real people, but he soon learnt the lesson of changing their names and he always publicly denied any real-life connection.[19]

Upon his return to Britain, Greene entertained himself and readers as the film critic of the *Spectator*, involving himself with a creative format that had always fascinated him, even more so when his novels *Stamboul Train* and *Gun for Sale* were made into successful films. The experience gave him the confidence to branch out as a film script writer. In 1936, he worked on *The First and the Last*, a story by John Galworthy. It was during the treatment of this picture that Greene encountered the film producer Alexander Korda, who had helped to secure lead parts for Vivenne Leigh and Laurence Olivier. The film suffered a number of severe edits and major reshoots and was finally released in 1940 by a different studio and under a different name, *21 Days*. Greene strongly objected to the cuts and gave it a poor review in the *Spectator*.[20]

Yet this was the start of a close and rather mysterious relationship with Korda, a Hungarian Jew who had been a prolific and successful producer of silent films in his troubled home country. In 1919, the Hungarian government was replaced by a short-lived Soviet Republic. It lasted just four months before far-right forces led by Admiral Miklós Horthy overthrew the communist government in a violent counter-revolution. During this so-called White Terror, tens of thousands were executed. Some 2,500 Jews, who were targeted as 'traitors and communists', were massacred in 1919 and 1921.

In October 1919, Korda, who had made five films supported and funded by the newly founded Soviet Republic, was arrested by the far-right militias and forced to leave Hungary for Austria. In Vienna, he continued making successful films before moving to Hollywood and then London, where he established himself with the huge hit *The Private Life of Henry VIII* (1933), which he also directed. He was naturalised as a British citizen in 1936, the same year he founded Denham Film Studios, Europe's biggest film studios located in 165 bucolic acres of a sprawling Buckinghamshire estate.

During this time, Graham Greene was a frequent visitor to Denham, where he became close to Korda, who commissioned the author to write more film scripts. But Korda was not simply a film mogul. He was also an Anglophile who, after his experiences in Hungary, recognised the importance of the British Empire as a bulwark against the rise of both fascism and communism.

The location for Korda's film studios and his London Film Company was no accident.[21] Denham was conveniently close to the home of Sir Robert Vansittart, head of the Foreign Office and resolute anti-appeaser of Adolf Hitler. Vansittart and Korda saw eye to eye on the threat from fascist Germany and Vansittart helped to arrange the financing of Korda's London Film Company.

Vansittart was not a typical Whitehall mandarin and retained strong links to MI5 and MI6.[22] One of his closest contacts was Claude Dansey, an irascible, ageing eminence grise of British intelligence who had run double agents in the First World War. Dansey had just been put in charge of a shadow counter-intelligence agency separate to SIS called Organisation Z, which specialised in the recruitment of businessmen agents.[23] Dansey and Z worked out of offices in Bush House on the Aldwych, and came into their own after the Venlo debacle at the start of the Second World War, which had wiped out most of SIS's operations on the continent. Vansittart joined forces with Dansey and they began beefing up their own private intelligence gathering operations in Europe. One of their first recruits was Nicholas Elliott, who would later work closely with Kim Philby.

The London Film Company was used by Dansey and Vansittart as a conduit for their international espionage missions – the wide distribution network gave cover to their agents and couriers.

Greene's own experience as an 'agent' in Germany and his contacts with the Communist Party, combined with his willingness to travel to the most dangerous parts of the world, made him an ideal candidate for 'Z'.[24]

Greene is characteristically silent about his dealings with this side of Korda's enterprise. Korda employed Greene as a script writer on a flexible contract that paid him handsomely for his film ideas.[25] It was a relationship that endured until Korda's death and culminated with the release of their best-known collaboration, *The Third Man,* a film set in a post-war Vienna caught between the forces of communism and the West.

Aside from Graham, the Greene family was steeped in espionage. His uncle Sir William Graham Greene had been Permanent Secretary to the Board of the Admiralty and had been instrumental in setting up the Naval Intelligence department. He continued to work with the intelligence services in the interwar period and was an unofficial adviser to the government during the Second World War. Graham's elder brother had a rather less distinguished career as a spy. Herbert Greene also had ambitions to be a novelist, but he very soon ran out of money and came close to bankruptcy. He spun fantasies about his life while sponging off his brothers and sisters.

In 1934, Herbert offered his services as a spy to the Russian embassy, but he was turned down.[26] The Soviet residency in London must have smelt a rat, and in any case they were running far too sophisticated an operation to take any risks with a dubious and opportunist character like Herbert. Moreover, they had a surfeit of vetted and field-tested spies including Kim Philby. So Herbert redirected his offer to the Japanese, who were far less discerning about their British agents, and he began working as a spy for Japanese intelligence, passing on 'secrets' about the American navy to the Japanese naval attaché Orata Oka (also known as Ichitaro Takata) who paid him generously.[27] Codenamed MIDORIKAWA,

Herbert Greene spent more than two years in the employ of the Japanese, receiving his instructions from Oka in correspondence signed 'Arthur' and addressed to Greene at Claridge's Hotel in London.[28]

Oka was particularly keen for Greene to head a propaganda campaign against the Americans by placing articles in the media.[29] Such an operation, Greene told Oka, required financing, but when the Japanese made clear they only had a small budget and wanted a sample of what Greene could offer in terms of a media presence, he decided to look for new paymasters.

On 16 January 1937, Herbert left Newhaven for Spain as a member of a team of ambulance drivers working for the Joint Committee for Spanish Relief. According to an MI5 report, his sister Elisabeth, who had recently been taken on by the Secret Intelligence Service, had helped her brother to find work in Spain.[30] It was the second year of the Spanish Civil War and the conflict had attracted young men from Britain to join the international brigades of the Republican and communist forces.[31]

Graham Greene had also responded to the call. He wanted to fly to Bilbao, where the Basques, supported by the Republicans, were holding out against Franco's forces laying siege to the city. Greene intended to report for the BBC on what he witnessed. However, his plans were frustrated when he couldn't find a pilot willing to brave Franco's anti-aircraft guns. Greene got no further than Toulouse. Perhaps his heart wasn't in it – as much as Greene despised the fascists, he could hardly support the Republicans, who were anti-Catholic and had instigated killings of the clergy who sided with Franco.

Chapter 4

The Vienna Circle

Kim Philby's time in Austria helping the communist cause took place outside the gaze of the British security and intelligence services. Even the Austrian police appear to have been hopelessly ill-informed about the communist groups at work in Vienna.[1] So during Philby's stay in the Austrian capital, when Suschitzky, Deutsch, Smolka and Lizy Friedmann were all active in communist circles, there was no trace of the Cambridge graduate being drawn into the orbit of the NKVD. Instead, we have to rely on Philby's own versions of his recruitment to the Russian intelligence service. In his book *My Silent War*, Philby says almost nothing about this process and mentions no NKVD agents at this time. But in January 2025, Philby's partial confession made to SIS officer Nicholas Elliott in Beirut in 1963 was released to the National Archives in London.[2]

It is the first genuine insight into the mind of Philby and his dealing with the Soviets during his recruitment and early years working for them. It is dated 11.1.1963 and begins with Philby declaring that the events he is describing 'occurred a long time ago and cannot therefore be taken as 100 percent accurate . . .'

Such an opening statement is in keeping with the character of a man who built several careers through disciplined ambiguity and self-serving imprecision. Philby claimed to Elliott that it was his wife Lizy who put him in contact with Arnold Deutsch, who he only knew as 'Otto'. Lizy, says Philby, arranged for Deutsch to meet Philby in Regent's Park on 21 June 1934.

'Otto,' Philby said, 'spoke at great length, arguing that a person with my family background and abilities could do far more for communism than the run of the mill party member sympathiser. In short, he proposed that I should work for an organisation which I was able to identify later as the OGPU.'[3]

This may be true, but Philby was careful to say no more about Deutsch than was already known to MI5. A deeper understanding of Philby's recruitment and what the Russians thought of him can be found in a report written by Deutsch's boss, Ignatz Reif, codenamed Mar(r). Reif, who had been in Vienna at the same time as Philby,[4] sent his report to Moscow the day after Philby and Deutsch met in Regent's Park.[5] It reveals that it was Reif who authorised Philby's employment, and it was Reif who codenamed Philby 'Sonchen' ('Sonny') in recognition of the fact that he was the son of St John Philby, the then famous diplomat and Arabist who was of much greater interest to the Kremlin.

And rather than Lizy, it was Edith Suschitzky, now the respectable Mrs Tudor-Hart, who had arranged his final introductions. Reif told the Centre, the headquarters of the NKVD in Moscow: 'Through Edith whom you know and who worked at one time for Siegmund in Vienna we established that an Austrian Party member with recommendations from Viennese comrades to "Edith" arrived on the island with her English husband from Vienna. She is also known to Arnold. Edith checked the recommendations and got confirmation from all our Viennese friends . . . Sonchen was never a member of the party and tried to hide his sympathies for the Party since he was planning a diplomatic career after Cambridge. Edith's references on Sonchen are highly positive.'[6]

Reif's Moscow report shows how important Edith was to the Deutsch network. She had extensive contacts in British society and was involved in Soviet recruitment while helping facilitate relations between the Communist Party of Great Britain and the Soviet embassy in London.

Reif concluded: 'I decided to recruit the fellow without delay (of course not for the organs directly, it's too soon for that) for anti-fascist work. Sonchen was supposed to take over his father's apartment and his wife would stay with Edith temporarily. Arnold and Edith and I developed a plan for Arnold to meet Sonchen before Sonchen and his wife moved into his father's apartment. I knew about the colossal role played by the father [in the Middle East] with Ibn-Saud . . .

'It turns out that Sonchen's sympathy for the party comes from the Socialist Club at Cambridge University, that the sons of many important Anglo functionaries sympathise with the club and did work for it. We will have the list of their names soon.'[7]

Philby and Lizy had only been in London three weeks and yet Moscow was already well on the way to recruiting the son of a famous British diplomat, which strongly suggests that the process had begun in Vienna. There was also a renewed urgency in Moscow, where the Centre was planning 'affirmative measures' against hostile countries like Britain. In July 1934, the OGPU was folded into the NKVD, an all-powerful agency that answered directly to Stalin, and embarked on a ruthless repression of its own people, committing atrocities across Russia and its satellite states in what became known as the Great Terror. The NKVD later directed the counter-intelligence operations of the Second World War.

In the pre-war years, the Kremlin instructed its network of 'illegals' based in Europe to penetrate deep into their enemies' state apparatus. Deutsch told Philby that, in order to cover his tracks and avoid suspicion, he must cut off all ties with his communist friends and all connections with the Party. That included separating from Lizy, by then a known communist. It was fortunate that Philby's attempts to join the Communist Party of Great Britain had been rebuffed by a member who had taken against middle-class Oxbridge types. This was the first and only time his class counted against him.

Philby's maiden 'mission' for his NKVD bosses was also a test of his loyalty to the Soviet cause. Moscow firmly believed that St John Philby must be a British spy whose influence in the Middle East was being used to further British interests. This conviction had been fuelled by the way that, aided by St John, Ibn Saud had become the dominant figure in Arabia, founding the Kingdom of Saudi Arabia in 1932.[8] Kim Philby was told to write to his father to convince him that he was no longer interested in communism. Having reclaimed a place in his father's affections, Kim was ordered to burgle the family's Kensington home, copy St John's private papers, then hand them to Deutsch.[9] Philby carried out the task without question, confirming his lifelong willingness to put Party before family, lovers, friends and country.

Once Philby had passed this test, Deutsch began schooling him in the art of spycraft.

When it came to security, Deutsch took no chances, meeting in Central London parks and busy cafés and pubs in Ealing, Acton and Park Royal.[10] Meetings were only to be arranged in person and the arrangements never written down. Philby was always to catch three taxis before arriving at a rendezvous and watches were synchronised with the public clock located at or near the chosen location.[11]

Having satisfied themselves of Philby's loyalty, diligence and obedience, the Centre asked Deutsch and Reif to deliver a list of acquaintances who might be traitor material.

Philby readily admitted to Nicholas Elliott in Beirut in 1963 that he had named more than six candidates. The six he could recall, or chose to recall, were: 'Donald Maclean, Guy Burgess, Stott, Stevens, David Guest, Tom [sic, his first name was Fred] Pateman . . . and others whom I have now forgotten.'[12]

Donald Maclean and Guy Burgess are two well-known

members of the Cambridge Five. The four other men appearing on his list were Denis Stott, a distinguished child psychologist, Wilfred Leslie Stevens, a government statistician, Fred Pateman, reporter and editor for the *Daily Worker*, and David Guest, the leader of a communist group who died fighting the fascists in Spain in 1938.

The list was one of many drawn up for the London 'residenzia' (the word used for the NKVD officers working out of the Russian embassy) that fatally undermines the notion that there were only five Cambridge spies.

In July 1934, another of the Austrian communists arrived in London, instructed by Moscow to engage with their important new recruit and the new opportunities for adding to the group.

Philby knew him only as Big Bill, a 'bull of a man who struck me as being quite ruthless.'[13] His real name was Alexander Orlov, a Russian spymaster senior to both Reif and Deutsch. Orlov operated under the cover of an American refrigerator salesman with offices in Regent Street.[14] His sudden arrival in London indicated how seriously the Russians were treating the Philby breakthrough.

Orlov's first task was to make an assessment of Philby's list of recruits. Philby told Elliott: 'A few weeks after I presented the list, Otto [Deutsch] turned up at a rendezvous with a senior official whom he introduced as Big Bill.' Philby immediately warmed to Orlov, who he said possessed 'a good sense of humour, and was always very pleasant with me.'[15] Philby recalled: 'Big Bill went over my list with me, concentrating finally on Donald and Guy. We had several meetings to discuss their potentialities. I was in favour of recruiting Donald, but entered strong reservations with regard to Guy, on the grounds of his unreliability and indiscretion. Finally, Big Bill instructed me to approach Donald, which I did.'

Philby claims that after contacting Maclean he 'passed out of my life,' adding 'although the OGPU officers constantly asked me to keep an eye open for potential recruits, Guy and Donald were the only two whom I actually recruited. I think this was deliberate policy on their part as they did not want to put too many eggs into my basket. In any case, my instructions were to have no contact with communists, so that my access to likely material was strictly limited – in fact, virtually non-existent.'[16] This is a very carefully crafted element of Philby's 1963 'confession'. There is plenty of evidence to show that Philby continued to suggest potential new recruits throughout his service to the Kremlin.[17]

After overseeing the selection programme, Orlov left London. He had been in Britain for just ten days and would not return until September later that year.[18] Deutsch and Reif were left in charge of running the British agents, an extraordinarily sophisticated spy network, perhaps the most successful ever assembled. They soon added two more Cambridge men, Anthony Blunt and John Cairncross, to the group, completing the so-called 'Magnificent Five'. In this role Deutsch was the mastermind, combining psychological profiling with human warmth and intellectual acumen. Above all, Deutsch treated the British men as Party comrades first and agents second.[19]

Deutsch is reported to have recruited 20 spies[20] and was in contact with a network of 29.[21] Under the strict NKVD rules of the separation of agents, Reif may have been involved with a similar number.

Towards the end of 1934, Deutsch suggested that Harry Smolka, the Austrian journalist who had lowered his profile after his early political activism in London and a spate of speeding fines, should establish an international news agency with Kim Philby. It would both give the Russians an influence over propaganda and serve as international cover for their spying. Seemingly confident of his place in British society, Smolka openly wrote to the Home Office asking permission to set up a 'London Continental News with a British colleague of mine H.A.R. Philby.'[22]

The Home Office, who cannot have consulted MI5 about Smolka, replied saying they had no objection to Smolka's involvement in the venture, but the application created a dangerous paper trail that would cause Philby severe difficulties during the war.

This uncharacteristic lapse of security by putting Philby and Smolka's relationship on the public record was followed by an even more serious one. Among the Deutsch and Reif recruits was a British agent Percy Glading, a well-known communist at the centre of a NKVD group, some of whom had worked at an armament factory at the Woolwich Arsenal in London and were passing on secrets to the Russians. It proved impossible to keep such industrial-scale espionage secret from the British home security agency, MI5, who already had Glading in their sights and had planted one of their own agents among his network.

Shortly after Reif had recruited Glading, the Soviet spy chief was called to the Home Office for an interview about his immigration status. It was not clear whether MI5 had been able to link Reif to Glading, although it appears Reif was about to be expelled by the British. Nevertheless, the interview triggered a security scare at the Kremlin and Reif was recalled.[23] In his stead, the Centre sent a replacement 'illegal' with orders to tighten security measures and step up the engagement of the Cambridge spies. The new man was the charismatic former Catholic priest Teodor Maly, who had recruited Lizy Friedmann and Edith Suschitzky in Vienna, where he had first been made aware of Kim Philby. Maly arrived in London in January 1936.

Maly, who used the name Paul Hardt and was referred to by the Austrian network as the 'tall man' on account of his 6ft 3in stature, was as erudite and security minded as Deutsch. But he was much tougher. He had fought with the Austro-Hungarian Army in the First World War when he was captured by the Russians. He later recalled: 'I was moved from one camp to another and starved along with other prisoners. We were all covered with vermin and many were dying of typhus. I lost my faith in God and when the revolution broke out, I joined the Bolsheviks. I broke with my past completely. I was no longer a Hungarian, a priest, a Christian, even anyone's son. I became a Communist and have always remained one.'[24] Maly instructed Philby to further distance himself from his communist past by writing pro-fascist articles and joining the Anglo-German fellowship, a pro-Nazi group.

It was during this time, in 1934, that Philby met a beautiful Russian émigré who many years later would be the instrument of his ultimate downfall as a Soviet spy.

Flora Solomon was the daughter of a wealthy Russian gold and mining dynasty and a friend of the Rothschild banking family, who had settled in Britain in 1914. When she met Philby, she was the mistress of the deposed Russian Prime Minister Alexander Kerensky, who was living in exile in London and Paris after being ousted in the Bolshevik-led Russian Revolution of 1917. Solomon claimed that Philby was 'infatuated' by her but denied having an affair with him. Victor Rothschild, himself a British intelligence officer, was adamant that she and Philby became lovers.[25]

Whatever the truth, a White Russian dissident like Alexander Kerensky was of great interest to the Russian secret service. And according to Solomon, Philby tried to recruit her as an agent to spy on 'White Russians'[26] but she says she refused. In openly making his approach, Philby had committed the ultimate sin in spycraft of revealing to Solomon his true colours. Solomon kept his secret and the two remained close, implying there was more to their relationship and that Solomon was already a Soviet asset.

Moscow was impressed with Philby's work in Vienna and had earmarked him as a field agent. So in 1937, when Philby secured a job as foreign correspondent on *The Times*, the Russians encouraged him to go to Spain so he could get close to Franco's fascists as one of the foreign press corps, a form of cover favoured by Deutsch. The Centre gave Philby an important if rather improbable mission – to assassinate the nationalist leader. Philby did not have the character to kill in cold blood, although he had no hesitation delivering fatal intelligence to his Russian masters that allowed others more suited to the messy business of assassination.

Maly managed the situation brilliantly, telling Philby to ignore the order while informing the Centre he did not think Philby was capable of fulfilling it. Philby returned to London in May 1937 having never set eyes on Franco.[27] In his report to Moscow on 24 May 1937, Maly wrote: 'Sonchen came back on 12th or 13 May in a very depressed state . . . I think, rather sense from my conversation with him, that even if he had been able to get to Salamanca and even if he had been able to get close to Franco, which is a separate matter, because only two or three journalists have been able to do that so far, then he, despite his willingness, would not be able to do what was expected of him. For all his loyalty and willingness to sacrifice himself, he does not have the physical courage and other qualities necessary.'[28]

In June 1937,[29] his Russian handlers sent Philby back to Spain with a more realistic mission – to infiltrate the Nationalists' high command by writing pro-Franco articles for *The Times*. In this Philby succeeded, and on 17 June 1937 the British journalist was granted an interview with Franco. No longer under orders to kill the fascist leader, he instead managed to prise from him an admission that his Nationalist army was not interested in negotiating a peaceful end to the war.[30] Philby faithfully reported this and much more pro-Franco propaganda back to *The Times* foreign desk in London. It must have been difficult for Philby to write these kinds of articles when he bore witness to so many atrocities carried out by Franco's men. It was yet another demonstration of Philby's cold ambition to serve the communist cause whatever the reputational cost.

A harsher physical test was to come on New Year's Eve 1937/38 when he was reporting on the frontline near Teruel and his car was hit by a Russian-made shell, killing four of his journalist companions. Philby was the sole survivor of the explosion. He showed great bravery by clambering out of the vehicle and then filing a report on the battle in very pro-Franco terms despite the eventual fall of Nationalist-held Teruel.[31]

Philby's distorted coverage of the war delivered its greatest reward on 2 March 1938, when Franco decided to present the British journalist with the Red Cross of Military Merit. It was well known that Franco did not care for the British so for him to bestow such an important medal on a young English journalist caused a minor sensation. The decoration was reported by the British and international media and questions were asked in the House of Commons about why *The Times* was in bed with the Spanish fascists.[32] It was ironic that the probing question was tabled by communist MP, Willie Gallacher, who had actually blackballed the 'middle class' Philby from joining the Communist Party of Great Britain but had somehow forgotten their meeting.[33]

'The decoration itself,' Philby said, 'meant nothing to me, but it opened many doors that I'd never dreamed would open for my main work. Once I had the decoration I could ask any question at practically any government level and get the most detailed and frank replies.'[34]

The value of this to Russian intelligence was immense. The Kremlin was not prepared to take any chances with the extraction of Philby and his hard-won intelligence so it was arranged that once a month he would leave Spain and travel to the south of France to meet his Soviet contact. That man would turn out to be 'Big Bill', Alexander Orlov, his old mentor – a reacquaintance that thrilled Philby who greatly admired the Soviet spymaster, later describing him as a communist 'Messiah'.[35]

Explaining his special respect for Orlov, Philby told the Russian journalist Genrikh Borovik: 'Theo [Maly] and Otto [Deutsch] were communists but Big Bill was a Bolshevik.' Orlov's mythology was only enhanced when he turned up at one of their rendezvous in Perpignan, France, with a semi-automatic rifle concealed under his raincoat. Big Bill had become a target for Trotskyist assassins. On one occasion, Orlov told Philby, he had used the rifle to kill two men who had entered his room when they thought he was asleep.[36] After reading Philby's latest report, Orlov told his protege: 'You know when I met you in London the first time, I thought nothing would come of you. But I see I was mistaken.'[37]

During these meetings, Philby also learnt about Orlov's role in Stalin's purge of the Trotsky elements fighting for the Spanish brigades.

Having secured his fascist credentials with Franco, Philby turned his attention to cosying up to the Nazis, becoming a frequent visitor at the German embassy in Salamanca and then Burgos, where he befriended the German ambassador. Philby claimed to know Joachim von Ribbentrop, the German foreign minister, and presented himself as a friend of the Nazis in the same vein as many British young men who had travelled to Germany to witness the birth of National Socialism and had stood in awe at the Nuremberg rallies.

More doors opened and he was introduced to the head of the German military intelligence, the Abwehr, in Spain: Major Ulrich von der Osten, who worked under the codename 'Don Julio'.[38]

The German spy chief invited the Englishman to his office at Abwehr headquarters where Philby was able to casually note details from military maps pasted to the walls, all dotted with coloured pins. Philby took complete advantage of the German's arrogance, later remarking: 'He invited me to his office and showed his maps in order to astonish me with his knowledge, hoping that I would tell some important people in the Third Reich what a good man he was. In his eyes I was a chum of Ribbentrop and Hess. The poor fellow had no idea that my real friends lived in a very different place.'[39]

Philby was able to call upon one of his well-connected

girlfriends to exploit the German's well-known weakness for women. The extremely attractive actress Frances Doble, who was in Spain visiting friends, had political ties to both Frances and the monarchists and soon became Philby's lover during his stay in Spain. Von der Osten had also recognised her political connections and approached her to ask her to spy for the Abwehr. She politely declined and reported the German's advances to Philby.[40]

In 1938, von der Osten was recalled to Berlin and given a new and very important assignment in America that would have implications for Japanese plans to attack Pearl Harbor. The Russians were also interested in Japan and Philby was put on standby for a secret mission to Tokyo.[41] Orlov was unable to tell his agent what the mission entailed, only that he had to leave immediately. Philby informed *The Times* that he intended to take some emergency time off from his journalism and waited for the Russians to give him the order to leave. But he heard nothing more about the Soviet plan.[42] On 10 July 1938, Orlov wrote to Moscow demanding to know whether the mission was on or off. Two days later Orlov broke with Moscow and defected to America.[43]

Orlov had been a guiding light and friend to Philby. Now he had suddenly disappeared, leaving Philby in the lurch and none the wiser as to his whereabouts or his defection. It was only after the Second World War that Philby discovered Orlov was living quietly in Cleveland, Ohio.

While Philby was fighting the Kremlin's war in Spain, another of Maly and Deutsch's British agents was about to threaten the security of Philby's own operations.

MI5 had begun winding up the Percy Glading network and sent three of them, including the ringleader Glading, for trial. Among the documents obtained by Special Branch was a receipt for a Leica camera in the name of Edith Tudor-Hart, the Austrian communist who had helped recruit Philby. The threads of the Soviet penetration were being pulled apart. Surely it was only a matter of time before the remaining members of the group recruited by Deutsch and Maly would be under lock and key.

Moscow certainly feared so and put the Russian 'illegals' on notice to pull out of Britain.[44] Their time served in the West meant they were all at risk of Stalin's Great Terror, the mass extermination of mostly imagined enemies of the Soviet state. Word reached Maly and Deutsch that among the Soviet agents executed was the former London 'illegal' Ignatz Reif, who had been put up before a firing squad as soon as he reached Moscow. Others were murdered before they reached Russia. Yet Maly and Deutsch were resigned to their fates.

Teodor Maly's religious background made him an obvious suspect. He accepted the order to return to Moscow in June 1937 and with a touch of idealistic fatalism confided to one of his comrades, 'I know that as a former priest I haven't got a chance. But I've decided to go there so that nobody can say: "That priest might have been a real spy after all."'[45] Maly was indeed executed. His Soviet file simply reads: '1936–1937. Resident of London residence. Maly Teodor Stepanovich. No 9705. Sentence in 1938. German Spy.'

Not all the 'illegals' were as compliant as Maly. Alexander Orlov and Walter Krivitsky, another NKVD officer who had had contact with the London residency, decided to save themselves. They embarked on separate ships for New York and gave themselves up to the Americans.[46] Orlov, who had been working in Paris and Spain, refused to disclose his secrets about the London residency, while Krivitsky sang like a canary. Krivitsky had been in Vienna in 1934 when he had married an Austrian communist at the height of the revolution and knew of an Englishman that matched Philby's description.[47] It was fortunate for Philby that Krivitsky did not know Philby's name and was only able to describe him as a 'young Englishman and journalist of good family' who had been sent to Spain to assassinate Franco.[48]

Philby believed that, like his other handlers, Maly and Deutsch,

Orlov had been recalled to Moscow for reassignment. But the timing of his defection is interesting. Orlov knew about Philby's work for the Russians yet kept the Soviet omerta, not out of loyalty to Philby but in the hope that his silence would save him and his family from Stalin's retribution. Only later did Philby discover Orlov's defection and the jeopardy in which it had placed him.

The departures left Arnold Deutsch nervously holding the fort in London, waiting for either Orlov or Krivitsky to name him as a spy or worse, for the Russians to declare him an enemy of the state. Deutsch's Jewish Austrian background and close association with Reif, Maly and Orlov made him an obvious target. Fearing the worst, Deutsch stepped up his efforts to regularise his immigration and employment status in the UK and applied to set up a research company in Birmingham. The Home Office declined his application on the basis that the work could be performed by a British national.[49] In November 1937, the Centre finally recalled Deutsch.

It is a moment – the breaking of ties with his old comrade Arnold Deutsch – that Philby chose to write about in his confession to Elliott in 1963: 'One evening, our telephone rang (22 Glenross, Belsize Road, NW6 in 1936), and Otto asked if we were alone at home. I replied that we were, and he told me that he could be round in half an hour. I was much astonished at this, since it was completely at variance with his normal security mindedness. He arrived in a state of great agitation with a suitcase. He used my telephone to book an air passage to Paris, and left the following morning. I never saw him again.'[50]

Deutsch was part of the communist generation born of the 1917 Russian Revolution who helped protect a new and fragile communist state from the interference of the West and nurtured a Soviet Union stretching from the Baltic to the Pacific. Stalin's Great Terror had perverted the cause of the international Comintern and ended the dream of a new world order in which everyone would have a fair stake, transforming the prospects of the proletariat. Philby remembered Deutsch for his 'strong humanistic streak ... he was a man of considerable cultural background.'[51] When Philby's first child was born in 1940, he named her Josephine, after Deutsch's wife.

Later, another of the Cambridge spies, Anthony Blunt, attested to the intellectual and ideological rigour of the 'illegals' saying, 'our generation was won over by the finest minds in Europe.'[52] Miraculously, Deutsch escaped a firing squad and unlike all the other foreign 'illegals' retained the trust of Stalin and his security advisers. Stalin instead chose to believe Deutsch had been betrayed.[53]

Stalin's Great Terror was now front-page news. Philby must have known, or suspected, the ignominious fate of his Soviet handlers.

The London residency was temporarily closed and Philby and the other agents were cast adrift, loosely supervised by the Paris residency who knew nothing of the great work done by Deutsch and the other 'illegals' in setting up the Cambridge spy ring.

In March 1938, the Nazis marched into Austria unopposed and annexed the country. All that Philby and the Austrian communists had fought for four years earlier was undone. A year later in July 1939, Philby returned from Spain, irritated by the rapid turnover of handlers although his commitment to international communism remained undimmed. A few weeks later, the loyalty of all the Cambridge spies faced an even greater test when the Soviet Union and Nazi Germany signed the Molotov–Ribbentrop Pact. The two governments agreed that they would not attack each other and secretly divided the territories that lay between them. Overnight Kim Philby found himself an ally of the Nazis, whose brutal brand of fascism had been the root cause of his decision to throw in his lot with the Soviets. Yet Philby was able to rationalise the fascist-Soviet alliance, more anxious that his own special talents were in danger of being wasted by the communists. Job satisfaction was more important to Philby than any moral certainty. He got a thrill out of deceiving people who trusted him in the exciting game of espionage in which he knew all the real secrets and in which he knew he could be found out at any moment.[54]

The successive disappearances of Reif, Orlov, Maly and Deutsch, as well as the successful conclusion of the Glading case, had satisfied MI5 that they had caught and dealt with all the agents involved in Russia's penetration of the British state. In January 1939, the year of the start of the Second World War, Major General Vernon Kell, the head of MI5, declared: 'Soviet activity in England is non-existent, in terms of both intelligence and political subversion.'[55]

This was a catastrophic miscalculation. Philby and the other British spies had signed up to the Soviet cause. They had been expertly schooled by Deutsch and Maly, who had given them the spycraft and resources to work their way into the heart of British intelligence. It didn't matter that the ideals of communism that had originally attracted them to the Party had been wholly corrupted by Stalin. For Philby and the Cambridge sleeper spies, they were in too deep and there was no going back.

Chapter 5

War of Words

In 1938, two of Graham Greene's passions, his love of travel and his pursuit of Catholicism, led him to the badlands of Mexico, where priests were being hunted down like dogs by the Republican government. It meant he almost missed the start of the Second World War the following year, bearing witness to a different kind of conflict, one being waged against the Catholic Church.

By then, Greene was an author with an international reputation. His sixth and most successful novel, *Brighton Rock*, his first overtly Catholic work, had just been published, while his travel book on Liberia, *Journey Without Maps*, had established him as an accomplished travel writer. Greene was navigating a personal exploration of his increasingly troubled relationship with his faith: a search for a spiritual reconciliation between Catholic dogma and everyday, sinful life. Latin America offered him a new landscape where he could settle these issues.

For the past 18 months, he had been working with the Catholic Church on a planned trip to Mexico that would help bring the plight of the persecuted clergy to world attention and perhaps serve as a penitence for his own adultery and other sins. Greene was moved by stories of martyred priests at the hands of a socialist government that regarded the Catholic Church to be counter-revolutionary and sympathetic to colonial powers who retained designs on the new republic. He may also have been antagonised by the atheism of Mexican president Lázaro

Cárdenas, who told his people: 'Man should not put his hope in the supernatural. Every moment spent on one's knees is a moment stolen from humanity.'[1]

Yet Greene found Mexican politics to be fascinating in its own right. The government had supported the Republican cause in Spain, opposed Germany's violation of Austrian neutrality in the wake of the Anschluss and had fallen out with Stalin by granting sanctuary to the Soviet leader's nemesis, Leon Trotsky. As usual, Greene was in the right place at the right time and he used the country and its politics as the backdrop for a new Catholic novel, *The Power and the Glory*, as well as a Mexico travel book *The Lawless Roads*. These two works helped to shape the literary landscape that was to become known as Greeneland, populated by anguished souls struggling with emotional and spiritual conflicts in far-away, troubled places.

However, Greene's more prosaic writing, the journalism from which he had earned a living, was about to terminate his Mexican adventure. On 21 April 1938, returning to Mexico City from one of his research expeditions among Mexico's rural Catholic congregations, he picked up his forwarded correspondence.[2] One letter was marked urgent and had been sent by his solicitors. It contained news of a high-profile legal action against him that had been instituted in the High Court in London. The year before, Greene had written a review in *Night and Day* of *Wee Willie Winkie*, a film starring the child actress Shirley Temple. In it, he suggested that Temple had been deployed to titillate the paedophile interests of 'middle-aged men and clergymen' who, he said, enjoyed 'her dubious coquetry' and 'the sight of her well-shaped and desirable little body, packed with enormous vitality, only because the safety curtain of story and dialogue drops between their intelligence and their desire.'

The makers of the film were not amused and issued defamation proceedings against both *Night and Day* and Greene, the magazine's literary editor and film reviewer. Once again Graham Greene had plunged himself into a zone of conflict, this time the reporting of the sexualisation of children.

His article resulted in a very damaging and humiliating legal defeat, amounting to fulsome apologies all round and an expensive £3,500 (£300,000 today) damages award. The judge was particularly annoyed that Greene was out of the country when his judgement was read in court and ordered Greene to be personally liable for £500 (£42,000 today) of the payment.[3]

When Greene returned to England in 1938, he discovered that the case had not blown over and that he might face criminal prosecution for libel, an offence that could leave a far more serious stain on his character and writing career as well as carrying a possible jail term.

To Greene's great relief, the Attorney General decided a prosecution was not in the public interest. Nevertheless, he still faced bankruptcy from the civil claim against him. The prospect of an impecunious survival in the coming war greatly focused Greene's mind and he embarked on a high-intensity writing programme. His marriage to Vivien, who in 1936 had given birth to their second child, was strained as Greene found himself unable to settle down to family life in Oxford. So, Greene rented a writing studio in Bloomsbury where he began an affair with the landlady's daughter, Dorothy Glover. Here he set himself a punishing writing regime that produced *The Confidential Agent*, one of his so-called 'entertainments' set in the Spanish Civil War. In the morning, he wrote the fast-moving thriller, devoting the afternoon to the more contemplative narrative of *The Power and the Glory*,[4] in which he reworked the schoolboy tormentors Carter and Wheeler into the drawn-out betrayal of the 'whiskey priest', the book's protagonist who is given up to the Mexican soldiers by his travelling companion.[5]

*

Greene completed *The Confidential Agent* in just six weeks, fuelled by Benzedrine tablets taken twice a day, the same pills that would be popped by Hitler's stormtroopers in their Blitzkrieg across France. The book was largely well received and served its purpose of offsetting some of Greene's debt. An interesting dimension to the book, again one that centred on the theme of betrayal, was that the characters were given letters. Mr K is the double agent whose true loyalties are never established. He is a character who took on living form in a real spy case featuring an agent also codenamed K and encountered by both Graham Greene and Kim Philby.

That was all to come. Greene's rush to finish *The Confidential Agent* and *The Power and the Glory* (he completed *The Power and the Glory* on 13 September 1939) may have been informed by his acute political senses, which warned him of the impending doom about to engulf Europe.[6]

On 1 September 1939, Germany invaded Poland. Following weeks of rising tension and failed diplomacy, Britain and France issued ultimatums to Adolf Hitler demanding the immediate withdrawal of German forces from Polish territory. Two days later, when these demands were ignored, both nations – bound by treaty to defend Poland – formally declared war on Germany, marking the beginning of the Second World War. Sandbags were piled high outside the ministry buildings and wailing sirens sounded an endless stream of false alarms. Anti-aircraft guns were hurriedly pitched on London's parks, including Clapham Common, close to Greene's home.

Those first weeks of turmoil swept millions of Britons into the service of their country. Greene accepted a post in the newly created Ministry of Information (MOI), the government's controversial propaganda agency that was also responsible for censoring the news. His job was to take charge of the 'authors' section'. Here he was reunited with Malcolm Muggeridge, with whom he regularly dined at his nearby Bloomsbury garret. Writing in *Chronicles of Wasted Time*, Muggeridge said of Greene: 'he took a highly professional view of what was expected of us, fully exploring the possibility of throwing stigmata and other miraculous occurrences into the battle for the mind in Latin America to sway it in our favour.'[7]

But that was not how Greene really regarded his new job, which he satirised in his 1941 short story *Men at Work* about a 'civil servant with his nose above water, happy to be no longer taunted by other men's success.'[8] Greene dismissed his time at the MOI as 'such rubbish' and discounted any merit in the job as 'propaganda being a means of passing the time: work was not done for its usefulness but for its own sake – simply as an occupation.'[9] George Orwell, who also worked at the MOI, drew much darker inspiration from his employment, recasting it as the Ministry of Truth in his novel *1984*.

At 1.30am on 18 October 1941, a Luftwaffe parachute mine demolished Graham Greene's three-storey London home on Clapham Common. The writer took the loss in his stride, telling Muggeridge that at least he no longer had the burden of the mortgage.[10]

His wife Vivien, their two young children and the pet canaries had been evacuated to the safety of Greene's mother's cottage in Crowborough deep in the Sussex countryside.[11] With the family out of the way, Greene was free to move in with his mistress, Deborah Glover, in her Bloomsbury studio. When the bomb dropped on their Clapham house, Greene was staying with Glover and Vivien bitterly reflected that it was her husband's adultery that had saved his life.[12] His new address was no safer than his last and a few weeks later he was awoken in the early hours of the morning to find the house next door had been flattened by another German bomb.

The Blitz's grim mix of destructive horror and adrenaline-charged excitement mesmerised and energised Greene. He volunteered as an

Air Raid Warden, helping to protect the capital from Hitler's bombs while also collecting human stories at close quarters. During one raid, Greene encountered his first dead body: 'One's first corpse ... was not nearly as bad as one expected. It seemed just a bit of the rubble. Looking back, it is the squalor of the night, the purgatorial throng of men and women in dirty torn pyjamas with little blood splashes standing in doorways, which remains. These were disquieting because they supplied images for what one day would probably happen to oneself.'[13]

Greene helped to rescue many Londoners trapped in collapsed buildings or bloodied by the flying glass and masonry, recalling one occasion when he was left helplessly watching a man manically 'laughing outside his house where his wife and children were buried'.[14] The Blitz experience inured him to the constant threat of death. Muggeridge, with whom he spent many nights on fire duty, thought Greene might be in the grip of his own death wish, saying 'I remember the longing he had for a bomb to fall on him.'[15]

Muggeridge was half right. The truth was that the quiet human catastrophes played out in the London darkness also offered a valuable descriptive resource to be deployed to great effect in Greene's first wartime book, *The Ministry of Fear*.

Greene had also found other ways of escape that helped to soften his nihilistic fatalism. The heightened seediness of London during the Blitz attracted Greene, who became a frequent visitor to the semi-naked dancing girls at the Windmill Theatre in Soho as well as the dives and clip joints of London's wartime underbelly. He soothed his depression by seeking out the services of the army of prostitutes working the capital.[16] Such was his addiction to paying for sex that he drew up a list of 47 women, each annotated with coded descriptions including: 'the one who wouldn't'; 'Russian boots'; 'Irish pole sucker'; 'real tough buggerer'; 'girl with stench and baby'; 'beautiful bottom in S'.[17]

Nevertheless, he took his war duties seriously and made many acquaintances among the warden volunteers and homeless families. On his fire warden rounds, he looked up the bookshop owners of Charing Cross Road whom he knew so well before the war. Perhaps it was then that he first considered the idea of bookshops as fronts for communist agents, a theme he put to work in his novel *The Human Factor*, published after the war.

While Greene hung around London waiting to play a part in the war, his literary standing received a huge and unexpected boost. The 1940 publication of *The Power and the Glory* in Britain and America had begun to attract positive reviews. His Mexican novel about the renegade priest in dual conflict with his spiritual beliefs and the communist atheist state prompted one reviewer to claim Greene was now the 'finest English novelist of his generation'.[18]

This literary success secured a sinecure at a firm of publishers called Eyre and Spottiswoode, who paid him a £100 annual director's fee.[19] Such was Greene's reputation as a mover and shaker in the literary world that paying Greene a fee simply to have his name associated with the publisher was considered very good business.

Chapter 6

Ace of Spies

When Britain and France declared war on Germany on 3 September 1939, many Britons expected a declaration of hostilities against Hitler's ally, Communist Russia, to soon follow. Yet no action was taken and Russia was allowed to pursue its war aims unmolested.

Kim Philby was *The Times*'s star foreign correspondent and he was sent to France to cover the war on the Western Front attached to the British Expeditionary Force (BEF)[1] where he had access to the British top brass and its planning. Moscow realised how important their neglected agent had become.

So a new 'illegal' was dispatched to the London residency to help facilitate the control and direction of Philby and the rest of the Cambridge spies. Anatoly Gorsky had joined the Soviet secret police in 1928 and worked in the internal political police. In 1936, he transferred to foreign intelligence and was sent to England as a cipher clerk and assistant to the London residency. When Gorsky returned he took the trouble to talk to Lizy about how best to use Philby, telling the Centre: 'According to 'Mary' [Lizy], Sonchen had formed numerous ties with very interesting people who have ties with the British intelligence service and has developed very good relations with them.'[2]

Philby assured the newly constituted Moscow residency in London that he was in the ideal position to pass on military intelligence about the British and French forces opposing the Germans. He must have known that this intelligence could end up in the hands of the Germans, Russia's ally and the country that now threatened to conquer and occupy Great Britain. The Russian spy began his assignment corralled with other war reporters at General Headquarters at Arras, northern France, under the strict supervision of censorship officers who had the job of ensuring no damaging intelligence was inadvertently released to the Germans. Philby deployed his immense charm and cunning to outwit his military chaperones, although while the German army stood behind the Maginot Line, there was precious little action to report. The only military offensive that took place at this time was Russia's invasion of eastern Poland.

Philby may have had little to fill his reports for *The Times* but he had plenty of information concerning the static location and military hardware of the BEF that he could secretly relay to a Russian handler in Paris, a city he frequented as often as he could.[3] Among his unwitting sources was Lord Gort, the head of the BEF, who he made sure he sat next to during liaison dinners with the press.[4]

Philby expertly covered his tracks by writing jingoistic articles about the mood and invincibility of the British forces, like this one that began: 'Today it is possible to travel hundreds of miles along the roads of Belgium without leaving the British traffic area. Bren guns guard vital points; British military police control the crossroads. Convoy work has been particularly brilliant.'[5]

To further disguise his treachery, he even deprecated the local communist politicians: 'The Belgium people are thoroughly aroused . . . When the British Ambassador entered the diplomatic gallery of the Belgium Parliament on Friday, the Deputies of all the parties, with the exception of one Communist, rose and cheered his coming . . . It is suspected that two communist deputies who have disappeared are in Germany.'[6]

The two communists concerned were Trotskyists, enemies of the Soviet state.

When the Nazis surprised the Allies by attacking through the Ardennes, bypassing the Maginot Line, it is possible that their panzer generals benefited from intelligence fed to them via Soviet agents operating among the British and French armies.

The German Blitzkrieg carried the Allies before it, forcing the British back to the towns and beaches of northern France. Philby found himself at Boulogne waiting for embarkation to England with elements of the routed BEF. It was here that he encountered one of the other Cambridge spies, Anthony Blunt, who was also serving on the Western Front. Blunt claims it was in Boulogne, on the eve of their departure for England, that he first told Philby he was working for the Russians, although it seems likely they were already aware of each other. They shared a mutual friend in Victor Rothschild, and France was well-trodden territory for Russia's European spy network of 'illegals' known as the Rote Kapelle (Red Orchestra). Among them was Henri Robinson who was reported to have made contact with Philby through the Paris residency.[7]

When Philby arrived back in England he was determined to get a job with British intelligence.

To support his cause, he was able to brandish an impressive CV that included a military decoration personally awarded to him by General Franco.

It was at this point that he became involved with the woman who was to be his common-law wife throughout the war, although he remained legally married to Lizy, from whom he'd been separated for many years. Aileen Furse worked as a store detective in the Marble Arch branch of Marks and Spencer. There she was befriended by Philby's former lover, Flora Solomon, who held a senior executive role in the firm. Soon afterwards Solomon introduced Aileen to Kim; before long she had fallen for the dashing war correspondent and the couple moved into a flat together.[8] What was it about Aileen, an ordinary middle-class woman with few political interests, that had captured Philby's heart? Flora Solomon described her as 'typically English, slim and attractive, fiercely patriotic, but awkward in her gestures and unsure of herself in company.'[9] She was also suffering from a debilitating neurosis that Solomon claims she had warned Philby about.

Could it have been that Aileen's then-boyfriend Frank Birch, a senior intelligence officer attached to Bletchley Park, the top-secret decryption station in the Hertfordshire countryside, was the real reason for Philby's interest in her?[10] Birch was a charismatic Cambridge history don who may have known Philby when he was an undergraduate. In the First World War, Birch had played a leading role in the breaking of German naval codes, and in 1939 he resumed this work at Bletchley Park heading up the German Naval Section when he was part of the Enigma team that broke the Nazi codes.[11]

Philby made sure that the new couple and Aileen's old boyfriend remained on close terms. Someone like Birch was important to Philby at this stage in his career as he was still seeking a position in British intelligence. By inveigling his way into Aileen's affections, he had picked up a very useful sponsor in Frank Birch.[12]

Under Philby's guidance, Aileen changed her name by deed poll to Philby so that it looked to the outside world that he was a respectably remarried family man. To support his application to British intelligence, he was able to call upon his own family standing and the ties of the old boy network. His father was friends with senior figures within British intelligence including Vivian Valentine, then deputy head of MI6. However, it was a female acquaintance charmed by Philby who he claimed had helped land him his first spy job. On a train back to London from France, he shared a compartment with the *Daily Express* war reporter Hester Marsden-Smedley. After a difficult Channel crossing by boat, the couple were so overjoyed to have got back safely that they toasted their good fortune with a bottle of champagne.[13] When Philby later told this story, he said that the conversation took place over lunch in the dining carriage, where they were drowning their sorrows over the fall of France.[14] Philby told Marsden-Smedley that he thought he would have to enlist with the army as he couldn't think of any other way of doing his bit. Falling for Philby's self-deprecating conversation, she said she might be able to help find him a role that kept him away from the front line.

Marsden-Smedley was from a military family, the daughter of Major-General Sir Reginald John Pinney. Her husband, the barrister Basil Marsden-Smedley, had connections in the Foreign Office. And according to Philby, Hester herself was employed by British intelligence.[15] A week later, Philby was contacted by a Whitehall civil servant who interviewed him twice at the St Ermin's Hotel, Victoria,[16] for a job at a top-secret government department known as Section D. 'D' was for destruction and was set up to carry out sabotage operations in occupied Europe, a forerunner of the SOE.

Among the new intake was Philby's fellow Cambridge spy Guy Burgess, who had been at Philby's second interview at the hotel just in case his application needed bolstering or threw up any last-minute hitches, such as questions about Philby's time in Austria working for the communists or in Spain reporting with the fascists.[17] After the war, Hester Marsden-Smedley denied playing any part in Philby's recruitment, leaving MI5 to surmise that Burgess's role[18] and that of Frank Birch[19] were much more influential.

The selection of Burgess and Philby for such sensitive posts in Section D was an egregious lapse of security. Burgess had been rejected for a teaching job at Eton after the school had contacted Cambridge seeking a reference only to receive the reply: 'I would very much prefer not to answer your letter.'[20]

Philby's recruitment was perhaps an even greater indictment of the standard of vetting at the beginning of the war.

The vetters were required to access both the MI6 and MI5 registries. Philby had known links to communists and fascists in Spain and Germany. He was also married to an Austrian communist and had been named as a fellow company director by Harry Smolka, an MI5 communist suspect, on Smolka's 1935 application to the Home Office to set up a foreign news agency. Perhaps most concerning of all were the political allegiances of his father, who just before the war had brokered a deal between the Nazis and Saudi Arabia whereby the Germans would exchange weapons for oil.[21] Philby senior's fascist connections were cemented when he co-founded the British People's Party, for which he stood as a candidate in the 1939 by-election in Hythe on the Kent coast, polling just 576 votes.

Nonetheless, Kim Philby's MI6 vetting card was positively stamped to show all his documents had been checked. The person most surprised by the superficiality of the checks was Philby who remarked 'apparently none of these facts was held against me.'[22]

MI6 and MI5 in 1940 were understaffed and so it was impossible to devote huge resources to the professional vetting of desperately needed linguists to work in intelligence. And of course, Philby's background – public school, Cambridge and the Athenaeum club – meant his face was a perfect fit. It wasn't until 1951, after Burgess and Maclean had defected to Russia, that MI5 was to piece together all the damning evidence.

At Section D, Philby and Burgess wrote the SIS syllabus for the new cadre of agents being trained at Brickendonbury Manor near Hertford and the SOE training camp at Beaulieu Abbey in Hampshire. Burgess was the spy school's political adviser, offering guidance on how to work with communist resistance groups in Europe. Part of his instruction even included screenings of the Soviet film featuring the 'heroic' revolt of the crew of the ship *Potemkin*. At Beaulieu, Philby instructed the agents on the workings of the Abwehr and the various resistance movements active in Europe.

Mindful of the fact that the Soviets were allies of the Nazis, Philby began his lectures: 'Gentlemen, I have no wish to prevent you blowing up the Russians, but I would beg you, for the sake of the allied war effort, to blow up the Germans first.'[23]

Among the recruits were trainee agents from Spain. One of the first proposals by Philby and Burgess for a Section D operation was the assassination of General Franco – the very job Moscow had given Philby three years earlier. There is no evidence that this operation got off the ground, although Philby was questioned about it in 1951 during his interrogation by Helenus Milmo of MI5.[24]

The rise of the two NKVD agents should have produced rich pickings for Russian intelligence, who were still allied to Nazi Germany. But Moscow's paranoia over the loyalties of its foreign agents had reignited suspicions about the London residency and its group of middle-class gentleman spies who had rejected their bourgeois lives in favour of communism. The Cambridge spy ring had all the hallmarks of an MI6 set-up, the kind of operation that Moscow knew British intelligence was capable of pulling off, partly because of the secret reports already sent back by Philby and the other British agents.

Moscow ordered the closure of the London residency and Anatoly Gorsky was told to end all contact with Philby and return to Russia.[25] Once again Philby was left out in the cold and at a time when he was facing family troubles. Aileen, pregnant with his first child Josephine, suffered from depression and the combination of the war and her pregnancy exacerbated her anxiety, forcing Philby to make emergency visits to the family home.

His father St John's fascist sympathies had finally caught up with him in Bombay, where he was arrested on 3 August 1940 under Defence Regulation 18B and deported to England for internment. This was not just embarrassing for the Philbys, it also drew unwelcome attention to Kim's own dalliance with the fascists as part of his attempts to disguise his communist loyalties.

Philby had outgrown Beaulieu and yearned for a more important role in the intelligence war against the Nazis. He needed to move on. It was at this point that the controversial detention of Philby's father, still held under the Defence of the Realm regulations by the Home Secretary, Herbert Morrison, would actually boost Kim's career prospects in SIS.

Valentine Vivian, who had served with St John Philby in India and maintained a friendship for 30 years, intervened to help secure St John's release.[26] Vivian secretly lobbied the Foreign Office and Morrison (grandfather of Peter Mandelson), saying he did not believe St John to be disloyal, merely 'insufferably arrogant'[27] and that the action taken against him looked like 'political malice'.[28] Vivian was supported in his campaign by Guy Liddell, MI5's head of counter-intelligence, who thought a 'gross blunder was being committed' and passed on Vivian's comments to the Foreign Office.[29]

During the course of their correspondence, Vivian told Liddell that St John's son Kim 'is one of our D officers ... who I have found both charming and capable,' adding, with respect to Kim's view of St John: 'He himself told me that his father had cooled down in the strength of his views in the last few years, but that would not appear to be so from the letters ... I mention young Philby simply because I think it will make it more difficult to take any repressive measures against the father.'[30]

The files show that neither Vivian nor Liddell made any reference to St John Philby's far-left past and his close ties to the Soviet spy Norman Ewer that predated Philby's move to the far-right. This is very odd since Liddell, who helped break up the Ewer cell when he was at Special Branch, had written to Vivian in December 1933 warning him that Philby senior 'was an intimate friend of Ewer'.[31]

St John Philby was finally freed on 14 March 1941. The case

served to make Kim Philby a sympathetic figure who it was felt had suffered unfair anguish over the treatment of his father.

A few weeks later, an opportunity arose that brought Philby into the heart of British intelligence.

Having won the war in France by defeating the British Expeditionary Force, the Germans set their sights on defeating the British spy agencies still operating in Europe.

By March 1942 the Abwehr, Germany's military intelligence, had infiltrated the entire SOE network operating in Holland, leading to the capture of all its agents. The Germans were also gaining the upper hand in espionage operations in Portugal and Spain, both officially neutral but in reality led by Nazi-friendly governments. There was growing concern that SIS did not have the resources to counter the Nazis in Lisbon and Madrid, where the Abwehr was able to organise spy networks that were sending enemy agents to Britain, some of whom had been captured by MI5.

The stakes were high. Should either Spain's leader Francisco Franco or Portugal's António de Oliveira Salazar agree to give the Germans a free hand on the Iberian Peninsula, Britain's sea routes and North Africa operations would be directly threatened. So, towards the end of 1941, it was agreed to look for SIS officers with personal knowledge of Spain or Portugal to carry the fight to the Abwehr.

While covering the Spanish Civil War for *The Times*, Kim Philby had cultivated a contact called Tomás 'Tommy' Harris, an Anglo-Spanish art dealer who was trading paintings and antiques bought up from refugees fleeing the conflict. The two men became firm friends. Back in England, Philby and Burgess managed to get Harris and his wife jobs as cook and housekeeper at Section D's Brickendonbury Manor. Harris's artistic leanings also brought him into contact with Anthony Blunt, the Cambridge spy and Marxist art critic, who helped to get Harris into MI5, where Blunt worked.[32]

Harris was at the centre of a hub of young intelligence officers from both MI6 and MI5 who met at his home at 6 Chesterfield Gardens, which he had recently inherited from his father. Members included Anthony Blunt (MI5), Kim Philby (MI6), Guy Burgess (MI6), Tim Milne (MI6), Desmond Bristow (MI6), Victor Rothschild (MI5), Guy Liddell (MI5), Richard Brooman-White (MI5) and Peter Wilson (MI6). When Harris found out that SIS and MI5 were looking for candidates for a revamped Iberian section, he immediately thought of his friend Kim Philby, still stuck in Hampshire. He informed his boss Richard Brooman-White, head of the Iberian section at MI5, that Philby, who spoke both Spanish and German, would be an excellent fit.[33]

Philby's name, as well as his 'charm and abilities', was already well known to Valentine Vivian, the deputy head of SIS, who was required to vet the candidate. Vivian decided to have lunch with his old friend St John Philby, now freed from internment. There was plenty to discuss as well as one or two concerns that needed to be allayed.

There was of course *The Times* report about Kim's visit to Austria and his marriage to Lizy, a known communist in 1934. The MI5 registry had also found a 1933 reference to Philby in *Labour Monthly*, the Communist Party of Great Britain's magazine that brought together Comintern and left-leaning thinkers and activists.[34] His name was one of several copied from an index card by an MI5 informant working in the magazine's offices. The MI5 file does not say exactly what the extract taken from the magazine said about Philby, but it would have at the very least highlighted his involvement in the communist movement. There is also a reference to a Special Branch report relating to 'Mr and Mrs Gerhadt Egge', who were the Philbys' housekeepers before the war. The Egges were German Jewish refugees who had raised concerns about the 'bohemian' home of Kim and Lizy Philby where they were working. In 1939, a report found its way to MI5 accusing the Egges of being

Nazis, which led to their internment throughout the war. The report's author was Harry Smolka (now Smollett), then a trusted employee at the Ministry of Information. The complainant was a Mrs Lizy Philby.[35]

And finally, there was Harry Smolka's 1934 letter to the Home Office applying to set up a news agency with Kim Philby.

Vivian's starting point for approving Philby's appointment would have been the original SIS vetting form when he joined Section D the year before (1940).[36] Whether Vivian had access to all the underlying intelligence is unclear as these reports may have been collated and attached to St John's file, a subject of interest to MI5. It probably didn't matter because Vivian intended to satisfy himself about Philby's ties to communism at Cambridge by seeking direct assurances from his father. When asked about these communist connections St John obligingly told him: 'That was all schoolboy nonsense. He's a reformed character now.'[37]

Two or three more large glasses of port later and all doubts about Philby junior had been quelled. Given that Vivian was MI6's expert on communism counter-intelligence and had been privy to the Krivitsky debriefing when the Russian defector had described an important Soviet agent almost matching Philby's description, this was at the very least an extremely serious oversight, one that would have catastrophic consequences for MI6 in the years ahead. Just a few months into the war, Kim Philby, the Soviet mole, had been anointed as a trusted man in the heart of British intelligence.

Chapter 7

Ways of Escape

Homeless after German bombs demolished his London house and keen to avoid the domestic complications of his failing marriage to Vivien, Graham Greene embarked on the search for a suitable refuge, a bolthole in town from where he could run his life.

He turned to his friend Herbert Read, the poet, literary critic and anarchist. Read, a recipient of the Military Cross (MC) in the First World War, knew just the place and duly wrote to the secretary of the Reform Club in Pall Mall proposing Greene's candidature: 'I have known Mr Greene for many years and strongly recommend him as in every respect eligible for membership of the club. In addition to being an author of considerable distinction he is at present acting literary editor of The Spectator.'[1]

Read said Greene was in 'urgent need of the amenities of a club' and requested that the 'nomination be considered soon.'[2] On 6 November 1940, the secretary wrote to Greene informing him that he had been duly elected to the Reform but that he need not pay £15 in fees until the turn of the year. This was due to the fact that the club had suffered bomb damage and was temporarily closed for repairs.[3] Greene's membership was seconded by another First World War veteran and another holder of the MC, the literary critic Rolfe Arnold Scott-James, grandfather of the historian and former *Telegraph* editor Sir Max Hastings.[4]

The Reform was less stuffy than the other London clubs. Its only stipulation, since its foundation in 1836, was that members were 'reformers' under terms of Rule VI committed to progressive political ideas. Greene simply signed the papers and added the word 'yes' in answer to Rule VI.[5] The author had joined a gentleman-only private members' club that provided him with a discreet retreat to write and socialise among a congenial companionship of writers, academics and War Office mandarins. He had also accidentally insinuated himself into a world of espionage.

The club's relaxed approach to membership had exposed the institution to a danger that its Victorian founders could not have foreseen.

Here the cream of British intelligence worked in the library and socialised in the bar and dining room.

But the Reform was also a favourite haunt of Soviet agents. Anthony Blunt and Guy Burgess joined on the same day in March 1937 and went on to assiduously exploit the Reform's long list of establishment figures as well as sponsor the membership of two senior MI5 officers: Roger Hollis, then in charge MI5's F Division, Soviet counter-intelligence, and Herbert Hart, the law academic recruited from Oxford University to help interpret and analyse the reams of secret decrypts pouring out of Bletchley Park. Guy Liddell, MI5's head of counter-intelligence, was a regular guest of Anthony Blunt.

Among Blunt and Burgess's own Reform sponsors was Alister Watson, the 'high priest of Marxist theory', a member of the Cambridge Apostles who was also suspected of spying for the Russians. After Blunt's 1964 confession, Watson was removed from his post as head of the Submarine Detection Research Section of the Admiralty Research Laboratory. Although there is no official record of Soviet agent Peter 'Harry' Smolka at the Reform, he must have been present in the later 1930s, working his way through the membership. Eric Kessler, a Swiss agent controlled by Moscow, claimed it was Smolka who introduced him to Blunt and Burgess at the club.[6]

*

In 1941, Blunt, Burgess and Eric Kessler used their combined influence in the club to enrol another member of the Reform spy ring,[7] Gorowny Rees, a military officer later serving with the Chief of Staff to the Supreme Allied Commander. Two more Blunt and Burgess sponsors – Dennis Proctor, a wartime civil servant, and Edward Playfair, the Permanent Secretary at the Ministry of Defence – later fell under suspicion for their Soviet sympathies. 'We were all meeting in the Reform,' said Blunt, by then a senior officer in MI5.[8]

On 22 June 1941 Hitler launched Operation Barbarossa, the invasion of Russia. It marked a seismic turning point in the war, shifting Nazi Germany's focus away from Britain and towards the Soviet Union. For the British agents working for the Kremlin, who had been unable to understand Stalin's alliance with fascist Germany, the attack, overnight, gave their espionage both moral and political purpose. The greatest value of the Reform to Moscow's war aims was the access it offered to key intelligence figures and military officers who unknowingly mixed with, and shared secrets with, the Russian spies. One of the most important was John Masterman, the architect of the Double Cross programme and Operation Fortitude, which fooled Hitler into believing the 1944 Allied invasion of France would take place in the Pas de Calais rather than Normandy. Masterman used the Reform address (and a mattress in the basement) as an alternative to his base at MI5 when he was supporting the private lives of his double agents operating in Britain.[9] There were literary sponsors, too. The most prominent among them was E.M. Forster, another of the Cambridge Apostles, who signed both Blunt and Burgess's ballot book nominations. It was Forster who famously proclaimed: 'If I had to choose between betraying my country and betraying my friends, I hope I would have the guts to betray my country.' Graham Greene never forgot Forster's principle for the ranking of loyalty, and when he wrote *The Third Man*, he invented a literary character based on the 'gentle genius' of Forster.[10]

The gregarious Guy Burgess was a permanent fixture in the club during wartime. He sat at a table on the second floor overlooking the club entrance, lying in wait for his victims, both sexual and political.[11] Since his Cambridge days Burgess had been a promiscuous gay man who used his sexuality to help him forge links with society and Whitehall contacts.

One member remembers how Burgess always waited excitedly for Blunt's arrival: 'As soon as he came into the bar the two of them went into a huddle.'[12]

Kim Philby eschewed the Reform Club for the nearby Athenaeum just along Pall Mall, although he still occasionally visited as Burgess's guest and may have even bumped into Greene before they were formally introduced at MI6.[13] The only record of Philby at the Reform was when he was hosted by *The Times*, who tried to woo him from MI6 halfway through the war to rejoin the ranks of the press corps. The Foreign Office politely told *The Times* he was too valuable in his current post.[14] By keeping a lower profile in clubland, Philby made sure he wasn't seen in the company of the other Soviet agents. He was right to be circumspect. In the first year of the war, Hugh Dalton, head of the newly formed espionage organisation, the Special Operations Executive (SOE), was appalled at the 'amount of quack quack which goes on in West End clubs ... Some of them say that the Athenaeum is a little safer than some other clubs but I doubt even this. It is always observed, I say, who is with whom, and intelligent guesses are then made as to why they are together.'[15]

Graham Greene used the Reform Club regularly and relied on it as a *post restante*.[16] His fondness for the club led him to set some of the key scenes there in his novel *The Human Factor*, a work about an MI5 officer's defection to the Soviet Union. He may have borrowed the name of the protagonist of his other book based on his experience of MI6, *Our Man in Havana*, from another Cambridge graduate Francis Wormald, a wartime civil servant who had been seconded to the War Office from the manuscripts department at the British Museum. The name of the MI6 agent in *Our Man in Havana* is Jim Wormold, and it has been unintentionally misspelt as Wormald by a number of literary critics. Francis Wormald's membership of the Reform was sponsored by Anthony Blunt, who worked closely with Professor Wormald shortly before Blunt was exposed by MI5 in 1963.

When MI5's spy catcher-in-chief, Peter Wright, came to investigate the extent of the penetration of the Cambridge spy ring in the 1960s, he used the Reform Club to interview some of the witnesses. Isaiah Berlin, the philosopher and public intellectual who had worked for the British diplomatic service during the war, expressly asked to meet Wright at the Reform because he told Wright that this was the scene of some of Burgess's 'greatest triumphs'.[17]

Wright didn't realise he was sitting on an intelligence goldmine. The MI5 mole hunters might have had more success in unravelling the Cambridge spy network if they had interrogated the ballot book of the Reform Club, especially as MI5's central registry of the names of Soviet suspects and other security risks, then housed in MI5's temporary headquarters at Wormwood Scrubs, was destroyed by the Luftwaffe in the Blitz – some claim after a tip off from Blunt.[18] The Reform ballot books remain open to this day and include the names of at least five Soviet spies, plus many more persons of interest closely connected to the Cambridge spies.

At the height of the Blitz, the Reform Club remained an important and popular sanctuary for Liberal-leaning members of the establishment who mixed with artistic and literary society, including Forster, Siegfried Sassoon, H.G. Wells and Hilaire Belloc.

Despite its reputation for non-conformism, the club membership also drew from the senior civil service of the War Office and a smattering of military families. One such family were the Brodies, several of whom had served in the First World War and enjoyed influential roles in British colonial Africa. Greene's relationship with one of the Brodie clan in Sierra Leone would shape the terms of his loyalty to his country and help deliver his greatest work.

Graham Greene had signed up to the Army Officers Emergency Reserve after the Munich crisis in 1938 when war with Germany seemed unavoidable.[19] Days after the declaration of hostilities one year later, he had been summoned to a meeting with the draft board.[20] What Greene feared most was conscription to the Artists' Corps or some similar outfit, so he volunteered for the infantry rather than intelligence, although he quickly had second thoughts about his suitability for frontline service.[21]

He managed to stave off call-up for active duty by asking for eight months' reprieve so he could complete his novel *The Power and the Glory*. The board did not know he had already written it and so agreed to his request.[22] Greene was on borrowed time but kept himself busy and profitable by writing book and film reviews for the *Spectator*. This was during the period of the 'phoney war' when Germany and Britain stood at arms waiting to see which of the opposing armies would blink first.

Greene felt the phoniness too as all around him friends and family were being called up without actually leaving London. Greene was an instant beneficiary of mass mobilisation, taking over as literary editor of the *Spectator* after the incumbent, Derek Verschoyle, received his service papers.[23]

Greene may have been keen to avoid frontline duty but he wasn't prepared to sit out the war in the stuffy comfort of the Reform dining room filing film and literary reviews for the *Spectator*. Not while members of his own family were doing their bit. Brother Hugh had met Adolf Hitler, reported for the *Daily Telegraph* on the frontline of the Nazis' conquest of Europe and returned to Britain to be recruited to RAF intelligence who gave him the job of interrogating captured Luftwaffe crews during the Battle of Britain.[24] Brother Raymond was a doctor who worked for Combined Operations and helped train the brave agents of Dalton's SOE.[25]

Graham's conscience dictated that he, too, needed to make a contribution to the war effort, but one that was commensurate with his literary talents. After leaving the Ministry of Information he had been offered five dreary propaganda jobs, one in Lisbon, Portugal, doing PR work for the War Office, but declined them all, holding out for something more interesting. In the end he turned to his younger sister for help. Following a mandatory secretarial course in London, Elisabeth Greene joined the SIS at Bletchley in November 1938 as personal assistant to Captain Cuthbert 'Curly' Bowlby, a First World War naval commander who had been recalled to head up the Inter-Services Liaison Department. Elisabeth was highly sexed – very attractive to men who she found it difficult to say no to. She also had protective sisterly instincts towards her four older brothers, especially Graham.[26] In 1941 she was part of SIS's G Section, responsible for overseas postings, and was in a position to find Graham a posting much more to his liking.[27]

She had done as much as she dared to keep 'black sheep' brother Herbert Greene, the fantasist who had offered his services to both the Russian and Japanese intelligence services, out of trouble and now she started the ball rolling for Graham's introduction to MI6.

In the summer of 1941, Graham Greene found himself at a cocktail party in the West End of London. His host was a mysterious 'Mr Smith'.[28] It was here that Mr Smith's friends had the chance to assess Greene's suitability as a potential recruit to the Secret Intelligence Service, aka MI6. Greene was of course a reasonably well-known author, but it was his character and class that was being judged, not his writing skills. His provincial public school in Berkhamsted and contacts at Oxford University meant his face was a good fit. More important was the Greene family's pedigree in espionage, particularly Greene's uncle, Sir William Graham Greene who after setting up the Naval Intelligence department during the First World War was still involved in intelligence in 1941. MI6 was, just like the Reform, a club of gentlemen who came from the upper echelons of the British class system. They all recognised each other and felt comfortable in each other's company. The unwritten rules that strictly governed the behaviour of their class were more important than adherence to the Official Secrets Act.

MI6 had started the war very poorly, losing two of its most experienced officers and the identities of many more agents to a spectacularly successful Nazi sting carried out in Venlo, Holland, on 9 November 1939. Two hapless MI6 station officers who had fallen prey to the German snare were typical of the 'monocle and spats' brigade who had come to characterise the British secret service. The Venlo calamity was a direct result of their amateurish approach to intelligence work. Someone like Greene, older, more worldly wise and yet from the same recognisable upper middle classes, must have presented an attractive proposition to the MI6 vetters looking for new men to enter the service in the newly professionalised world of the modern spy. As the stoopingly tall Greene mingled with the other guests in the West End town house, he was able to impress them with his adventures in Germany, the Baltics and West Africa.

One of the MI6 assessors later introduced to Greene recognised exactly what the writer had to offer. Kim Philby was a young intelligence officer who shared much of Greene's background and outlook. It was a meeting that would shape both their lives and give rise to one of the most enigmatic relationships of the 20th century.

Philby claims not to have known Greene was a writer as he had spent most of the pre-war years out of the country on his own adventures and had not read any of Greene's books.[29] Greene would have only known Philby by whatever alias he chose to go by during the vetting process.

Like Greene, Philby, who stood out in his favoured army combat jerkin instead of the customary tie and blazer, had no time for the amateur buffoonery that had so harmed the service's ability to fight a professional spy war. Philby reported back to his superiors at Broad Street that Greene was just what the service needed.[30]

Even so, Greene's application remained stuck in the system, perhaps because of the misdemeanours of his brother Herbert or concerns about Graham's celebrity literary status and the libel suit brought by the directors of *Wee Willie Winkie*.[31]

It was already 18 months into the war and Greene was impatient to get started. He could count on positive soundings from a number of influential figures working with the War Office and the world of British intelligence, including his friend Alexander Korda, whose film studios were closely aligned with MI6, and Claude Dansey, the shadowy spook who ran a freelance spy network for the Foreign Office. Dansey had a house in St James's and may have been the mysterious 'Mr Smith' who took charge of the vetting parties.

Finally, Greene's application was personally cleared by Valentine Vivian, the deputy head of SIS.[32] Vivian, in the face of much publicly available detrimental evidence, had rubber stamped the appointments of both Philby and Greene.

Greene's previous travels in the region made him a suitable candidate as a station chief on the West African coast and at first he was slated for Liberia. But his forthright observations of the Liberian government in his book *Journey Without Maps* made such a posting undiplomatic[33] and he was instead proposed for the head of station in Freetown, Sierra Leone.[34]

This was an important job. Freetown's deepwater harbour and strategic location on the convoy routes between the colonies, Commonwealth countries and Britain made Sierra Leone an important staging post during the Battle of the Atlantic and the ground offensive against the Vichy Africa states.

On 20 August 1941, Greene wrote to his mother informing her he was travelling to West Africa for the Colonial Service.

But first he had to undergo a bespoke training programme devised by the chief staff officer that included personal briefings from the SIS section heads. Greene was instructed in codes and wireless protocols and writing in secret ink before he was sent to Oriel College, Oxford, for basic training in weapons handling, uniform and saluting.[35]

Greene regarded the training, mostly aimlessly marching up and down the parade ground in full battledress, no more favourably than he had the OTC back at Berkhamsted. He was unable to slope arms and crashed his army motorbike on at least three occasions.[36]

One of his fellow trainee spies reported that he was 'everyone's comic notion of how *not* to drill'.[37]

A much more serious impediment to his new career as a professional spy followed a routine medical in which the MI6 doctor wrongly diagnosed diabetes. 'I had to pay a specialist to disillusion him,' Greene told Philby after the war. 'I was suffering slightly from lack of sugar rather than too much sugar – a diagnosis which my critics would probably agree with.'[38]

Back in London, Greene finally crossed the portals into the secret world of British intelligence. The innocuous sign at the bottom of the nine-storey office block at 54 Broadway read Minimax Fire Extinguisher Company. Since 1936 this had been the headquarters of MI6, located in easy reach of Downing Street and the War Office. From the basement, secret tunnels ran under the road to St James Underground Station and to a secret door close to the Cabinet Office. Broadway, as it was always referred to, was the nerve hub for espionage, counter-espionage, and clandestine operations during the Second World War. It was here that Greene took his first notes about how to be a spy in a foreign territory from Frank Foley, one of the best intelligence officers in the service.[39] While it was left to Kim Philby to brief the new recruit on the specific espionage threat he would face in Sierra Leone and the neighbouring African states that were in the hands of Vichy forces. Philby told Greene's biographer Norman Sherry of his first impressions of Greene:

'After very few sessions, I came to like and respect him as someone quite out of the ordinary run of SIS trainees. As I try to remember Graham's reactions to such training, the word "bewilderment" occurs to me most readily. The mechanics of the work presented no problem to a man of his intelligence. But he showed, in flashes, profound doubts about the relevance of whatever he might do in Freetown to the war against Hitler. I confess I shared his doubts, although at the time I tried to dispel them with the suggestion that any of the ports of West Africa (Dhaka, Bissau, Conakry) might harbour enemy agents doing us no good in the Battle of the Atlantic, and that Freetown should be a good observation post. He listened with invariable courtesy, but I am quite sure he remained unconvinced. I am also fairly sure that he sensed my own scepticism, though again he was too polite to say so. Or perhaps he realised that I was just saying my piece and extended to me a slice of charity.'[40] This is a telling account that reveals Philby and Greene were well acquainted in 1941, two years before it is generally accepted that they had their first face to face meeting in St Albans, where SIS's counter-intelligence Section V was based. Philby's counselling of Greene about his imminent posting reassured the writer that he would be engaged in a war of intelligence of some importance to British interests.

Philby was also on the up and in October 1941 he was placed in charge of SIS's Iberian desk, the VD section, under another India police service officer, Felix Cowgill, Vivian's deputy. Philby's accelerated promotion to lead such an important desk confirmed the confidence in which Vivian held the young intelligence officer.

Philby's appointment to VD was a relief to Cowgill who, on top of shouldering the growing political responsibilities of leading the section, also had day-to-day control of the whole Iberian operation.[41] Cowgill, who had begun the war as an expert on the threat posed by communism[42], would later discover that beneath Philby's self-effacing stammering charm lay a steely ambition. Under Cowgill, Philby's VD remit was expanded to include Spanish and Portuguese islands and colonies as well as British interests in West Africa, where Graham Greene was soon to be 'our man in Freetown'.

Before his departure for Africa, Greene contacted the film producer Alberto Cavalcanti, who he persuaded to make a film of his short story *The Lieutenant Died Last*. The resulting feature was released as *Went the Day Well* and told the drama of a Surrey village called Bramley End that had been captured by German paratroopers in a prelude to the invasion of southern England.

By the time it was in cinemas Greene, now officially MI6 officer 59200, had boarded a 5000-ton cargo ship from the Elder Dempster Line at Liverpool and set sail for Africa with just 12 other passengers on 9 December 1941.[43]

He left behind a wife, two children and a mistress. Partly comforted by his lucrative film deal and improving sales of *The Power and the Glory*, he could look forward to his African adventure knowing he had taken care of the family finances and that, at last, he was about to play his part in the war.

Chapter 8

Station Chief

The Mediterranean and the Suez Canal were too perilous for Allied shipping bound for West Africa and British bases in Asia and Australia. In December 1941, when Greene embarked for West Africa, convoys were forced to take the longer route around the Cape of Good Hope.

That meant that Freetown was now the main port of call for the South Atlantic convoys. Cargo ships headed for Britain sailed independently from South America, Africa and India to Sierra Leone where they formed up in large convoys, codenamed SLs, before beginning the perilous onward leg to Liverpool and Glasgow, a journey that made them highly prized targets for the free-roaming Nazi U-boat wolfpacks.

On his voyage to Freetown from Liverpool, Greene took his turn operating one of the ship's machine guns and keeping watch for enemy submarines, a task given heightened tension knowing the ship's cargo was TNT and the news that the Japanese had sunk the battleship HMS *Prince of Wales* and the battlecruiser HMS *Repulse* off the coast of Malaya (Malaysia). These losses came just days after the Japanese attack on Pearl Harbor on 7 December and the United States Congress declaration of war on Germany.

Greene occupied himself during the long days and nights of the four-week sailing doing what came naturally to him – chatting, boozing and writing. In his cabin he penned a modest history of English theatre and then began sketching out the themes for his new novel, *The Ministry of Fear*, which he intended to complete in Africa. The book was a psychological spy thriller in which a group of Austrian refugees operating a charity in London turn out to be part of a dangerous Nazi spy ring. If the Austrians had been communists, this was exactly the kind of network that Kim Philby had been drawn into.

Warming to his new role as a British spy, Greene got to know the crew and the other passengers very well. He discovered that the chief steward was of a particularly anxious disposition as his previous ship had been torpedoed just nine days out from Freetown, while the second steward had survived three sinkings. Greene was especially interested in two of the passengers – an elderly American civilian who was an expert in Byzantine art and a mysterious chess-playing Dutchman who 'collects scraps of information'.[1] The Dutchman turned out not to be Dutch at all but a Pole born in Georgia who fought for the Russians in the First World War.[2]

A terrifying reminder of the dangers of the war in the Atlantic came on 20 December when the convoy passed Brest and a huge explosion was heard from one of the other ships. In the initial panic it wasn't clear whether this was an act of sabotage or a torpedo, but the following day a destroyer passed Greene's ship dropping depth charges.[3]

Freetown sits beneath the 'Lion' (Leone) mountain range (Sierra) that runs parallel to the sea for about 25 miles on the west coast of Africa. Founded in 1792 by freed slaves, it became a refuge for oppressed Africans and West Indians, but the much-coveted Sierra Leone River estuary meant their freedom was only ever transitory. Sixteen years after its creation, the African free slave state was forced to submit to British colonial rule and its port, the largest natural deep-water harbour on the continent, became the regional base for ships of the Royal Navy.

At the time of Greene's arrival in 1942, the city was run along ethnic lines. The colonial elite and expatriates inhabited grand buildings overlooking the harbour while the local African population lived in sprawling mosquito-infested shanty developments.

The harbour was a hub of thriving international trade in bauxite, diamonds, gold, palm oil, rubber, timber and fish – all threatened by Vichy-occupied French Guinea on Sierra Leone's border. As a result, security was strict and all visitors were viewed with suspicion.

War had swelled the number of harbour ships to more than 200 craft of all sizes sitting at anchor. Crews and cargo were ferried to the quay by fleets of lighters although since the start of the war crews from neutral vessels were generally barred from disembarking.[4]

Above the harbour, a squadron of Boulton Paul Defiants based at HMS Spurwing, the Royal Naval Air Station cut out of the thick Sierra Leone bush, kept watch over the convoys.

The arrival of Greene's ship was met by a loud and enthusiastic welcome from the Freetown hawkers, peddlers and traders who gave the well-known writer a personal greeting: 'A kitchen orchestra of forks and frying pans played me off the Elder Dempster ... The red Anglican Cathedral looked down on my landing as it had done in 1935.'[5]

Much had changed since Greene's last visit to this genteel African port seven years earlier before he had set off on foot to explore neighbouring Liberia. An MI5 report summed up the military situation:

'The importance of Freetown has steadily increased as a result of the course of the war. Apart from being probably the biggest convoy assembly point for the United Nations,[6] it is the port of call for water and fuel on the route around the Cape, even for those vessels which can reach Cape Town without refuelling. The entry of Japan into the war has resulted in return traffic from the Far East retracing the outward route instead of returning via Panama. In addition it is the focus for shipping utilised in deploying US troops and war material in Central Africa. As a result of this combination of factors the port of Freetown regularly affords harbourage for hundreds of ships and hundreds of thousands of tons of vital shipping of all kinds.'[7]

German agents freely blended with crews serving on neutral ships docking at Freetown, while Vichy agents visited Sierra Leone across the land border with French Guinea. Intelligence picked up by MI5 had to be sent to the Commissioner of Police whose job it was to detain suspects on visiting ships without giving away the intelligence source. MI6 business had also been in the hands of the local police chief but now Graham Greene was on the ground to follow up the intelligence leads. Greene had entered a war zone, a zone of conflict where the Germans were not the only enemy.

In a territorial contest between the British security and intelligence services, MI5 was battling it out with MI6 and the Secret Operations Executive over the control of intelligence in West Africa. Whatever Philby had told Greene about his posting, he could not have prepared him for the internecine nature of the war between the three British secret services. The question of an expanded role for MI6 had been simmering throughout the interwar years. And in the latest act of territorial trespass, SIS had tried to recruit agents from the mounting number of anti-Nazi refugees arriving in Britain. MI5 considered counter-intelligence to be its domain and under its 'overseas control' department[8] dispatched MI5 officer Col Maurice Haigh-Wood to Lagos, Nigeria, using the codename 'Operation Wagon', with orders to establish a beefed up MI5 security presence in West Africa.[9]

Haigh-Wood was the brother-in-law of the poet T.S. Eliot and would have been known to Greene, who had admired and met

Eliot in London. Since Haigh-Wood's arrival, Lagos had become militarily less significant, and by 1941 it was Freetown that was the most important colonial port, on a par with Gibraltar.

Tensions between MI5 and MI6 were running high. Sir Arthur Jelf, head of MI5's overseas control office and a former mayor of Hythe, Kent, warned David Petrie, the new head of MI5: 'What is now recommended, and I am convinced is now necessary, is the appointment of an MI5 officer for each colony. I feel that MI5 in West Africa must either "get on or get out". There seems to be some danger of our being supplanted by SIS.'[10]

Valentine Vivian, deputy head of MI6, had written to Jelf on 13 December 1941 after Greene had set sail for Freetown, informing MI5 that his man was on his way and cheekily requested assistance in bedding him in under the cover of their own Wagon operation in West Africa. Vivian wrote: 'My dear Jelf. Mr Graham Greene, who was born in 1904, is ex-literary editor of The Spectator and a director of Eyre & Spottiswoode, is being sent out by SIS to West Africa to join staff with the eventual object of being established under xxx as our representative at Freetown. Graham Greene has been under training in SIS for the last month or two and, on arrival at Lagos, will stay there for an extra few weeks of local training with xxx.'[11] The 'xxx' notes a redacted name.

Vivian then approached Jelf about the sensitive business of Greene's security cover for his SIS role: 'The question of his cover in Sierra Leone has arisen and xxx has suggested that it would be convenient and desirable if he could authentically work in with your proposed representation in Sierra Leone. Before suggesting precise details we should be grateful if you would let us have your views on this suggestion in principle.'[12]

It took Jelf, perhaps put out by SIS expectation that MI5 should facilitate MI6 territorial expansion, a whole month to reply:

'My dear Vivian. I must really apologise for not having replied earlier to your letter dated 13 12 41 on the subject of Graham

Greene's working with xxx in Lagos undercover of our representative there but the letter from Heywood coded by xxx was mislaid and has only just reappeared. There is no objection at all in principle to the suggestion so please go ahead as proposed.'[13]

Greene arrived in Freetown three days before MI5 had approved his cover, causing confusion and delay to the start of his SIS placement, something that perhaps Jelf had anticipated. Greene's first priority was to establish himself as His Majesty's representative in Sierra Leone. But it was six days before anyone contacted him about his secret posting, a period when Greene was forced to quarter himself in his cabin on the Elder Dempster.[14] There he waited anxiously for his contact to show himself.

Eventually he was offered accommodation by Dr John Martyn, who Greene said was a Food Controller. It was generosity Greene repaid by assassinating Martyn's character in his private journal: 'a pompous little man very inclined to show off: monocle dubiously unnecessary.'[15] The anxious waiting appeared to be sharpening Greene's pen. A day later, a Major 'with a large moustache' invited Greene for a walk. Greene obediently followed him along a dirt track out of town, before stopping at a large rock away from prying eyes: 'Got a message for you. Signal came in Friday. You're an inspector in the DOT [Department of Overseas Trade].'[16]

But the major's good news had been overtaken by interdepartmental politics and the DOT had declined to grant Greene a cover role. The same thing happened with the British Council, the Air Ministry and the Admiralty – an obdurate Whitehall response to SIS's presence in the region that had more than a whiff of MI5 meddling.

In the end, after much arm twisting, Greene had to settle for the cover of a CID Special Branch officer, a newly created role to investigate crimes committed by members of the white population of Sierra Leone. A black CID officer was already in charge of crimes concerning the black community. British apartheid rule meant even crime in the West African colony was investigated along racial lines.

It was Philby, the SIS senior officer responsible for both North-west Africa and the Iberian Peninsula, who briefed Greene on his intelligence role in Freetown. He later wrote: 'it was my business to tell him what we knew of the German intelligence services and of their connections with the corresponding services of the Vichy French. The latter, and a few Germans in the Spanish and Portuguese possessions in West Africa, were to be the main objects of his attention.'[17]

It was further impressed upon Greene, presumably by Philby, how important it was to secure intelligence about the seaworthiness and potential plans for the movement of the formidable Vichy French battleship *Richelieu* that was being repaired 1,000 miles north along the coast at Dakar, Senegal. But since this was too far away for Greene to keep under surveillance, he focused his attention on the crews of the visiting ships to Freetown and the enemy agents stationed in the Vichy colony of neighbouring French Guinea.

Before Greene could begin his spy work in earnest, he was sent to Lagos for three more months of training under the tutelage of Sidney Smith, SIS's man in charge of the four SIS officers posted to West Africa.[18] Here he learnt writing with secret inks or bird droppings if the ink ran out[19] and how to conceal and use a potassium cyanide suicide pill should he be captured by the enemy. Greene shared the training accommodation with another intelligence officer. The two trainee spies distracted themselves from the boredom of monotonous code-learning by playing a game called 'cockroach hunting', in which they used their shoes to splatter cockroaches that crawled over the bedroom and bathroom walls.[20]

When he returned to Sierra Leone, Greene was issued with a second-hand Morris car, a local driver, and a small bungalow two miles outside Freetown in a marshy area below the main hilltop inhabited by the Europeans. On his left hand he wore a gold ring, which he dipped in warm wax to seal his secret correspondence to London and the SIS station in Lagos.[21] In the bungalow was the 'office' safe where he stored the SIS codes and encrypted documents that he received from Lagos and London and a novel by Theodore Powys, the Christian fantasy writer.[22] In London the decryption officer had the same book to read Greene's coded messages. He was not, however, authorised to carry a gun. His day-to-day living conditions were far from ideal. Greene's new home was adjacent to a Nigerian transport depot and an open-air public lavatory and he had to contend with rats, mosquitoes and vultures that roosted on his corrugated roof.[23]

Despite all the privations, Greene was happy here and based one of his most successful novels, *The Heart of the Matter*, on his experiences in wartime Sierra Leone. But he was performing the duties of both MI5 and MI6 and complained of being 'overworked' while he coped with the increasing flow of coded messages between Lagos, London and Freetown.[24] The security lapses and corruption in Freetown must have been only too apparent to Greene. Without a permanent MI5 officer in the city, he was being pressed by his boss in Lagos to take up the slack.

Sidney Smith was an old SIS hand, but totally unacquainted with Africa, who was nearing the end of his professional service.[25] He was also a sick man now having to deal with a cocksure amateur agent starting up a station 2,000 miles away in Freetown. Greene says that the two men had got off to a difficult start when Greene, who liked to question unnecessary orders, arrived in Lagos for his training.[26] Smith had been persuaded to view the security situation from an MI5 perspective and appears to have been receptive to the MI5 man Haigh-Wood, who was working alongside him in Lagos as part of the British combined intelligence operation. Smith did not trust the local security authorities in Freetown, thus placing greater pressure on Greene to carry out tasks normally handled by MI5.[27]

*

Greene did not see it as his job to take part in the routine detention of suspicious crew from visiting ships, and he badly fell out with his boss over this aspect of his duties, leading to Smith pulling the plug on Greene's funding, forcing him to seek financial help from the Commissioner of Police.[28] During one 'long silence' when Smith cut his salary and payments to his sub-agents, Greene reflected: 'I had plenty of time to wonder again why I was here. Our lives are formed in the years of childhood, and when a while ago I began writing an account of my first 25 years I was curious to discover any hints of what had led a middle-aged man to sit there in a humid solitude far from his family and his friends and his real profession.'[29]

The truth was that Greene and Smith, a long-in-the-tooth intelligence professional with little experience of Africa, had 'disliked each other on sight'.[30] As relations continued to deteriorate, a note of sarcasm crept into Greene's reports to Smith: 'Finally we came to open war – I had a rendezvous [with one of his agents] at Kailahun on the Liberian border and he sent me a telegram forbidding me to leave Freetown.'[31] It meant Greene had to renege on a promise he had made to the district commissioner who already took a dim view of the secret services operating in Africa.[32] Moreover, MI6 would miss out on a vital opportunity to make use of a clandestine radio being operated by American missionaries who were about to cross the Vichy border.[33]

Greene was now so distraught and 'fed up' by the episode and the breakdown of relations that he tried to resign his position.[34] It was Kim Philby who came to Greene's rescue by ruling in the novelist's favour, cutting Smith out of the Freetown chain of command and making Greene directly responsible to London and Philby. Greene's morale was further boosted by the arrival of MI6 officers on stopovers to postings in all parts of the world. One of these was Philby's close friend Nicholas Elliott, an MI6 officer who was bound for Lagos and no doubt passed on Philby's reassurances of London's confidence in its station chief. Greene took the opportunity to plead with Elliott for spare condoms because he said he was running low and so the MI6 officer arranged a discreet collection onboard ship.[35]

Greene repaid Philby's loyalty by embarking on an enterprising approach to spycraft that owed more to his talent as a novelist than a newly trained MI6 officer.

His first idea was to establish a brothel in the Portuguese territory in Bissau, further down the West Africa coast, where he planned to install a British-friendly madame. Bissau was 650 miles closer to Dakar and the battleship *Richelieu*, and Greene, perhaps rather optimistically, expected to harvest valuable intelligence from the Vichy French sailors who liked to visit Bissau on leave.

Prostitutes held a fascination for Greene ever since he had encountered them in Paris during his adventures abroad in the 1920s and then went on to develop his coding system for their identification in London.

In Freetown, he was a frequent visitor to the city brothels (hence the need for Elliott's condoms) and must have recognised how much of the passing trade were British officers and civil servants, all with secrets to spill. So why not get the British government to open a brothel and tap this enemy resource in Vichy territory? He had even lined up a woman for the role, writing to London: 'I had found an admirable Madame, French by origin but very patriotic, who was ready, given the money, to open the brothel. I felt valuable information could be obtained from many of her visitors.'[36]

Greene's detailed report was read by Philby, who found it worthy of serious consideration and put it up to Felix Cowgill as a viable operation. In the end it was rejected for being too expensive and too difficult to manage.

Philby later recalled: 'For kicks, I put the plan to my superiors and we discussed it seriously before rejecting it as unlikely to be what is now called cost effective. When later I told Graham the story, he was loudly gratified.'[37]

'Not cost effective' may have been a Whitehall euphemism for hare-brained.

There is every indication that Greene and Philby had already struck up a ribald correspondence. When London asked Greene whether he could make an appointment with an SIS officer visiting Africa, Greene took great delight in sending this coded message: 'Like the Eunuch I cannot come.'[38]

Greene's second idea for an espionage operation was on much more solid ground and betrayed his willingness to suspend his objection to the use of unscrupulous practice when pursuing objectives that served the nation's wartime interests. The operation centred on an African associate of the British publisher Victor Gollancz, who is not named by Greene, but who had been interned in Freetown under the same emergency laws used to imprison Greene's cousin Ben in England.[39] Greene's plan was to arrange the escape of the man, who had travelled widely in Vichy territory, with the help of a group of men purporting to be communists, and get the freed man to pass on fairly benign secrets about the Vichy.

'When we had sufficient of this, we would blackmail him and threaten to show it to the French if he did not provide more interesting material,' Greene revealed for the first time just weeks before his death in 1991.[40] Once again when Philby put the idea to his superiors it was turned down, this time on the grounds that should it go wrong it might attract questions in the House of Commons that could uncover a government-sanctioned blackmail plot.[41]

The rebuff from London must have disheartened Greene. He had devoted time and energy to the project and elicited support for the operation from the Commissioner of Police, Captain Patrick Ian Brodie, who was willing to provide the agents and resources needed to carry it off.[42]

Brodie was Greene's closest companion and confidante during his time in Freetown. London's failure to support Greene in his ventures contrasted with Brodie's generous counsel and willing assistance, and only deepened their friendship.

Brodie, the son of an Inverness wine merchant, had travelled to Africa to join the British South African Mounted Police. In the First World War, he bravely served with the King's African Rifles; he was mentioned in dispatches three times and was awarded the Military Cross and Distinguished Service Order.[43] Eighteen years older than the famous author, Brodie had been in post for nearly two decades. No colonial officer knew the lay of the land or its people better than Brodie. He was a teetotal loner who adopted a cynical approach to his dealings with the British government that must have appealed to Greene.[44]

But the new burdens placed on Brodie by MI5 at the start of the war exposed shortcomings in his command of 300 officers for all of Sierra Leone. While Brodie was greatly valued by the colonial governor, many of his senior officers were not up to the job. Some took bribes from the Syrian-based diamond traders, others drank too much and almost all of them failed to grasp the security implications of the war-sensitive intelligence they often had access to.[45] It was a problem that gravely worried both Sidney Smith and MI5.

In July 1942, seven months after Greene's arrival, Maurice Haigh-Wood sent a telegram to his boss Sir David Petrie, head of MI5.

'In view of the risk indicated in paragraph 5 of my letter 14 July I suggest that information derived from sources needing very careful protection should not be sent until the appointment of a security service representative in Freetown. Meanwhile information derived from SIS sources is received by Smith here, who passes it on to his man at Freetown [Greene] . . . Headquarters and to government with grave danger of compromising SIS's sources and causing the enemy to shut down on channels of communication known to SIS and to start some other racket which it may take infinite trouble and time to get a line on. This is what Sidney Smith is very worried and dissatisfied about. As a temporary expedient I have thought of trying to get Brodie himself to take command as such searches come on but even if he could be persuaded to do so I very much doubt if he could exercise a necessary authority over the navy and army, and I also doubt whether he has the requisite imagination or experience for this sort of job.'[46]

In 1942 the security crisis in Freetown was coming to the boil and the assistant colonial secretary asked Greene to confidentially report to him about the calibre of Captain Brodie's staff. Although Greene had only been in post for a few months, he happily rose to the task, dissecting the inadequacies of Brodie's officers in a verbal and then a written confidential report. He began with a vicious character assassination of the assistant superintendent of police, an officer called 'Rodder', recently transferred from Mauritius.

'He is a foolish man,' Greene baldly stated without any introduction, 'who puts up an enormous personal bluff and regards himself as too big for his job. On his way up from the Cape he boasted that he was going to Freetown to succeed Brodie – a foolish boast as the senior assistant superintendent happened to be on the ship. He fancies himself as an "intelligence" officer [Greene's job] and mixes as much as he can with army and naval officers, including the S.O.E. and his department. Unfortunately as things are at present he goes on the Portuguese ships to examine passports and help the FSP [Field Security Police] Officer in his search and this officer is a little inclined, I think, to respect Rodder's swagger.'

Greene, now in full flow, described how once on board: 'Rodder behaves in a terribly "cloak and dagger" fashion. He does not "drink" but he is liable to call attention to and pinpoint anyone who he may get to know as either suspect or friendly. He telegrams, and one feels that nothing is kept really secret from him, although my opinion of him is shared privately by the commissioner [Brodie] and Lucas [Brodie's personal assistant].'

Next in Greene's sights was Lucas, who had recently transferred from Palestine: 'Lucas, who is not intelligent, is inclined to drink too much and has no conception of security. Unfortunately what is passed to the Commissioner is passed by him to Lucas (it is impossible for Brodie to deal with everything himself), and Lucas is quite ready to gossip – I won't say to all and sundry but to another police officer or to anyone else in a confidential position, such as the censor or the keeper of the secret files at the secretariat. It is impossible therefore to confine the knowledge of any subject passed to the Commissioner to one man or even two men.'

Russel-Jones, another transfer from Palestine, is described by Greene as a 'useful man in a rough house but certainly not a man to have any access to confidential material and one can never be certain in the present set-up how much confidential material is in verbal circulation among the police.'

Age and experience were no protection from Greene's cutting analysis of the station's security woes. Senior Assistant Superintendent Tuach, the prosecution officer in the Sierra Leone law courts, had served longer than Brodie – 22 years. Greene reveals 'his relations with the Syrians are very suspect, he drinks a great deal but on the other hand is well enough pickled to hold it, because of the general insecurity of the police force and through his friendship with the Syrians.'

The only two officers in whom Greene placed any confidence were Brodie's deputy, Inspector Peter Turnbull, and Rutland, an assistant superintendent. But he warned that Turnbull spent too much time up country dealing with diamond and weapons trafficking and Rutland was about to go on leave.[47]

All of these real-life officers of the crown, their security shortcomings and personality defects, made their way into *The Heart of the Matter* in some form or other, most barely changed from Greene's description in his confidential report to the assistant colonial secretary.

However, it was the long-suffering, teetotal Brodie who Greene said shouldered the heaviest burden, declaring that 'he has to depend for help with the new work which has been thrust upon him on his junior staff – and with perhaps one exception that staff is unreliable.'

Throughout his time in Sierra Leone, Greene continued to rely on Brodie, finding him honest, trustworthy and an invaluable guide to the cultures, castes and classes of the people and the colonial civil service that ruled West Africa during the war. He was particularly struck by Brodie's admission that he could not eat meat for many weeks after he had presided over a hanging.[48] After the war, Greene reported how Brodie's 'friendship was the human thing I valued most during 15 rather lonely months.'[49]

He was also in financial debt to Brodie, who had bailed him out when Greene's funds were cut by Lagos.

In *The Heart of the Matter*, Brodie became Henry Scobie, the incorruptible commissioner of police and the novel's protagonist, although some of Scobie's character and beliefs, including his Catholicism, are also Greene's.

For nearly two years, Captain Patrick Brodie had been at the centre of a spy war between Britain and Germany in which he had been ordered to arrest and detain a number of Nazi and Vichy agents in Freetown working on neutral ships identified by Philby and his Section V officers in London. One of these agents would turn out to be one of the most perplexing and mysterious cases of the Second World War that would draw in both Greene and Philby. The affair would also raise questions about Russia's penetration of British intelligence and the true loyalty of officers working for the Secret Intelligence Service.

The agent in question was so secret that British intelligence only refers to him as 'Josef K'. His real name was Vladimir Kusnecoff, a 31-year-old Polish boatswain.[50] His ship, the Dutch merchantman

SS *Parklaan*, had docked in Freetown on 19 March 1941. When the ship arrived, Kusnecoff had reported on-board sabotage to the authorities (a small bomb had exploded causing minimal damage) and had assisted Brodie in his investigations, leading to the removal of three suspects from the ship: Dutch seamen Steen, Meyer and Lagerward. Kusnecoff also told Brodie how he had foiled an earlier attempt at sabotage when he alleged a member of the crew had stolen some TNT.

Brodie sent a report to London informing MI5 of the result of his interrogations and London responded by ordering Brodie to interrogate the three suspected saboteurs, allowing Kusnecoff to rejoin the *Parklaan* on its journey to Canada. But a few weeks into the voyage there was another attempt to blow up the ship, this time in Bermudan waters. A Mills bomb had gone off close to a store of cordite, causing minor damage. It appeared that the helpful Polish sailor was not who he seemed. MI5 in London ordered Kusnecoff to be arrested on arrival at Halifax, where he was closely interrogated by the Canadian Royal Mounted Police. The Canadians came to a very different view of Kusnecoff from Brodie, concluding that he must be a German saboteur. The officer in London dealing with the case was Victor Rothschild, MI5's expert on matters of sabotage. He was also a member of the Cambridge Apostles and friends with Kim Philby and Anthony Blunt.[51]

Rothschild deemed that this was much more than an ordinary case of sabotage on the high seas, as it appeared the Germans were running a sophisticated operation out of Buenos Aires for the recruitment of seamen to act as saboteurs against British shipping. He wrote to SIS urgently requesting they investigate claims Kusnecoff was working with a British spy who he may have met in Buenos Aires at a club called the Belgrano.[52] If his suspicions were correct then many British ships and lives were at risk.

Rothschild also obtained a statement from a Lieutenant Long of the SS *Parklaan* who had warned the ship's captain after arriving at

Freetown that Kusnecoff could not be trusted as 'he talked too much' and had maliciously accused the captain's wife of being a spy. How could Brodie have got it so wrong about Kusnecoff?

On 13 June 1941, MI5 wrote to Brodie criticising his interrogation: 'It is considered that this incident [sabotage] is connected with the previous one. Kusnecoff is strongly suspected . . . This would appear to differ from the details given by you on this matter in paragraph two of your report of the 23rd of March 1941.'

A week later Brodie filed a second report: 'The news of fresh attempts at sabotage on the Parklaan while en route from Bermuda to Halifax arouses fresh doubts as to whether Steen, Meyer or Lagerward were responsible for the Sabotage on the 24th of the second 1941 . . . I consider that statements made by Kusnecoff, the boatswain, should be treated with extreme caution. Nothing is known of his antecedents. He talks in a mysterious manner about his secret work for Russia in South America. He made certain allegations against Steen, Mayer and Lagerward, allegations which were not corroborated. Kusnecoff or some other person has deliberately staged an attempted sabotage in order again to delay the ship in Canada while further investigations are made.'[53]

The three Dutch seamen who had been arrested on Kusnecoff's testimony complained bitterly to their government, prompting a humiliating apology on behalf of MI5 that was delivered to the Dutch security service.[54]

When Graham Greene first arrived in Freetown from Lagos in March 1942, this case was still very much on Brodie's mind, so much so that he may have felt it his duty to share the details with Greene, the MI6 man. The troubled commissioner must have suspected that repercussions would follow. Greene would also have cause to regret his own personal dealings with the strange case of Kusnecoff when he returned to England.

*

Much of Greene's time in Sierra Leone was taken up searching ships for illicit diamonds smuggled out of Portuguese-controlled Angola. These were used by the Germans in their precision tooling industry, so stopping the supply was important to Britain. Greene also arranged long trips to the Guinea border where he met his agents, who reported back about Vichy military installations.

Sustaining long-distance relationships with his wife Vivien and mistress Dorothy added to the strain of his onerous duties in Africa, where he often worked from early morning right through until he went to bed.[55] Distressing personal news, upon which Greene does not expand, had brought him to a point of despair: 'I had always thought that the war would bring death as a solution in one form or another, in the Blitz, in a submarined ship, in Africa with a dose of blackwater, but here I was alive, the carrier of unhappiness to people I loved, taking up the old profession of brothel-child.'[56]

The war appears to have triggered Greene's bipolar depression, and a reckless attitude to life, almost a death wish. During these desperate days, Greene's friendship with Brodie, who offered him a fatherly ear, must have been a great comfort while he faced down his demons and settled into his post. The police commissioner was facing his own troubles, hounded by MI5, partly over the Kusnecoff affair and Greene could see it.[57]

Greene had experienced in Freetown that year something similar when he had been tasked with interrogating a suspected German agent who had also been sent from Buenos Aires:

'I knew from a report about the girl he had loved in Buenos Aires – a prostitute probably, but he was really in love in his romantic way. If he came clean he could go back to her, I told him, if he wouldn't speak he would be interned for the duration of the war.'[58]

Greene asked the spy: 'And how long do you think she'll stay faithful to you?' He later wrote that the interrogation had 'sickened' him, especially as he was forced to go through the suspect's personal correspondence and the 'squalor' of his suitcase: 'It was a police job, an MI5 job again. I was angry that I had been landed with it. It was a form of dirty work for which I had not been engaged. I gave up the interrogation prematurely, without result, hating myself. He may even have been innocent. To hell, I thought then, with MI5.'

Notes in Greene's private journal, which SIS had forbidden him to keep while working in Freetown, suggest he may have indeed uncovered an incriminating letter being carried by the 'German agent'. Greene decided to burn it.[59] In *The Heart of the Matter*, Scobie faces a similar moral dilemma and also chooses to destroy an incriminating letter he found among the belongings of a German agent facing allegations of diamond smuggling.

In London, the Kusnecoff case had raised further concerns about the calibre of the colonial police officers who were overseeing investigations on behalf of MI5. David Petrie decided to send three officers to assess the security situation at the port. The first was Thomas Argyle Robertson (known as TAR) who conducted a security assessment of the harbour in June 1942. He was followed by Colonel Haigh-Wood and then Reggie Gibbs, of MI5's Overseas Control, who were given the job of evaluating the performance of the security personnel, including the work of the police commissioner.

On 10 July 1942, Haigh-Wood reported to David Petrie: 'The special circumstances of Freetown make the problem of security there peculiarly diabolical as my note of 9th of February 1942 and other letters have indicated.' During his visit he had found: 'evidence of subversive and hostile influence in the Syrian and Lebanese Communities of Sierra Leone complicated by the suspicion of corruption by Syrians of officers of the Sierra Leone police; suspicious activities of certain of the French inhabitants of Freetown; the suspected existence of illicit WT [wireless telegraphy] transmission in

Sierra Leone and periodical visits of Portuguese ships with enemy couriers on board signalled by agents in Portuguese colonies or onboard ship.'

Haigh-Wood concluded: 'In a nutshell there are, we may take it as certain, enemy agents among the European peoples in Freetown and that it is dreadfully easy for them to pass information to the enemy by means of couriers across the land frontiers which would take no more than three days even if they were not able to do so by still more rapid means.'

Gibbs and Haigh-Wood saw Brodie as the main obstacle to restoring the necessary security conditions. Haigh-Wood reported to London: 'As regards the police, Brodie is reliable and solid but not a man of great intelligence, imagination, or initiative. He is getting on in years and has been in Sierra Leone some 20 years and can hardly be expected to be a very live wire.'[60]

Brodie took the interference from London very badly and Greene describes the visits by Haigh-Wood and Gibbs as 'disasters'.[61]

Greene's verdict on the hounding of his friend and mentor whose 'humanity and knowledge' had meant so much to him, was damning: 'I remembered the morning in the rains when he went out of his mind under the pressure of overwork, the strain of controlling corrupt officers, the badgering of MI5 bureaucrats from home.'[62]

Chapter 9

Philby's War

Local townsfolk enquiring about the mysterious comings and goings at a grand stately home in St Albans, where a group of young men and women had suddenly taken up residence, were told the building was being used by archaeologists working on the Roman site of Verulamium.[1]

In fact, Glenalmond House and the nearby Prae Wood House were the secret headquarters of MI6's beefed-up counter-intelligence unit, Section V. MI6 had chosen St Albans because the town was close enough to the War Office in London without risking the daily attacks from Luftwaffe bombers.

The VD section, headed by Kim Philby, had been given the job of defeating the heavily resourced and increasingly belligerent German intelligence service that was running operations from bases in the pro-fascist nationalist states of Spain and Portugal and their colonies.

Philby wasted no time bedding down and seeking the recruitment of loyal officers such as his Westminster School friend Ian 'Tim' Milne. The scale of the task facing Philby's section was summed up by a SIS report on 1 August 1942 that must have been written by Philby. In it he says that the German intelligence agency in Spain was running a wide range of sophisticated operations, including 'sabotage, naval intelligence, shipping movements and aircraft production'.[2]

The port of Lisbon, said Philby, 'offers by far the best field in

Portugal for the recruitment and contacting of agents destined for the Americas, Africa, the UK and shipping between all those places. There is therefore in Lisbon a large field organisation [Abwehr] existing side-by-side with the KO [Kriegsorganisation] Portugal and it is on that field organisation that our organisation naturally and regularly impinges.'[3]

Of just as great concern was the German threat to Gibraltar and the straits so vital to the Royal Navy who guarded the British convoys. The Abwehr had financed, trained and equipped saboteurs to attack British naval assets in the Gibraltar harbour, and on 8 January 1942 they sank the trawler HMS *Erin* and badly damaged the auxiliary minesweeper HMS *Honjo*, killing six British seamen.[4]

Philby relied on the Gibraltar station chief Lt Colonel John Codrington to keep him informed of the German operations on the British Rock.[5] Intelligence reports from the Iberian Peninsula revealed that SIS was struggling to get to grips with the nuts and bolts of the Abwehr espionage machinery and hadn't even established the full identities of the German spy chiefs in either Madrid or Lisbon. In one letter to Philby, MI5 officer Cecil Liddell, brother of counter-intelligence chief Guy, asked for help identifying a collaborator known as 'Sheldon' who was passing intelligence to the Germans about Allied shipping from a bar in Cadiz:

'Sheldon,' replied Philby, 'is a Gibraltarian who at one time tried to become a Spanish subject, but appears to have since given up this idea. He has lived many years in Cadiz and is well known as a thorough scrounger and ne'er do well.'[6] And when T.A.R. Robertston, who had returned from Freetown, asked Philby about a significant German intelligence officer he had identified as Lambrecht Pohlmann, operating out of Madrid, Philby had to admit 'we know very little about this individual,' adding confusingly 'it is not however certain that Polmann is identical to Pohlmann.'[7]

This worrying picture of vital gaps in intelligence is further illustrated in other correspondence between Philby and Robertson, who were struggling to identify a German called 'Pablo' only to concede that there must be two agents of the same name.[8] As the confusing and fruitless quest for the identities of 'Pablo' and the other German agents continued, Philby apologised to Robertson for having 'put so much speculation in one letter'.[9]

Philby knew that, in the absence of much deeper cooperation with MI5, he and his officers were working with one hand tied behind their backs. Moreover, the Section VD chief realised that without MI5 input, SIS was failing to take full advantage of the cypher breakthroughs at Bletchley Park that had generated so many intelligence leads.[10]

Aggravating the situation, Philby's boss Major Felix Cowgill, who was in overall charge of Section V, had made himself unpopular with MI5 by shielding from them the secret encrypts of German intelligence codenamed 'Ultra', the product of the breaking of the Enigma codes, adding to the already considerable tension between the two agencies.[11]

In July 1943, Guy Liddell, head of counter-intelligence at MI5 and Cowgill's opposite number, complained to the head of SIS, Stuart Menzies, also known as 'C': 'As long as he [Cowgill] remained in charge of section V there was bound to be constant friction between our two departments . . . it was quite impossible to have any sort of rational conversation with him.'[12] Philby recognised that only full cooperation between the two agencies would defeat the German intelligence service and he set out to urgently mend fences with his MI5 colleagues by passing some secret material under the table, bypassing the cumbersome bureaucracy set up by his boss. Cowgill 'revelled' in his isolation at Glenalmond House, creating an 'excessively cosy' working environment where MI6 officers and their secretaries were all on first name terms. He maintained an aloof proprietary presence, like a headmaster of a minor public school, by overseeing the work from his nearby office apart from the main section desks. Cowgill's detached approach to the management of his officers during this busy and critical period in the war played into Philby's hands.[13]

'Cowgill,' said Philby, 'did not mind how or when the work was done, provided it was done – itself no mean requirement considering the volume of paper with which we were flooded.'[14] Crucially it left Philby free to travel up to SIS's headquarters in Broadway Buildings in London and pay unannounced visits to other government departments. Twice a month, Philby volunteered for night duty at Broadway, where he had the job of monitoring the telegrams and secret messages that came into SIS in the early hours. Throughout this period Philby was loyally committed to defeating Nazi Germany, the principal enemy of both Russia and Britain.

MI5's London headquarters in St James's Street was a short stroll across St James's Park from the SIS offices in Broadway. His visits to MI5 impressed Philby, particularly the calibre of the MI5 staff:

'The officers sat at desks uncluttered by dog-eared paper. At most, half a dozen neat files, each nicely indexed and cross indexed, would be awaiting treatment. MI5 wore an air of professional competence that Broadway never matched. It may have even been over-staffed, as Cowgill frequently complained, but the result of such over staffing was that most of the officers knew what they had to do, and how to do it. The same could not be said of Broadway.'[15] Philby's cooperative attitude, chumminess and physical presence in the MI5 offices won him friends and influence. Among his most useful contacts was Herbert Hart, one of the Oxbridge academics recruited by MI5 to bolster the department's capacity for analytical examination of the mountain of coded messages and reports pouring in from the field.

Hart, who until the war had been working as a Chancery barrister, shared an office with Anthony Blunt in Blenheim Palace, Oxfordshire, where MI5 had transferred the bulk of its operations after the bombing of its station at Wormwood Scrubs. It was Hart who became Philby's unofficial port of call whenever he needed help with a line of enquiry or access to a piece of intelligence held by MI5.[16]

Where Cowgill had kept his MI5 colleagues at a professional distance, the pipe-smoking Philby invited them to Glenalmond House for congenial case conferences.

As Philby later admitted: 'I cultivated MI5 assiduously and before the end of the war I could claim many personal friends in St James' Street [where MI5 kept a central London office]. It was in every way necessary for someone to soften the collision between Cowgill and our opposite numbers and as few others were willing to take the lead I took it upon myself.'[17]

Regular visitors included officers Victor Rothschild and Tomás Harris, the only MI5 officer to address his senior SIS counterpart in official correspondence as 'Dear Kim'.[18] Through Rothschild, MI5's resident expert on sabotage, Philby learnt how German agents operating out of Spain were using bottles of hair cream to carry explosive material.[19]

The Americans believed they had much to learn from Britain's MI6, and had sent a small team of intelligence officers to join Philby and Cowgill at Section V in St Albans in 1942.[20] Philby masked his instinctive dislike of the Americans[21] and began aggressively cultivating the Yale-educated spies who had a fondness for English and American poetry. Among them were Norman Pearson, a Boston aristocrat, and later James Jesus Angleton, the head of the CIA's counter-intelligence department from 1954 to 1975. Pearson taught Angleton poetry at Yale and they both counted modernist poet Ezra Pound as a personal friend.[22] The later arrival of Graham Greene from Sierra Leone only added to the literary appeal of Section V's hard-nosed limey spies. Greene fondly recalled being told how the first contingent from the Office of Strategic Services (OSS), a forerunner of the CIA, arrived at Bristol Airport 'with revolvers on their hips (I can't imagine Professor

Pearson with a revolver) and demanded special transport to London, claiming "we are the American secret service".'[23]

Greene, however, was wary of the Americans, later saying he had 'never been a member of the English-speaking Union', and guarded against being drawn into literary discussions that strayed into his professional work.[24]

'My conversations with Professor Pearson, as I remember them, always began with literature, I think we disagreed about the merits of professor [Cecil] Day-Lewis, but they would nearly always end with some query about some unpronounceable character in the by-ways of Lisbon.'[25]

The more amiable Philby happily schooled the American spies and then charmed them into sharing American secrets.

In these early days, the greatest challenge facing combined British intelligence operations on the peninsula was the poor quality of the agents recruited by MI5 and MI6. One of the worst was the aptly named Agent Careless, Clark Korab, a Polish pilot captured by the Germans at the start of the war. MI5 tried to run him as a double agent, but after being detained for failing to follow orders, he got into even hotter water by fraudulently signing his own release form in the name of his controlling MI5 officer.[26]

Philby invited John Gwyer of MI5 to Glenalmond to see if Careless's Spanish contacts could be salvaged. Demonstrating the extent of this new cooperative working relationship between Section VD and MI5's Section B, Gwyer wrote to his colleague at MI5: 'When I was down in Glenalmond, Philby asked me whether we could find out if the telephone number used by Careless in Madrid could possibly be 58062, which is a number very familiar to them. You remember that Careless said that the number began with 62. I do not think this is a very important point but I told Philby that we would clear it up if an opportunity arose.'[27]

A few days later Gwyer and Robertson wrote to Philby with copies of case histories for 20 suspected Abwehr officers and their agents.[28] Gwyer added: 'I hope that we shall be able to send you others presently as the information is gradually extracted from files here.'[29]

Cooperation between the two services paid dividends when Philby was able to inform Robertson that the mysterious 'Pablo' was a German officer who had 'carefully manicured nails, wears double breasted suits and drives a maroon coloured Citroen four-seater with a folding roof and a "BMW"'.

More significant was intelligence that revealed Pablo's real name was 'Sommer', and that he worked out of offices opposite the Hotel Nueva York in Madrid from where he headed SS operations on the Iberian Peninsula.[30] The best of the intelligence picked up about German operations in Spain and Portugal was obtained from the interrogations of captured Abwehr agents rather than SIS sources or even Bletchley decrypts. It was obvious to Lt Col Robin 'tin eye' Stephens – who was in charge of these interrogations at Camp 020, Latchmere House in Ham Common, south London – that Philby and his section needed to go on the offensive if they were going to crack the Abwehr on the peninsula:

'My attitude,' argued Stephens, 'is that information on the structure of the German SS activities in Portugal and Spain should be the result of active British SIS espionage in those countries. In point of fact such information is either non-existent or not available and I am therefore left in a counter espionage centre, to piece together as best I can intelligence derived from certain spies who are with us at the present time. Much of this information is valuable, and much of it is true, but I do not conceal the fact that I have a number of pieces of a jigsaw puzzle without any conception of the size of the puzzle itself.'[31]

Philby set about completing the intelligence picture. He had two advantages over the other officers. He was a veteran reporter from the Spanish Civil War, where he had got close to Franco, so he was familiar with the key Spanish intelligence and police officers working with the Germans.[32] Moreover, he was able to supplement British intelligence with information supplied by the Kremlin, who still eyed the Iberian Peninsula as a potential Soviet sphere of influence.

In return, Philby was able to hand over to the Russians the crown jewels of British intelligence which he acquired on visits to Broadway. Once a week he turned up with a 'bulging brief case and long visiting list.'[33]

Broadway was a dingy building, a warren of wooden partitions and frosted glass windows. It had eight floors served by an ancient lift. Philby had to negotiate the offices and corridors with care:

'On one of my early visits I got into the lift with a colleague whom the lift man treated with obtrusive deference. The stranger gave me a swift glance and looked away. He was well built and well dressed but what struck me most was his pallor: pale face, pale eyes, silvery blond hair thinning on top – the whole impression of pepper and salt. When he got out of the fourth floor I asked the lift man who he was. "why sir, that was the chief", he answered in some surprise.'[34]

Philby soon discovered he could achieve more at night and volunteered for fortnightly night duty where he had the job of monitoring communication traffic, telegrams and wire messages, coming in from MI6 stations all over the world.

During these night shifts, Philby copied and squirrelled away key documents to pass on to his Soviet handlers. One of the overnight files he stumbled on contained all the War Office communications with the British military mission in Moscow.[35] It meant the Kremlin knew, if it didn't already, the military secrets Britain was withholding from the Soviet Union. Philby could also call upon Anthony Blunt, Guy Burgess, Donald Maclean and a host of other Soviet agents operating in Europe to assist him in his intelligence work. In the National Archives in Kew there is an exchange of letters between

Philby and Blunt that illustrates this synergy. In it, Philby passes on a report from Madrid about claims of an intelligence leak from the Swiss embassy in London. The leak in question pointed the finger at one of the Soviet agents working with the Cambridge spies, Eric Kessler, a Swiss diplomat. It was a dangerous moment for the British spy ring.

Blunt's response was to kill the report and issue this instruction to MI5: 'C.G &C.S. [Bletchley Park] say there are no cipher telegrams which could fit this and from what we know from Orange [Eric Kessler] of the general form of the Swiss [diplomatic] bag I am confident that no cipher messages could be sent in it without the knowledge of the Minister. I originally intended to make enquiries specifically of Orange, but have omitted to do so. Do you think that we can now decently put this away in some well chosen and if possible obscure file?'[36]

Who knows whether the burying of the report also served the interests of the British war effort. At this stage of the war, February 1943, the interests of Russia and Britain were strongly aligned. The Russians had turned the tide on the Eastern Front with victory at Stalingrad, which marked the beginning of Germany's retreat. In May, the German army in North Africa surrendered to the British and Americans. Victory was in sight.

Philby had absolutely no qualms about serving both masters, nor any confusion over which took priority. His conviction that communism must end the war as the ultimate winning ideology had never wavered. He did later admit to having reservations about Stalin's reign of terror but said: 'It is a sobering thought that, but for the power of the Soviet Union and the Communist idea, the old world, if not the whole world, would now be ruled by Hitler and Hirohito.'[37]

One of Philby's closest Soviet contacts at this time was the inscrutable Peter 'Harry' Smolka who had risen in the Ministry of Information to head the Russian section and had known of Philby from his time in Vienna.³⁸ Throughout the war the two men met regularly at Whitehall receptions and cocktail parties. Philby devised a crude communication system whereby whenever Smolka had any important intelligence to impart he would offer Philby two cigarettes, telling him: 'I'll take one and you'll keep the other and that will be the signal that you want to tell me something important.'³⁹

Philby's dedicated charm-offensive towards MI5, with its split locations at nearby St James's Street and Blenheim Palace, was achieving considerable success in the intelligence war against Germany. The biggest breakthrough in this new climate of cooperation between the two agencies had rather humble beginnings but ultimately changed the course of the war.

On 5 February 1942, Desmond Bristow, a member of Philby's Section V D, arrived for work at Glenalmond House where the daily bag of telegrams and memos from London awaited his attention. A telegram from the SIS man based at the British embassy in Lisbon immediately caught his eye: 'Lieutenant Demarest US naval attaché has informed me he has been approached by a Spanish national wanting to work for us in Britain. He has a story about sending messages to Germans from Lisbon.'⁴⁰

The man's name was Juan Pujol García, a Catalan chicken farm manager. It was the start of a remarkable story that gave rise to the legend of Agent Garbo, the most famous double agent of the war.

Bristow soon discovered that Pujol was in fact known to MI5 as Agent Arabel who had been working for the Abwehr pretending to be based in Britain where he was sending his imaginary reports about British military and intelligence back to Berlin. When Bletchley Park first started decrypting Arabel's messages, MI5 was worried there was a real German agent operating out of London with contacts in Whitehall. But as Arabel's secret reports became more and more fantastic (one report said 'during the summer months MI6 decamps to Brighton' and 'the Royal Navy are carrying out naval exercises on Lake Windermere.'[41]) concern had turned to amusement.

Bristow was excited and wanted to tell his boss, Kim Philby, about the potential new agent. But Philby was on one of his bridge-building trips to London at the offices of MI5. So Bristow took his news to Felix Cowgill. The head of Section V did not share Bristow's excitement, raising the distinct possibility that Pujol was a German double agent. Bristow begged to differ and insisted on finding out.

'We wait for Philby to return,' came Cowgill's reply.[42]

Philby returned from London later that afternoon and almost before he had stamped off the snow from his motorcycle boots and hung up his leather jacket, Bristow thrust the Lisbon telegram into his boss's hand. 'I think we have something rather big here. I think it might be Arabel.'[43] Philby, immediately realising that Arabel was the mysterious agent who had been misleading the Germans, slapped Bristow on the shoulder: 'By God, Desmond, I think you're right.'[44]

Without a word to Cowgill, Philby swung into action. He arranged for Ralph Jarvis, the head of the SIS station in Lisbon, to have Pujol interviewed by his top agent Gene Risso Gill in the grand seaside resort of Estoril.[45] Gill and Jarvis were quickly able to confirm Philby and Bristow's hypothesis that Pujol was indeed Arabel. Pujol's background chimed with Philby's. During the Spanish Civil War he had served both sides without ever firing a bullet. First he joined the Republicans then he switched to the Nationalists. He claimed this experience had instilled a hatred of both communist and fascist ideology. But as Philby could testify, such double dealing was straight out of the Soviet playbook.

A week later, Pujol was given the codename 'Bovril' and sent to London where Philby shepherded him into the arms of his friend Tomás Harris and the Double Cross Committee, the joint MI5 and MI6 department responsible for running double agents, who changed his codename to (Greta) Garbo on account of his astonishing acting skills. To make doubly sure he was kept abreast of all the plans for his new star agent, Philby secured a place for Bristow on the XX Committee so he had a direct line into the Garbo briefings.

It meant the Spanish-speaking Bristow was given the job of debriefing Pujol: 'I spent the next four hours translating the messages he had sent to the Abwehr into English. In the afternoon I started the preliminary debriefing. As the representative of MI6, it was my task for the next eight days to interrogate this enigmatic Catalan.'[46] Together, Harris, Bristow and Pujol wrote 315 letters addressed to a post-office box in Lisbon supplied by the Germans. Gradually the British team built up a convincing network of fictious spies all working for Pujol. He fed a vast amount of false intelligence to the Germans, including descriptions and locations of British and American military units, insights into Churchill's thinking and what British intelligence knew about German activity. According to the *Official History of British Intelligence in the Second World War*, Pujol's Abwehr handlers were so overwhelmed that they made no further attempts to recruit any additional spies in the UK. In the run-up to D-Day, Garbo and his group of fake agents would make a critical contribution to the most important operation of the Second World War. And Philby had played a crucial part in his recruitment.

Chapter 10

The Heart of the Matter

Towards the close of 1941, MI6 scored a major intelligence coup by planting its own agent in the office of the head of the Germans' West Africa spy network operating out of Lisbon.[1]

As a result, British intelligence detected and deciphered seven coded wireless communications between Lisbon and Portuguese Guinea between February and May 1942. All the reports related to Freetown harbour, detailing the arrival and departure of Allied vessels, their cargo, the naval escorts and security around the port.

The critical Battle of the Atlantic had placed Sierra Leone at the heart of the intelligence War. The Colony itself was of little interest to the enemy but accurate information about the Allied convoys and military hardware routed through the West African ports to support operations in North Africa would determine the next phase of the war.[2]

The product of MI6's intelligence successes soon washed up on the shores of Freetown where Graham Greene was enjoying his new-found freedom after escaping the controlling hand of Sidney Smith, who had been effectively sidelined by Philby. Under Philby's direction from London, Greene had emerged as a proficient and hard-working SIS officer in the British colony, guarding a strategically vital port. Although Greene later played down his contribution to the war effort, and he focuses in his memoirs on the comical or absurd aspects of the job in West Africa, he scored some remarkable triumphs that have never been told before.

THE HEART OF THE MATTER

In August 1943, Greene felt able to write to his sister Elisabeth in an upbeat mood telling her: 'I quite enjoy my work now – which is more varied and interesting than what I did at first.'[3]

Greene did not mix well with the other colonial types but he was not, as he liked to make out, a solitary intelligence operative cast adrift by Lagos and London. Shortly after his arrival in Freetown, he received some vital assistance in the form of a young woman called Doris Temple. Greene never identified her by name in any of his writing or correspondence. She is, however, revealed by his brother Hugh Greene in a letter written to Graham after Temple had visited Hugh to be briefed about the famous MI6 author. Hugh described her as a 'very nice piece' who would make an ideal companion for his brother. Graham wrote back to his brother pretending not to know anything about her.[4]

In reality, Doris Temple was an MI6 secretary assistant sent by London to help Greene cope with the burgeoning bureaucracy of an increasingly important SIS station. Temple was mostly employed by Greene in the laborious task of encrypting secret reports and memos sent back to 'the office'. It's not difficult to see Philby's hand in her posting, part of his effort to ingratiate himself with the great author while also smoothing security operations in Freetown. After the war, Greene told his biographer Norman Sherry that he encouraged Doris to mix with the Europeans so she could report back to him any useful intelligence. Doris became Greene's personal and indispensable eyes and ears in the British colony.[5]

On 16 October 1942, Philby passed on a piece of intelligence concerning an important German agent who he said was arriving at Freetown on the SS *Quanza*, bound for Portugal. He told MI5 and, presumably Greene, that this agent must be detained and interrogated before he was allowed to leave the African port.[6] The agent's codename was 'Tome' and the tip-off had come from messages encoded by the German Enigma machines, decrypted at Bletchley Park.[7]

Tome's real name was Manuel Mesquita Dos Santos: he was a Portuguese journalist working for the Abwehr in West Africa. According to MI6 he was an 'exceptionally well-equipped spy' carrying with him two kinds of secret ink and a wireless receiver. He had undergone training by German intelligence in Rio where he had been issued with four different cover names.[8]

Dos Santos's mission was to discover whether the US army had a base in Takoradi, Ghana, and then report on British 'military installations in South Africa'.[9] Greene, who did not know about Dos Santos's secret orders, was only able to tip off Captain Brodie that MI6 believed the ship was 'carrying' valuable intelligence'.[10] The Home Secretary signed the requisite warrants and the SS *Quanza* was boarded by Freetown police and officers from the Field Security Police, who searched the ship and entered Dos Santos's cabin on the pretext that members of the crew and passengers had told the search party that he had been heard making pro-Nazi statements. This was important, otherwise the Germans would have been alerted to the real source of the intelligence – Ultra decrypts. Inside the cabin, they found evidence of a spy who liked to travel in style. Among Dos Santos's belongings were a selection of cravats, linen suits and shoulder pads. More significantly the search party retrieved 'a picture book of Royal Navy and US Navy ships'.[11] It was just the excuse Brodie needed to have the man arrested and questioned.

MI5 officer Reggie Gibbs had arrived in Freetown just in time to help Greene and Brodie with the SS *Quanza*. Gibbs decided that Dos Santos was so valuable he should be sent to the UK for a full interrogation at Camp 020 by Lt Col Robin Stephens.[12] MI6 had expected to secure the arrest of a second, and more dangerous, spy who Philby had been informed was accompanying Dos Santos on the return trip to Lisbon. But the Freetown police found his cabin empty, and they now pinned their hopes of catching him on a second Portuguese cruiser headed for Freetown.[13]

This second Abwehr agent was Armando Borges De Avila, another Portuguese journalist, this time based in Lourenco Marques (present-day Maputo, Mozambique), described in an MI6 report as a 'bad character ... without morals, willing to sell his mother-in-law, to say nothing of his wife, to the highest bidder.'[14]

Herbert Hart and Anthony Blunt had tracked down Avila's address in Lisbon and passed it on to Philby.[15] Philby, with the help of Bletchley decrypts, identified Avila's secret courier as the ship's barber serving on the SS *Colonial* and SS *Angola*, two Portuguese ships that were due to dock at Freetown on 31 October 1942.[16] On 25 October, Blunt cabled Captain Brodie and the Sierra Leone Governor, Sir Hubert Stevenson, asking them to apprehend the SS *Colonial*'s barber and the ship's 'nervous looking' female manicurist, who were both suspected German agents.[17]

Blunt added: 'Please interrogate all the above persons and detain any who arouse your suspicions.'[18]

When Brodie's boarding party started interviewing the SS *Angola* passengers they made a startling discovery – one of the passengers was travelling under the name of Armando Borges De Avila. In his desire to return to Portugal as quickly as possible, the brazen German spy was not only travelling under his real name but was on the same ship as his own couriers.

Brodie telegrammed Sir David Petrie reporting on his remarkable discovery. 'He [Avila] was interrogated by Captain McCowatt and myself over a period of two hours and 10 minutes. The interrogation disclosed that he is the editor of the following newspapers ... he gave his address in Lisbon as Luiz De Comes 67, Lisbon.'[19] When word reached Philby of Avila's surprise appearance in Freetown, he realised SIS had been presented with a golden intelligence opportunity. Thanks to Brodie, MI6 now had Avila's secret address in

Portugal from where the Abwehr ran many of their agents across Africa and South America.

Instead of arranging for Avila's detention, Philby decided it would be better to let him run and see who else they could uncover by having him tailed in Lisbon.[20]

Brodie's report also revealed that Avila, hoping to ingratiate himself with the British, had told them that he was close friends with the British vice consul whom he had met in Lourenco Marques, not realising that this was actually British intelligence officer, Malcolm Muggeridge.

Greene must have been highly amused that his old friend and fellow MI6 officer had been so successful in gaining the confidence of one of Germany's most dangerous agents.

Under MI5/MI6 direction, Brodie and Greene were told to question and then release Avila without arousing any suspicion.[21] But the pair went one better and uncovered Avila's address book hidden among his belongings. Brodie arranged to have the address book sent ashore and copied and then carefully replaced without Avila noticing. Philby was now in receipt of the names and addresses of 46 contacts associated with the German spy ring.[22]

On 16 November, Philby triumphantly informed Hart that MI6 had 'met' Avila in Lisbon where they were working on him to attain as much intelligence as possible about the 'German intelligence set up' although they considered him 'far too unreliable to run him as a double agent'.[23] A week later, Avila's fellow agent, Manuel Mesquita dos Santos arrived at Camp 020, where he was interrogated by Stephens who warned him that he faced a death sentence for spying. Dos Santos made a full confession in which he provided intelligence on an astonishing 344 contacts and addresses, as well the secret workings of German intelligence across West Africa.[24]

The combined fruits of the interrogations of Avila and Dos Santos amounted to a huge coup for Philby and MI6. It was also testament to the smooth efficacy of Greene and Brodie's working relationship. The MI6-led counter-intelligence operation had neutralised a vital German spy ring operating against Britain's key sea routes between West Africa, Britain and America and handed the British government a diplomatic victory: the Foreign Office could now prove to the Portuguese President Salazar that German agents were using Portuguese cover to spy on British interests. This was hugely important as the German operations risked Salazar's cherished policy of neutrality.

Philby informed senior officers at MI5: '... we can now give them documentary evidence that the German espionage activities are directed against Portugal as well as against Great Britain.'[25]

Philby was careful to share credit for his success with both the Foreign Office and the Home Office, who had directly benefited from his more cooperative approach to joint intelligence operations.

Yet all was not well in Freetown, where the counter-espionage breakthrough had raised the profile of the former intelligence backwater and added impetus to the turf war raging between MI5 and MI6. Philby was pushing for a greater SIS presence in the country.[26] An unfair impression emerged, or was allowed to emerge, that the MI5/6 breakthrough had been achieved in spite of and not because of the Sierra Leone Commissioner of Police.

David Petrie, the Director General of MI5, wanted to replace the ageing Brodie with one of his own officers, but the police chief had influential allies who did not want to lose such an experienced officer. Lord Swinton, the resident British Minister in West Africa, told Petrie that he regarded Brodie as 'an exceptionally good commissioner of police ... with a sound appreciation of security problems and he works well with everyone.' He insisted: 'For all these reasons I think Brodie should continue as security officer. I think he may well need help, and that it is desirable, at the present time that there should be a MI5 officer in Freetown as an assistant to Brodie who can devote himself entirely to security work.'[27]

For the time being, Brodie was spared from a humiliating forced retirement. Petrie, however, was determined to find evidence that would allow him to replace Brodie with a more malleable police commissioner. He sent Reggie Gibbs and Maurice Haigh-Wood to Freetown to do his dirty work. Haigh-Wood was billeted with Brodie, and Gibbs with Graham Greene.

Greene immediately took against his 'slimy' visitor after surreptitiously reading the man's diary in which he had written that Greene's accommodation was a 'rat hole' and Greene himself 'not up to the job'.[28] Brodie took violent exception to both men, describing them as 'dirty spies', which they were, and after several weeks had ordered them out of his office, although he was later forced to write a letter of apology.[29] Their prying presence had pushed Brodie to the edge, causing him to suffer a minor breakdown, an episode that left a lasting impression on Greene. Greene's 'slimy' MI5 guest and the MI5 visit took literary form in his novel *The Heart of the Matter*. Greene cast Gibbs as Edward Wilson, the MI5 officer who is sent by London to spy on Henry Scobie and ends up having an affair with his wife.

David Petrie's investigators had not only failed to dislodge Brodie, they had also antagonised the SIS man and the colonial staff in Sierra Leone. Gibbs had accepted Brodie's apology, and the embarrassing episode had appeared to have been laid to rest. Yet Petrie's 'Brodie problem' was unresolved, leaving responsibility for security and intelligence matters in Freetown to be ceded to SIS. Or so it seemed.

Then on 9 December 1942, Petrie received a report written by an intelligence officer stationed in Africa, which gave the MI5 chief the ammunition he finally needed to bury the Sierra Leone police chief for good. Curiously it had been sent to MI5 via Major Felix Cowgill of MI6 who said 'I am enclosing a copy of a report from our representative in Freetown which I think you will like to see.'[30] The author of the report was Graham Greene, who said that he was putting his thoughts in writing after the assistant colonial secretary 'asked me for a confidential verbal report on the Freetown police from the security standpoint . . . which may supplement the report of the MI5 representative [Reggie D Gibbs] when he returns.'

Greene declared: 'Brodie has 19 very hard years in this colony, often in the most difficult times with only one white officer on whom to rely. The war has added enormously to his work but no adequate extra assistance has been given him. He is now an elderly and very tired man on the verge of a breakdown. He lives alone, goes out practically not at all: he is quite aware of the normal gaps and faults in his organisation, especially as far as MI5 is concerned . . .'

This part of the report was very much in keeping with the way that Greene publicly and sympathetically expressed his views of Brodie after the war.

Then Greene added a more objective and professional observation: 'He has a very strong and very natural anti-government bias. Although they are now, presumably as [a] result of the MI5 representatives' visit, showing anxiety over the state of the police, they have in the past shut their eyes to Brodie's needs and felt very little responsibility towards him and no concern for his health. No attempt has been made to appoint a responsible second in command.'

Halfway through his report, the tone darkened with Greene saying that he had recently become concerned about the security situation in Freetown after 'two pieces of information came back to me in this last week via a member of the censorship [committee] who had heard it from police officers: one was information of a dangerous piece of local convoy gossip which I passed to the commissioner for action of a confidential kind (it is more than usually necessary to safeguard one's informant in a colony as small as this), the other of the detention of two men from a Portuguese ship last week.'

Greene now decided to put the interests of his country before his close friendship and loyalty to the man who had done so much to help him during his difficult stay in Freetown:

'Since Brodie's breakdown at the time of MI5's representative's visit,' Greene told Philby and his other bosses in London, 'the position has worsened a good deal. The situation which arose must be known by gossip to both the police and the Field Security Police [FSP] and one feels they have closed their ranks against the outside organisation. Brodie is inclined to manifest his hostility to MI5 by rather pointed cracks and criticisms of their telegrams and I feel his action in taking off two passengers last week without direction from London and without advising me beforehand was a symptom of his hostility to MI5. This attitude is having its effect on the FSP who are more and more inclined to take the bit between their teeth. I must emphasise that my relations with Brodie are and have always been completely amicable but this is now at the cost of keeping as much as possible outside his MI5 activities – a state of affairs which cannot continue.'[31] Greene's quiet professional damnation of the police commissioner was loudly endorsed by Greene's boss Kim Philby, who now described Brodie as a 'sub-tropical boozer of sub-homicidal tendencies'.[32]

David Petrie scrawled on the cover note to Greene's report: 'It looks as if Brodie could be retired.'[33] Relying on Greene's report, Petrie asked his office to inform Lord Swinton that because of the 'exceptional importance of Freetown' and the 'necessity for action on information from delicate sources [Greene's report]' Brodie should be relieved of all his security duties.[34] Brodie was indeed retired,[35] although he continued in post and worked with Greene for a few more months, always oblivious to the fact that it was his friend, an inexperienced SIS officer who had regarded him as something of a father figure, who had stabbed him in the back.

Graham Greene had stood by Brodie for as long as he could but the police chief's paranoia had simply become unmanageable, forcing Greene into an impossible position where he had to do something.

The episode offers a rather different perspective of Greene, a man willing to betray his friend for the sake of the security of his country. It is an act of betrayal that seems particularly stone-hearted given Greene had days earlier received the devastating news (4 November 1942) that his own father had died.[36]

Greene's betrayal of Brodie is played out in thinly veiled detail in *The Heart of the Matter*.

The inexperienced intelligence officer, Edward Wilson, who is posted to the African colony and befriended by the ageing police commissioner Scobie. Wilson repays Scobie's friendship by reporting him to the Colonial Secretary over an alleged diamond bribe and then revealing the true cause of Scobie's death to be suicide. In Greene's hierarchy of treachery, this final act is the most heinous of all as it means the Catholic Scobie will suffer eternal damnation. Is this how Greene felt about his own treachery towards Brodie?

After Brodie's departure in 1943, Greene was helped by Peter Turnbull, who he had praised in his secret report to London. Deputy commissioner Scobie's passing over for promotion is analogous with Brodie's sacking and replacement by Greene's proposed candidate Turnbull.[37]

So what drove Greene to denounce his only true friend in Freetown?

Could it have been that Brodie had tried to freeze Greene out of the fruits of the interrogations of Avila and Dos Santos? Or was Greene professionally concerned about the threat to the security of British convoys at this critical juncture in the war when the Allies had advanced plans to use the Sierra Leone convoys in Operation Torch, the codename for the invasion of Vichy territories in North Africa.[38] These high-risk Anglo-American amphibious landings were so secret that Philby had only been informed of the operation in August.[39] If it was to succeed, absolute secrecy and tactical surprise were paramount. Loose talk in Freetown really could have cost thousands of lives. Torch marked the first major Anglo-American operation of the Second World War, the first large-scale Allied amphibious landing, and the beginning of the end of Axis power in North Africa, paving the way for future offensives in Europe. The stakes could not have been higher.

Kim Philby and Graham Greene's work in disrupting the Abwehr's operations in West Africa had been important in helping to prepare the ground for the invasion. But the job was not done.

MI6 had received reports of at least eight German wireless stations located close to the Straits of Gibraltar, gathering intelligence on Allied ship movements and convoys being assembled under the invasion task force.

The Germans were aware of the Allies' build-up of shipping in Gibraltar and knew that something was being planned, but they had no concrete intelligence as to what it might be.

Philby's section reported: 'The means of communication used [wireless telegraphy] ensured extremely rapid transmission of news . . . any movement of shipping in the Straits was in the hands of German naval HQ both in the Atlantic and in the Mediterranean within a few hours of observation . . . only on moonless nights – and even then never with any certainty – could shipping hope to escape undetected.'[40]

Briefed by Gibraltar Station Chief John Codrington, Philby feared that the Germans were about to place infra-red ship detection equipment on the approaches to the Straits.[41] This was of precarious concern because the Torch convoys were to set sail under cover of night. It was surely only a matter of time before the Germans cottoned on to what was being planned and vectored packs of U-boats to the North Africa convoy routes. Philby's section swung into action by compiling a dossier of German espionage activity in Spain that was to be used by the British government to put pressure on Franco to curb Abwehr operations in the run-up to Torch.[42]

Armed with Philby's dossier, the British ambassador, Samuel Hoare, put the case to Franco that German actions threatened to draw Spain into the war. While Franco recognised the danger, he refused to intervene, pointing out that the British also ran agents on Spanish territory, including some communists (perhaps recruited directly by Philby) who opposed Franco's government.[43]

Philby's dossier had failed, leaving the British to counter the German wolfpack threat to Torch by mounting an extensive deception operation, planting false reports of a build-up of shipping bound for the beleaguered Mediterranean island of Malta as well as false plans for an attack on Italian territory.

In the run-up to Torch in October 1942, Hitler's U-boats, patrolling the Atlantic and Mediterranean, presented a very serious danger, and the success of the top-secret operation was hanging perilously in the balance. In a desperate high-risk gambit to try to lure the U-boats away from the waters that lay between Gibraltar and the intended invasion beaches of Morocco and Tunisia, the Admiralty devised a deeply controversial plan to deploy a decoy convoy.[44] Convoy SL (Sierra Leone) 125 was to be the 125th convoy of merchant ships since the start of the war to leave Freetown harbour bound for Liverpool. Thirty-seven merchantmen departed Freetown on 16 October 1942, and they were joined at sea by five more.[45] This was the same day that Philby had passed on to Greene the intelligence about the arrival in Freetown of the dangerous German agent Manuel Mesquita Dos Santos. The convoy's presence was well known to German cryptographers who had decoded naval message traffic. Wolfpack Streitaxt (Battle Axe), comprising *U-103, U-134, U-203, U-409, U-440, U-509, U-510, U-572, U-604* and *U-659*, was assembled on 23 October with orders to intercept the convoy west of the Canary Islands.[46]

On 27 October, *U-409* found and transmitted the location of the main convoy to the rest of the pack. The U-boats were ordered to launch ceaseless attacks on the merchant ships and their escorts all the way back to British waters. By the time Convoy SL 125 arrived in Liverpool on 9 November, 12 merchant ships had been sunk by the Kriegsmarine with the loss of 407 lives, the greatest death toll suffered by any Sierra Leone convoy. These losses were justified by the knowledge that the naval sacrifice had achieved its objective, diverting German submarines from the Operation Torch troop ships that took part in the successful Allied invasion of North Africa on 8 November 1942.[47]

The lost lives were a high price to pay, but had the German wolfpacks been let loose on the invasion fleet, hundreds of thousands of Allied troops and seamen may have perished and the Axis forces would have maintained their hold on North Africa, prolonging the war.

Was Graham Greene privy to the vital importance of Operation Torch and the significance of the timing of the sailing of Convoy SL 125? Was this the intelligence he knew was at risk when he found out about the lax security in Freetown for which he blamed Brodie? If so, then the interests of war demanded that Greene sacrifice his old friend. Greene was careful in his public writing not to disclose any details of the top-secret work he undertook for MI6 during his posting in Sierra Leone. Instead, he preferred to give the impression that his contribution to the war effort was negligible. In his autobiography however, Greene gives away the significance of the North African landings when he describes being caught up in a 'scurry' of intelligence that 'affected even my remote coast with cables at all hours'.[48] Graham Greene, under the diligent tutelage of Kim Philby, helped prevent the Germans from discovering the truth about the role of the convoys in the Allied invasion of North Africa.

Almost overnight, Operation Torch's overwhelming success rendered MI6's presence in West Africa obsolete. The Vichy threat was mostly eliminated in the region and merchant shipping was no longer reliant on the protection of the SL convoys. As Philby succinctly summed up 35 years later: 'After the North African landings, SIS interest in West Africa waned and we left MI5 in possession of the field.'[49] Graham Greene appeared to be out of a job.

Chapter 11

Mole Hunt

While the Western Allies were basking in the success of Operation Torch, two MI5 officers in London had started to pick up the trail of the Cambridge spies and Russia's secret penetration of the British state. Unusually, the two officers involved in the investigation were both women, the only women to hold senior posts in MI5 at the time. Kathleen 'Jane' Sissmore was a barrister and the first female officer to be recruited to MI5 in 1929.[1] She was now Jane Archer after marrying widower Wing Commander Joe Archer, the Air Ministry liaison intelligence contact who had been working on the Herbert Greene spy case.[2] Critically Archer had interviewed Walter Krivitsky in London and had drawn up a list of suspects for Krivitsky's 'young Englishman and journalist of good family' who had been sent to Spain to assassinate Franco.

The second officer was Milicent Bagot, another excellent investigator and a stickler for meticulously correct officer procedure, terrifying some younger officers to whom she pointed out their shortcomings. Her strength was her 'extraordinary memory for facts and files . . . which passed into Service folklore.'[3]

Working in MI5's counter-communist F Division alongside Roger Hollis and Roger Fulford, Bagot would later be the inspiration for the Connie Sachs character in John le Carré's 'George Smiley' novels.[4] Bagot had noticed that there was a reference to a Kim Philby having once been a member of the Cambridge University Socialist Society before later switching to the far-right

Anglo-German Fellowship.[5] Archer and Bagot were slowly but surely closing in on Kim Philby.

In 1942, Bagot began reevaluating the Austrian communists who had arrived in England before the war. One name was of particular interest to her – Edith Tudor-Hart, the Soviet agent who had helped to recruit Philby. Bagot ordered a round-the-clock watch on Tudor-Hart's north London photographic studio, shopping trips and her visits to the special needs nursery where she picked up her disabled son Tommy. The Special Branch surveillance team even reported on her daily glass of port at the Wallace Head public house.[6] Bagot's breakthrough came when she was handed a letter written by Tudor-Hart to a refugee called Leopold Hornik, who had been detained by the Home Office at the Oratory Central Schools in Stewart's Grove, off Fulham Road. Hornik was better known as head of the Austrian Communist Party, a dedicated Viennese communist.[7]

The long chain of correspondence extended to Hornik's later detention in Canada and showed a deep political relationship.[8] It was evidence that Tudor-Hart was an active communist agent.

Three months later, another member of the Austrian communist circle connected to Philby became a subject of even greater interest to Bagot. MI5 had kept a watch on Harry Smolka (Smollett), now a senior officer in the Ministry of Information in charge of the Russian section. The problem for MI5 was that, although the telephone taps and close quarter observation had turned up a multitude of Smolka's links to Russians and suspected Soviet agents, they could all be justified as part of his job at the ministry. It would only later emerge that many of these contacts were in fact active Soviet agents working against British interests.[9]

Among them was Andrew Revai, a Hungarian art expert and journalist who had been recruited to the Soviet cause by Guy Burgess and Anthony Blunt. Revai had worked with Graham Greene at the Ministry of Information[10] and Greene and Revai remained good friends long after the war.[11]

MI5 decided to take a closer look at Smolka's background to see if they could uncover anything more conclusive.[12]

On 8 September 1942, Roger Fulford, armed with the fruits of Bagot's digging, arranged to have lunch with Richard Brooman-White, who knew Philby had liaised with MI6 on Iberian Peninsula cases, to discuss Peter 'Smollett'. Two days later, Fulford wrote to Brooman-White: 'You will remember that when we were having lunch on Tuesday I mentioned to you the case of a man called Henry Peter Smolka @Smollet [sic] in which F2 is interested. I see from our records that in Nov 1934 a Smolka formed a small press agency called LCN ltd with a certain HR Philby. I think that is almost certainly our mutual friend in section V. I should be extremely grateful if you could ask Philby for any information he would let us have about this man. Smolka is at present employed in the MOI and there can, I think, be no doubt that he has good connections with the C.P.GB [Communist Party of Great Britain], which explains our interest in him.'[13]

Brooman-White wasted no time following up Fulford's enquiry and directly approached Philby, his opposite number at MI6. It would have been a chilling encounter for the Soviet spy, and Philby must have reproached himself for his failure to follow Deutsch's strict spycraft edicts about breaking all ties with other agents. Only Philby's sangfroid could save him.

Just 48 hours after their meeting, Brooman-White reported to Fulford: 'I spoke to Philby about Smollett. The press agency in question never actually functioned but Philby knew Smollett quite well at the time. He says Smollett is an Austrian Jew who came to this country about 1920, did well in journalism and is extremely clever. Commercially he is rather a pusher but has rather a timid character and a feeling of inferiority largely due to his somewhat repulsive appearance. He is a physical coward and was petrified when the air raids began. Philby considered his politics to be mildly left wing but no knowledge of CP link up. His personal opinion is

Smollett is clever and harmless. He adds that in any case the man would be far too scared to become involved in anything really sinister.'[14]

By destroying Smolka's character Philby had smothered any suspicion that Smolka had the moral fibre to be working as an enemy agent. Yet Smolka and Philby were part of a network of Soviet spies that represented the deepest ever penetration of British intelligence by a foreign agency. The sad irony for Philby was that, while he had been bravely passing on intelligence to his Moscow masters and cooly deflecting MI5, who had come perilously close to exposing him, the NKVD had reached an alarming conclusion about Smolka. Moscow suspected him of being a British plant and began investigating Philby's contact with Smolka.[15]

Philby now found himself in the very difficult position of having to defend his relationship with Smolka to both Russian and British intelligence. He must have rued the day he had first met the inscrutable Austrian. Smolka remained a scheming and insouciant operative who, just like Philby, enjoyed double dealing and playing the intelligence services off against one another. The only difference was that it was impossible to know where his true allegiances lay, although he must have believed the Russians would win the spy war.

The British were happy to accept Philby's explanation for his relationship with Smolka at face value; the Russians, however, were not. Yelena Modrzchinskaya, a formidable 'blue-eyed blonde' investigator working in the Information Service of the Intelligence Directorate of the GUGB, the section looking after counter-intelligence against Great Britain, had long believed Philby and the other British spies were MI6 double agents.[16] According to the Russian writer Borovik, who inspected the KGB files after the war, Modrzchinskaya's education, knowledge of the English language and blind faith in her own conviction meant she was a force that had to be reckoned with. She asked whether

British intelligence could really be so stupid that no one had noticed so much precious intelligence was leaking to Moscow? How was it possible that Philby, with his communist opinions, his work for the communists in Vienna and his Austrian communist wife, had sailed through SIS vetting procedures?[17]

Modrzchinskaya's closer inspection of his file led to further troubling questions. Philby's father was 'obviously' a British spy and yet Philby had retrieved very little from his burglary mission of the family home. He had also failed in his mission to assassinate Franco, and his handlers, Deutsch and Maly, had been denounced as spies while Orlov had defected to the Allies.

A cross reference of a secret document copied and sent by Philby with the same document secured by another Russian agent revealed that Philby had omitted one important section. Modrzchinskaya concluded: 'He is lying to us in the most insolent manner.'[18]

In the paranoid offices of the Lubyanka, where falling victim to an enemy's espionage meant a one-way trip to the basement, Modrzchinskaya's view held sway. Moscow central told Gorsky to hold off further contact with Philby and the other British agents until they had been cleared by the Centre. They also sent an NKVD surveillance team to monitor the British agents in London to make doubly sure the Cambridge men weren't batting for both sides.[19]

Gorsky tried to soften what must have been a serious blow to Philby's morale, assuring him that the paranoia and suspicion always passed. He must bide his time and carry on with his work until some sort of resolution had been achieved. Philby did as he was told.

Russia's distrust of their Cambridge agents was to the advantage of Britain's wartime aims. This cooling-off period allowed Philby to dedicate himself to MI6 counter-intelligence operations and defeating the Abwehr on the Iberian Peninsula. Moscow's paranoid logic had the unintended result of unfettering the talents of SIS's most accomplished counter-intelligence officer. At the time Philby was careful not to show any bitterness regarding this episode. But in Moscow 50 years later, he still believed that the Centre had been wrong to judge him on his relationship with Smolka who he said turned out to be a very 'trustworthy' agent.[20]

On 7 February 1943, Valentine Vivian, the deputy chief of SIS, visited Kim Philby in his office at Glenalmond. Vivian said he wanted to discuss with Philby important matters concerning Soviet espionage.

The Russian spy sensed danger. And he had every reason to. Vivian had discovered that the Russians had been tipped off about Operation Torch in advance of the landings, confiding in Philby that the Kremlin had 'accurate intelligence on the codes, beaches, medical supplies etc.' He suspected: 'senior officers involved had gone straight from their desks at the War Office to clandestine rendezvous with Communists.'[21]

Which was exactly what Philby had done.[22]

Philby reported the meeting with his MI6 boss to Gorsky saying that Vivian's tone seemed to be one of 'indignation and surprise; he thought it curious that Russia should be spying on one of its allies.'[23]

But Vivian's greatest fear was that the Russians had infiltrated Bletchley Park. Philby reported: 'There was some feeling that the Russians, being very interested in Bletchley Park, might have made contact with some of the younger people on its staff with the aim of utilizing them at some future point. Vivian said, however, there was no reason to think that they had been successful in doing so.'[24]

Of more personal danger to Philby, Vivian said he had been speaking to Roger Hollis, who now commanded the counter-Soviet operation at MI5 and was of the view that the people the Russians were likely to have taken an interest in were 'those who belonged to

University Communist clubs and societies, subscribed to Labour Monthly, and so on.'[25]

This of course perfectly characterised Philby's early flirtation with communism. It was apparent to Hollis that MI5 had merely caught the tip of the iceberg.

In October 1943 Hollis's dire estimation of the Soviet threat was passed on directly to Winston Churchill, who was told: 'These agents differ fundamentally from the very poor type employed by the Germans who belong to the dregs of civilisation. Communist agents are inspired by altruistic, idealist motives, their first duty is to the Soviet Union.'[26]

Hollis was already on to Blunt, who he suspected was up to something no good, even if he couldn't put his finger on exactly what it was.[27]

Roger Hollis was educated at Leeds Grammar School and Clifton College in Bristol before going up to Oxford at the same time as Graham Greene and was also a member of the Reform Club. Greene's great friend Evelyn Waugh remembered Hollis as being a 'good bottle man.'[28] Before the war he had been a journalist and then an executive at the British American Tobacco Company posted to the Far East. Christopher Andrew, the former official historian of MI5, considers Hollis, who had authorised an elaborate bugging operation of the Russian embassy in London, to have had a 'remarkable insight into Soviet penetration' at this time.[29] Hollis was also suspicious of Kim Philby's friend Guy Burgess, who had stunned him one day with an uncharacteristic demonstration of a remarkable knowledge of the structure and working of the Comintern.[30]

Philby was well aware of the threat posed by Hollis, who he said had been 'successful at obtaining an intimate picture of the British Communist Party.'[31]

The Soviet spy liked to keep his enemies close and after navigating

Hollis's 'cautious' nature was soon 'exchanging information without reserve on either side.'[32] In November 1944, Hollis was passed a file concerning one of Philby's SIS colleagues, Kenneth Syers, who MI5 believed was a communist with links through marriage to the niece of Soviet minister Maxim Livinov. The case against Syers was weak and purely circumstantial but Philby risked his own position by defending Syers as 'being remarkably unfortunate in his choice of friends!,' adding 'I have had several conversations with him recently . . . it would seem, therefore, his connections with communists are less sinister than might be supposed.'[33] The case against Syers was not unlike one that might be raised against Philby, so by providing an innocent explanation for Syers' 'unfortunate' associations, Philby was laying down a useful precedent for a defence of his own past communist connections should they ever be called into question.

It was Valentine Vivian who had first passed on concerns about Syers to Hollis. Vivian revealed to Philby that he had the Russians squarely in his sights by announcing 'Anglo-Soviet Alliance, notwithstanding, the Russians had demonstrated their guilt by having an espionage organisation here working against the British armed forces.'[34] Then he coolly confided in Philby that he and senior MI6 man Frank Foley knew who the communist-sympathetic officers were.

Was Vivian bluffing or was he on to Philby and the rest of the Cambridge spies? Two days later, Philby received a telephone call from Peter Brown, the officer chosen by Vivian to be attached to Section V and whose sole role was the investigation of Soviet espionage. Brown wanted a meeting with Philby.

Philby immediately reported to Moscow: 'I will see him on Wednesday. If he wants to do the new job I intend to press for him to be appointed since we get on well and I am quite sure that he will pass on to me everything of real interest.'[35]

The Russian agent was confident he had countered the threat

from Vivian. After all, if Vivian did suspect Philby of working for the Soviets, he would hardly put him in direct contact with his chosen mole hunter.

Later Philby smeared Brown by describing him to MI5 investigators as 'mad as a coot' with 'extremely pronounced Marxist leanings'.[36]

Chapter 12

Our Man in Greeneland

Graham Greene's time in Sierra Leone had run its course. The success of Operation Torch meant he was no longer needed in an SIS station whose importance to the war effort had been overtaken by events.¹ Greene's last act before departing his beloved Freetown was to dump his codebooks, letters and files into a steel drum in the back of his cottage garden and set them alight.² On the same day that Kim Philby was heaping praise on Peter Brown and promising to support him in his new role, Graham Greene arrived in Liverpool from Freetown.

Greene was apprehensive about his return to the 'office', writing to his sister, the only member of the family who could really empathise about his work worries: 'I'm not quite sure whether or not I'm going home under a cloud. I think not as I'm not being replaced. This is a quite useless spot [after the Operation Torch landings]. Anyway you'll probably hear of me yet cleaning latrines on Salisbury Plain.'³

The truth was Greene had acquired 14-months' valuable wartime experience in the field, experience that was demonstrably absent from the CVs of Philby and most of the other Section V officers. Greene was, well, no longer green. His efforts in Sierra Leone breaking up Axis spy rings and protecting Allied operations were rewarded with an appointment to the head of the Portuguese desk in Section V, working under Kim Philby. He had done his candidacy the power of good by reporting on Patrick

Brodie and thus helping Cowgill and Vivian shore up their relations with MI5, who had used the report to oust the troublesome police commissioner. At this stage in the war, Portugal's neutrality was vital to keeping the Iberian Peninsula free from Nazi influence and Philby recognised that he had found the right man in Greene for this sensitive and challenging role.

The returning intelligence officer was permitted a two-week break spent in joyful reunions with his family and mistress, Dorothy Glover, as well as rekindling professional relationships with his agent and publishers. By 1943, Greene was a celebrated author with a string of popular works to his name. His most pressing concern was the dramatisation of his hit novel *Brighton Rock* that was opening in the New Theatre in Oxford. Greene was appalled at the way the director had mangled the story and casting, and insisted his name be withdrawn from the production. He was also being besieged by movie executives fighting over the film rights to his novels, including Alberto Cavalcanti, the director of *Went the Day Well*.[4]

Yet Greene forewent all film projects in order to focus on his duties at MI6, vowing to work long days in the service of the war effort at the expense of his literary output. That began on his first visit to Glenalmond House, where he was to join Philby and the rest of Section V. Greene's sense of the absurd must have been tickled when he realised the British intelligence department for whom he had been working for the previous 14 months was codenamed 'VD', and he was to be VD5.

Greene was to fill a vital role in the Iberian section which Philby was concerned had been underperforming. The 'weak link', Philby reported to his Moscow handlers, was his good friend, Desmond Bristow, who he said was 'immature and had an inferior brain.'[5]

The arrival of the great author at Glenalmond did not go unnoticed. At 37, Greene had published popular thrillers such as *Stamboul Train* (1932) and *A Gun for Sale* (1936), as well as his more ambitious novels like *Brighton Rock* (1938) and *The Power and the Glory* (1940). Many of his books had been made into films. His adventures in Liberia, his run-ins with MI5 in Sierra Leone and his rather fantastic plan for an MI6-run brothel only served to enhance his celebrity status at Glenalmond.

Only one other MI6 officer could possibly match Greene in terms of reputation. That was of course Kim Philby, the hero of the Spanish Civil War who had survived a direct hit from a Republican shell and had been personally awarded a gallantry medal by General Franco. The two men had other claims to notoriety through their families. Philby, at 31 the younger man, was still known as the son of the interned fascist St John Philby. Greene's family fame included an association with the author Robert Louis Stevenson (a first cousin to Graham), close friendships to well-known writers like Evelyn Waugh, and a series of public disputes with J.B. Priestley, Noel Coward (whom Greene repeatedly derided for leaving the UK during the Blitz) and the Hollywood filmmakers behind Shirley Temple's *Wee Willie Winkie*.

Greene and Philby had much else in common, some known to them, some not. Greene's cousin Ben, like Philby's father, had been imprisoned under the emergency detention legislation, while both Greene and Philby had dabbled in communism at university and afterwards widely travelled in Austria and Germany. Both men had sisters working for MI6. Philby had secured a job for his younger sister Helena as a filing clerk with Section V when she was 18 years old.[6] She remembered all the secretaries were 'terribly in awe' of Greene.[7] Greene's own sister Elisabeth had a well-established career in the service.

Working in St Albans, Greene and Philby were ostensibly family men with wives and children set up in suburban houses.

Philby was charming and wry while Greene was mischievous and cynical. The surviving secret memos, telegrams and letters written by them when they were working together and now transferred to the National Archives, stand out for their colourful language in a grey sea of bureaucracy of institutional espionage administration.

In the years after the war, both Greene and Philby were at pains to stress the mutual respect that they had for one another while working purposefully to defeat the Nazis.[8] Philby was the leader of his Section V team inside and out of the office. He created a hardworking but relaxed working environment, organising cricket matches and long drinking sessions in the many popular hostelries of St Albans. He liked to play at being the everyman, often seen drinking with junior members of staff, one of whom had access to the all-important Registry, from which Philby borrowed files that had no bearing on his Iberian work.[9]

In his foreword to Philby's 1968 book *My Silent War*, Greene was effusive in his praise for his former boss: 'Noone could be a better chief than Kim Philby when he was in charge of the Iberian section. He worked harder than anyone and never gave the impression of labour. He was always relaxed, completely unflappable. He was in those days of course, fighting the same war as his colleagues: (the extreme strain must have come later, when he was organising a new section to counter Russian espionage though he was fighting quite a different war) . . . he maintained his craftsman's pride.'[10]

Philby told Greene's biographer Norman Sherry that while he was aware of Greene the author he had not read any of his books, which Philby claimed was 'hardly surprising' as he had been away in Spain working as a war correspondent.[11] On a personal level, it was Philby's human qualities that left a lasting impression on Greene: 'If one made an error of judgement he was sure to minimise it with a halted stammering witticism.'[12]

Philby was equally praising, saying that he regarded Greene as being 'out of the ordinary run' of SIS officers; that his experience of working with Greene was 'wholly delightful'; and that he particularly enjoyed Greene's 'sniping' at the Americans and making 'tart comments' about incoming correspondence from other agencies.[13] Probably because of Greene's acerbic character, Philby recalled that Greene's presence could be 'corrosive' but concluded that he greatly 'added to the gaiety of the service'.[14] Both men shared a contempt for British middle-class hypocrisy.[15]

The head of VD oversaw a band of six officers working on Portugal, Spain and the remnants of SIS interests in West Africa after Operation Torch. This convivial group of spies, who could share nothing of their work with friends and families, inevitably became very close.

The horrors of war were far away and only intruded into their armchair espionage in the secret telegrams and reports sent to Britain by their agents.

At lunch times, Philby led the whole group to the local pub, The King Harry, where the boss held court and they all enjoyed 'warm beer and sandwiches'. Greene remembered those days in St Albans 'with pleasure . . . when the whole subsection relaxed under his leadership for a few hours of heavy drinking.'[16] This did not mean that the rest of Section VD could take liberties. Philby found ways of letting them know that, while he tolerated a degree of subversive frivolity, he was still the boss. Secretaries who made administrative errors would find themselves solemnly standing in front of Philby's desk having to account for themselves. Greene was not exempt from a stiff telling-off and one of his colleagues remembers how one day she found him 'gripping the chair and his eyes glinting with anger'. Greene's explanation was: 'I've just had a caning from the headmaster.'[17]

There were also dashes to London at the weekends for parties and the thrills and spills of the West End, often led by Philby who rode pillion on the back of Desmond Bristow's motorbike.[18] Greene was in his element in London. His writing had made him relatively well-off, although still not comfortable in terms of ensuring the long-term financial security of his family, and he was able to call on the very best contacts in the entertainment business. While he had been away in Sierra Leone he had lived off SIS expenses, leaving his £1,000 salary (worth £60,000 today) virtually untouched, apart from what he gave to Vivien and the taxman.[19] Added to this were the mounting royalties from his books and his stipend with Eyre and Spottiswoode, which had helped pay off his Shirley Temple libel debts.

In the late summer of 1943, when the outcome of war was tilting favourably towards the Allies, there seemed no reason to keep Section VD so far away from its London HQ. Cowgill, who liked the isolation because it gave him political control, was forced to confront the growing case for a move. He wrongly judged that his staff, like him, would prefer to stay out in the sticks away from the interference of Broadway and so put the option of a return to the capital to a free vote.

Philby had always resented St Albans, which placed him further away from both the centre of political power and his Soviet handlers, so he exploited Cowgill's gesture of democracy.

'Characteristically, Cowgill overestimated his hold on the situation,' wrote Philby. 'I assumed that the free vote entitled me to a little lobbying and I got busy accordingly, not neglecting the secretarial staff, many of whom had begun to tire of the cloistered life in billets.'[20] Two-thirds of the staff voted for the London move, a result that completely dumbfounded Cowgill.

Two weeks later, in July 1943, Section V was installed at 14 Ryder Street[21], two minutes' walk from MI5 and fifteen minutes from Broadway. Here the group upped the entertainment and socialising in the nearby pubs, their favourite being the Unicorn on the corner of Jermyn Street.[22] This would not be the first time that Philby outmanoeuvred his boss. The next occasion would culminate in one of the most successful coups ever played against British intelligence.

*

In London, it soon became clear to Philby that he and Greene had something else in common: they both held down messy private lives. Philby was living with Aileen Furse and their children but had not divorced Lizy. It was a secret that he tried to hide from work. Likewise, Greene was juggling his family life with Vivien in the country and his relationship with Dorothy Glover in Gower Mews.

One afternoon in 1943, Philby was given a glimpse of Greene's adulterous second life.

Greene's secretary asked Philby to attend Greene's office where he was writhing around in great pain on the floor, holding his stomach. 'He told me not to worry,' recalled Philby, 'it was an internal haemorrhage which he had had before; could I send him home? I got a taxi and went with him to some address in Bloomsbury. On the way there he asked me a favour. "If when we get to my place you notice anything irregular, please keep it to yourself".'[23]

Philby promised he would. When Philby rang the doorbell Dorothy was there to receive them and without a word of introduction, scooped Greene up and helped him upstairs. Philby remarked that he 'wondered at such sensitivity from the tough man of the pub talk'.[24]

Perhaps Philby was the only friend who could truly suspend judgement on Greene's morality.

It's quite possible though that this piece of potential Kompromat made it into Philby's reports to his Soviet handlers about agent 'Loran', the Soviet codename for Greene, when he recorded the foibles and vulnerabilities of his colleagues. Very few escaped Philby's personalised and often trenchant secret reports. He described Cowgill as having 'large grey eyes set rather close together' and a 'face that gives the impression of intensity coupled with a great weariness,' adding that he had 'few social graces . . . but his capacity for work is enormous.'[25]

Philby informed Moscow that Cowgill's wife was employed as his personal secretary and that his children had been sent to Canada:

'I suggest Cowgill should be carefully watched. It should have interesting results.'[26]

On his old school mate Tim Milne, Philby reported: 'A good brain, though inclined to inertia.'[27]

Geoffrey Trevor-Wilson's 'chief weakness was women',[28] while his new friend Nicholas Elliott was 'ugly and rather piglike to look at'.[29] Felix Russi, who had only recently joined Philby's section, was a 'total moron'.[30] Russia's secret archives have so far failed to yield Philby's report on Greene.[31]

It was at this time that Greene had a chance encounter with another of the Cambridge spies.

On a train from St Albans to London, he noticed the passenger sharing his compartment was reading his novel, *England Made Me*. Greene proffered his opinion that it 'was not a bad book', to which the man replied that he believed the author had written better novels, citing *The Power and the Glory*. Greene agreed that 'it is a fine piece of work' before revealing that he was the author of the work.[32] The two men struck up a conversation during which they discovered they both worked for SIS and knew Kim Philby.[33]

The other man's name was John Cairncross, an aspiring writer and recently private secretary to Lord Hankey, the Chancellor of the Duchy of Lancaster and a member of Churchill's cabinet.

He was now working for Section V after a transfer from Bletchley Park where he had been acting as a translator in the German section,[34] and Greene was now technically his boss.[35]

By the time they reached London, the two men had become well acquainted.

Greene did not know that Cairncross had already done great harm to British intelligence by passing over 1,454 documents to the Russians giving away Cabinet secrets as well as the workings of Bletchley Park.[36] He had been recruited by Teodor Maly in 1937[37] and assigned the codename 'Liszt' on account of his love for classical composers. But the grammar school-educated Cairncross was not like the other Cambridge spies. His family was not upper-middle class, nor did he move in the same social circles. In fact, he harboured a deep loathing for the English class system. Perhaps this was why Greene became so interested in him and why they remained firm friends until Greene's death.

Or could it be that Graham Greene knew much more about John Cairncross than he ever let on? To maintain one life-long friendship with one Cambridge spy might be considered a misfortune but for it to happen twice looks, at the very least, suspicious.

Chapter 13

Josef K and the Canaries

Graham Greene returned from West Africa to take charge of MI6's Lisbon desk and immediately discovered one case of espionage had followed him home.

Imagine Greene's surprise when he was informed that the dangerous German double agent who the British had codenamed 'Josef K' was now working for MI5. To Greene's knowledge, Vladimir Kusnecoff (also spelled Kosnecoff) was the saboteur who had tried to blow up the Dutch ship *Parklaan*.[1] Kusnecoff had fooled Greene's friend Captain Patrick Brodie but had been apprehended by the Canadian Mounted Police in Halifax before being sent to the UK for questioning. His interrogation had been undertaken by MI5's Victor Rothschild and T.A. Robertson, who found that there was much more to Kusnecoff's espionage than the Canadians or Brodie had been able to establish.[2]

Kusnecoff admitted to being a Soviet agent who had been trained by the OGPU in Kiev in 1933. He was employed by Russian naval intelligence as an expert in wireless, codes and photography. He was also trained in the use of explosives and military sabotage and had served with the communists in Spain.[3] And he candidly admitted that in 1938 he had arrived at the Orkney Islands on a Russian ship as part of a spying mission, reporting to the Russian embassy in London, to identify Royal Navy submarine bases and break naval codes.[4]

He claimed that, when the *Parklaan* had docked in Buenos

Aires, he was told by his Soviet handlers to report to the German embassy where he was given explosives and orders for a mission to blow up the ship. He insisted that as Russia was allied with Nazi Germany, British shipping was a legitimate target. But when he later heard during the voyage about Hitler's invasion of Russia and that Britain was now an ally of the Soviet Union, he had switched sides and decided to help the British by drawing attention to the lax security on ships sailing between British controlled ports.[5]

His story appeared utterly bewildering to Rothschild and Robertson (one MI5 officer was so shocked when he heard Kusnecoff's story that he thought Kusnecoff must be an 'exhibitionist').

They concluded: 'From an examination of the evidence, we feel that there was a strong possibility that Kusnecoff had committed the acts of sabotage. The motives however were not clear. First, he might have been a German agent; secondly, he might have been a Russian agent; thirdly, he might have committed these acts of sabotage, which in one way might be considered trivial, in order to draw the attention of the British authorities to what Kusnecoff considers are the gravely inadequate counter sabotage precautions taken by the British authorities in foreign ports.'[6]

MI5 lawyers advised that there was a reasonable prospect of convicting him on the sabotage charge. But Rothschild and Robertson argued that his unique history made him of interest to them as a possible British asset, and it was 'decided not to attempt a prosecution'.[7] When Kusnecoff was given the choice between working for MI5 and spending the remainder of the war interned on the Isle of Man, he chose life as a double agent.[8] It didn't seem to matter to MI5 that he might still be working for the Russian NKVD. Josef K was to be the first agent to be run exclusively by MI5 in Europe, the strict domain of MI6. This was MI5 flexing its muscles in the ongoing power struggle with SIS over the right to control its own foreign field operations.

Kusnecoff's first mission was to infiltrate the Irish republican movement in London so that he could be sent to Dublin to make contact with the German and Japanese embassies. This operation was to be headed by Anthony Blunt, the Soviet double agent, but was abandoned when MI5 decided the counter-intelligence rewards would be multiplied if he was re-tasked to target the same embassies in Portugal, where the intelligence stakes were higher.

He was dispatched to the Glasgow docks, where he posed as an experienced seaman looking for passage on a ship sailing between Scotland and Lisbon. Unknown to MI5, Kusnecoff's handler in Scotland was an MI5 officer with a chequered past. Bill Hooper had been recruited by the Russians in Holland before returning to Britain after the German invasion and finding work with MI5. Both Kusnecoff and Hooper had known Walter Krivitsky when he was the senior 'illegal' in Holland.[9] Where their true loyalties lay now was anyone's guess.

Hooper instructed Kusnecoff to contact the Japanese in Lisbon and offer his services as a spy against the British. After securing safe passage to Lisbon, Kusnecoff spent several weeks in the Portuguese capital talking to the Japanese. He held meetings in local cafés and bars with the Japanese head of intelligence but failed to persuade them he had the calibre of a double agent capable of carrying out acts of sabotage against British dockyards. He had however managed to arouse the suspicions of a British embassy official who he had tried to pick up at a dance organised by the British seamen's institute. She reported him to MI6 complaining that he was very drunk and very anti-British.[10]

Although Kusnecoff was working as a foreign agent in Portugal, MI5 had deliberately not told Kim Philby about his mission. The embassy official's report immediately alerted Philby to Kusnecoff's presence in Portugal and after some rudimentary checks Philby learned that the agent was being run out of Glasgow and London by MI5. Philby was furious that he hadn't been told about Kusnecoff and wrote to T.A. Robertston saying that his man 'was spilling the beans' in Lisbon and he was clearly a 'rabid communist'.[11] This drew an immediate apology from Robertson for both trespassing on Philby's turf and for Kusnecoff's oafish behaviour in Lisbon.[12]

To placate Philby, MI5 agreed to Philby's suggestion to allow Graham Greene to handle the MI6 side of the 'Josef K' operation. MI6 gave Kusnecoff the codename 'Rhubarb'. Greene was teamed up with the experienced Richman Stopford, a former banker who had actually been MI6's man in Lisbon at the start of the war under the cover of financial attaché at the British embassy until he was urgently recalled to help run the Iberian desk at MI5. As a result, Greene regarded him more MI6 than MI5, a factor that helped to smooth their relationship.[13]

A few days later, Hooper reported that Kusnecoff had made a major breakthrough in Lisbon.

The Japanese had finally, and perhaps reluctantly, agreed to set up Kusnecoff as a saboteur and had put him in contact with an explosives expert, part of a Hungarian intelligence team in Lisbon that the Japanese said had the capabilities to carry out an attack on Royal Navy dockyards in Liverpool and Glasgow. Kusnecoff reported back to his British handlers that he was to meet the Hungarian saboteur in Lisbon in July 1943. Although Kusnecoff had only the barest details about the Hungarian demolition expert, MI5 attached paramount importance to finding him and smashing the ring of potential saboteurs. This could only be achieved with the help of MI6 and so Stopford reached out to Greene for any local intelligence that might help them with their investigation.

On 8 August 1943, Greene and Philby wrote to Stopford saying possible suspects for the Hungarian explosive expert had 'come tumbling in', adding that 'our Lisbon representative suggests Ferenczhalmi as chief saboteur'. Greene added that Ferenczhalmi was 'assistant military attaché at the Hungarian legation in Lisbon and is believed to be working in close contact with the Japanese . . . and engaged by the Hungarian War Office to help the German Intelligence Services.'[14]

Philby was even able to procure a photograph of Ferenczhalmi, whose real name, said Philby, was 'Halmi'.[15] But two days later when Stopford showed the photograph to Kusnecoff, the agent said this was not the man he had met.[16] Kusnecoff didn't recognise another likely candidate, a Hungarian agent named 'Fulop', a picture of whom was also sent over by Greene and Philby.[17] Desperate to identify the saboteur, Stopford suggested to Greene that he should arrange for the Japanese embassy in Lisbon to be placed on a round-the-clock watch.[18] This drew a sharp response from Greene, who had perhaps lost patience with the trespassing MI5. He rejected the idea out of hand, saying: 'Even MI5 on their home ground would hesitate to embark on such an enterprise!'[19]

The timorous Japanese quietly dropped plans for a sabotage operation to blow up British dockyards. Kusnecoff had no more meetings with the Hungarians and told his handlers that he believed the Japanese did not possess the resources to pull off such an ambitious operation.

Yet Kusnecoff still retained the confidence of Japanese intelligence chiefs in Lisbon who MI5 wanted to target with deception material. The Double Cross committee sanctioned important 'traffic', a mix of genuine and fake intelligence, sent by Kusnecoff to the Japanese that fooled them into believing major Royal Navy aircraft carriers and battleships were located in parts of the world where they weren't.[20] This helped to give Britain an advantage in its naval war in the Pacific.

Meanwhile, MI5 stepped up its counter-intelligence operations in Lisbon and set up a number of seaman agents and couriers to help 'Josef' to keep in contact with his Japanese spymasters. One of them, codenamed 'Irma', reported that he had been followed by a suspicious taxi everywhere he went in Lisbon. Stopford asked

Greene if he could get MI6's representative in Lisbon, Charles de Salis, to try to find out who the taxi driver was working for.[21]

This enquiry drew a blank. Then in December 1943, de Salis passed back very disturbing intelligence to Greene about Rhubarb/Josef that raised serious concerns about the whole MI5 operation in Lisbon.[22] One of de Salis's agents had uncovered a Nazi plot to capture and interrogate an unnamed British double agent in the Portuguese capital by drugging him with quinine. The quinine was to be smuggled into Lisbon by a German spy, a fireman or stoker, who would be aboard the *Baron Forbes*, a cargo ship on which Kusnecoff frequently sailed.[23]

On 29 December, Greene wrote to Stopford: 'I am sorry that the Christmas season has delayed my written confirmation of our telephone conversation on the subject of the fireman on SS Baron Forbes. The facts are as follows: on December 18 our Lisbon representative reported that a fireman on the Baron Forbes was bringing quinine for a German agent in Lisbon, probably unconsciously. There was a possibility that he would be asked to do espionage on his return. After speaking to you we cabled to our representative asking whether this report could possibly be a garbled version of Rhubarb's activities. We have not yet had a reply to this but our representative on December 20th reported that the fireman bought four canaries in Lisbon and this may assist you to identify him. Your secretary has promised to reserve me one canary!'[24]

Greene's request for a canary was a serious one. When Greene had moved his family out of London to the country just before the start of the war, his two children had not been allowed to keep their pet canaries. Greene hoped to make it up to them.

But his suggestion that MI5's Kusnecoff might somehow be implicated in the quinine plot drew this response from Stopford:

'Dear Greene, many thanks for your xxx of 11th January 1944 about the fireman in the "Baron Forbes" who was said to be bringing quinine to Lisbon for the Germans and returning with canaries. I have made careful inquiries from Rhubarb and I think there is little doubt that no canaries were brought home in that ship. The fo'castle where the firemen live in the Baron Forbes is so diminutive and so limited in its accommodation that there should be little possibility of even getting the canaries' cage into it, and certainly none of having it there without everybody else knowing about it and probably sitting on it! This is confirmed by my port officer who handles Rhubarb and knows the ship well.'[25]

When it later emerged that one of MI5's seaman couriers working with Kusnecoff (Agent Plato), had been spotted bringing canaries home with him from Lisbon, Stopford wrote to Greene pouring cold water on Greene's theory that the MI5 agents could somehow be involved in a German operation to kidnap and interrogate a British double agent.

'Further to my letter of 14th January and the reference, here is a bit more bird seed for your canaries,' wrote Stopford. 'I think we must wait until you get a little more specific information from the other end. Our agent Plato said that he bought one canary in Lisbon on the day of sailing. No one tried to get him drunk during the time he was in Lisbon and no one mentioned or suggested quinine. Plato was the only one in his ship who brought home a canary. He has brought canaries to this country before and every time for the same girlfriend. He suggested that there is a possibility that a member of the crew of ship SS Master Elias Kulekundis may be the person for whom we are looking. Plato visited this vessel and noticed that the donkey man of that ship had a number of canaries in his cabin and amongst them was a white one. There must have been ten others. Plato states the Greeks' ships putting into Lisbon are running a charter for the Swiss Government and Plato thought it very likely that a lot of the smuggling must go on between Argentina, Lisbon and Switzerland.'[26]

*

Stopford confided in Greene: 'The story to me has a very phoney ring about it and my impression is inclined to be the same as yours in thinking that it smells like a plant; and rather a variation of old Weltzein's well known tactics of creating a nuisance for the British by trying to discredit some quite harmless person.'[27] Kuno Weltzein was ostensibly the Lisbon representative of the German engineering company Krupp in Portugal but really headed up a Nazi spy ring. Weltzein's main business was recruiting agents to be sent to Britain.[28] There was nothing phoney about Weltzein, who was very well known to Philby as one of the German spymasters he had been targeting for the last two years. Weltzein had outfoxed Philby on several occasions, including an MI6 tip-off that led to a raid on his business premises. Philby recalled: 'We staged a raid on Weltzein's office with the object of stealing his whole [spy] card index. Weltzein however was not caught off his guard and the raid was a big fiasco.'[29]

Philby later arranged for Weltzein's picture to be attached to the written confession made by Mesquita dos Santos (who Greene had helped entrap) to be sent to the Portuguese president Oliveira Salazar as part of the British diplomatic operation to force Salazar to liquidate the Axis spying machine operations in Portugal.[30]

MI5's complacency in dismissing repeated SIS tip-offs about German plans to kidnap British agents working in Lisbon would place one brave agent in real danger and threaten the security and success of the whole Double Cross operation.

Chapter 14

Betrayal of Trust

On 17 July 1943, a year after the recruitment of Agent Garbo (Juan Pujol García), British intelligence had the good fortune of a second 'walk-in' from the enemy lines. This time the agent wishing to switch sides was a highly placed German intelligence officer who had the full confidence of the senior ranks of the Abwehr, including its head Admiral Wilhelm Canaris. Johannes-Nielsen 'Johnny' Jebsen was an avowed anti-Nazi who, like Pujol, claimed to be running a spy network of agents in London. He even told his handlers he had personal links to MI5's Lord Victor Rothschild.

MI6's man in Madrid, Kenneth Benton, found a very anxious chain-smoking Jebsen waiting for him in a room at the top of the British embassy in central Madrid.[1] 'The Gestapo,' explained Jebsen, 'are on my tail because I made a report on their dealings in forged banknotes.' He might have added that the Abwehr were also looking at allegations that he had been skimming off from the agents' fund and taking backhanders from Spanish and Portuguese officials in his own financial wranglings.

Benton reported: 'He told me that he suspected the Gestapo of lining their pockets with forged banknotes but I was never quite sure it was not the other way around.'[2] Jebsen's loyalty, however, was not in question. One of Jebsen's real agents (Dušan 'Duško' Popov) was, unknown to him, already working for MI6 and had provided corroborative intelligence about his genuine allegiance to the Allies.

From a British point of view, Jebsen was a talking 'dictionary' of the German intelligence set-up who had direct knowledge of Abwehr espionage operations as well as contacts with their senior officers and agents.[3] Kim Philby recognised the unique opportunity that an Abwehr double agent presented to both MI6 and his Soviet masters, and moved Jebsen out of harm's way, arranging for him to be interviewed in Lisbon by Charles de Salis. Philby wanted to keep Jebsen in the peninsula and under his personal control, rather than lose him to MI5 as he had with Garbo. However, he was bigfooted by one of his own MI6 colleagues. In 1943, Frank Foley was the outstanding star of MI6, whose reputation was built on his brave work saving Jews from the Nazi concentration camps when he was head of the SIS station in Berlin before the war. Such was his standing within intelligence circles, Foley had been the officer chosen by the British government to conduct the interrogation of Rudolf Hess, the deputy leader of Germany (Deputy Führer), after he arrived in Scotland in 1941 on his 'peace' mission.

Foley saw the same potential in Jebsen as Philby did, and Foley had no trouble easing Philby off the case. He gave Jebsen the code-name 'Artist' and, with the help of MI5 officer Ian Wilson, kept Jebsen in Lisbon, where he passed on secrets of Abwehr operations and sowed deception material with the Germans, just like Garbo was doing in London.

Jebsen liked to pose as an umbrella-swinging, 'spats and monocle' Anglophile who counted P.G. Wodehouse as a friend. To complete his English playboy persona, he cultivated the image of a hard-drinking, casino-gambling womaniser. The Germans only tolerated his appearance and behaviour because they thought it was part of a disguise to convince the British he was on their side.[4]

In the spring of 1944, Berlin decided Jebsen had outlived his usefulness and devised a plot to kidnap him called Operation Dora.[5] On 29 April 1944, Jebsen and his friend Heinz Moldenhauer accepted an invitation to the office of Aloys Schreiber, the head of German counter-intelligence in Lisbon. Schreiber gave the reason for the meeting as the official notification of a medal of service to the Third Reich (KVR First Class) that was to be bestowed on Jebsen.

As soon as Jebsen arrived, the affable Schreiber invited his 'guests' to be seated. Then Schreiber's mood suddenly changed and he told Jebsen he had orders to take them both to Berlin 'by force if necessary'. Fearing the worst, Jebsen made a bolt for the door, but Schreiber was too fast and laid him out with one clean punch to the head.[6] The German injected Jebsen with a sleeping drug laced with quinine, just as Greene had warned, and two Gestapo thugs helped Schreiber bundle him into a wooden box that they placed in the boot of a large saloon car.[7] When Jebsen awoke, he found himself in a prison cell at the Gestapo headquarters in Berlin. His prospects looked very bleak indeed.

London was only alerted to the disappearance of Agent Artist when he failed to turn up to a meeting with an SIS officer in Lisbon. This was confirmed by an Ultra message from Schreiber sent to Berlin which read simply: 'undertaking is a success.'[8] The news sent shockwaves through the XX Committee, the MI5 and MI6 officers who were running Operation Fortitude, the critically important deception plan for D-Day.

How much did Artist know about Garbo and his fictitious network who had been feeding lies to the Germans for months? When the Committee met a few days later, the potential scale of the disaster was obvious. Jebsen had known Garbo in Spain and already suspected that he was a bogus agent. The verdict of John Masterman, who led the XX Committee, was damning: 'The fact Artist has been removed to Berlin ... threatens the whole cover plan,' adding, 'if all agents are blown then we will have to abandon Fortitude.'[9]

Ultra decrypts revealed that Jebsen was being held with another Abwehr agent captured at the same time as Jebsen, Heinz

Moldenhauer, who the British knew very little about. The D-Day planners wanted to know as a matter of urgency the risk of Jebsen and Moldenhauer breaking under interrogation. They also wanted to know more about Moldenhauer.

Graham Greene, who had been following the case closely, was asked to investigate Moldenhauer's links to agents in Madrid and London.[10] Who was he working for and what did he know about Fortitude? Greene quickly discovered that Moldenhauer was, like so many agents working for the Abwehr, not what he appeared to be.

Moldenhauer had been so desperate to avoid being called up for German military service that he had set up his own spy ring running through the Iberian Peninsula to London. This had alarmed MI5 because one of Moldenhauer's 'agents' had been detained at the Oratory Schools in London, where he was being interrogated. This 'agent' said he had known Moldenhauer in Madrid, where he had worked undercover as a travelling rep for the Austrian café chain Meinl.

Two weeks before the Gestapo kidnapping, Philby was given an address found in a document at Moldenhauer's house in Madrid. It was the address of a woman called 'Doris' who lived in Notting Hill, West London.[11] But when Greene read the interrogation report of the agent being held in the Oratory, it was clear the man was entirely innocent, and the Notting Hill address was invented.[12] Moldenhauer was no German spymaster at all.

In fact, Moldenhauer's so-called agent had found Moldenhauer's company so boring he made efforts to avoid him in Madrid because all Moldenhauer ever talked about was his business affairs. He never once mentioned anything about espionage. It soon became obvious that Moldenhauer's British agents were no more real than Jebsen's.

Graham Greene had a longstanding abhorrence to the mistreatment of enemy agents and the blundering activities of MI5 that stretched back to his time in Sierra Leone. He was clearly unconvinced by the case against Moldenhauer and Moldenhauer's alleged 'agent' wrongly detained by MI5 in London. When MI5 requested further intelligence on Moldenhauer from MI6's man in Madrid, Greene obfuscated, leading to complaints of feet dragging. One MI5 officer complained in a memo to colleagues that he had spoken to Greene but had still not received 'any information from the other side [MI6]'.[13]

The truth was that Moldenhauer, like Jebsen, had been conning the Germans and now the Gestapo were on to them. Both men were being held in the Gestapo headquarters, a block of cells and torture chambers used to extract confessions and intelligence from the most obstinate of suspects. Whatever pitiful sympathy Greene had for these two brave men soon turned to anger when he discovered that they could have been saved.

In the days leading up to Operation Dora, Jebsen had become very concerned that the Gestapo were trying to trap him by inviting him to leave Lisbon for a meeting in Biarritz. But when he confided in Ian Wilson about his fears, Wilson batted them away saying: 'Artist is apt to get into a state of nerves where he quite genuinely imagines traps which do not exist.'[14] Frank Foley had taken a similar view about Jebsen's exaggerated fears of his safety on 17 February 1944.[15]

Yet Ultra messages picked up from German intelligence in Lisbon, revealed that Berlin suspected Jebsen and Moldenhauer of being traitors who were about to flee to London and the SD (the Sicherheitsdienst, the SS security agency) were planning to interrogate Jebsen in Lisbon.[16] German intelligence was particularly alert to such treachery after the defection in February 1944 of Erich Vermehren, an anti-Nazi diplomat based in Istanbul whose family was close to Jebsen.[17] Wilson had seen these messages and now knew that Jebsen was at risk, but instead of giving him a direct warning, Wilson decided to simply tell him to take care in his dealings with another Abwehr officer called Hans Brandes, who the Ultra message showed suspected Jebsen of working for the British.[18] Although it was apparent to the British that Brandes had betrayed his friend to the SS, Wilson concluded: 'It seems clear that no immediate action can be taken by us . . . we cannot strengthen our warning without danger to our sources.'[19]

What MI5 and MI6 feared most was that too precise a warning might alert Jebsen to the existence of Ultra and the knowledge that the British had broken the German codes. Foley, Masterman, T.A. Robertson and Wilson met to discuss whether they could warn Artist before his meeting with Charles de Salis in Lisbon on 17 April 1944. Wilson coldly reported: 'It was decided that time was inadequate to brief Lisbon, and no action was taken.'[20]

The tragic train of consequences flowing from such abject failure to protect one of British intelligence's most valuable and bravest agents blew up into an almighty row between MI6 and MI5, with Foley asking Robertson for full background on the Jebsen warning.[21] Graham Greene must have been all too aware of the Jebsen predicament. MI6 correspondence held in the National Archives include memos written by Greene passing on valuable intelligence to MI5 about Hans Brandes, including his intention to escape the Nazis by obtaining a Mexican passport and starting a new life in Central America.[22]

De Salis had come to trust and know Jebsen very well while they worked together in Lisbon. An extract from an MI6 memo dated 1 June 1944 demonstrates the rawness of the MI6 man's own anger at London for the betrayal of Jebsen and the way they had lied to him. De Salis asked: 'Why lead me up the garden path?', explaining that it would have been simple for de Salis to justify a more explicit warning that would have made it clear that Jebsen's life was in danger. 'If I cannot be trusted to act a little comedy as simple as this,' said de Salis, 'I should not be here at all.'[23]

De Salis's outburst forced Wilson and Robertson to justify their actions, with Robertson meekly protesting that he had done all that he could without jeopardising Most Secret Sources (Ultra).

While MI5 were clearly culpable, so was Frank Foley who had taken the decision not to tell de Salis the full story.[24]

Philby hardly appears in the Jebsen case papers, but he was nevertheless acutely aware of the threat to Artist. He had been part of the team that secured the defection of Erich Vermehren and his wife, who were both close friends of Jebsen. Philby was approached by Vermehren the year before when the young German diplomat was posted to Portugal and had tried to switch sides. Then he had little to offer, but in 1944 the German held a plum job in the German embassy in Istanbul. In February 1944, Philby and his MI6 colleague Nicholas Elliott arranged a secret operation to fake a kidnapping and bring Vermehren and his wife to London, where they stayed with Philby's mother Dora in her Kensington flat.[25]

The defection was leaked to the Germans, possibly by Philby or the Russians, who rounded up all the Abwehr officers associated with Vermehren, gifting Hitler an advantage over his anti-Nazi opponents, thus helping to end any plans for a post-Hitler settlement with the Western Allies.

Philby had wanted to act on Jebsen's idea of approaching Brandes and make him a similar offer to Vermehren, although Philby suggested lacing it with blackmail by threatening to tell the Nazis that not only was Brandes lying about his British spy network but that he was also hiding his Jewish religion.[26]

It is easy to understand how the Jebsen case might have had a profound effect upon Graham Greene, who had always stood up for the agent stuck out on his own wholly dependent on the care and protection of the service. After all, Greene was one of the very few MI6 officers based in London who had served in the field working with vulnerable agents. Indeed, Tim Milne remembered how Greene had become fixated around this time on the 'human injustices' suffered by MI6 agents and one unnamed agent in particular who had been captured in Lisbon but in whom 'we [MI6] had lost interest'.[27] Milne recalls how Greene 'bombarded everyone for weeks with pleas and arguments on his behalf'. Could this have been Jebsen?

Johnny Jebsen spent the next three months in the custody of the Gestapo. In those first weeks Foley, Wilson and Robertson scoured the Ultra intelligence that poured out of Berlin for any reference to the fate of their agent. Their chief concern was not his personal welfare but whether the Nazi interrogators had forced him to talk about Garbo or any of the other agents involved in Fortitude. The matter was so important to the next phase of the war that Winston Churchill was kept informed about the case.[28]

As the weeks ticked by, it became increasingly clear that Jebsen had not only held out against his interrogators but had managed to switch the focus of the questioning away from his alleged work for the British to his fraudulent financial dealings.[29] To this day, his fortitude remains a stand-out example of selfless heroism against the Nazis and their brutal interrogation techniques.

In July 1944, Jebsen was moved to Sachsenhausen concentration camp. He was badly beaten, sustaining several broken ribs. Yet he still harboured thoughts of escape. He told Allied soldiers in the camp that he had been accused of helping the British and when he had refused to talk, his financial fraud had been investigated. Eventually, he got a message to London via British Commando Jack Churchill, but the War Office had no record of Jebsen's name and so the plea for help went unanswered.[30] The British had failed him a second time.

The last person to see Jebsen alive was Frau Petra Vermehren,

Erich Vermehren's mother, who was at Oranienburg Concentration Camp. She told MI6 in 1947 that an SS escort was sent from Berlin to Oranienburg to collect Jebsen and Moldenhauer, but only Moldenhauer returned (on 12 April 1945). Jebsen, who was just 27 years old, was never seen again, executed by the SS.

The proof that Jebsen's terrible ordeal played heavily on Greene's mind can be found in an obscure film treatment he attempted in 1945 under a contract with MGM that had been negotiated with his friend Ben Goetz, the MGM rep in London. Greene says he signed the contract because: 'I feared when the war came to an end and I had left government service that my family would be in danger from the precarious nature of my finances. I had not before the war been able to support them from writing novels alone. I had indeed been in debt to my publishers until 1938, when *Brighton Rock* sold 8,000 copies and squared our accounts temporarily. The *Power and the Glory*, . . . about 3,500 copies, hardly improved the situation.'

He candidly admitted: 'I had no confidence in my future as a novelist and I welcomed in 1944 what proved to be an almost slave contract with MGM which at least assured us all enough to live on for a couple of years.'[31]

The first of these contracted film plots was called *Jim Braddon and the War Criminal*. Its conceit centred on an ordinary American civilian being physically mistaken for a Nazi war criminal. Greene named the Nazi 'Schreiber', the same name as the German who had kidnapped Johnny Jebsen in Lisbon a few months earlier. In his film treatment, Greene described Schreiber as the 'Nazi Inspector-General of concentration camps'.

At the time, Aloys Schreiber, whose German codename was 'Harry', was still wanted for his war crimes. Greene thought the outline to be a good premise although it was just six pages long and nothing came of it.[32] The film was to be set in Mexico where Greene's fictional Schreiber had fled after the war (just as Hans

Brandes had been planning). The innocent American in the script suffers from a severe form of amnesia and comes to believe he committed the crimes. He is saved from the gallows because of his genuine expression of shock and horror at sitting through a graphic film of Buchenwald concentration camp, a reaction that cannot be reconciled with a monster like Schreiber.

Jebsen's case also inflamed Greene's burning enmity towards MI5. When Greene came to write *The Heart of the Matter* in 1946–48, he used the name Wilson for the MI5 officer investigating Scobie in Sierra Leone who ends up betraying him to the authorities. Ian Wilson was the real MI5 officer who ignored Jebsen's own fears about the Gestapo and effectively betrayed him to the Nazis.

Johnny Jebsen had been in contact with one genuine German agent who had a direct influence on another of Greene's masterpieces, *Our Man in Havana,* a story about a spy whose reports are all fabricated. It was a relationship that may have hastened Jebsen's capture, interrogation and execution.

Paul Georg Fidrmuc was a German Czech, educated in Vienna, who was working for the Abwehr in Lisbon during the Second World War. He was given the codename 'Ostro' and had built up a ring of agents, one who he claimed was based in London, reporting on the secrets of the Allied war effort. His intelligence was well known to Greene because Fidrmuc began his spying career reporting on convoys sailing from Freetown and he had alerted Hitler to the secret Allied plan to invade the Azores.[33]

At the start of 1944, Berlin considered Fidrmuc to be one of their best agents, with some of his reports being personally read by Hitler. The same reports were being carefully monitored by British intelligence, who had come to believe that they were works of fiction and that, just like their own controlled agent Garbo, Fidrmuc had no real agents at all.[34] One of the first to suspect Ostro of fraudulent reporting was Johnny Jebsen who, to bolster his own standing with Berlin, had made his suspicions known to the Abwehr.³⁵

Jebsen's report was met with hostility by the Abwehr.³⁶ Aloys Schreiber was the Abwehr officer in charge of Fidrmuc and had the most to lose from Jebsen's meddling in the affair.³⁷ Schreiber had passed on all Ostro's material to Berlin without changing a single comma, effectively attesting to their credibility. Ostro's reports were so trusted by Berlin that they were being used by the Germans to question the authenticity of their own agents' deception material, supplied by Garbo and others, which was vital to the success of D-Day.³⁸

Ostro's guesswork was so close to the truth that the XX Committee decided to try to neutralise him.

The British planned to use Jebsen to expose Ostro's fabricated intelligence to the Germans.³⁹

The plan failed when the Gestapo chose to believe Ostro over Jebsen, sealing the British agent's fate. It is at this moment that Kim Philby, curiously absent from the Jebsen and Ostro files, makes a timely re-appearance. Philby was now running an important and growing intelligence section at MI6, and had been given instructions by the Centre to secure a deeper penetration of British intelligence. The Russians were particularly interested in Mr and Mrs Vermehren, who Philby had safely accommodated with his family in the UK. The German defectors were at the centre of an anti-Nazi movement that included many opponents of communism committed to forming a new Christian democrat government should Hitler be toppled.⁴⁰ Vermehren was a Catholic convert, and Philby skilfully extracted from the couple a list of names of Catholics and democrats, which he passed on to Moscow.⁴¹ When the Red Army entered Berlin at the end of the war, the Russians used this list to round up and execute suspected anti-communists. The part Kim Philby's intelligence played in this murderous elimination of opposition to Soviet rule did not trouble the conscience of the Russian spy. He later wrote that the Vermehrens were 'so god-awful conscientious you never knew what they were going to do next.'[42]

Philby believed that the ends, in this case the establishment of an East European communist bloc, justified the means, even if this meant the liquidation of scores of innocent Catholic Germans. Had the Catholic Greene known of this part of Philby's treachery, he may not have held his boss in quite such high esteem. Instead, Greene was sucked further into Philby's scheming.

Erich Vermehren's defection triggered another unintended bloody consequence that led to the deaths of scores of non-Nazi German intelligence officers working for the Abwehr. His treachery had convinced Hitler that the leadership of the Abwehr shared the views of the traitor. Two weeks after Vermehren's defection Hitler ordered the break-up of the Abwehr and later the arrest of its leader Admiral Wilhelm Canaris.[43]

This turned out to be an unexpected coup for British intelligence, who suddenly no longer faced the canny Canaris and the Abwehr's counter-intelligence apparatus. But it was an even bigger boon for Philby and his Russian masters, who had always feared an anti-Nazi plot led by Canaris to unseat Hitler and make peace with the British and Americans, leaving the Russians out in the cold and a long way from Germany, the conquest of which was Stalin's main war objective.

Philby later set out his reasoning for opposing a peace deal in his memoir *My Silent War*: 'It often appeared that the British wanted a simple return to the status quo before Hitler, to a Europe comfortably dominated by Britain and France through the medium of reactionary governments just strong enough to keep their own people in order and uphold the cordon sanitaire against the Soviet Union.'

Philby had already devoted considerable efforts to ensuring this didn't happen. He had even proposed to his MI6 bosses a plan to assassinate Canaris, an idea that was turned down because of Canaris's potential value to the Allied cause.[44] So when Canaris visited Spain in 1943 to make contact with the British, Philby made sure that the two sides never met.[45]

Convinced that Germany would lose the war, Canaris had sent out feelers for a possible meeting with his opposite number, 'C', Sir Stuart Menzies. According to the MI6 officer and historian Hugh Trevor-Roper, the resulting secret report was suppressed by Philby who 'forbade its circulation' in MI6.[46]

Graham Greene, head of SIS's Portuguese section, was roped in by Philby to help him frustrate the German intelligence chief's peace mission. Philby had instructed Greene to alert the Portuguese international police, who were trying to hold a line of neutrality between the Germans and the British, whenever Canaris or one of his officers stepped foot in the country.[47] Forty years later it still troubled Greene that Philby had played him as a patsy in a Soviet counter-intelligence operation against Canaris, and he told his biographer Norman Sherry in 1983 that he wondered whether Philby had used him to undermine any peace deal that would keep the Russians out of Germany and Eastern Europe. How much these concerns about Philby were bothering Greene in 1944 is deliberately left open.

This was not the only anti-peace intrigue being orchestrated by Philby. He similarly suppressed, as 'unreliable', a report from the important German defector, Otto John, who had contacted one of Greene's agents in Lisbon revealing that a conspiracy was being hatched against Hitler.[48] This would turn out to be the 20 July 1944 plot (codenamed 'Valkyrie') to kill Hitler in the Wolf's Lair, the Fuhrer's headquarters in Poland.

Hugh Trevor-Roper claims that Greene and his fellow MI6 officers were: 'baffled by Philby's intransigence, which would yield to no argument and which no argument was used to defend. From some members of Section Five, mere mindless blocking of intelligence was to be expected. But Philby, we said to ourselves, was an intelligent man: how could he behave thus in a matter so important? Had he too yielded to the genius of the place?'[49]

Philby kept Otto John away from London until after the plot had safely ended in failure. The blast from the bomb, placed by the lead conspirator, Claus von Stauffenberg, next to Hitler in a meeting room, was muffled by a wooden table leg and the Fuhrer escaped with minor injuries.

Hitler's revenge was brutal and absolute and began at the top. Admiral Canaris was led to the gallows naked and executed on 9 April 1945 at the Flossenbürg concentration camp, just weeks before the end of the European war. Many of the plotters fled to Madrid and Lisbon, where the Abwehr officers stationed there were known to be sympathetic to Valkyrie. The only member of the plot to survive Hitler's retribution was Hans Brandes, the Abwehr officer who had betrayed Jebsen to the Gestapo. He was arrested and held in detention but miraculously survived the war.[50] He did not, however, escape a grisly end. On 15 April 1971, Brandes was found poisoned in his car on a quiet road just outside Schäftlarn, Bavaria.[51]

Chapter 15

Island Agents

As the Second World War was careering to its climax, Graham Greene was to play a pivotal part in the secret counter-intelligence war being waged against the German agents operating from Portuguese territory.

At the end of 1943, Kim Philby had signalled his intention for Section VD to go on the offensive, taking on the Abwehr spy networks spread across the Iberian Peninsula and the vitally important Portuguese and Spanish islands that acted as transport hubs for the North Atlantic convoys. Greene had been working with Charles de Salis, like Greene an Oxford University man who had been personally recruited by Philby.[1]

But in August 1943, de Salis was sent to Lisbon with orders to find agents to infiltrate German intelligence. In de Salis's absence, Greene was promoted from VD5 to VD4 and given a new priority task of gathering intelligence about German spies operating in the Portuguese-held islands of the Azores.[2] In the run-up to D-Day, this would turn out to be a very important job.

Philby assigned Greene the key job of compiling a 'purple primer', a kind of 'who's who' of the German intelligence set up in the Azores. This meant locating and identifying all the enemy agents, their characteristics, contacts and vulnerabilities. The 'purple primers' were the major documents from which MI6 worked and briefed ministers. Their compilation took many months, each detail double sourced and tested against countervailing intelligence. To assist him in his mammoth task, Greene had access to the highly sensitive 'Ultra' material, decrypted secret messages of the Abwehr and other German commands.

Philby told Greene that he should return the completed dossier to him so that he could write an introduction to the report.[3] This not only gave Philby control over the intelligence, it also permitted him one final chance to cast his eye over the dossier before handing a copy to his Russian handlers.[4]

The Azores are nine volcanic islands in the middle of the Atlantic covering 910 square miles (2,355 square km), located 800 miles from Europe. Salazar had worked hard to ringfence the islands and keep them out the hands of either the Axis or Allied powers, but they were weakly defended. Should the Azores become enemy-controlled territory, the Allied convoys would be vulnerable to German U-boats operating from the islands. In May 1943, Churchill and Roosevelt met at the Third Washington Conference to plan the next phase of the war. Churchill understood that the U-boat menace needed to be neutralised before attempting the high-risk transport operations necessary for the final assault on Hitler's Fortress Europe. The two leaders agreed that the Portuguese Azores would offer the Anglo-American forces the perfect base from which to cover the Mid-Atlantic Gap, an undefended zone outside the reach of Britain's Coastal Command aircraft, which had seen a deadly rise in merchant shipping losses.

Britain drew up two war plans, Operations Brisk and Alacrity, to take the islands by force. It would be a perilous seaborne assault that relied on total surprise. If the Germans got wind of the operation, the British ships would be cut to pieces by the wolfpacks. Section VD had the task of identifying the German military presence on the islands and the Portuguese Nazi spies and sympathisers who were passing back to Berlin intelligence about the convoys.

Greene had inherited a threadbare report containing what little MI6 knew about the German intelligence presence. By the time Greene began the task of compiling his 'purple primer', Philby was able to add to it the fruits of an intelligence breakthrough the year before that included the break-up of a German spy network operating in the heart of Lisbon using agents strung out across the Portuguese colonies.

Philby had managed to infiltrate the Lisbon group by identifying an important agent who had been endangering British convoys through his access to telegrams and letters relating to Allied ship movements sent by someone based in the Azores.[5] The intelligence trail led Philby to the Bremen Eins Marine Organisation in Lisbon run by Hans Grimm, a German Abwehr officer posing as a cotton trader in Portugal. Grimm, very tall, well built with swept back black hair, had been a thorn in the side of British intelligence from the previous year when he had reported on the build-up of Allied forces in Freetown in preparation for Operation Torch.[6] One of his intelligence reports helped the Germans locate and sink the aircraft carrier HMS *Eagle* in August 1942, caught sailing between Gibraltar and Malta, for which he was awarded a medal.[7] Grimm, who used the codename 'Eduardo', had contact with a German wireless engineer called Johann Majewicz, an ardent Nazi who had worked for a cable company in the Azores island of Fayal (Faial) for more than 12 years.[8]

Majewicz's agents included Portuguese workers at the islands' whaling stations, whom he bribed to pass on reports of British convoys, many of them bound for Freetown. Under the codename 'Augusto', Majewicz also gathered reports of Portuguese military defences and any intelligence he could pick up from British seamen whose ships docked at the islands' ports.[9] He then telegraphed this intelligence back to Grimm's HQ in Lisbon.

By spring 1943, Philby had gathered enough incriminating material to hand it over to British ambassador, Sir Ronald Campbell, who was now armed with direct proof of the German espionage operations against Portugal. When Sir Ronald approached Salazar with Philby's findings, the Portuguese dictator was this time forced to acknowledge the extent of the German penetration. Salazar reassured Campbell that the Portuguese authorities 'will be able to do a good job' in winkling out the German spies and agents operating in Portugal territory.[10] Grimm was arrested and interrogated by the Portuguese International Police. He made a very partial confession saying that he had received 'nothing of value' from Horta, the largest settlement on the Azores.[11]

Philby had been certain the Portuguese would find a clandestine wireless station at Grimm's premises, but none was found and Grimm and the other German agents were released.

The Portuguese government assured the British it had shut down the Azores spy ring, but MI6 knew of at least two agents who had escaped detection. One was codenamed 'Corsepius' and another 'Kessner', whom Philby described as 'short, fat, fair, bandy legs with a round blue enamel badge on the lapel'.[12] There were bound to be others, and these Portuguese fifth columnists and their German masters posed a serious threat to British plans to take military possession of the islands.

Greene and the rest of the VD officers began the painstaking business of locating the 'missing' agents and their Lisbon contacts with the aim of having them kicked out of Portuguese territory.

On 17 August, acting on behalf of Philby, Greene wrote to Dick White of MI5 with some very good news: 'Dear White, the long awaited departure of Ernst Schmidt [an Abwehr agent] has at last been reported by our Lisbon representative [de Salis]: with frau Schmidt he left Portugal by train on 4th August. Hans Scholz has also been deported, and Arturo Omerti has been served with an expulsion order and is expected to leave within the next week.' Scholz was one of Grimm's accomplices, while Schmidt was an SS man working out of Lisbon and reported to be 'the most dangerous German agent in Portugal'.[13]

Ten days later Greene was able to tell White: 'We have just had the satisfactory news from our Lisbon representative that the expulsion order against Arturo Omerti was carried out on August 17th.'[14] Omerti was a member of the Italian secret service, confirming British suspicions that the enemy's intention to capture the Azores was part of an Axis-wide operation. In a further major coup, the network's lynchpin, Hans Grimm, was finally given his marching orders.

Philby was not entirely convinced that the danger in the Azores had been eliminated, and he wanted to know from Greene what had become of Majewicz and 'Corsepius' and the other agents who remained on the islands. An MI6 effort to work with the Portuguese to trap the Abwehr spies on the Azores failed when the German agents spotted a radio detection van coming down the street just as they were about to transmit a message to Lisbon. MI6 suspected they had moved their operations to another part of the island.[15]

While D-Day remained the next big Allied operation, the Azores were an important staging post for the transportation of troops and supplies across the Atlantic. If German agents were still at large, they would be able to report on the British and American build-up of forces. Greene decided to send his own agent so that he had someone on the ground whom he could secretly direct against the German spies. However, the agent chosen by Greene turned out to be an intelligence disaster. His name was Paul Mathews, a former MI5 officer who had transferred to MI6 in June 1943, joining Section V at St Albans. As soon as Mathews arrived on the islands he broke off all communication with Greene. It is not clear why this happened. Perhaps he didn't get on with Greene, perhaps he wasn't up to the job, or perhaps he just rather enjoyed being thousands of miles from London on a sub-tropical island. Whatever the reason, the situation was an acute embarrassment to Greene and MI6, who were being chased by MI5 for intelligence about the German operations there.[16]

Philby said the dispute soon became a bone of niggling contention between MI5 and MI6. The two MI5 officers most concerned about the intelligence deficit were Richman Stopford and Herbert Hart, who had the job of fitting the Azores into a bigger intelligence picture in the run-up to D-Day. According to Philby, MI5 launched a protest, possibly accusing the aloof and increasingly prickly Greene of incompetence, and when the row threatened to boil over, Philby was forced to come to his subordinate's rescue.[17]

Philby had rowed in behind Greene the year before when Sidney Smith had tried to bully Greene and withdraw his funding in Freetown. Now once again, Philby defended Greene against the professional corps of intelligence officers who thought they knew better than the novelist and amateur spy.

There was something in Greene's psyche that caused him to seek out the path of greatest resistance when he came up against smallminded colleagues or obdurate bureaucracy. In truth, Greene liked a spat. As his fellow spy Malcolm Muggeridge testified: 'Greene is a Jekyll and Hyde character, who has not succeeded in fusing the two sides of himself into any kind of harmony. There is conflict within him, and therefore he is liable to pursue conflict without.'[18]

When MI6's head of station in Lisbon showed a dense and blundering understanding of a developing intelligence matter, Greene wrote in the margin of one of the many memos that poured in from the Portuguese capital: 'Poor old 2400, Our Man in Lisbon, charging around like a bull in a china shop, opening up vast vistas of the obvious.'[19]

Greene and Philby's attitudes to field agents were in tune. Philby had strong and prejudiced views about the kind of agents who offered their services to MI6: 'The motives in working as agents are various, ranging from the heroic to the squalid. The great majority are paid for their work, though not too well. On the whole, SIS prefers their agents on its payroll since the acceptance of pay induces pliability. The unpaid agent is apt to behave independently, and to become an infernal nuisance. He has almost certainly his own political axe to grind, and his sincerity is often a measure of the inconvenience he can cause.'[20] According to Muggeridge, Greene was very skilful at handling these agents: 'He was tremendously good at dealing with agents and working out cover plans and things like that and justifiably was very highly thought of.'[21]

Philby also had a high regard for his junior officer's analytical and espionage skills, later praising Greene for working 'quietly, coolly and competently'.[22] And in the Azores case it was Greene who had the last laugh in the bust up with MI5. After several weeks of digging, and presumably engaging more competent agents, Greene had managed to smoke out three of the German spies still operating in Horta and passing on intelligence to the Germans.

One can only imagine Greene's satisfaction when he updated Herbert Hart on his success in the case:

'Dear Hart, You will be interested to hear that we have received some news of the arrest at Horta of Humberto Azvedo and his associates Joaquim Costa Martins de Amaral Domingos Silveira by our representative attached to British forces. They left Horta for Lisbon on February 2nd in SS CARVALHO ARAUJO [a small Portuguese luxury liner].'[23]

Hart was clearly in the dark as to the significance of this development and it was left to Richman Stopford to scribble a note on Greene's letter explaining to Hart that, having spoken to Greene, he now understood that Azvedo was the wireless operator, the important German agent sending all intelligence back to Lisbon.

Stopford added: 'G.G. does not want us to acknowledge the letter and will let us know if he hears any more.'[24]

There was more to hear a few days later. A Portuguese police report on Azvedo shows that he was arrested by the Portuguese security agency as soon as he arrived in Lisbon.[25]

*

A Nazi occupation of the Azores had be successfully averted and Salazar signed an agreement with Winston Churchill granting the British air and naval bases on the islands. Shortly afterwards, the German news agency reported that the German Consulate on the Azores was being closed and German nationals were leaving. Section V D had played its part in helping to persuade Salazar that Germany's espionage activities presented a threat to Portugal's sovereignty as much as it did to the Allies' war aims.

MI6 had scored a huge hit against their German adversaries in Lisbon, neutralising their espionage networks and forcing Salazar to come off the fence and expel some of the most dangerous agents working for the Abwehr and the SD. An SIS document entitled the Lisbon Offensive, which may well have been drawn up by Greene, sets out in detail these achievements and makes for very impressive reading.[26] Erich Schroeder, the head of the SD working with the Portuguese police, conceded after the war that SIS operations were extraordinarily successful in Portugal, stating that they had 'destroyed 50%' of his organisation.[27]

Greene played down his contribution to the intelligence campaign of the Second World War. Nevertheless, he was fiercely proud of his work and angrily defended the record whenever his efforts were misrepresented. This was demonstrated after the war when the *Sunday Times* made out that he had failed to send an agent [Mathews] to the Azores in time to assist the British occupation of the islands.[28]

The same error had crept into a footnote of a draft of Philby's memoirs, which Greene had agreed to read before publication. He told the editors: 'I didn't forget to send an SIS man to the Azores, although he nearly failed to catch the convoy. However he utterly failed to make his wireless work with result there was a long delay before any news arrived and when he did communicate he communicated through the MI5 radio. I suggest it would be more accurate if the footnote read: "Philby once defended Graham

Bill Brandt © Bill Brandt Archive

The writer and the spy: during the Second World War, Graham Greene worked as an MI6 officer under Kim Philby in Sierra Leone, St Albans and London, until he inexplicably resigned on the eve of D-Day.

The Vienna spy ring. Above, Lizy (Litzi) Friedmann; below left, Alexander Orlov; below right, Kim Philby. Philby married communist agent Friedmann in Vienna in 1934 and was himself recruited by NKVD officers Arnold Deutsch and Orlov the same year when Philby and his new wife were forced to leave Vienna in the wake of the fascist victory in the Austrian civil war.

(Left) Arnold Deutsch was the NKVD agent credited with orchestrating the recruitment of the Cambridge spies.

(Below left) Philby's second wife, Aileen Furse. One of Furse's relatives had served as private secretary to Winston Churchill. In 1940 when Furse and Philby first got together her boyfriend was working at Bletchley Park, the government's top secret code-breaking establishment.

(Below right) Philby's younger sister Helena had worked for MI6 and fell under suspicion after her brother's defection in 1963.

Movie Poster Image Art/Getty

(Left and above) Graham Greene's 1949 film noir *The Third Man (Der Dritte Mann)* was set in Vienna and featured Orson Welles playing penicillin racketeer Harry Lime. Lime, who seeks refuge in the Soviet sector, is betrayed by his old friend and novelist Holly Martins, a character partly based on Greene.

(Right) While writing his novella for *The Third Man*, Greene took time out to speak at the Palais des Beaux Arts in Brussels on 16 January 1948 under the banner '*Is the Christian civilization in danger?*' Greene, seen here with French Catholic writer Francois Mauriac, used his talk to warn of the looming danger of Soviet communism.

Associated Press/Alamy

Bettmann/Getty

Bentley Archive/Popperfoto/Getty

(Above) Kim Philby deployed his famous self-deprecating charm and sangfroid to allay suspicions that he was a Soviet agent. At a press conference staged at his mother's London flat in 1955, Philby continued to deny that he was the so-called 'third man' who had helped fellow Cambridge spies Guy Burgess and Donald Maclean defect to Moscow. It was only after he too defected in January 1963 that the British public and his friends at MI6 knew he had been lying.

(Right) Philby had the ambition and the right credentials to be the next head of MI6 but was forced to resign after the Third Man affair in 1951. The same year he bought a London taxi which he used to chauffeur his friends (including Anthony Blunt) around the city. During these journeys he wore 'a cabbie's cap and a wide grin on his face', according to the MI5 watchers who had the job of tailing him.

(Left) Greene's heavy drinking lifestyle caught up with him in 1949 during a trip to New York where he was finalising the production of *The Third Man*.

(Below) Greene with director Carol Reed, who rushed Greene to hospital where Greene received three diagnoses following a haemorrhage.

Kurt Hutton/Getty

Larry Burrows/The LIFE Picture Collection/Shutterstock

Bournemouth News and Photo Service

Our men in Havana. (Above) Kim Philby travelled to Moscow-friendly Havana in 1978 where he was treated as a celebrity by Fidel Castro's government. While a guest of Castro he wrote a postcard to Graham Greene describing himself as Greene's 'greatest fan'. It was the start of a rekindled relationship, culminating in Greene making four visits to see Philby in Moscow.

(Right) Greene in 1959 on the filmset of *Our Man in Havana*, which MI5 Director General Roger Hollis had tried to ban because the book made fun of British intelligence.

Everett Collection Inc/Alamy

Ts/ZUMA Press Wire/Shutterstock Laski Diffusion/Gett

(Above left and right) Graham Greene and Kim Philby finally met in Moscow in 1986 after twenty-three years' separation by the Iron Curtain. Philby was never fully trusted by his Soviet bosses. Graham Greene was his oldest friend and the only link to the old world.

(Left) Mourners at Graham Greene's graveside in Vevey, Switzerland, on the vine-covered slopes overlooking Lake Geneva in 1991. (L–R) Greene's wife Vivien Greene (née Dayrell-Browning), who he never divorced because of his Catholic faith, his daughter Caroline Bourget and his last lover Yvonne Cloetta pay their final respects to the enigmatic author who took many of his secrets to the grave.

Sipa/Shutterstock

Greene when the latter was involved in a row because his agent sent to the Azores after the takeover failed to communicate. The result was etc".'[29] He also told the *Sunday Times* journalist Leonard Russell that the fact his agent couldn't make the radio work was not 'my responsibility: Perhaps something was wrong with his radio, perhaps he had been badly trained . . .'[30]

In 1977 Tim Milne wrote to Greene pointing out that Paul Mathews was close to Philby as he had been billeted with the Philbys in St Albans when he first joined Section V. Defending Mathews and Greene he asked: 'No-one forgot anything, at least that is my recollection, and I wonder if yours differs at all?'[31]

After the war Greene's only public reference to his secret work with Section V D was his claim to authorship of the 'purple primer'. He also incorporated it into the espionage of MI5 defector Maurice Castle, the central character in *The Human Factor*. In his memoirs *Ways of Escape*, Greene says: 'The only relic I left behind me when I resigned was a Who's Who limited to 12 copies, if I remember right, compiled by myself, of German agents in the Azores . . . and a contribution by Kim Philby on radio communications, for the use of our invasion forces. Does a copy still exist somewhere on the files? It would have a certain value today.'[32]

In *The Human Factor* Castle says the most secret information he ever knew was the 'date for the invasion of the Azores'.[33] When Britain was at war, Graham Greene regarded himself as a professional MI6 officer working diligently and patriotically in the defence of the realm. He rarely ever spoke about his secret spy work. Those who dared question his competence or loyalty were met with a dagger stare from those famous blue ice-chipped eyes, quickly followed by a cutting rebuke.

Johannes-Nielsen 'Johnny' Jebsen (Agent Artist). Graham Greene's sense of personal responsibility and loyalty towards the agents working for MI6 during the war remained with him all his life. One of the bravest was Johnny Jebsen who was kidnapped in Lisbon in April 1944 by the Nazis when MI5 and MI6 failed to warn Jebsen that the Germans were investigating him.

(The National Archives, KV2-862)

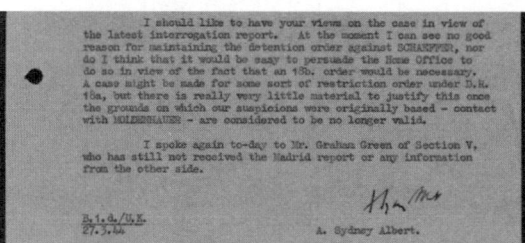

(The National Archives, KV2-857(2))

(Above) Greene liaising with MI5 in the case of Heinz Moldenauer who was kidnapped with Jebsen.

(Right) Rare correspondence: Kim Philby's secret memo to Captain Anthony Blunt (MI5) keeping him abreast of espionage cases on the Iberian Peninsula.

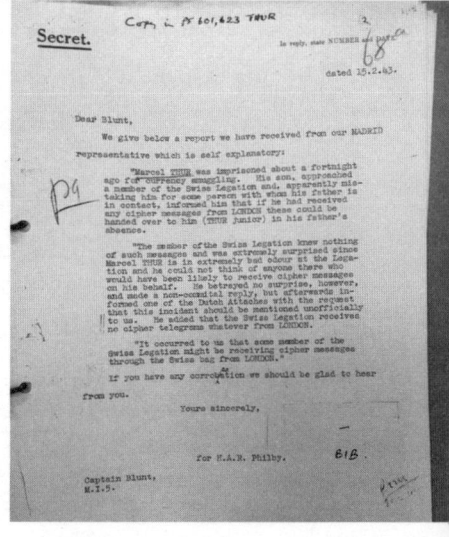

(The National Archives, KV2-2270)

(Torre do Tombo, PIDE, Serviços Centrais, Registo Geral de Presos, liv. 78, registo no. 15475)

Humberto Azvedo was a Portuguese wireless operator working for the Abwehr in the Azores, Portuguese islands key to both Allied and German interests in the Battle of the Atlantic as well as during the build-up of forces before D-Day. The British and Americans feared the Germans would try to seize the islands. Kim Philby gave Graham Greene (codename VD4) the job of compiling a 'purple primer' that identified all German agents and suspects operating out of the Azores.

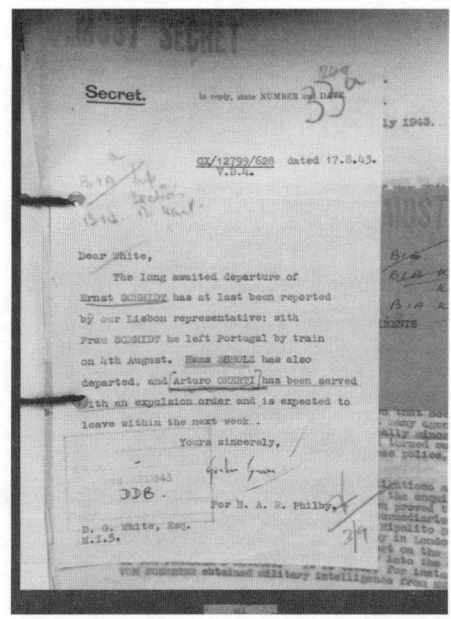

(The National Archives, KV-3-175 p.33b)

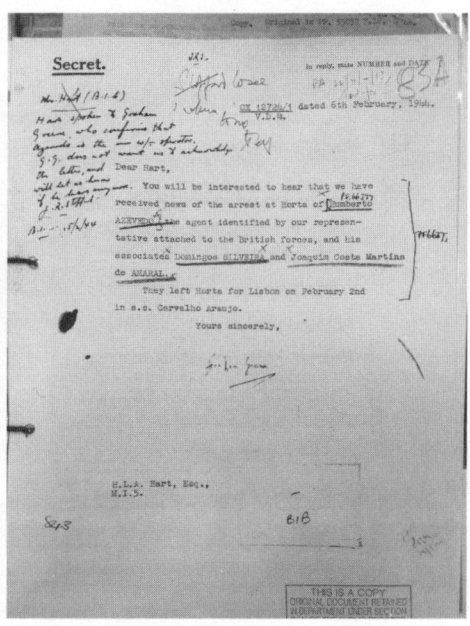

(The National Archives, KV-3-270 p.83a)

(The National Archives, KV2-862)

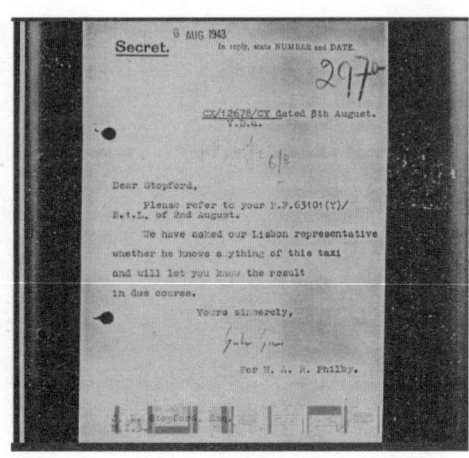
(The National Archives, KV-2-2271 (4) p.24)

(Above left) Dusko Popov was another brave British agent working out of the Iberian Peninsula where MI6 and MI5 were running agents. Popov's flamboyant lifestyle and good looks made him a natural model for Ian Flemming's James Bond. Graham Greene remained friends with Popov until his death, regularly dining with him near Greene's flat in Antibes, south of France, and helping him publish and promote his memoirs.

(Above right and below) Greene takes up the mysterious case of Agent Rhubarb, the canaries and the quinine.

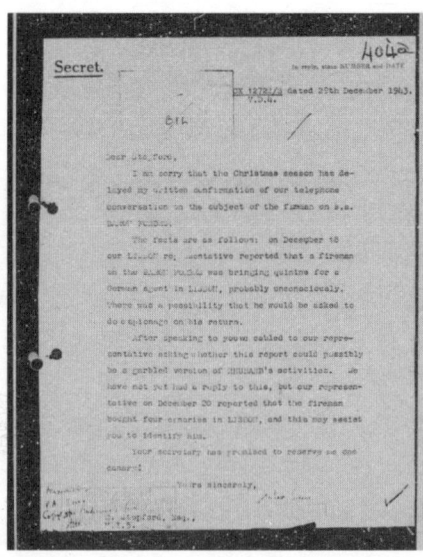
(The National Archives, KV-2272 (4) p.36)

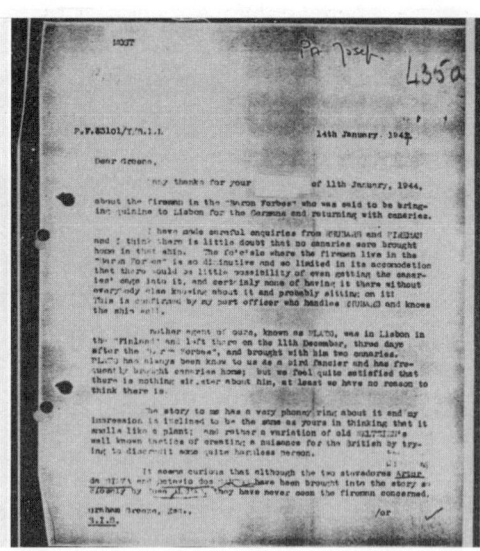
(The National Archives, KV-2272)

(The National Archives, KV-4-424 p.70c)

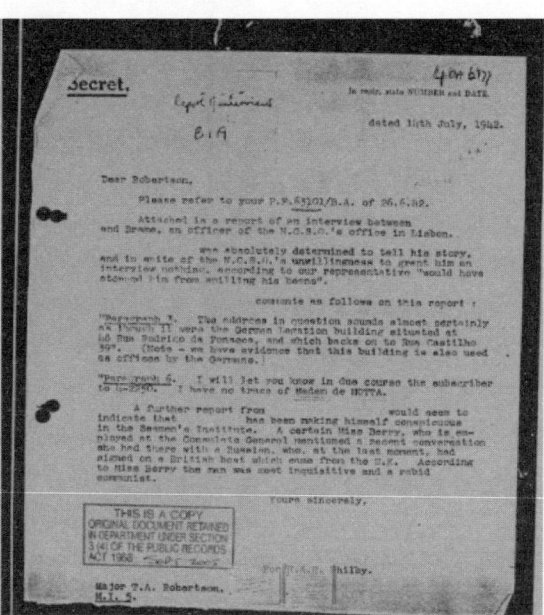

(The National Archives, KV-2-2267 (2))

Vladimir Kusnecoff (aka Josef K and Agent Rhubarb) was perhaps the most enigmatic spy of the Second World War. Trained by the Russians, Kusnecoff carried out sabotage operations against Allied ships docking at Freetown, Sierra Leone, where Graham Greene was MI6 station chief. After his detention and interrogation by MI5, Kusnecoff agreed to work for British Intelligence who used him against the Axis spy agencies in Portugal.

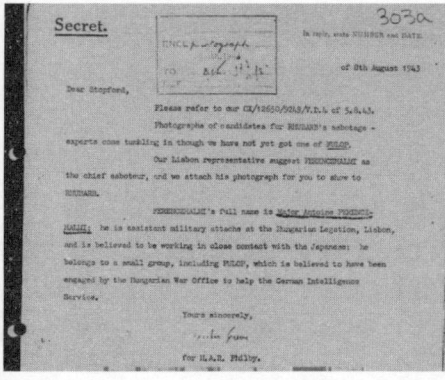

(The National Archives, KV-2-2271 (4) p.16)

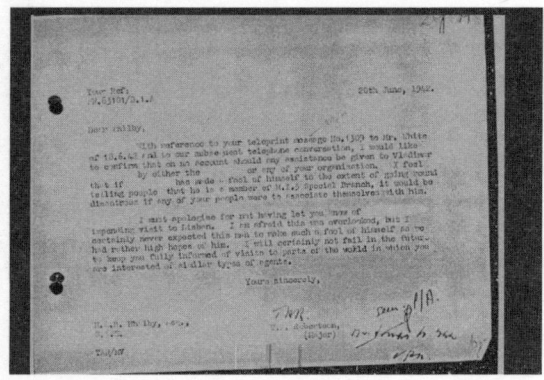

(The National Archives, KV-2-2267 (3) p.40)

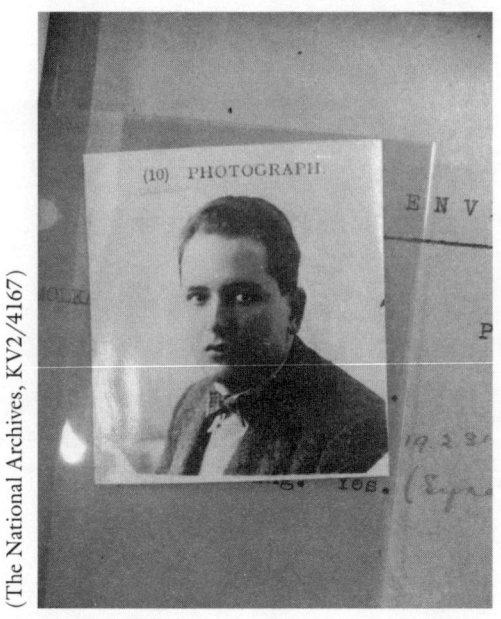

(The National Archives, KV2/4167)

The Third Man: Austrian journalist Harry Smolka was a Russian secret agent and childhood friend of Kim Philby's first wife Lizy (Litzi) Friedmann. He set up a press agency with Philby and was a regular visitor to the Philby's London family home. After the war Smolka returned to Vienna where he met Graham Greene and advised the British writer on his new film *The Third Man* about an American racketeer called Harry Lime, a character Greene is believed to have based on Kim Philby. Smolka, who changed his name to Peter Smollett, first came to the attention of MI5 before the war but was cleared by Philby (see below) in 1942 of any malign activities.

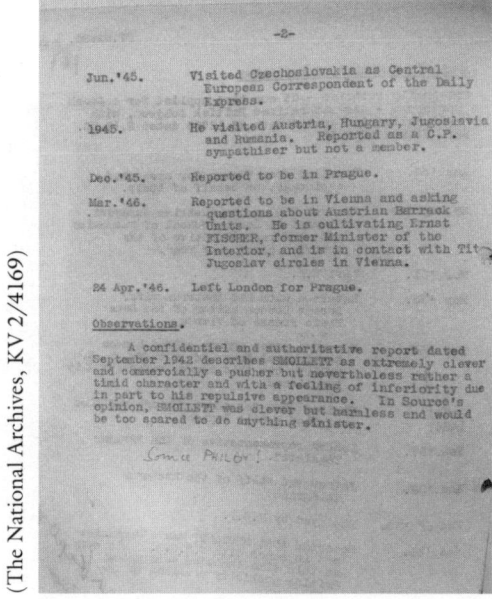

(The National Archives, KV 2/4169)

INTERNAL MEMORANDUM.

A.D.F. Mr. Fulford.   To B.1.G. Mr. Brooman-White

You will remember that when we were having lunch on Tuesday I mentioned to you the case of a man called Henry Peter SMOLKA @ SMOLLETT, [B?].2.a. is interested. I see from our records that in November [19]34 SMOLLETT was said to have formed a small press agency called "London Continental News Limited" with a "certain H.R. PHILBY". I think that that is almost certainly our mutual friend in Section V. I should be extremely grateful if you could ask PHILBY for any information he would let us have about this man. SMOLLETT is at present employed in the Ministry of Information and there can, I think, be no doubt that he has good connections with the C.P.G.B., which explains our interest in him.

10.9.42.   Signature R. Fulford

(The National Archives, KV 2/4169)

Kim Philby's close relationship with Harry Smolka raised suspicions about Philby with MI5.

INTERNAL MEMORANDUM.

B.1.G. (R. Brooman-White)   To A.D.F. (Mr. Fulford)

I spoke to Philby about SMOLLETT. The press agency in question never actually functioned but Philby knew SMOLLETT quite well at the time. He says he is an Austrian Jew who came to this country about 1920, did well in journalism and is extremely clever. Commercially he is rather a pusher but has nevertheless a rather timid character and a feeling of inferiority largely due to his somewhat repulsive appearance. He is a physical coward and was petrified when the air-raids began. Philby considered his politics to be mildly left-wing but had no knowledge of the C.P. link-up. His personal opinion is that SMOLLETT is clever and harmless. He adds that in any case the man would be far too scared to become involved in anything really sinister.

12.9.42.   Signature R. Brooman-White

(The National Archives, KV 2/4169)

(Alamy, photographer Ron Harvey, Contributor Everett Collection Inc.)

Commissioner of Police Captain Patrick Brodie was the real-life figure Greene based Heny Scobie (here played by Trevor Howard) in his novel *The Heart of the Matter* set in West Africa.

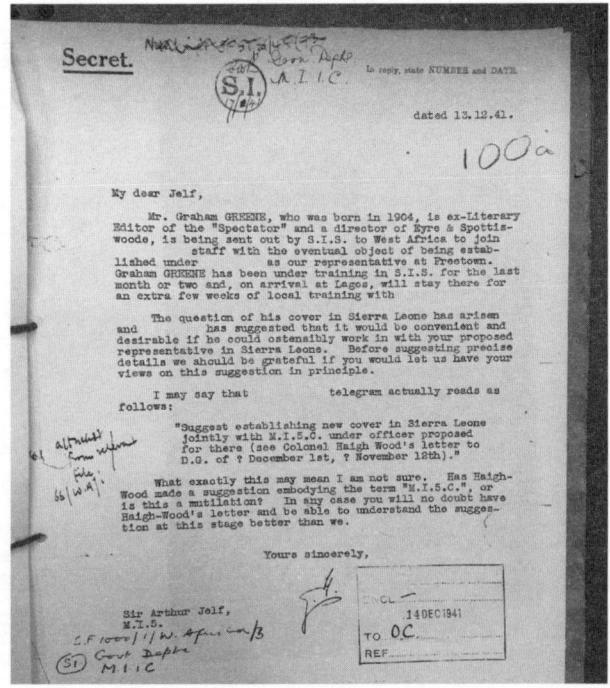

(The National Archives, KV4-310)

D.G.S.S. through D.B.

This report by the S.I.S. representative in Freetown on the available security machinery there, throws a rather disturbing light on the decision which is being taken to employ our normal police contacts in the West African port areas. On the other hand, although Brodie may himself be tired and somewhat disgruntled, were we to place a full time representative of this office in Freetown, he would presumably have to work with Brodie and use his resources. Probably Gibbs will give us some further clarification of the position in Freetown when he returns.

A.D.B.1. D.G.write.
9.12.42.

(The National Archives, KV4-311)

Greene was sent to Freetown by MI6 (see left hand page) where he formed a close friendship with Patrick Brodie. But he ended up betraying him in his secret report on the poor security situation in Sierra Leone.

C O P Y   9.11.42.

1. As the Assistant Colonial Secretary has asked me for a confidential verbal report on the Freetown police from the security standpoint I think I had better let you have an enlarged report on the position which may supplement the report of the M.I.5 representative when he returns.

2. The police officers with whom I have official contact are only the Commissioner, Capt. Brodie, and his personal assistant, Lucas (Assistant Superintendent of Police). Unofficially I have seen something of the following: Rodder (Senior Assistant Superintendent), Tusch (Senior Assistant Superintendent), Turnbull (Assistant Superintendent), Russel-Jones (Assistant Superintendent), and Rutland (Assistant Superintendent) who is now on leave.

3. Brodie has served 19 very hard years in this colony, often in the most difficult times with only one white officer on whom to rely. The war has added enormously to his work but no adequate extra assistance has been given him. He is now an elderly and very tired man on the verge of a breakdown. He lives alone, goes out practically not at all: when he is not at his desk he is alone in his house. He is quite aware of the enormous gaps and faults in his organisation, especially as far as M.I.5 is concerned, but he has to depend for help with the new work which has been thrust upon him on his junior staff – and with perhaps one exception that staff is unreliable. He has a very strong and very natural anti-Government bias. Although they are now, presumably as the result of the M.I.5 representative's visit, showing anxiety over the state of the police, they have in the past shut their eyes to Brodie's needs and felt very little responsibility towards him and no concern for his health. No attempt has been made to appoint a responsible second-in-command as has been done in the Gambia where far less work has to be done.

4. Brodie has two good junior officers – Turnbull and Rutland. Rutland is a ranker from the Ceylon police and acted as his personal assistant when I first arrived. He is now on leave. Turnbull is stationed at Waterloo to control the human traffic between the Colony and the Protectorate.

5. Lucas, who acts as the Commissioner's personal assistant, is a young man transferred from Palestine. He is not intelligent, is inclined to drink too much and has

/no conception

(The National Archives, KV4-311B)

Chapter 16

Dramatic Pause

In the weeks leading up to D-Day, Graham Greene had become incensed by the slack security among the contingent of American secret service (OSS) officers, who shared Section V's Ryder Street offices. One of Greene's duties was to take his turn as night fire officer maintaining security after everyone had left the office. 'Security,' explained Greene, 'was a game we played less against the enemy than against the allies on the upper floor,'[1] and he decided to take it upon himself to highlight the Americans' flawed approach to office housekeeping by removing files from the locked cabinet and placing them on the desk of the OSS officer he considered the most security careless, brash or just too American. When the morning security team made their routine checks, the OSS officers were upbraided and threatened with sanctions for their lax handling of top-secret papers. Greene repeated this week after week until the Americans instigated their own counter-security operation and narrowed down a list of suspects with Greene the prime suspect. Fearing imminent exposure, Greene sought out his boss Philby who he knew shared his contempt for the Americans and made a full confession. Over a lunchtime pint in the Kings Arms, Piccadilly, Philby agreed to have the matter dropped and to protect Greene from any repercussions.[2]

Greene greatly valued Philby's support, but his loyalty to his employers, MI6, had become considerably strained. The case of

DRAMATIC PAUSE

Johnny Jebsen, whose tragic fate was determined by a far more costly professional misjudgement than any of Greene's, had ended in the execution of a brave and valuable agent. Greene blamed MI6 and MI5 for the Jebsen betrayal, but never Philby.

Greene's animus towards MI5 ran particularly deep. When a friend once wrote to him mistaking him for an MI5 officer, he sourly replied: 'You insult me when you suggest that I was ever MI5. I've never spied on my own countrymen!'[3] Even in to his eighties, three years before his death, he told a personal correspondent: 'I don't think I have ever had a friend in MI5, thank God'.[4]

Such antagonism had its roots in the 'young puppy from MI5', Reggie Gibbs, sent to Freetown in 1942, who Greene claimed had driven Captain Brodie to his nervous breakdown.[5] While the internment of his cousin Ben on dubious evidence adduced by MI5 still rankled with him.

Greene's sense of personal responsibility and loyalty towards the agents who had worked for him during the war remained all his life. He kept in contact with one of the bravest, Dusko Popov, until his death, taking him out to lunch near his flat in Antibes and helping him publish his memoirs.[6] He later said: 'He was sent to England by the German secret service, but he was already working for us. From time to time, he returned to Lisbon to report to his [German] chiefs. It was thanks to him that we had sight of the questionnaire furnished by the Japanese to the Germans, which indicated they were preparing for the attack on Pearl Harbor. He passed these documents to Hoover, who unfortunately left them in a drawer.'[7]

Dusko was also the agent who worked closely with Johnny Jebsen and testified to his loyalty.

But what of Graham Greene's loyalty to Kim Philby, a communist and Russian agent?

Ever since the lunch in the Café Royal in June 1944 when

Greene announced his early departure from MI6, his biographers and fellow intelligence officers have speculated about what he knew of Philby's Soviet connections. In 1968, Greene himself offered a tantalising glimpse of the real motives behind his actions when he wrote the foreword to Philby's own memoirs, praising MI6 for doing all it could to defend Philby after his defection in 1963 while lambasting MI5 for 'forcing him into the open'.[8] He reasoned: 'A spy allowed to continue his work without interference is far less dangerous than the spy who is caught.'[9]

It is an intriguing statement that introduces an intriguing possibility. Had Greene raised his suspicions about Philby with MI6 and then walked out? Given the subsequent damage done by Philby to both British and American intelligence, such a notion seems hardly plausible. That is unless of course Greene was merely biding his time, waiting for the right moment to finally expose Philby or to draw out from him all his secrets of the Soviet operations in the UK.

In 1983, Greene spoke about how it would be possible to turn a KGB agent like Philby. He said the defection of a Russian agent 'would never surprise me because the profession can become a sort of game as abstract as chess: the spy takes more interest in the mechanics of his calling than in its ultimate goal – the defence of one's country. The game (a serious game) achieves such a degree of sophistication that the player loses sight of his moral values. I understand a man's temptation to turn double agent for the game becomes more interesting. Perhaps my childhood experience of divided loyalties has helped me to sympathise with people like Kim Philby, who have gone to the limit with their divided loyalties.'[10]

For Greene the notion of loyalty had both personal and national dimensions. His bitter experience in Sierra Leone, when he had betrayed his only friend, Captain Patrick Brodie, by writing a secret report to MI6/MI5 exposing Brodie's professional and personal failings, left a deep scar. He had stood by Brodie for as long as he could, defending his behaviour as a man under pressure and urging MI5 to provide him with more resources. When this was not forthcoming he was forced to choose between Brodie and the security of British operations at a critical point in the war. In the end Greene had allowed his country to come before a close friendship and helped to send Brodie home to a sad and empty retirement, a forgotten casualty of the internecine war between MI5 and MI6.

He elliptically referred to such a treachery when he confessed to Marie-Francoise Allain, the daughter of his old friend and French resistance leader Yves Allain, in 1981: 'I've betrayed a great number of things and people in the course of my life, which probably explains this uncomfortable feeling I have about myself, this sense of having been cruel, unjust. It still torments me often enough before I go to sleep.'[11]

In an extended essay on the business of espionage written in 1968, Greene tried to justify the brutality and human victims of his trade: 'Anyway, moral judgments are singularly out of place in espionage. "Sent men to their death" is the kind of stock phrase which has been used against Philby and [George] Blake. So does any military commander, but at least the cannon fodder of the espionage war are all volunteers. One cannot reasonably weep at the fate of the defecting spy Volkov [a Russian would-be defector betrayed by Philby] who was betraying his country for motives less idealistic than Philby's.'[12]

In June 1944, which values did Graham Greene cherish most? What moral code did he adhere to? Was he a spy who put friends before country or a loyal and professional MI6 officer prepared to sacrifice friendship in the interest of the nation?

As with so much surrounding Greene's motives, the truth is opaque and his loyalties at this time were mixed, fluid and emotionally complex. He had started out as the MI6 technician and suffered the consequences of his undeviating service to his trade: the betrayal of his closest and most faithful friend Brodie, the man to whom he said he owed so much during his difficult time in Sierra Leone. If a year later he had suspected Philby of being a double agent, he was not going to repeat the treachery. He was going to stand by Philby, yet at some point, after much agonising, he knew he would have to act.

Greene teasingly said that had he known Philby was a Soviet agent, he 'might have allowed him 24 hours to flee as a friend and then reported him'.[13] This was exactly what MI6 officer Nicholas Elliott did when he confronted his old friend Philby in Beirut in January 1963. Greene first made this statement in an interview with the *Sunday Telegraph* in 1978, and stood by it a year later when Andrew Boyle, the writer and former MI6 officer who exposed Anthony Blunt, challenged him about it.[14] In fact, he went further and told Boyle he saw 'nothing fishy in the rise of Philby' whom he described as a 'very able man'.

There is another reason Greene might have let Philby run or have been prepared to turn a blind eye. Philby's work for the Soviets may not have troubled Greene very much at all. Like many British intelligence officers, Greene was sympathetic to the Russian ally whose losses fighting the Nazis far dwarfed those of Britain and America. He was a former member of Oxford University Communist Party who retained a socialist, if not a communist, outlook.

Then there was the strange case of Vladimir Kusnecoff who Greene knew very well. Even a casual glance at the Josef K file revealed that Kusnecoff was a Russian agent who was serving both London and Moscow. This was something that MI5 only woke up to in 1955 when they suspected Soviet penetration may have gone much deeper than they first appreciated.[15]

Reopening the Vladimir Kusnecoff case to investigate Blunt's double agent role, MI5 officer Courtenay Young said 'the gun against Blunt has backfired' but MI5 should interrogate Kusnecoff again.[16]

MI5 had chosen to employ Kusnecoff as an agent, trusting him with important missions, in the full knowledge that Kusnecoff had candidly told them he would return to the Soviet fold after the war. They had turned a blind and negligent eye to the danger.

If British intelligence had no issue with such a duplicitous arrangement, how could Philby's own split loyalties be considered treacherous? Indeed, Greene may not have characterised Philby's under-the-table sharing of secrets with Moscow as an act of disloyalty at all. Greene later said that Philby justified his actions because he believed they would benefit the United Kingdom in the long run.[17] Perhaps Greene thought so, too. After all, he shared Philby's dislike of Britain's rotten class system and contempt for the elites who had led Britain into two world wars in a period of less than 20 years.

Greene also owed a personal debt of loyalty to his boss. Philby had three times risked his own reputation and career speaking up for Greene when he had got himself into serious trouble at work. When Greene was in Sierra Leone in 1943 Philby had intervened to protect the author from the repercussions of a spectacular falling out with his senior officer in Lagos over operational matters.[18] And when Greene's alleged mishandling of his agent in the Azores had drawn fire from MI5 in 1944, Philby had been there to provide cover. Much closer to home, in MI6's central London offices, Philby had saved Greene from the Americans who were close to exposing his office sabotage.

Whatever his reasons for abandoning British intelligence at the war's most critical moment, Greene soon found civvy street a much duller place. His new offices at the Political Intelligence Department (PID), a cover for the Political Warfare Executive, in the upmarket playground of Mayfair's Grosvenor Square, were only a short stroll from the lush greens of St James's Park, his former home at Section V. Greene may have been recommended for his new job by his brother Hugh who was the BBC's MI5-vetted point man in charge of liaison with PID's black propaganda unit.[19] At PID, Greene ran the editorial section, another propaganda department that produced culture and lifestyle magazines to be dropped over occupied France.[20] The work was less taxing but hardly rewarding. Greene wasn't ever sure whether his 'Reader Digests' promoting Western Allies' values reached their destination, commenting: 'The aeroplane crews probably threw them away rather than waste time dropping them.'[21]

In his new post, he was constantly bumping into the many shared acquaintances he had acquired during his SIS days. Among his new Whitehall colleagues at PID was the wife of an Austrian communist who was well known to Kim Philby. Lotte Smollett, wife of Peter Harry Smolka/Smollett, had been successfully vetted and working as a Political Warfare Executive research assistant since 1942.[22]

Throughout everything, Greene was happy to keep up his friendship with Philby, while Philby certainly bore Greene no grudge for leaving his section in the lurch, and they continued to meet by 'arrangement' and through mutual contacts. Greene was close enough to Philby to be introduced to Aileen, an intimacy conferred on very few of Philby's work colleagues. Greene said he found her to have a 'gentle character' and enjoyed her company.[23] Whether he knew about her troubled mental health is not clear.

Philby said he had missed Greene's 'good company, trenchant talk and outbursts of amused exasperation', which he said was equivalent to 'a lot of stiff whiskies'.[24]

The two friends had shared interests outside the office, particularly a taste for Soho dancing girls and the wilder West End cocktail party scene.[25] Philby stuck to his regular Piccadilly stomping ground, boozing with his MI5 and MI6 cronies in the Three

DRAMATIC PAUSE

Crowns pub on Babmaes Street and dining at the Athenaeum Club in Pall Mall.[26] Greene and Philby had become close enough for Greene to champion Philby's membership of Greene's new bolt hole, the Authors' Club at Whitehall Court. Philby claimed the mischievous Greene decided to nominate him on two grounds: 'that he wasn't an author and the club was the seediest in London.'[27] Philby continued to use the Authors' Club as a more discreet rendezvous to the better-established Athenaeum right up until he defected to Moscow, settling club bills sent to him after he moved to Beirut.[28]

Throughout June 1944, Greene continued to live with his mistress Dorothy Glover in Gordon Square while visiting Vivien and the children in Oxford at the weekends. When he was back in town he made sure he kept a close eye on the workings of Philby's Section V, meeting his former colleagues at the Authors' Club. On June 30 he lunched with Desmond Pakenham, now in charge of the Iberian desk, who told him that Greene's successor at Ryder Street was a 'comic professional from the Azores'.[29] Could this have been the accident-prone Paul Mathews?

After D-Day the Germans unleashed flying bombs on London and Greene's diary records almost daily attacks. On the day of his meeting with Pakenham, Greene wrote in his diary: 'another big explosion during lunch'. And four days later: 'A bad night with over 40 explosions . . . when a bomb falls very close there is a crunching sound like walnuts being broken against each other in the fist.' [30]

Greene believed it was his patriotic duty to remain in London and wrote that his old editor at the *Spectator* was 'ratting' because he was exploring a move to Manchester.[31] But a few weeks later Greene removed himself from the war effort altogether.

On 14 July 1944, Greene wrote to his mother, 'my half time release from government service came through: starting on Monday as a publisher.' He had taken up an offer first made to him in 1940 by publishers Eyre and Spottiswoode (E&S), the

King's Printer and publishers of the Bible. Greene had been approached by managing director Douglas Jerrold, who promised him £1,000 a year and control of the publishing firm once Jerrold had retired in 18 months' time.

It meant he was finally able to concentrate on securing his family's financial future, something that had preyed on his mind ever since he had begun his adulterous affair with Dorothy.[32] Greene was still chained to a desk, albeit as a big wheel in a London publisher where he was given the job of raising a list of authors. Among them were Mervyn Peake, author of the gothic fantasy trilogy Gormenghast, the German author Anna Seghers, and the Indian novelist R.K. Naryan.

He may have insulated himself from the war, but he could not hide from it entirely. The mandatory fire service regulation meant Greene 'volunteered' as a fire warden before falling out with the administrators, resigning a few weeks later over what he said was the shambolic organisation of the fire watchers' service, complaining 'I have arrived at blackout half an hour early but no-one was there'.[33]

Greene and Glover, who had ambitions to be a writer, took a top floor flat in Gordon Square, cheaper than the floors below because of the greater exposure to the feared doodlebugs that Greene had foreseen in a dream.[34]

London stood defenceless against Hitler's secret super weapons – the V1 and even more destructive V2 rockets. In his novel *The End of the Affair*, published in 1951, Greene wrote about the couple's tender love making during the evening rocket raids: 'The moment of absolute trust and absolute pleasure, the moment when it was impossible to quarrel because it was impossible to think . . . the V1s didn't affect us until the act of love was over. I had spent everything I had and I was lying back with my head on my stomach and I had her taste in my mouth . . . when one of the robots crashed down on the common.'

These were dangerous times, and Greene seemed to be addicted to the terrifying excitement of the fragility of his existence, just as he had in the first year of the Blitz. It was as if he was playing Russian roulette all over again, this time with Hitler's rockets.

In the offices of E&S, Greene tackled his working day with gusto. His single-minded business-like approach was far removed from the tortured consciences and sensitivities of the characters he wrote about. E&S director Douglas Jerrold recorded exactly how Greene organised his daily tasks: 'He would settle down to the serious business of the day (at his director's desk), telephoning with rapid succession to his bank, to his stock broker, to his insurance agent, to his literary agent, to a film company or two, and, if it was really a busy morning, to two or three editors.'[35] Whenever he wished to escape the mundane routine of the office, Greene pretended to receive a phone call from a fictitious 'Mrs Montgomery' who would urgently require his presence at a meeting in an out of the way part of London.[36]

Greene was burning the candle at both ends and had completed the permanent switch from his favourite dining haunt, the Reform Club, to the Authors' Club in Whitehall Court.[37] Yet, as Jerrold recalled, Greene always arrived early in the office as a man who 'had not been particularly early to bed and might leave again at any moment to get rid of his hangover at The Dog and Duck . . . when I asked him how the evening had passed off he always replied with a look of intense pleasure "it was perfectly ghastly"; his club must be what he calls "the seedy club": if he goes to a party it must be "simply appalling" or "perfectly ghastly", even a quiet cocktail with two or three friends becomes on leaving [the office] "a dreary little drink".'

Throughout the last year of the war, Greene, perhaps immersed in bringing on new authors and running a thriving publishing house, struggled to make a serious contribution to his own writing. He had wondered at the start of the war whether he would ever be able to resume where he had left off and confided in his mother in 1940: 'I may not feel like writing anymore books, except very occasionally.' Desmond Pakenham described Greene as suffering from an 'inexpressible melancholia – it seemed as if all the sorrows of the world were known to him and he couldn't get the horror out of his eyes.'[38]

It is quite possible that he was still troubled by the 'human factor' of wartime espionage – the betrayals of Brodie and Jebsen and all the other innocent, brave agents who had become casualties of the war. Greene had begun to calculate the terrible price he and the nation had paid for an Allied victory. His disenchantment with the spying game was evident in his first piece of writing since stepping down from MI6 and now under contract to MGM.

In the summer of 1944, he began a film treatment called *Nobody to Blame*. It was a piece of writing that betrayed his preoccupations and feelings towards the war. Greene had come to realise that a common feature of the espionage of the Second World War was that very few spies were bona fide agents serving a single master. Garbo, Ostro, Jebsen, Brandes, indeed almost all the British and German agents with whom Greene had been involved, invented networks of pretend agents. He had done so himself when he was in Sierra Leone, relaying 'intelligence' from 'agents' who could barely speak English and whose identity Greene was never sure of.[39]

But it was the Abwehr that had been the biggest victim of the phantom spy rings and the multifaceted deception operations that were run out of London. In *Nobody to Blame,* Greene decided to write about a British spy who fooled MI6 by filing intelligence reports to London from a series of spurious agents. Greene's main character was Richard Tripp, a British sales representative for Singer Sewing Machines working in Tallinn, Estonia. Tripp sends back to

London bogus intelligence about German military and espionage activity in Tallinn and asks MI6 to send him rare stamps, the currency he uses to pay his agents.⁴⁰ This was the espionage trick played by the real spy, Paul Fidrmuc, codename Ostro, who fooled Aloys Schreiber into sending him valuable stamps to pay his non-existent agents in London.⁴¹ Ostro was the only German spy to use this form of currency.

Greene's plan to set up a brothel to elicit intelligence from unsuspecting enemy soldiers in West Africa was rejected by MI6 as too risky, although Kim Philby thought it might have worked.

In the pages of *Nobody to Blame*, Greene put this plan into action so that Tripp successfully asks London to fund a 'madame' who runs his own fictional brothel in Tallinn.⁴² Tripp is eventually rumbled when MI6 sends another officer to Tallinn to help him to capitalise on his successful spy ring and channel the fruits of his intelligence in the run-up to the Second World War. London soon discovers that none of Tripp's agents exist and he is summoned home to face the music. Then, in an almost carbon copy of Ostro's lucky break on the eve of D-Day, Tripp accidentally predicts the date and location of the German invasion of Poland, and the start of the Second World War, hugely boosting his credibility among the British chiefs of staff, although the message comes too late for them to do anything about it. This is uncannily close to what happened over D-Day, when Ostro accidentally predicted the Normandy landings, although the Germans failed to act on it. Greene is clearly making fun of MI6 and the Abwehr, but it is a wartime satire that the British were not quite ready to appreciate. The fighting hadn't finished and Greene's attempts to have *Nobody to Blame* made into a film was rejected by the government's film censorship board.⁴³

Greene reluctantly put *Nobody to Blame* in a drawer and forgot about it for 14 years when it became the framework for his famous novel *Our Man in Havana*.⁴⁴ Tripp transforms into MI6 officer

Jim Wormold, a vacuum cleaner salesman given the serial no. 59200/5 – the same number assigned by SIS to Greene when he was dispatched to West Africa in 1941.[45]

Later asked why he had switched the book's location, Greene explained that a Secret Service comedy about an expatriate vacuum cleaner salesman who gets 'sucked up' into espionage would be more credible in pre-Castro Havana, with its louche nightclubs and promise of tropical oblivion, than in dreary Soviet-occupied Tallinn:

'I already knew Cuba [and later met Fidel Castro twice] and my sympathies were with the Fidelistas in the mountains . . . One could hardly sympathise with the main character if he was to be involved in the Hitler war.'[46]

It was this unique geopolitical paradox, the free-living Caribbean state under strict communist rule, that also attracted Philby. After he escaped to Russia in 1963, Philby wrote a postcard from Havana to Greene in 1979 signing off as one of Greene's 'greatest fans'.

Perhaps Philby, who had read most of Greene's books after the war, recognised how much of himself was in *Our Man in Havana*. The Cambridge spies all imagined themselves playing a part in a Graham Greene novel. When Leo Long, a Russian agent recruited by Anthony Blunt who passed military secrets to the Soviets during the war, was interrogated by MI5 he confessed: 'Walking around London with George [the codename for his Russian handler] was like being in a Graham Greene film.'[47]

The pipe-smoking and stammering Carter – the enemy agent killed by 'our man' Wormold at the end of the novel – was pure Philby, a real-life pipe-smoking stammerer. Carter was also the name Philby assumed in MI6 when he had helped recruit Greene at the start of the war and the name MI6 had used when they sent an agent to Portugal to approach Paul Fidrmuc (Ostro) in Lisbon in an attempt to recruit him to the British side.[48]

Ostro later told MI5 interrogators that when he had been approached in the summer of 1944 it was by a British spy called Carter who asked him to work for British intelligence. The subject of double agents and spycraft was still a sensitive one for British intelligence in 1958 when *Our Man in Havana* was submitted for publication. Greene was warned that MI5 were not happy about it: 'There is no censorship for novels' he later wrote, 'but I learned that MI5 suggested to MI6 that they should bring an action against the book for a breach of official secrets. What secret had I betrayed? Was it the possibility of using bird shit as secret ink?' In 1958 Roger Hollis was head of MI5, and it was Hollis who wanted to prosecute Greene. Hollis had failed to catch Philby and Greene's book was rubbing the failure in his face. Greene added: 'But luckily C, the head of MI6, had a better sense of humour than his colleague in MI5, and he discouraged him from taking action.'[49] The episode merely added to Greene's contempt for MI5.

Throughout 1944 and into 1945, Greene's writing interests were still firmly focused on the absurdity of wartime espionage and the pitiful sacrifice of agents like Jebsen. The novel he attempted next was *The Tenth Man*, a story that Greene considered to be one of his best. Like *Nobody to Blame* and *Jim Braddon and the War Criminal*, it began life as a film treatment and concerned the terrible choices faced by those who lived in Nazi-occupied Europe.

The story opens in a French prison, where 30 inmates are caught by a Nazi decimation order that requires three of them to be selected by lottery for execution in the morning. One of the three chosen is a rich lawyer named Chavel, who desperately offers his entire wealth to any man willing to die in his place. A young man, Michel Mangeot, known as Janvier, who is dying of tuberculosis, accepts his offer and is executed under the name of Chavel in the morning. After the war Chavel is alive and free, but destitute. He returns to the house he sold for his life and finds it occupied by Janvier's mother and sister Thérèse. Assuming the false name, Charlot, he becomes their servant. It is powerful stuff, demonstrating how acts of wartime heroism and cowardice are decided by existential ambiguities.

Greene has Chavel telling Thérèse: 'We think there's a meaning and then we find out the facts are wrong – there just isn't one.'[50]

Thérèse, explaining why she no longer goes to church, reveals: 'I've lost my faith – it's the hate that keeps me away.'

An impostor named Carosse arrives, claiming to be Chavel and wanting the house back. Carosse denounces Charlot in the hope of winning the favour of Thérèse and staking his claim on the property. In the denouement Charlot, having fallen in love with Thérèse, must save her from Carosse.

In one telling exchange Charlot says: 'Anybody's liable to play the coward once. Most of us do and forget about it, it was just the one in his case proved – well spectacular.'[51]

Is Greene remembering Brodie? Or is he facing up to his failure to tackle Philby over suspicions that he was a Soviet mole because he feared the consequences of his actions? He is certainly exorcising the ghosts of the many brave agents who died while working for Greene and Philby and all the other MI6 officers safely stationed in London. Finally, Charlot forces the imposter Carosse to shoot him so that he can die in the arms of Thérèse after confessing to being the real Chavel, the coward who bought his life from her brother. It is a heroic suicide that is also Charlot's redemption.

Greene's manuscript lay in a cupboard unread until 1983, when Greene was approached by a publisher who had uncovered a copy the author had given to MGM while under contract.[52]

Greene believed the story had aged well and professed to preferring it to *The Third Man*, the film that made him internationally famous, written two years later in 1948.[53] It was finally published in 1985.

At the end of the war, Greene picked up his notes for another, much more substantial novel that also had its roots in his wartime service. *The Heart of the Matter* would be as close to real life as anything he had ever written. It was to be set in Sierra Leone, a place he said had 'got under his skin', although he didn't identify the West African country in the book.

He had assembled the cast of characters – Scobie, Wilson, Louise and Yusef – and was two-thirds through the plot when his own personal life crashed into his writing schedule.

Greene was still juggling family life with Vivien and his mistress Dorothy but remained unfulfilled in both relationships. He characteristically reacted to his discontentment by adding a further layer of jeopardy by beginning a relationship with a prostitute. They became close and the woman started telephoning Vivien in Oxford enquiring of Greene's whereabouts, causing further tension in the family. So, it seems extraordinary that he should choose this moment to take on another lover. Catherine Walston was married to Old Etonian Harry Walston, a wealthy aristocrat farmer and aspiring Liberal and later Labour politician. Catherine was an adventurous American beauty who among her claims to fame was a qualified pilot. She was also Greene's goddaughter and the mother of four young children, as well as a friend of Vivien.

None of this was a bar to Greene falling in love with her on an aeroplane flying from Cambridge to Oxford: 'A lock of hair touches one's eyes in a plane with East Anglia under snow and one is in love . . .'[54]

The relationship quickly blossomed with Greene making regular visits to the Walston family estate at Thriplow, Cambridgeshire. Vivien discovered the affair when one of Greene's many love letters to Catherine was reposted to Oxford stamped 'return to sender'. He later wrote to Vivien: 'the fact that has to be faced, dear, is that by my nature, my selfishness, even in some degree by my profession, I should always, and with anyone, have been a bad husband. I think, you see, my restlessness, mood, melancholia, even my outside relationships, are symptoms of a disease and not the disease itself, and the disease, which has been going on ever since my childhood and was only temporarily alleviated by psychoanalysis, lies in a character profoundly antagonistic to ordinary domestic life. Unfortunately the disease is also one's material. Cure the disease and I doubt whether a writer would remain. I dare say that would be all to the good.'[55]

The 'disease' bore fruit in *The Heart of the Matter*. The hurt, guilt and misery over Greene's tortured love life was given expression in Scobie (Greene), Wilson (Greene again), Scobie's wife Louise (Vivien) and Scobie's young lover Helen (Catherine and Dorothy). Nevertheless, Greene managed to make Scobie the victim of his own adultery.

Greene's passionate affair with Catherine had lit a creative fire under the novel, which he rattled off as quickly as he had his 'entertainments' when he was powered by the stimulus of benzedrine.

The end of the war and the 1945 General Election had forced the people of Britain to seriously think about what kind of government should rule the victorious but economically crippled nation, a topic that had seemed almost abstract during the existential struggle against the Nazis. At the heart of the debate was the question of which values mattered most in the governance of post-conflict Britain. The electorate's resounding answer was – socialist ones. Churchill, the wartime saviour, had served his purpose and was dumped in favour of a Labour leader who would be able to reshape a less class-ridden society. Given how popular socialist ideology had been before the war, the election result should not have been surprising. Britons rejected a rapacious capitalist society that served the already wealthy and voted for a state interventionist government that promised to share the spoils of war fairly among the people – heroes, cowards and bystanders alike.

*

Graham Greene was the most prescient of writers who had been writing mostly favourably about communism and its effects throughout the 1930s. He had even briefly joined the Communist Party. The war, however, had altered his outlook. Greene told a friend on the day of the election that he 'didn't care' who won the election and reported to his mother that he would be voting Conservative because 'The Socialists are such bores.'[56] Yet there was more to his electoral apathy than disenchantment with Clement Attlee and the Labour Party.

As an MI6 officer, Greene had witnessed Stalin's ruthless conquest of Eastern Europe and by the end of the war recognised what life under Stalin's totalitarian rule really meant.[57] When George Orwell published *Animal Farm* in August 1945, Greene was quick to praise it for the brave stance Orwell had taken against Britain's wartime ally.

He acknowledged that during the struggle with Nazism there had to be a 'measure of appeasement' towards Russia but now the war had been won it was time to break from Stalin.[58] This could also have been the moment Greene broke from Philby and his lingering support for Moscow and the ideal of universal communism. Greene no longer saw eye to eye with the Oxbridge intake of spies who championed Soviet ideals.

Chapter 17

Moscow Calling

In an unnamed London park in the early summer of 1944, Boris Krotenschield (aka Krotov, Krechin) was waiting patiently for his agent to arrive.[1] Because of the strict counter-surveillance measures demanded by Moscow – the changing of buses, the ducking into shops, the tracking back on oneself – Krotenschield knew that it was not always possible to be absolutely on time. A few minutes late for the rendezvous, there was no mistaking the shuffling swagger of Kim Philby, every inch the congenial Englishman enjoying a stroll in the early summer sun.

Krotenschield, who had replaced Anatoly Gorsky as the Cambridge spies' handler,[2] was ambitious for himself and his agents. His warmth, humanity and intellect had made a positive impression on Philby, who described him as 'a splendid professional and wonderful person'.[3] The two men found they shared an interest in sport. Philby was an Arsenal man,[4] while Krotenschield was in love with English football. Philby knew Krotenschield only as 'Max'. A couple of years older than Philby, Max made light of the business of treachery, in contrast to Gorsky, reassuring his charge that everything would work itself out in the end and that he should look forward to the final victory.[5] But these were dark days for the Cambridge Five, when Moscow had turned its face against the British spies, not sure whether to trust them or cut them loose. In his briefcase, Philby carried a document that he hoped would convince his Soviet spymasters of his true worth. It was an MI6 report authored by a revamped counter-intelligence department called Section IX that told the unvarnished truth about what Britain really thought of its Russian ally: 'The contradictions between Great Britain and the Soviet Union are as great as those between Britain and Nazi Germany,' the report began. 'Soviet Russia is our friend only while it can obtain benefit from this friendship. It does not trust us and will exert all efforts in espionage activities against us even in years of friendship. When it will obtain everything it can from a friendship, it would inexorably activate all the secret forces against the ideals for which Britain struggles. In this way our most dangerous enemy after the war can turn out to be the secret aggression of Soviet Russia.'[6]

A few weeks later Krotenschield and Philby met again. The Russian had good news. Moscow was able to corroborate Philby's report with other documents and had informed the London residency: 'This is a serious confirmation of S's [Sonchen was Philby's Russian codename] honesty in his work with us, which obliges us to review our attitude towards him and his entire group. Further contact with them should be based on the consideration of their great value to us, and any possibility of failure must be excluded from work with them. On our behalf express much gratitude to "S" for his work, especially for passing us the aforementioned file. If you find it convenient and possible, offer "S" in the most extremely tactful way a bonus of £100 [worth £3,870 today] or give him a gift of equal value.'[7]

After Krotenschield had passed on the money, which Philby used to buy an Austin Reed suit and an Anthony Eden hat,[8] Philby wrote to Moscow profusely thanking them for their reassessment of his loyalty: 'I am deeply grateful for your communication and the gift which was passed to me by Max. This communication inspires and excites me deeply and binds me more closely than ever to those whom I always considered my real comrades and friends, although I never saw them. More than ten years have passed since our collaboration began. And during this decade of work I have never been so deeply touched as now with your gift and no less deeply excited by your communication. Both the communication and the gift permit me to be absolutely sure that I have made a certain contribution to the greatest achievements of the Soviet people. Accept my heartfelt thanks.'[9]

Rehabilitation of the Cambridge Five also meant the rehabilitation of Boris Krotenschield, who knew only too well what happened to illegal residents who fell out of favour with Moscow.

Philby's position was further helped when Yelena Modrzchinskaya, the chief architect of Moscow's distrusting attitude towards the Cambridge spies, was promoted out of the NKVD and ended up writing books about the evils of capitalism at the Institute of Philosophy of the USSR Academy of Science.[10] For the next few weeks, Philby said 'virtually all of my discussions' with Krotenschield 'concerned the future of Section IX'.[11]

The man then heading the inchoate MI6 Soviet counter-intelligence unit was John Curry, an MI5 secondee who was hard of hearing and close to retirement.[12] Everyone knew that he was keeping the post warm until a senior SIS officer could be found to replace him. Philby told Krotenschield: 'If I was offered the post . . . it would mean a significant promotion and improve my chances of determining the course of events.' Krotenschield informed Philby that the Centre did indeed want the British spy to apply for Curry's job. Or as Philby put it: 'I must do everything, but everything, to ensure that I became head of Section IX.'[13]

This was no easy task. The obvious candidate was Felix Cowgill, Philby's boss, and an expert on Soviet espionage who had grown pathologically opposed to communism. Philby wrote rather disingenuously in his autobiography: 'I liked and respected Cowgill, and I'd much to thank him for. But he was a prickly obstacle in the course laid down for me, so he had to go.'

Before Philby could begin his campaign of intrigue against Cowgill and Curry, he had to defend himself from communist ghosts of his past.

John Curry was old and wise enough to realise that the success of a counter-Soviet intelligence department after the war would depend upon its working relationship with the Americans.[14]

Curry's early entreaties to the FBI for the sharing of all communist intelligence gathered by the Americans had delivered a document that concerned the espionage activities of Teodor Maly, Philby's old spymaster.[15] Maly, 'the long man', was of interest to the Americans because he was linked to Earl Browder, head of the Communist Party of the USA and grandfather of anti-Putin campaigner Sir Bill Browder.[16]

Before the war, Maly had sent several Soviet agents to Washington. The FBI had begun tracing Maly's US network and some of them were beginning to talk.[17]

Curry passed on this gem to Roger Hollis and Milicent Bagot, who were now heading MI5's own counter-Soviet intelligence section, F1, the branch investigating communist subversion.[18] How could Philby be sure that one of Maly's agents would not implicate him?

The defection of 'Big Bill' Alexander Orlov just before the war meant Philby had already been forced to anticipate just such a dangerous scenario. Philby hoped Orlov, now cut off from Moscow, would be ignorant as to how far his 'Three Musketeer' British agents had travelled into the heart of British intelligence. In fact, the Russian defector was struggling to get by in Cleveland and had decided to publish a version of his story, a damning indictment of Stalinism, to generate some much-needed cash.[19]

How could Philby be sure that Orlov wouldn't accidentally name Philby as one of his pre-war communist acquaintances? There were also whispers that two of Philby's other Russian handlers had not perished behind the Iron Curtain. Arnold Deutsch was reported to have followed Orlov on a ship bound for New York,[20] while MI5 had evidence that Maly had been seen in Moscow and that he may have even joined his own agents in America before the start of the war.[21] Deutsch and Maly could of course also identify Philby.

Forewarned is forearmed, and so Philby began establishing an early warning system among the American secret service, the OSS, operating in Britain. He skilfully relieved the 'fawning Yanks' of all the intelligence they had, including progress reports on the FBI's investigation into Maly's cell of stay-behind Soviet agents who might yet help MI5's Hollis and Bagot in their efforts to track down the London moles. Philby's deep penetration of the American secret services would serve him well after the war, when it would be the CIA, not MI6, who posed the greatest threat to the expanding Soviet empire and Stalin's ambitions.

Around this time, another apparition from his communist days materialised out of the ether. Philby had never divorced his first wife Lizy but, as part of the strict Soviet protocols, the couple had separated from each other's lives. So it came as something of a surprise when one day an MI6 vetting officer requested to see him to discuss Lizy.[22]

Tim Milne says it was the only time he ever saw his ice cool school friend 'slightly disconcerted'.[23] Approaching Philby, the MI6 vetting officer explained: 'Sorry to bother you, Kim – Mere formality. It's about your wife's application for a job – she's quoted you as a reference. I just need the usual good word.'

Lizy hadn't warned her husband she was seeking work. Milne, who was standing next to Philby, said Philby looked 'utterly blank' before shooting back 'yes, she's OK'.[24]

It was Lizy who suggested to Moscow that her husband would be most useful to Russia as a penetration agent at the heart of the British government[25] and she remained an important, perhaps the most important, link between the Vienna circle and the Cambridge spies. She was close to Guy Burgess, Anthony Blunt and Harry Smolka, and she also knew Graham Greene's friend

Claud Cockburn.[26] She met Soviet contacts all over Europe and in 1937 Deutsch sent Guy Burgess and Lizy to Paris to collect a suitcase of cash, which they brought back to the UK to fund Russian espionage.[27]

When the group later lost touch with Moscow after the liquidation of Deutsch and Maly, it was Lizy who brought them back in from the cold. Anthony Blunt described her as the key fifth member of the group at this time, making the so-called 'fifth man'.[28] 'I'm sure Lizy was the link there,' Blunt later told MI5 when they were formulating their theories about the Cambridge spies. 'You don't know and can't know I suppose when the phrase circle of five was invented.'[29]

During MI5's interrogation of Anthony Blunt in 1965, Arthur Martin told the Russian spy it 'seems reasonable to say that the initial recruitment of Kim produced a ring of five'. But Blunt countered 'oh no that seems to me arbitrary deduction, you see what I mean doesn't Lizy count in this? Now I had always assumed that with a certain vanity, Kim, Donald, Guy and myself were four but if one assumes that, Lizy was the fifth.'[30]

Philby was saved because the vetting officer hadn't bothered querying why Philby was still married to a rabid communist. The degrees of separation between the registries of MI5 and MI6 made it difficult to make such enquiries. But it may have been that Philby, with the inadvertent assistance of his younger sister Helena who worked in the MI6 registry in St Albans, had had this piece of inconvenient information judiciously weeded. The incident sufficiently rattled Philby to commit to regularising his personal life. When the time was right, he would tell Menzies about the wartime marital anomaly.

There was, however, one further figure who could also be traced back to his Austrian communist days, whom Philby was unable to shake off. Philby must have hoped his expert character assassination of Peter 'Harry' Smolka/Smollett had buried MI5's interest in the suspect civil servant. But Smolka's high-ranking penetration of the Ministry of Information made his Russian links a high-profile security risk. In 1944, Smolka was being championed by Churchill's close personal adviser and the head of the Ministry of Information, Brendan Bracken. Aided by Bracken, Smolka was able to help persuade Churchill that Stalin's intentions were benign while also handing the Russians invaluable insights into British foreign policy. Smolka organised pro-Soviet events across the country including the celebration of the 25th anniversary of the formation of the Red Army in 1943. Packed cinemas showed a short Pathé film called *Russia 1918, Anniversary of Red Army,* which depicted Lenin signing the document to create the Red Army followed by the Red Army marching into Kiev in 1919. The resonances of 1918 and 1941 were powerful as was the impression of Russia's overwhelming might and resources. In London, thousands gathered at the Albert Hall for this celebratory event, which included readings by the leading British actors Laurence Olivier and John Gielgud.[31] KGB defector Oleg Gordievsky later described Smolka's takeover of the MOI Russian section 'the NKVD's most remarkable "active measures" coup'.[32]

Philby had already introduced Smolka to Guy Burgess, explaining the 'winking' code they used when the Austrian had useful intelligence to pass on. Smolka appeared to be embedded with the Cambridge Five. Yet Smolka's true loyalties were not so clear cut. While MI5 suspected him of being a Soviet spy, Moscow had come to believe he might be a double agent working for the British.

The Centre did not like the way he had such open access to both Philby and Burgess. In a letter dispatched from the Centre to London dated 25 October 1943, the NKVD had warned the residency that Smolka was an experienced 'enemy agent' who was being 'planted' in the GRU network by the British.[33] The Russians blamed Philby for his recruitment and told him to drop Smolka immediately. If Moscow was right, Philby was now horribly exposed and must have wondered if Smolka was even a true communist.³⁴

Philby had little choice but to gamble that the Centre was wrong, that Smolka would remain loyal to the Cambridge Five, if not to Moscow, and focus his efforts on the job in hand – securing the Section IX position. According to his autobiography, Philby instigated a Machiavellian campaign of intrigue that would live on in Soviet spycraft folklore and became the centrepiece of Philby's many future lectures to the KGB academy of aspiring spies.³⁵

Philby had closely studied the main players in MI6 and was now ready to exploit their weaknesses. To destroy Felix Cowgill's chances of taking over Section IX, he had to subtly undermine his boss's credentials. First port of call was the 'enfeebled' Valentine Vivian, who had confided in Philby that he resented Cowgill's empire building, which threatened Vivian's own position. 'On past occasions,' wrote Philby, 'he had wept on my shoulder on account of his lost influence, embarrassing me deeply. But now I welcomed these sentimental little scenes, and it was not long before Vivian was asking me quite improperly, "what to do about Cowgill".'³⁶ This question was answered by Cowgill himself, whose blocking of MI6 intelligence-sharing with MI5 and OSS had made him a hated figure among both agencies. Since the IX job would require a candidate who could work well with the Americans and MI5, he had effectively ruled himself out of the position.

All that remained was to persuade Sir Stewart Menzies, the head of MI6, of Cowgill's unsuitability, while planting in his mind the idea that Philby was the best man for the new counter-intelligence command. Certainly, Philby could pray-in-aid his highly fruitful working relationship with MI5 that dated back to the days of Glenalmond House, as well as his blossoming relations with the Americans. Nevertheless, Philby decided a direct approach was not the best idea, so he started courting Menzies' principal staff officer, the ageing but influential Christopher Arnold-Forster, a

Royal Navy Lt Commander and an Assistant Director of Naval Intelligence.

Arnold-Forster had an office across the corridor from Menzies, who regularly consulted him on MI6 structural and personnel matters. Philby hoped: 'He would soon grasp the impossibility of the situation in which the head of SIS counter espionage section [Cowgill] was permanently at loggerheads with MI5. It might be tolerated in the short run under the stress of war but to prolong it indefinitely into peace time is a different matter. If Arnold-Forster got the point, I had little doubt that he would press it.'[37]

Philby suggested to Vivian that Arnold-Forster should have a full and frank meeting with Guy Liddell, who he knew was no friend of Cowgill.[38] In early September, Philby was summoned to the fourth floor of Broadway where he waited in the secretaries' office for the green light to flash up indicating that the chief was ready to see his visitor. Menzies, well-built with a weak moustache and a big, pale forehead, liked to remain aloof from his underlings. Philby had only spoken to him half a dozen times during the past year, instead dealing directly with Vivian and Cowgill.

Menzies addressed his visitor by his nickname, Kim, which Philby took as instant affirmation of his promotion to the IX position. His highly trained instincts were correct. Menzies said that he had chosen Philby on the basis of Vivian's recommendation after taking soundings from MI5. Philby said he was careful that he 'left him [Menzies] in the hope that he would claim, and perhaps more than half believe, that the whole credit for the idea was his own.'[39]

Philby's scheming was so successful that he even persuaded Menzies to allow him to write his own terms of reference: 'It gave me responsibility, under the chief, for the collection and interpretation of information concerning Soviet and communist espionage and subversion in all parts of the world outside British territory. It also enjoined me to maintain the closest liaison for the reciprocal exchange of intelligence on these subjects with MI5.'[40]

Within a matter of weeks Philby, a 32-year-old intelligence officer with little experience in communist or Russian intelligence, found himself in charge of the UK's Soviet counter-espionage operations, an achievement described as the greatest intelligence coup ever perfected by a spy agency against its principal enemy.[41]

Philby had not only been promoted ahead of his boss Felix Cowgill (who resigned from MI6 shortly afterwards) but also in preference to the candidature of Jane Archer, who had re-established herself inside MI6 and whose experience and skill-set should have made her a much more obvious choice for the post.

Such was the secrecy surrounding Philby's appointment that Menzies told him he was on no account to let the United States' services know about his role nor even the existence of Section IX – in case the Americans inadvertently leaked the information to the Russians.[42]

But of course, the news had already been greeted with cold, steely delight by Philby's Soviet spymasters in Moscow. This was how the Centre responded to Philby's success: 'The new appointment is hard to overestimate. First of all it is important to see the significance the British attached to working against the fraternal intelligence services all over the world and our service. To all appearances, "S" [Philby] is moving up in his institution, he is respected and valued. He must retain this position and work so that his reputation continues to grow.'[43]

Philby wrote back thanking Moscow for another 'marvellous gift' promising: 'The prospects that have opened before me in connection with my recent change at work inspire me to optimistic thoughts, and all that remains is to realise them in concrete form.'[44]

However, almost as soon as the mutual exchange of back-slapping missives had ended, Philby sensed that defeat was about to be snatched from the jaws of his extraordinary victory, in the form of plans for a new combined British security and intelligence agency. Throughout the war the Foreign Office, Home Office and the Cabinet had considered options for the amalgamation of MI6 and MI5 to create a single Secret Service.[45] The exigencies of war meant the issue had been kicked from department to department. But with victory in sight, MI6 and MI5 were engaged in a bitter struggle to be the dominant force in a new supreme intelligence and security agency.

MI5's Director General David Petrie had long criticised MI6 for its unwillingness to work more closely with MI5, citing examples of failed intelligence sharing, which he claimed had led to serious security gaffes that had threatened the UK.[46] Felix Cowgill's intransigence and ultimate demise had served to weaken SIS's position, and the case for MI5 to play the part of senior partner in the new agency was gaining ground. Its lead proponent was Guy Liddell.[47] MI5's head of counter-intelligence believed there should be one organisation answerable to one ministry with two separate departments for defensive (home security) and offensive (foreign) operations, but with much closer cooperation.[48]

Liddell arranged for Herbert Hart to draw up a plan for full fusion between the two services.[49] Menzies asked his close adviser Chris Arnold-Forster to look at the proposal, which he initially thought was a good one, although he regarded himself as the natural head of a super spy agency.[50] One of the key elements of a proposed fused service was a combined Soviet counter-intelligence (detection of foreign state threat) and counter-espionage (neutralisation of foreign state threat) division, combining MI5's F Division and Philby's Section IX.[51] It is at this point that Philby, realising control of his new unit countering Soviet espionage abroad was about to be wrested from him, steps into the picture.

Philby relied on his special relationship with MI5 and its counter-intelligence head, Liddell, to subvert the amalgamation plan on the basis that fusion would weaken both services. To carry the argument with Liddell he had two advantages. The first was Liddell's historic sympathy for the MI6 officer after the harsh internment of his father St John Philby at the start of the war. The second was Anthony Blunt, a fellow Cambridge spy and Liddell's wartime personal assistant, who remained close to his former master and could report back to Philby what Liddell was thinking.

Armed with this insider knowledge, Philby believed he had done enough to dissuade Liddell and Petrie from their course of action. Yet he couldn't have been more wrong. On 3 November 1944, Liddell noted in his diary: 'Kim seems to have the idea that we are definitely opposed to total amalgamation. I told him that this was not so. We had only been worried by the tremendous difficulties to be overcome and by the possibility that if alternative proposals were made the whole thing would be put into the wastepaper basket, leaving us in the present muddle for another 20 years. Apart from this we thought that even if total amalgamation could be achieved there would have to be a subdivision rather on the lines that we were suggesting.'[52]

Philby's post-war characterisation of Liddell as the best intelligence officer in the country was proving very apt.[53]

The Russian spy's only hope was that the inherent antagonism between Menzies and Petrie would fatally undermine any plan that left either agency in control over the other.

In the meantime, Philby went ahead recruiting for his section. He approached the task with his customary blend of charm and ruthless efficiency. Having culled Curry's own team (a 'mental case' called Harry Steptoe and a woman officer who had 'toasted her eyeball' while watching an eclipse of the sun) he was careful to gather around him a mixture of loyal friends and uninquisitive types.

First pick was Graham Greene's brother-in-law, Lt Col Rodney Dennys OBE (1934), who had been recalled from intelligence duties in Cairo. Dennys, who was even taller than Greene, stood as a candidate for the Liberal Party before the war and was known for his 'cultivated taste and unfailing courtesy'.[54] His occasional absent-mindedness and distracted manner belied a considerable shrewdness and guile. But in 1944, he had recovered from the removal of one his kidneys to an unspecified disease contracted in Holland at the start of the war.[55] In Cairo he had enjoyed excellent tranquil relations with the other intelligence agencies, oblivious to the internecine fighting among the intelligence departments of Whitehall.[56]

Though quintessentially English and descended from an old Devonian family he was born in Ipoh in the British protected state of Perak, where his father was serving in the Malayan Civil Service. He was fond of recalling that the first words he spoke were Malay, taught to him by his amah; English came later.[57] In this respect, he had much in common with the Punjabi-speaking Kim Philby. After the war, he succeeded Philby as head of station in Istanbul in 1950.[58]

In the forced absence of Graham Greene, Philby made Dennys his number two, assistant head of section. Then in quick succession, he brought in Major Anthony Milne, brother of his old school friend Ian, who was having an affair with Philby's first wife Lizy, an indiscretion and failure of disclosure for which he had to resign after the war but one no doubt Philby fully exploited.[59]

Further recruits were Lord Victor Rothschild, one of the so-called 'Group' who socialised with the Cambridge spies; Charles de Salis, the former Lisbon head of station; and Sir Colville Barclay, an Etonian aristocrat and adventurer.[60] Not all appointments were Philby's. Valentine Vivian insisted on foisting on Philby the one person better qualified than him for his job. Vivian remembered Jane Archer's expertise in Soviet matters from the time they had worked together on the Maly case before the war and the Krivitsky interrogation in 1940. Archer may have been outspoken and at times difficult to work with, but Vivian knew how single-minded she had been in tracking down communist agents.

Philby had already taken steps to distance himself from Archer when he discovered that she lived in a flat in Ealing close to the location for his clandestine meetings with his Russian handler. He made sure he steered clear of Ealing.[61] After the war Philby could still recall the shock of having to accommodate Archer in his new section, knowing she still believed what Krivitsky had told her was still true – that a 'young English journalist who the Soviets sent to Spain' was the mole at the heart of MI6.[62]

'After Guy Liddell,' Philby later wrote, 'Jane was perhaps the ablest professional intelligence officer ever employed by MI5. She had spent a big chunk of a shrewd lifetime studying Communist activity in all its aspects . . . and here she was plunked down in my midst.'[63]

Naturally Philby had a plan to sideline Archer: 'To keep Jane busy, I put her in charge of the most solid body of intelligence on Communist activity available to the section at the time. It consisted of a considerable volume of wireless traffic concerning the national liberation movements in Eastern Europe.'[64]

If this was meant to bury her in paperwork, it didn't work. Only a few weeks after arriving at the Section IX offices in Broadway, Archer asked to speak to Philby in confidence. What she had to say to him was deeply sensitive and concerned a possible communist mole. Philby's heart must have skipped a beat or two while he waited to hear the particulars of her accusation. She confided in her boss that she believed the old Etonian Colville Barclay matched Krivitsky's description of an aristocratic British traitor working in MI6.[65]

Philby reacted with pragmatic haste, happily assisting Archer in leading MI5 up the garden path, and agreed to pass on Archer's suspicions to Guy Liddell, which he duly did.[66]

Yet Archer's suspicions must have spooked him because at the same time he used the opportunity to ask Liddell for access to other dormant communist files that might hold clues to Soviet penetration.

Liddell innocently recorded in his diary: 'Kim was very anxious to get hold of the old records of the John King case [a pre-war Soviet agent who had been convicted of espionage in the UK] in order to satisfy himself that he was on sound ground. I have put him in touch with Roger Hollis.'[67]

Philby's hope that the merger problem would resolve itself was realised when Sir Neville Bland, a former ambassador to Holland, who had witnessed the Venlo debacle at close hand, completed a report into the future of SIS that recommended 'its continued autonomous existence'.[68] More good news followed when David Petrie dropped his support for full amalgamation.[69] But Liddell still clung to the idea that his department would take over Sections V and IX, a proposal supported by Chris Arnold-Forster and Peter Loxley of the Foreign Office.[70]

By 9 November, Liddell's plan had run into serious opposition: 'Arnold-Forster asked me once more for a copy of my proposals for the absorption of sections five and nine by our organisation. I said that I was in a difficult position in giving him this because in fact my own chief [Petrie] did not agree with many of the proposals which I had made.'[71]

By the new year, Liddell was fighting the prospect of a reverse takeover of MI5 by MI6. The matter was settled for good by a new enquiry set up by Sir Findlater Stewart, a former member of the XX Committee and Security Executive, which focused on the future performance of the Security Service, rather than SIS.[72]

*

There were no obvious signs of intrigue beyond the warring of the two agencies. But somehow Philby had silently assassinated the hostile takeover bid by MI5 and seen off its formidable counter-intelligence chief Guy Liddell – and even turned it to his advantage. The idea that MI5 would ever have control over domestic and foreign counter-espionage was buried forever. If Liddell, Hollis and Archer had taken charge of a joint counter-Soviet operation, it would surely have only been a matter of weeks before the treachery of Philby and the other Cambridge spies was uncovered.

Instead, on January 1 1946, Philby, still only 33 years old, was awarded an OBE for services to his country – the only post-1939 recruit to MI6 to be decorated for their wartime service.[73]

Chapter 18

The Start of the Affair

Life outside MI6 in peacetime London allowed Graham Greene to focus on his twin passions – writing and his forlorn affair with Catherine Walston. At the best of times, his two loves forged a creative symbiosis that spurred him on to complete his masterpiece, *The Heart of the Matter*, and in September 1947 he was able to send the finished manuscript to his publisher Heinemann. At the worst of times, it triggered black depressions. Henry Scobie's struggle with his faith and adultery were also Greene's, as were the police commissioner's thoughts of suicide. Unable to reconcile his private life with his Catholicism and knowing the harm he had caused the three women in his life, Greene also contemplated suicide, an act of eternal oblivion and damnation that interested him more in the abstract than in the actual deed. When Vivien Greene confided in her local priest about her fears over her husband's written suicide threats, the clergyman's response could not have been more damning: 'People who talk about it never do it.'[1]

Kim Philby was not the only one of the Cambridge spies who Greene kept in contact with after the war. John Cairncross, the so-called 'fifth man', had left SIS and returned to the Treasury where he remained in touch with Greene, who fondly referred to him as 'Claymore', the Scottish Highland broadsword. They were unlikely friends: the working-class Scotsman and lapsed Calvinist who harboured a deep suspicion of the ruling elites; and Greene, the senior intelligence officer and celebrated author who was part of the milieu that so antagonised Cairncross. Yet his feelings for Greene ran deep.

How far their relationship had developed since the encounter in the train carriage on the way to London, and what Greene got out of it, is far from clear as neither wrote further about their wartime interaction. But in 1946–47, Cairncross recounted how he 'would often run into Graham' on Treasury visits to the capital: 'I never forgot to collect miniature bottles of whiskey for him – some of which would turn to good account in the film of his novel *Our Man in Havana*. He was always grateful for these and wrote "I consider the Stratford on Avon whiskey the sinister gem of the collection". I had a marvellous evening with him in London when I was entertained by him together with a French novelist. We were first taken to see *The Rake's Progress* and ended up with a splendid late dinner at Rules. We also met at the Old Vic where Laurence Olivier was acting in a Shakespeare play and was, Graham thought, jazzing up his role. Then I met him again with a beautiful Australian girl whom I had previously seen in the company of the philosopher Freddie Ayer.'[2]

By 1948, Cairncross had moved to the Exchange Control Division, where he was appointed deputy treasury representative on the Western Union finance committee, a forerunner to NATO.

Always surprised that such a 'distinguished writer' should have taken an interest in him, Cairncross dedicated his memoir to Greene saying: 'Graham Greene was for me not just a superb writer but a wonderful and loyal friend.'[3]

Another Cambridge spy who Greene would have come into contact with was Anthony Blunt, an old friend of Catherine Walston and a priggish bon viveur in post-war London.[4] Blunt had recruited his fellow Cambridge graduate, the American Michael Straight, to the NKVD before the war, and played the role of go-between when Straight later courted his future wife, Catherine's sister Belinda. Greene was also friends with the Hungarian writer Andrew Revai, a Soviet agent and art dealer who was very close to Blunt. The Cambridge spy may have sensed that Greene was suspicious of the group, and when Revai suggested he come round for dinner to meet Greene, Blunt made his excuses.[5]

Yet it was Kim Philby, the leader of the group, with whom Greene was most intrigued. At the turn of 1945, Philby was working very closely with Greene's brother-in-law, Rodney Dennys, at Section IX. It was an important position and Philby offered it to someone he trusted implicitly. Greene's relationship with his sister Elisabeth Dennys was, by the nature of their shared wartime secrets and Greene's shared personal confidences about his own tortured love life, exceptionally close. He also clearly thought very highly of Elisabeth's husband, writing of his sister's engagement in the summer of 1942: 'The man is very nice and intelligent. I was afraid she was emotionally tied up with the middle-aged married sailor [her boss in Cairo, Cuthbert Bowlby].' Elisabeth's love life and experiences in the Middle East helped inspire the author Michael Ondaatje when he came to write his best-selling novel *The English Patient*.

When Elisabeth got cold feet in the desert and broke off the engagement to Rodney, it was to Graham whom she turned for advice. He wrote from Freetown: 'I'm sorry things have not gone too well. Things can be hell, I know. The peculiar form it's taken with me has been in loving two people as equally as makes no difference, the awful struggle to have one's cake and eat it, the inability to throw over one for the sake of the other . . . yours is different and I imagine just as hellish. I always used to laugh at emotional situations and feel they couldn't, any of them, beat toothache. One lives and learns.'[6] He advised her to wait it out to see how she felt about Dennys when they had returned to England. The couple married shortly afterwards.

Greene's ties to Rodney and Elisabeth brought him into closer contact with his old boss Philby, who attended family events and parties after the war. The two friends also met regularly at office get-togethers organised by mutual colleagues from Greene's MI6 days.[7] How close Philby and Greene had been in the immediate years after Greene's resignation from MI6 is not altogether clear. But Philby acknowledged they had remained friends up until Maclean and Burgess escaped to Moscow in 1951, when Philby broke off the friendship out of his desire not to embarrass Greene.[8]

As Britain entered the new Cold War era, Rodney Dennys was able to apprise Graham Greene of the way Section IX was shaping up under the leadership of their shared acquaintance. Philby had inherited a poorly organised and under-staffed section whose Soviet files held at MI6's central registry were in a truly 'chaotic situation'.[9] This much Dennys could tell Greene. But behind the scenes, the Soviet spy was building a platform to launch a counter-intelligence offensive against both Britain and America.

As a result of Churchill's strict diktats, which had applied while Russia and Britain were allies, there was an almost complete absence of British agents in communist-held territory.[10] This suited Philby because he could work from a clean slate. He had also insinuated himself into the heart of the committee that was planning to shape the post-war strategy and organisation of SIS.[11]

Philby knew how critically important this was since the committee's 'sole purpose' was 'to facilitate penetration of the USSR from the north, south, east and west.'[12] It was ostensibly chaired by Menzies, but 'C' mostly left this to Chris Arnold-Forster.[13] Philby made sure that his own placeman Rodney Dennys, number 2 at Section IX whom he described as a 'first class draughtsman', took the influential role of secretary to the committee.[14] An SIS report from July 1945 on the performance of the committee members offers an insight into Philby's stealthy operating practice: 'Philby sticks to a moderate line. He has decided that his approach will be to hear the committee's point of view first and then support whichever line seems to offer the most effective results, mindful above all of avoiding even the slightest risk to his own position. He avoids mistakes and never argues with anyone.'[15]

The key paper on the methods and objectives of intelligence penetration of the USSR was written by Dennys. It began by declaring that, for the deployment of secret agents in Russian territory, '...our security needs to be perfect,' adding, 'to achieve perfection the cover needs to be perfect.'[16] But of course, SIS security was imperfect and already compromised. Philby handed Dennys' report to his Russian contact Boris Krotenschield along with a detailed, if rather prosaic, CV and appraisal of his friend: 'Dennys joined SIS in 1938. He was section V's head of station in The Hague and worked in section V after evacuation from Holland. At the end of 1941 he was posted as section V's head of station to Cairo, where he ran counter-intelligence across the entire Middle East. He has SIS symbol 8 9 7 0 0. He was recalled to London at the beginning of 1944 and began to prepare for the post of counter-intelligence department representative in the Far East. Health reasons prevented him taking up the job and he remained in section V. He was transferred to section IX at the beginning of this year.'[17]

By VE Day, Philby had secured a total grip on Britain's Soviet counter-intelligence operations. Section V had been folded into Section IX, leaving Philby in command of a beefed-up department focused on Russia and comprising 32 officers – SIS's entire London staff was 307 officers.[18]

Philby's dominance over Soviet affairs had not come a moment too soon. On 4 September 1945, a Russian diplomat walked into the British consulate in Istanbul. His name was Konstantin Volkov, Vice Consul for the Soviet Union, and for the right price he was willing to defect to Britain.[19] In return for £50,000 (£2 million today)

THE START OF THE AFFAIR

and political asylum, Volkov offered to provide the names of three high-grade Soviet agents working in Britain.[20]

One of the first to receive the news of what became known as the Volkov 'sales catalogue' was Russian-speaking John Reed, a senior diplomat who had been at Cambridge at the same time as Philby: 'I was serving in our embassy in Turkey in 1945,' he later recalled. 'One morning this Russian walks into reception looking very nervous and asks to see the acting consul-general . . . He says he wants a laissez-passer for himself and his wife to Cyprus and £27,500. In return he is offering the real names of three Soviet agents working in Britain. He says two of them are working in the Foreign Office, one the head of a counter-espionage organisation in London.'[21]

Volkov actually described the third spy as someone who 'fulfils the duties of a head of a department of English counter-espionage in London'.[22]

The urgent message from the British embassy in Istanbul sent to London began: 'I am quite prepared for the following to be a complete mare's nest but I think you must have it all the same.'[23] Naturally Sir Stuart Menzies passed on Volkov's proposition to the head of his Russian department, Section IX, Kim Philby, who immediately recognised the threat to himself.

'I had scarcely settled down to my desk one August morning when I received the summons from the chief. He pushed across at me a sheaf of papers and asked me to look them through . . . I stared at the papers rather longer than necessary to compose my thoughts. I rejected the idea of suggesting caution in case Volkov's approach should prove to be a provocation. It would be useless in the short run, and might possibly compromise me at a later date. The only course was to put a bold face on it. I told the Chief that I thought we were onto something of the greatest importance. I would like a little time to dig into the background and, in the light of any further information on the subject, to make appropriate recommendations for action.'[24]

Philby persuaded Menzies that the situation was so serious he would need to go to Istanbul personally to arrange for Volkov's exfiltration.

It took the British intelligence officer two weeks to reach Turkey by which time Volkov had mysteriously disappeared, never to be seen again.

Philby's formal report to Menzies on the case wrongly suggested that the Russians, who bugged Volkov's office and living quarters, had already rumbled Volkov.[25] The much more likely possibility, that the Russians may have been tipped off by one of the three moles Volkov was planning to expose, never made it into Philby's final report. Neither did Volkov's description of the British 'head of the counter-intelligence department'.

In January 2025, the National Archives in Kew released the full text of Philby's report into the Volkov affair. It is a masterpiece of deception and reads:

'It is exceedingly difficult to guess which parts of his [Volkov's] statement were true and which parts were exaggerated or false,' intoned Philby. 'We regard the figures of 250 and 314 for NKGB [People's Commissariat for State Security responsible for foreign agents] agents in the UK and Turkey respectively as wildly exaggerated. We tend strongly to the opinion that Volkoff [sic] was mistaken, possibly honestly, in asserting that NKGB cryptographers were reading Foreign Office and SIS telegrams. On the other hand, information from other sources leads us to take seriously his statement that there are two NKGB agents in the Foreign Office and seven in the British Intelligence Service. It is extremely unlikely (although of course it is impossible to speak with certainty) that indiscretion in the British Embassy in Istanbul was the cause of Volkoff's exposure to the Russians. The more probable explanation is that Volkoff betrayed himself . . . Finally, I would like to draw your attention to the fact that Volkoff's information as to the existence of NKGB agents in official positions is so vague that it is improbable that we shall succeed in identifying them ... It is in the USSR itself, and in its diplomatic commercial missions outside its boundaries, that the roots of this activity are to be found. If we want the information, we shall have to go and get it.'[26]

Not everyone bought Philby's account. John Reed still couldn't understand why it had taken Philby so long to reach Istanbul. He told journalist Phillip Knightley that he believed: 'Either Philby was criminally incompetent or he was a Soviet agent.'[27] Philby later admitted the Volkov affair nearly ended his 'promising career'. He was partly saved by Menzies, who was understandably reluctant to launch a formal investigation into Volkov's claims about Soviet moles in the heart of his own organisation. However, seven days before Volkov disappeared, MI5 was tipped off about the Volkov affair by Tom Bromley, SIS officer/diplomat at the Istanbul consulate, who clearly thought something was awry. He wrote to Roger Hollis, in charge of countering Russian penetration operations, describing the events as 'extraordinary', adding: 'It is rather difficult to know what to make of it, but I send it over to you urgently for any observations you may have. It may conceivably tie up with the Canadian business. I do not know whether you have anyone suitable who could check the Russian document. You may perhaps wish to mention the matter to Captain Guy Liddell.'[28]

The 'Canadian business' to which Bromley was referring concerned a second Russian defection – a successful one.[29]

On 5 September, the day after Volkov walked into the British consulate in Istanbul, Igor Gouzenko, a cypher clerk working at Russia's embassy in Ottawa, Canada, defected. This time Philby had no time to stall or tip off his handlers about the danger. All he could do was to sit tight for the Canadians to pass on any intelligence they had gleaned. It must have been a nervous wait for Philby, made more worrying when the first name Gouzenko produced was a British nuclear scientist, Allan Nunn May, working in Canada but now back in Britain.[30] The situation facing Philby darkened further when the Canadian intelligence services revealed that 107 documents taken by Gouzenko from the Ottawa Rezidentura implicated 18 more agents.

Guy Liddell sent Roger Hollis to Canada to find out exactly what Gouzenko knew.[31] It was on his journey to meet Gouzenko that Hollis was told that Volkov had mysteriously disappeared. He wrote back to London: 'After Philby's arrival . . . calls were made to the Soviet Consulate in an attempt to contact Volkov. The first was answered by the Russian Consul General, the second by a man speaking English who claimed to be Volkov, but clearly was not, and the last by the Russian telephone operator who said Volkov had left for Moscow . . . inquiries showed that Volkov and Mrs Volkov did leave by plane to Russia on I think September 26th.'[32] An MI6 agent on the ground reported back to London that Volkov was heavily sedated and bandaged from head to foot.[33] Hollis urgently telegraphed Liddell asking permission to pass on 'the story of Kim's recent trip' to William Stephenson, SIS representative in North America, and to the Canadian authorities.

Liddell answered: 'Yes, but on a strictly confidential basis owing to remote possibility agent's [Volkov] return.'[34]

Hollis came back from Ottawa with a new name, an agent codenamed 'Elli', who Gouzenko claimed to be a high-grade Soviet mole working at the heart of British intelligence.[35] Philby later recalled: 'The first information about Gouzenko and Elli came from William Stephenson. "C" [Stewart Menzies] called me in and asked me my opinion about it. I said Gouzenko's defection was obviously very important and we treated it as such. But it was a disaster for the KGB and there was no way I could help. The Mounties had Gouzenko so well protected that it was impossible for the Russians to do anything about him, bump him off or anything like that. So he was able to give away a big Canadian network, and the telegrams he brought with him when he defected would have been of great help to Western decrypters.'[36]

Understandably, Philby's nerves were frazzled as he feared the imminent prospect of exposure. He called an urgent meeting with 'Max' (Krotenschield), who reassured his prize agent: 'Don't worry old man we have seen a lot worse.'[37]

Krotenschield's sangfroid proved to be the right response as the British investigation into Elli soon fizzled out. No one appeared to be pursuing the idea that Gouzenko's agent Elli or Volkov's mole at the heart of British counter-intelligence might be Kim Philby.

Philby could at last afford to reflect on his achievements – in 1938 he had been honoured by the Spanish fascists with the order of the Red Merit and at the turn of the year, January 1946, the British had awarded him an OBE. Twenty years later the Russians bestowed on Philby an equivalent honour, the Order of the Red Banner. No other spy has been so highly rewarded and certainly none can claim to have 'medals' from three opposing sides. Confident in his position at SIS, Philby decided the time was now right to formalise his personal life and he approached Sir Stewart Menzies seeking permission to divorce his wife, Lizy Friedmann, and marry Aileen, who was expecting their fourth child Miranda. Menzies appears to have treated the request as a formality that would iron out the creases of the private life of one its star officers and so made no effort to remind himself of Lizy's communist background.

Philby was now head of an enhanced counter-intelligence department, R5, that combined the work of Section IX and his old Section V.[38] But his meteoric rise presented a unique and rather unforeseen conundrum. In a speech to a select group of KGB officers in 1977 in Yasenov just outside Moscow, Philby explained: 'Whenever an agent succeeds in penetrating a hostile intelligence service, it is generally assumed that the higher the position he gets the better it is for us . . . as soon as I had taken up my new post, I was landed in situations of horrible complexity. I could not afford to fail all along the line because I should have been sacked. Yet if I achieved too much success I would damage our own interests.'[39] Philby then explained how he solved the puzzle: 'In general I would try to drag out decisions, to give me time to consult my Soviet friend; and, if possible, to give him time to consult Moscow. But sometimes decisions had to be taken quickly within hours. In such cases I had to use my own judgment.'

Nevertheless, Philby's subversive activity and pre-emptive strikes against double agents had drawn suspicion and unwanted attention. Rodney Dennys, who shared an office with Philby for six months in 1945, was said to be 'uneasy' about his former chief and had moved on to the Foreign Office, where he worked for Ernest Bevin, the Labour Foreign Secretary. Dennys later claimed: 'While we continued to remain friends, our relationship was at arm's length.'[40] Whether Dennys had become suspicious of Philby's rise in MI6 has never been made clear. Yet a small number of SIS officers serving with Philby at this time had an inkling that something may not be quite right about the charmed life of SIS's rising star. Charles Arnold-Baker, who left MI6 for a career at the Bar, said he found Philby 'nasty' while Hugh Trevor-Roper said he was never taken in by the famous Philby charm. Those less critical and much closer to him knew of his interest in communism. Tim Milne had known it since the early thirties when Philby was an open student of Marx and an admirer of Lenin.[41] Trevor-Roper says that he had regarded Philby as a crypto communist ever since he had been told of Philby's political orientation before the war.[42] Yet none of them had woken up to the enemy within.

While MI6 looked the other way, Philby, now head of a beefed-up communist counter-intelligence department, was having considerable success thwarting British efforts to combat Russian spying. His main achievement was shaping Britain's counter-intelligence strategy by closely working with MI5's Roger Hollis and Millicent Bagot and MI6's Jane Archer.

In correspondence with Hollis and Bagot, who were helping to draft a Cabinet paper on the nature of the post-war threat posed by Communist Russia, Philby encouraged Hollis to regard the Comintern as independent from the NKVD and therefore much more benign. Philby even persuaded Archer to modify her own conclusion on the danger of international communism, knowing that Archer's opinion on the subject of Soviet intelligence carried great weight.[43]

In a long memo to Hollis on 19 July 1945, Philby wrote: 'The generalisations about "Soviet power politics", the "Teachings of Karl Marx", the "long-term policy of the Comintern", "opportunistic Tactics" etc have a dismally familiar ring, but I doubt whether any useful meaning can be attached to them.'

Not all his efforts to undermine British counter-intelligence operations were successful, especially the tracking of known Soviet agents. On 10 July 1945, Hollis picked up on one of Philby's red herrings: 'As a small point of detail I think I've recently seen that Wilhelm Pieck [the future communist president of East Germany 1949–1960], who is given in the paper as still in Moscow, was in fact recently in Berlin.'

Hollis had little faith in MI6's capability in tackling the Soviet menace, and midway through the war he told a colleague, 'I can think of no document produced by SIS which makes it appear that international communism has been seriously studied by them since the outbreak of war. We, on the other hand, have started, rather belatedly, to follow the activities of the Comintern wherever it appears . . . It may be said that our job is internal security, and that we are going outside our charter.'[44]

It is hard to believe that, by 1945, a professional spycatcher such as Roger Hollis who had been tasked with finding Russian moles in the heart of British intelligence had not got Philby in his sights. He had seen the Volkov letter identifying a Russian agent 'who fulfilled the role as head of the counter-intelligence department in London' and he had spoken to Gouzenko who told him about a Russian mole in London codenamed Elli. Indeed, Hollis was so focused on who Elli might be that when he got back to the office from Canada he had turned to Anthony Blunt and formally addressed him as 'Elli', hoping to catch-out one of his key suspects playing the part of the Russian mole.[45]

Was Philby also on Hollis's list of Elli suspects? Philby must have thought so as Blunt had warned Philby about Hollis's increasingly probing interest in Blunt. Philby admitted to MI5 in 1951 he knew that Hollis was 'vaguely unhappy' about Blunt and his Marxist background.[46]

There is evidence Hollis at this time had been keeping a 'restricted access' file on Philby, the existence of which only emerged after Burgess and Maclean defected to Moscow in 1951.[47] It contained suspicions first raised by Milicent Bagot and Jane Archer about Philby's illogical switch from his interest in communism at Cambridge to his subsequent membership of the Anglo-German Fellowship and alignment with Franco in Spain.[48] These suspicions were stirred up again in 1946 when it became apparent that he was married to the Austrian communist agent Lizy Friedmann. The hunt for a Soviet mole was gaining momentum, and on 22 March 1946, MI5 wrote to Philby asking him whether SIS had any further intelligence about 'Harry Peter Smollett alias Smolka' who they suspected was now working with Soviet agents in Vienna.

Philby, understandably worried about where these enquiries might lead, decided not to reply. Instead, a week later, another SIS officer picked up the enquiry and after digging into the Smollett/Smolka files, told MI5: 'Our representative in Vienna has sent us the following information about Harry Peter Smollett alias Smolka who is now Daily Express correspondent in Vienna. There are indications that he has been asking questions about [our] Austrian Barracks unit

THE START OF THE AFFAIR

and our representative in Vienna [Peter Lunn]. Also that he is cultivating Ernst Fischer, former minister of education and his wife and is in contact with Tito Yugoslav circles to Vienna.'[49]

On 10 May 1946, M.B. Towndrow of MI5's F2a wrote to Philby about another communist who had known Smolka in London and was now a leading member of the Communist Party in Vienna, where he entertained members of the party.[50]

'Dear Mr Philby, please refer to previous correspondence about Dr Walter Hollitscher ending with our pf 54073/f to a b/BS. As of possible interest to you we have been reliably informed that Hollitscher is staying at Peter Smollett's flat in Vienna. Smollett you will remember, was last referred to in my pf 39680/f2a (b)/MBT dated 2 May 1946.

Yours sincerely M B Towndrow.'

Philby does not appear to have answered this enquiry either.

Less than six months later, towards the end of 1946, Philby was 'summoned' to see General John Sinclair, Director of Military Intelligence at the War Office. He was informed that he was to be relieved of his command of R5. Whatever fears Philby had that he may have been rumbled were partly allayed when Menzies reassured him that the change of post was not motivated by any black mark. Philby was to be posted to the SIS station in Istanbul so he could gain in-field experience, considered an essential requirement for any officer tipped for future promotion within the agency. Nevertheless, from Philby's perspective the transfer to the intelligence backwater of Istanbul was a huge disappointment as his new job would be of far less value to Moscow. After the Volkov affair, the Russians had deep cleaned their Turkey operations and removed any further potential defectors.

Philby pointedly noted: 'The three senior officers of the service, the chief [Menzies] vice chief [Vivian] and assistant chief, had no experience of counter espionage and no practical knowledge of work in the field. But I was not senior enough to benefit from any such dispensation.'⁵¹

Philby's replacement heading up R5 was Douglas Roberts. Roberts was the MI6 officer first chosen by Menzies to fly to Istanbul to bring Volkov in from the cold, but an acute attack of air sickness had allowed Philby to step in at the last minute and take over the sensitive mission, with catastrophic results for Volkov personally and for British intelligence more generally.

Roberts was to be supported by a young officer recruited from a Middle East intelligence mission in Cairo where he had worked with Rodney Dennys. His name was Maurice Oldfield, another rising star among MI6 and a future 'C'.

Philby recognised the danger of relinquishing his old post to a new team who would have access to all the case files managed and worked on by him. He had tried to be thorough in covering his tracks, but he could not be certain he hadn't left behind a paper trail that betrayed his own treachery.

In the grammar school-educated Oldfield, a Soviet mole hunter who was very much not one of the old boys, Philby may have sensed his own vulnerability. Oldfield had long been troubled by a 1945 case in which Soviet Hungarian defector Dr Alexander Rado had approached the British embassy in Cairo seeking sanctuary.⁵² While he had been in Oldfield's custody, Rado had been so fearful of being sent to Moscow that he had attempted to take his own life. Realising that Rado had vital intelligence on the Russian spy network in Europe, the Red Orchestra, Oldfield repeatedly contacted London in the hope of saving him, but each time he encountered determined opposition, leading Oldfield to believe that someone 'was anxious to get Rado to Moscow'.⁵³ Rado was indeed extradited to Russia, where he was sentenced without trial to ten years hard labour.

Oldfield had also been troubled by the case of Erich Vermehren as he believed that at the time of his defection to the West, Admiral

Canaris was on the verge of doing a deal with the Allies.⁵⁴ A 'noisy' leak of the Vermehren defection, that must have come from within MI6, triggered the Nazi shut-down of the Abwehr, the arrest of Canaris and ending hopes for a separate peace settlement with the Germans.

In both the Rado and Vermehren cases, Kim Philby was the MI6 officer involved. Oldfield had not been able to make the connection, but in August 1946 he had been granted access to the files that, if properly interrogated, held all the clues.⁵⁵

Philby's Istanbul send-off party was a raucous affair and well-attended by officers from Broadway and St James's as well as a contingent of Americans from OSS.⁵⁶ Two of Philby's closest friends, Rodney Dennys and Graham Greene, may well have been among the throng of well-wishers to cheer 'good old Kim' on his next adventure. But beneath the smooth charm and sangfroid of the Soviets' most valued double agent, there was a growing fear that his enemies were closing in for the kill.

In Leconfield House, Mayfair, London headquarters of MI5, it was dawning on Roger Hollis that Smolka and Philby may have been much more than casual acquaintances. Special Branch officers had recovered the full accounts and documents from the St Paul's branch of the Westminster Bank relating to the news agency set up by Smolka and Philby before the war. It turned out not to be quite as fleeting an association as Philby had described it to Richard Brooman-White in 1942. London Continental News Limited was incorporated on 3 November 1934 and had capital of £100 divided into 100 shares, all of which had been fully taken up.⁵⁷ The majority were paid to Smolka, but Philby, who gave his name as Andrew Ralph Philby⁵⁸, had been granted a percentage of the business interest. And rather than being a still-born venture, the company ran for four years and showed net annual profits for each of those years.⁵⁹ More significantly, the two directors, Smolka and Philby, drew salaries of £88, £325 and £795 (£48,000 today), although Philby was supposed to be a 'nominal partner'. The report said the business, which operated from city offices in Printing House Square where Philby's employers *The Times* was based,[60] had provided Smolka with sufficient income to rent a plush 'maisonette' in Fitzjohns Avenue, Hampstead, not far from the Philbys' new home in Acol Road.[61] How long before the MI5 investigators would be able to connect the dots?

In Istanbul, Philby settled his family into a 'delightful villa' in an area called Beylerbeyi on the Asiatic shore of the Bosphorus and away from the prying eyes of the rest of the diplomatic corps camped over the water in the Istanbul metropolis. From here the SIS station chief commuted daily by ferry to his office on the European side of the strait.[62]

Philby was given the cover title of First Secretary of the British Embassy under the code BFX/51. In one of the first operations he sanctioned, Operation Climber 1, he arranged for Georgian emigres to cross the Russian border and bring back intelligence about Soviet military installations.[63] Having first established a surveillance mission that he comically named Operation Spyglass, a codename he had invented for his childhood adventures[64], Philby briefed two agents on a penetration mission.[65] Philby later callously recalled: 'So the two Georgians went off under the escort of a Turkish officer to Adahan and points north. All I could do was bite my nails in Erzurum.'

A few days later Philby received a telegram telling of the men's fate: 'The two agents had been put across at such and such a time. So many minutes later, there had been a burst of fire, and one of the men had fallen – the other was last seen striding through a sparse wood away from the Turkish frontier. He was never heard of again.'[66] The spies had been betrayed by Philby, the first of an unknown number of 'victims' during his short tour in Turkey.

THE START OF THE AFFAIR

On 7 August 1947, a converted RAF bomber left Berlin's Tempelhof airport and three hours later touched down at RAF Northolt in West London.[67] The plane carried three passengers, two British intelligence officers and an RAF NCO identified on the flight's manifest as 'Corporal Forde.' His real name was Alexander Allan Foote, an RAF wireless operator who had deserted to fight for the communists in the Spanish Civil War. In Spain Foote was recruited by Russian intelligence and later played a key part in the Red Orchestra, the network of Soviet agents who operated across Nazi-occupied Europe during the war sending vital intelligence back to Moscow. He had worked closely with Dr Alexander Rado in Switzerland and had accompanied Rado on the flight to Moscow that had made a stop-off in Cairo where Rado had tried to defect. Foote had wisely distanced himself from Rado and continued to the Russian capital, convincing the Russian Intelligence Service of his own loyalty. In 1947 he was rewarded with a transfer to Berlin and earmarked for a mission to Argentina where he was to 'organise all RIS activity in America.'[68]

But Foote had grown disillusioned with Stalin's Russia where he said the working classes continued to suffer terribly.

In London there was no hiding MI5's glee in their prize defector. 'Foote has not only given us a considerable quantity of valuable information about the workings of Russian intelligence,' wrote Roger Hollis, 'but it has been possible to use him as a "reference book" in the best conditions, and to re-examine his evidence at our leisure.'[69]

Hollis's excitement was equally shared by Maurice Oldfield who had not forgotten the suspicious circumstances that had let Rado slip through his hands two years earlier. What could Foote tell them about the other Russian agents working against Britain? According to the MI5 files the RAF corporal was on 'friendly terms' with several of the Soviet spies.[70]

Before the war Foote had visited the Lawn Road flats in

Hampstead where he had been tasked by Arnold Deutsch's Soviet cell for his mission in Switzerland. He was willing to spill everything he knew about his communist recruiters.[71]

Three months later a Russian scientist highly placed in the world of Soviet intelligence left his home in Berlin with his wife and daughter and crossed into the British sector. Lt Col Gregori Tokaev (Tokaty), who personally briefed Stalin, became the first high-ranking Russian to defect directly to the British side. There wouldn't be another until Yuri Krotkov's defection in London in 1963. Tokaev was an idealist who had also become disillusioned with Stalin's brand of communist authoritarianism.

Such was the value placed on Tokaev by MI5, he was given the codename 'Excise' and granted 24-hour police protection. His secret debriefing lasted almost a year. Tokaev was part of Russia's rocket programme, as well as being extremely well-connected with the Kremlin, and was able to hand over to the British the names of dozens of Russian generals, scientists and spymasters.[72] The sudden appearances of two Soviet agents in London posed a serious threat to the NKVD spies who had so successfully infiltrated MI6 and MI5, especially the Cambridge spy who was being tipped as the next head of the Secret Intelligence Service.[73] But Kim Philby was stuck in Istanbul and unable to repeat his textbook elimination of the last Russian to attempt a defection to London, Konstantin Volkov, in 1945.

Once again Philby had to sit tight and hope neither Foote nor Tokaev had been told or found out about the son of a British diplomat who had been sent to Spain to assassinate Franco and then promoted to head up MI6's Soviet counter-intelligence department.

Chapter 19

The Third Man

Graham Greene's desertion of MI6 on the eve of D-Day did not mean he had stopped working as a spy.

Buried in the bowels of Whitehall there is a Cabinet Office report stating that Greene continued to serve SIS informally until the early 1980s: 'In exchange for expenses, he gave his help to the organisation in many places – most notably Vietnam, Poland, China and Russia. And whether a particular trip was subsidised by SIS or not, he routinely gave its officers information from his foreign visits when he believed it might be useful.'[1]

Greene, whose SIS contact at this time was Kim Philby's close friend Nicholas Elliott,[2] was also one of the first writers out of the blocks to pay visits to Moscow in the late 1950s.[3] His welcome was almost guaranteed after his anti-American book *The Quiet American* was published in 1955. His controversial and highly publicized comment 'I would rather end my days in the Gulag than in California' curried even more favour with the Soviets.

Greene himself admitted that, in the first years after the end of hostilities, 'my wartime connection with the SIS used to bring me useful dividends in those days.'[4] Some of these 'dividends' were routed through Claude Dansey and after Dansey's death in 1947, the film mogul, Alexander Korda, who had been asked during the war by Winston Churchill to set up offices in America that could be used as a cover for British agents sent all over the world.[5]

During one of his periods in the political wilderness before the war, Churchill had been employed by Korda to write film scripts.[6] Churchill was joined in Korda's lucrative film development projects by the Foreign Office senior official Sir Robert Vansittart, who ran his own private spy network during the war in tandem with MI6.

Vansittart had been virulently opposed to communism before the war but, like Churchill, had set his hostility to one side while the Russians were allies of the British. After the war Vansittart was one of the first politicians to speak out against Stalin, warning of the Russian dictator's plan for communist subjugation of Europe. In 1946, he stepped up his witch hunts for communists in the Church of England, the BBC and most notably the newly elected Labour government. His anti-communist zeal earned him a comparison to the American congressman Joseph McCarthy.[7] So it is strange that Vansittart, the avenging angel against communism, should champion an Austrian political dissident whom MI5 suspected of being linked to communist subversion in the UK. Vansittart had supported Harry Smolka in his appointment to the head of the Ministry of Information's Russian section and had stuck by his man after the war.[8]

As soon as the fighting ended, the slippery Smolka left Britain for Czechoslovakia (he had been London correspondent for *The Prague Tagblaat* since 1937) to take up a position as the central European correspondent for the *Daily Express*.[9] A few months later, another member of the Vienna circle, Lizy Friedmann, the former Mrs Philby, followed suit and settled in east Berlin with her new husband. The communists were returning to their continental roosts.

Graham Greene had once dismissed Alexander Korda as a mere 'publicist', claiming the movie mogul 'had put over so many undistinguished and positively bad films as if they were a succession of masterpieces'.[10] Yet at the end of 1946, it was Korda to whom Greene turned to bankroll his film projects. Korda had moved his operations (film and intelligence) back from America to Piccadilly, the headquarters of London Film Productions.

A victim of communist persecution in his home country of Hungary, Korda divided his work between intelligence gathering for the British and producing big budget films. The one-time Hungarian dissident was keen to support Greene in his film endeavours and introduced him to the British director Carol Reed, one of the few directors Greene respected, describing him in a *Spectator* review as having 'more sense of the cinema than most veteran British directors'.[11] Reed had served in the Second World War with the Royal Army Ordnance Corps and the Army Film Unit. His first cinematic project after the war was *Odd Man Out* (1947), a film noir starring James Mason about an IRA man on the run, which Greene greatly praised. Greene's *Nineteen Stories*, a collection of his short stories from before the war, was published in 1947. Among them was 'The Basement Room', and it was this that Greene and Reed developed as a treatment for their first co-production, *The Fallen Idol* (1948), a story of the corruption of childhood innocence and betrayal. It was an instant success, winning a British Academy Film Award for best picture, and cemented their working partnership.

Korda encouraged Reed and Greene to come up with a follow-up film, a thriller that would appeal to a wider international audience by taking in the tumultuous and dangerous times the world was now facing. It would be the crowning glory to the cinematic careers of Reed, Korda and Greene. And it was also one of the most controversial spy films ever made, although what it is really about is still hotly debated to this day.

From the cooling embers of the burnt-out battles of the Second World War emerged a new conflict that pitched the victorious Allies against each other. The Cold War may have been less bloody than the one that had gone before it, but in a nuclear age the stakes were much higher.

Graham Greene had just sent the finished manuscript of *The Heart of the Matter* to his publishers. To protect himself from last-minute libels, he declared that none of the characters represented anyone he knew and that the African country in which the story was set was wholly fictional. He did not want any repeats of previous legal mishaps that had marred the launches of his works. Yet it was a clumsy attempt that failed to tackle obvious name approximations like 'Scobie' and 'Brodie' and the character traits of British intelligence agents with whom he had worked. Malcolm Muggeridge and Anthony Powell, who both served with Greene in MI6 during the war, were confident they could identify most of the minor characters in the book.[12]

Once *The Heart of the Matter* had been sent to the printers, Greene wrote a letter to Catherine Walston complaining that the experience had left him bereft of any creative spark: 'I have no ideas for another book and feel I never shall . . . I feel very empty and played out.'[13]

Two days later everything changed and he wrote to Catherine again: 'I believe I've got a book coming. I feel so excited that I spell out your name in full, carefully sticking my tongue between my teeth to pronounce it right. The act of creation is awfully odd and inexplicable like falling in love.'[14]

As Greene tells it, inspiration for his story came to him while spending time solo dining and then drinking in the bars of Piccadilly.[15] He took dinner at a restaurant favoured by Catherine and then walked down to the Café Royal, where he sat drinking beer and reading a travel book about the Aran Islands off the west coast of Ireland. At 10pm he left the bar and reached a public lavatory in Brick Street, where he claims the creative juices started to flow.[16]

Eager to record his train of thought before it was smudged out by the alcohol, he wrote down everything he could remember on the back of an envelope. The genesis for *The Third Man* thus began: 'I had paid my last farewell to Harry a week ago, when his coffin was lowered into the frozen February ground, so that it was with incredulity that I saw him pass by, without a sign of recognition, among the host of strangers in the Strand.'[17]

A few days later, Greene met Alexander Korda at the movie mogul's penthouse apartment of Claridge's hotel, which he was renting as his office.[18] Over dinner Korda invited Greene to come up with an idea for a new film to be directed by Carol Reed.[19] In his preface to the novella of *The Third Man,* Greene claims the scrap of paper scribbled after his visit to the Piccadilly lavatory was all he had to offer Korda for the basis of the story. Yet in his letter to Walston he says the idea was almost fully formed: '. . . suddenly in the Gent's, I saw the three chunks, the beginning, the middle and the end, and in some ways all the ideas I had – the first sentence of the thriller about the dead Harry who wasn't dead, the risen-from-the-dead-story, and then the other day in the train all seemed to come together.'

Not sure how long this rich vein of inspiration would last, he said he wanted to start writing the book immediately and so he took Catherine to a cottage in the Aran Islands, where he began to lay down the first sketch of his novella.[20] Whom had Greene recognised during his inebriated stroll down Piccadilly that brought such a vivid story to life? Who of his old acquaintances had stepped out of the shadows and into the pages of his new book?

Korda liked Greene's idea about a man risen from the dead. All he wanted changed was the location. Instead of setting the film in London, Greene and Korda agreed the film should be shot in the ruins of Vienna amid the backdrop of an embryonic Cold War. Korda explained that not only did he think it would make for a better picture, but he could also cash in on some of his financial 'assets', including interests in Wien-Film, held in Austria and subject to strict new laws preventing him from removing them from the country.[21]

Vienna was at the centre of a spy war being fought by Communist Russia and the Western Allies, and Korda may have had espionage 'assets' in the country that he wished to liquidate. This was probably the real reason for choosing Austria as the base for his next project. The new battleground between east and west was the partitioned zones of the bomb-damaged grandeur of the Austrian capital where the 'fighting' was being conducted by proxy armies of spies, agents and provocateurs. On 20 April 1945, the Soviets, without consulting their Western Allies, had imposed a provisional government on Austria policed by Stalin's intelligence agency, the NKVD. The British and Americans had forcefully protested the Soviet coup and succeeded four months later in forcing the Russians to accept the Allied Council of the four military governors in Vienna. The Allied occupation force in the city peaked at around 150,000 Soviet, 55,000 British, 40,000 American and 15,000 French troops. But the Russians still wanted the Austrian capital for themselves.

In April 1947, Austria's failing economy left the country ravaged by famine, and on 5 May Vienna was shaken by violent food riots orchestrated by communists, which turned the protests into a pogrom against the city's Jews. The world appeared to have taken a dark step backwards. Among Vienna's post-war ruins, black market racketeers profited from the squalor while gangs of Soviet-commissioned agents carried out kidnappings of Austrian scientists wanted by the Russians for their nuclear and rocket programmes.

Two years after the end of the war, the staging of a film in a bombed-out city with little supporting structure was a colossally expensive enterprise that would have tested the logistical resources of any of the occupying armies, never mind a London film company. Yet the wealthy and resourceful Korda was determined that Greene should fly immediately to Vienna to assess the lay of the land. Greene was fascinated by the creative potential of the location for the film, especially when Korda explained that the finer working arrangements of the shared control of Vienna meant the centre of the city was patrolled by military jeeps carrying four soldiers, one from each of the four occupying powers.

Greene had heard enough. In recognition of their rekindled partnership, Korda arranged for the London Film Productions to pay Greene £1,000 for his idea of 'Harry risen from the dead' and a further £3,000 for any ongoing work on the project. It was money that secured Greene's participation, while his admiration and respect for the movie mogul was given freely. As the writer Jerome Chodorov said of Korda: 'Working for Alex Korda was like working for no one else in the world. He was a sultan, a pasha. He was something. Nobody ever treated a writer like he treated a writer . . . he knew about writers. And he knew that without the writing there wasn't going to be any picture.'[22]

On 11 February 1948, Graham Greene arrived at Vienna airport where he was met by a young English woman working for London Film Productions. Elizabeth Montagu had been recruited by Korda after the war to act as his European agent to forge contacts across central Europe for both his film company and his intelligence network.[23] Montagu, a member of the English aristocracy and the older sister of Lord Montagu of Beaulieu, mixed in literary circles, and knew Evelyn Waugh, H.G. Wells, Colette and Ezra Pound. When war came, she volunteered for the Mechanised Transport Corps (MTC) in France, where she drove ambulances until the German advance forced the corps back to Bordeaux. Instead of escaping with the rest of her unit, she went to Berne, Switzerland, where she was recruited by MI6 and then by the OSS under Allen Dulles, a future director of the CIA. Her most important work was with Hans Bernd Gisevius, the German vice consul and Abwehr agent in Switzerland. He was pivotal to the opposition to Hitler and under instructions from Wilhelm

Canaris, worked with the Americans and British to coordinate a German coup against Hitler.

Montagu's job was to debrief Gisevius, often plying him with copious quantities of whiskey. During these sessions and her liaisons with both MI6 and OSS, she learnt about the anti-Nazi peace overtures. Gisevius was not working alone. In Berne, he was joined by another anti-Nazi Fritz Kolbe, who, after being rebuffed by the British, had approached Dulles with intelligence that would expose many of the Abwehr's spies, including a mysterious agent named Josephine run from Stockholm, as well as important Gestapo and SS operations. Kolbe said his key aim was to win American support for an assassination attempt on Hitler that he hoped would usher in a separate peace settlement with the German people.[24]

Once Dulles had properly appreciated the significance of Kolbe's documents, he passed copies to MI6, where they shuffled their way onto the desk of Kim Philby. Philby saw almost immediately the threat posed by the German anti-Hitler movement that included Canaris, Gisevius and Kolbe. He had blocked previous German attempts to dally with the Western Allies that cut out the Russians. Yet Philby, wishing to put the kibosh on Kolbe's peace plans, was unable to resist pressure to 'circulate the [Kolbe] documents as genuine'.[25]

In June 1945, Dulles informed President Truman about Kolbe, telling him that the 'usually sceptical and conservative British intelligence officials rated this contact as the prize intelligence source of the war.'[26] Nevertheless, Philby continued to find ways to resist and frustrate anti-Nazi Germans presenting peace proposals to the British. Whether Montagu or Dulles understood what Philby was really up to is not clear. But Montagu knew Philby when he was head of Section V and remained close friends with Nicholas Elliott, Philby's MI6 even closer associate. She was also friendly with another Cambridge spy, Anthony Blunt, with whom she mixed at social events in London.[27]

*

In February 1947, Philby arrived in Istanbul to be installed as the First Secretary at the British Consulate, the scene of his surgical liquidation of Volkov two years earlier.[28]

A year later, Graham Greene was met by Elizabeth Montagu at Vienna airport.[29] Korda had telegrammed her a few days in advance of Greene's visit instructing her to put herself at the writer's disposal. Montagu was assisted by another of Korda's agents and an SIS colleague of Kim Philby. Lt Colonel John Codrington, the former head of the Gibraltar SIS station in the war, not only procured all the necessary documentation for Greene's stay, but also booked him a room in the Hotel Sacher, behind the Vienna Opera, where the British officers were billeted.[30]

Vienna was at the centre of a spy war. MI6's new head of station, Peter Lunn, had just arrived in the city. Lunn, in his mid-thirties and a champion skier with an excellent war record, had orders to get on top of the Russian spy networks.

Peter Lunn tried to recruit his own double agents inside the Soviet sector.[31] One of these agents was a black marketeer, an Austrian Nazi who remained invested in the imminent return of the Third Reich. The British codenamed him 'Subaltern' and put him to work seeking out Russian defectors. Lunn soon discovered that whatever the British government was willing to pay for Soviet traitors, the Americans could double or even treble it.[32]

So Lunn decided to embark on one of the most audacious espionage operations of the Cold War. He had recently learned that a telephone cable ran under Aspangstrasse in Vienna's Landstrasse district, carrying most of the Soviet military telephone traffic as well as the international lines to Prague, Budapest, Sofia and Bucharest.[33]

Lunn decided to dig a tunnel opposite Aspang railway station (the goods station for Vienna) into the Russian Zone and tap the Russian communication lines, using as cover a terrace of single storey warehouses with large cellars.[34]

The arrival of Korda's film crews presented Lunn with a tempting opportunity – take advantage of the filming of *The Third Man* to distract the Russians from the industrial tunnelling operation at Landstrasse, which became known to the British sappers as 'Smokey Joe's' on account of the choking, cramped conditions in which they had to work.[35] The tunnel turned out to be a very secret British victory, allowing the Allies to eavesdrop on Soviet activity in the city for three years until the Russians rerouted their communications cables.[36]

Greene was a famous author and his arrival at the airport had stirred up some press interest, forcing him to dodge a photographer and reporter.[37] The drive into the city gave Greene his first glimpse of the unimaginable bleak backdrop to his Cold War thriller. Rubble lay piled outside the once-grand Viennese boulevards that now served as bombed-out refuges for the war-weary population during the harsh Austrian winter. Greene described it as a 'smashed dreary city of undignified ruins'.[38]

Queues for basic foods and fuel doubled back on themselves up and down the streets. It didn't take long for Greene to draw inspiration from the frozen squalor. At the city's cemetery gates, he encountered a scene that would mark out the film's famous opening, the funeral service for Harry Lime: 'Today it's been snowing for 24 hours and everything looks lovely under the snow . . . The monuments looking grotesque – white moustaches when there shouldn't have been and white bonnets skipping over eyes of stone women who should have been stark naked.'[39]

This, the Central Cemetery, was where 'a couple of friends and a Catholic priest watched the diggers smash their way into the frozen ground and lower Harry Lime's coffin into the dark'.[40]

Greene was now buried in the creative business of turning Vienna's post-war wasteland into a psychological Greeneland. For Greene being a writer was just like being a spy: ' . . .every novelist has something in common with a spy: he watches, he overhears, he seeks motives and analyses character, and in his attempt to serve literature he is unscrupulous.'[41]

Rollo Martins is the British author, part-based on Greene, who is invited by Harry Lime to Vienna to work for him in a refugee aid venture he claimed he was setting up. After the burial scene, Martins, a writer of trashy novels and Lime's closest school friend, ends up in Vienna's Sacher Hotel, where Greene had stayed researching the film script.

The Hotel Sacher placed Greene at the centre of an information and intelligence hub as the hotel served as the headquarters of the Information Service Branch and the Political Intelligence Department of the British Foreign Office. Here Greene had the chance to witness at first hand the tensions between the British and the Soviet administrators.[42] Greeneland thrived on the use of first-hand intelligence, cross-border gossip and real-world characters, which helped to give Greene's writing its unique verisimilitude. Vienna, with its black marketeers, political tensions and shadowy spies, was Greeneland writ large.

It was in the Oriental Bar of the Hotel Sacher that Greene was introduced to a man who was to gift his film both an irresistible character and an intelligence and insight beyond anything he could possibly glean from the British officers who were drawn to the writer's post-war celebrity and his generous hotel bar allowance.

Greene must have suspected that the meeting was important because in his diary for 17 February he had allotted six hours – from 7.15 until 'one or two in the morning'. The only clue to the source's identity was the simple description: 'The Times' correspondent'. His allotted time with the 'correspondent' was part of a packed itinerary and immediately followed on from an hour's catch-up with Greene's Austrian publisher and a short interview with the local American police chief in Vienna.[43] Elizabeth Montagu had made the introduction, but it had been ultimately sanctioned by Alexander Korda.

The man sitting in the hotel bar when Greene arrived was short – about 5ft 7in tall – and podgy, with large brown eyes and full lips. Wearing a tweed brown suit and a bow tie, he could have walked out of the pages of one of Greene's novels.

Peter Lunn considered this man to be the 'master of the unholy triumvirate of the Communist British press in Vienna'.[44] MI5 said he was known, even among his friends, as 'brilliant, ambitious and completely unscrupulous'.[45] Yet the most authoritative and more benign opinion was written by an MI6 officer who knew him for being 'extremely clever and commercially a pusher but nevertheless rather a timid character and with a feeling of inferiority due in part to his repulsive appearance'.

The author of this last character assessment was Kim Philby, and the man he was describing was his old associate Harry Smolka, now being closely watched by the British in Vienna.

In the same month Greene had arrived in Vienna and Philby had been relocated to Istanbul, Smolka, according to an MI5 report, was appointed the Vienna correspondent for *The Times*, taking over from another communist journalist and fellow member of the 'unholy triumvirate', Micky Burn, a former Colditz inmate captured by the Germans during the successful 1942 attack on the docks at St Nazaire. Bisexual Burn had had a fling with Guy Burgess during the 1930s and so knew all about the Cambridge communists.

In February 1948, while Smolka and his contacts were being closely watched by MI6, it must have come as something of a surprise to the SIS station chief to discover that one of MI6's most high-profile former officers and now one of Britain's foremost authors was meeting the dangerous communist agent. Greene may have officially left SIS four years earlier, but by his own admission he was still closely linked to the agency. Could the Smolka/Greene get-together have been arranged by British intelligence? Or was this Moscow's doing? However the meeting came about, it was

Smolka's knowledge of Vienna's dark underbelly, its racketeers, criminal networks and Russia's NKVD kidnap operations that most interested Greene the writer.

There was no one better qualified for passing on Vienna's shameful secrets than Harry Smolka. The Austrian agent was born in Vienna and had escaped the city just before the fascists crushed the communist uprising in 1934. It was his studies of the labyrinthine underground sewers that Kim Philby and the other revolutionaries had relied on to make their own escape that same year.

Greene's decision to clear the whole evening for their meeting proved to be the most profitable investment of his time during his first week's stay in Vienna. After a two-hour initial conversation, the three spies, Greene, Smolka and Montagu, hit the city.[46] For Greene this meant a tour of the seediest bars and shadowy dives that 'dreary' Vienna had to offer. Smolka, who was partially crippled by the early onset of multiple sclerosis, happily hobbled on behind. Montagu recalled how Greene insisted on the group visiting tawdry sex shows featuring naked women cavorting on stage. When Montagu challenged Greene about how he squared getting drunk in brothels with his much-professed Catholicism, he simply replied that he had 'found ways'.[47]

Greene wasn't embarrassed by his fascination with the darker side of the city, rather he embraced it, accepting it as an immutable predilection of his psychological make up.[48] Greene had a highly charged sex drive, yet he was determined to remain faithful to Catherine Walston. Even when the leading lady in the film Alida Valli (regarded as the most beautiful actress in the world at the time) made an appearance in Vienna, Greene managed to curb his interest. He told Catherine: 'I'm giving lunch to the beautiful wife of the unfaithful man on Wednesday (he's in England), but my heart is not in the game: so far avoided the 21 year old actress.'[49]

Smolka and Greene had much in common. They had both worked for *The Times*, Greene before the war and Smolka now as the Vienna correspondent. They had both been employed by the Ministry of Information, and Smolka's wife Lotte had been with Greene at the Political Warfare Executive. Moreover, Smolka knew Greene's great friend from MI6, Kim Philby, another veteran of *The Times*. It is very likely that Smolka and Greene had met at one of the many Whitehall/Fleet Street cocktail parties or impromptu 'office' leaving dos held in London during the war.[50] As they toured the Vienna bars, fascinated by their mutual connections, it is easy to see how Philby's name might have come up in conversation, if only as an icebreaker. Smolka's communism was an open secret in Whitehall. George Orwell, who in 1948 was putting the finishing touches to his dystopian *1984* novel that warned of the dangers of Stalin's totalitarianism, had drawn up a secret list of 135 dangerous communists and Soviet assets who threatened British democracy. The first name on his list was Harry Smolka, who Orwell warned: 'gives a strong impression of being some kind of Russian agent. Very slimy person.' Orwell, who corresponded with Greene and dined with him in literary London, said if he had published his list earlier he might have been able to 'stop people like Peter Smollett worming their way into important propaganda jobs where they were probably able to do us a lot of harm'.[51]

Orwell and Smolka had history – Smolka was almost certainly the MOI official on whose advice the publisher Jonathan Cape decided to turn down *Animal Farm* as subversive anti-Soviet propaganda.[52] Orwell was now being supported by a newly created shadowy government body called the Information Research Department, (IRD) which had been given the task of countering Soviet propaganda all over the world.[53] The IRD was well known to Graham Greene's brother Hugh who in 1948 was working as head of the BBC's own propaganda service in the British controlled sector of Berlin. One of his first acts was to sack any member of his German staff who had communist links.[54]

Smolka's own highly questionable past and dubious contacts

in Vienna's Russian sector must make him a candidate for Greene's Harry Lime. But he was important to Greene in one other way. What Harry Smolka could tell Graham Greene about Russian intelligence would settle any lingering suspicions Greene harboured about his former boss's loyalties and motivations.

In January 1948 Greene arrived in Brussels to address an international gathering of Catholics. It should have been a strictly theological speech, but Greene turned it into an attack on communism and Joseph Stalin: 'We can no longer take lightly the danger that threatens Christian civilization. Between 1933 and 1945 civilization was almost completely destroyed in Germany. That abscess has been lanced, but the totalitarian poison can still spread to countries which escaped the first infection. It is terrifying to think of the distance Russia has travelled in less than 100 years . . . And then think of the Moscow trials and of Prosecutor Vishinsky and that inaccessible grey figure in the Kremlin with his skin-deep bonhomie reserved for state banquets and the dark in the depths of his eyes.'[55]

Greene now intended to travel to Italy to be reunited with Catherine and start writing up a first draft of *The Third Man*, before returning to Vienna to complete the novella, remembering that Smolka had promised to arrange a visit to the Russian sector and a walk under the city along the famous sewer system. Before they parted, Smolka told Greene he had written his own book about corrupt Vienna and would appreciate the author's help getting it published.[56] The two men each had something to trade.

Greene did not go directly to Italy but mysteriously made a detour to Prague, another European city in turmoil and threatened by the Soviets. He had heard rumours of revolution and later claimed he didn't wish to miss out on 'an exciting story'.[57] On the flight, he was accompanied by two newspaper men who had also been tipped off that revolution was in the air.

The atmosphere in Prague was tense as government sentries

guarded important buildings and furtive citizens approached Greene to warn him about an insidious transfer of power as the apparatus of a free state was being systematically dismantled. Greene later recalled: 'Already the bitter humour of defeat was circulating – mainly jokes about the weight of the fat wife of Gottwald, the Communist leader.'[58] On the day Greene visited his publisher, he noticed a soldier standing outside: 'My publisher was soon to vanish into prison for ten years.' A Catholic politician sent Greene a note requesting a secret meeting, reminding Greene of the religious persecution that presaged all communist coups.[59]

When Greene took his onward flight to Rome a week later, a final indignity left him in no doubt about the impending catastrophe about to befall the people of Prague. An immigration officer called him back from his plane and demanded to check his passport one more time, leaving Greene to wonder whether 'I would be able to keep my rendezvous in Rome – I remembered the armed sentry at my publisher's office . . . the deputy [Catholic politician] hidden in a tortuous street of the old city waiting for the right number of rings at the door that indicated a friend.'[60]

Yet Greene's explanation for his curious week-long diversion from his pressing film writing does not make much sense.

The mystery deepens when flight manifest records show Harry Smolka, with OBE prominently stamped in his British passport, followed Greene to Prague and, according to an SIS report[61], was still there after the Russian-backed Czech Communists took control on 25 February. The coup would turn out to be a key moment in the Cold War that accelerated the Marshall Plan to save Berlin from Soviet control and pave the way for the division of Germany into its Eastern and Western states. Less than one year later, the Western powers banded together to establish the North Atlantic Treaty Organisation (NATO).

Many Western observers thought Vienna would be the next city to fall to Soviet control and Greene had now seen at first hand on the streets of Prague what a communist-staged coup represented. The disturbing events he witnessed in Prague and the comfort of his reunion with Catherine permitted Greene to quickly settle into the development of his plot for *The Third Man*. For the first time in his writing career, inspired by a re-reading of Dickens' *Great Expectations*, he felt able to tell a story in the first person.[62] He was going to write it from the perspective of the first man.

In Colonel Calloway, the British military police officer, he had a character who gave him authority over a narrative of betrayal and retribution set in a ruined city broken by political turmoil.

The two central characters were clearly sketched in his mind, Rollo Martins, the writer of pulp fiction Westerns, and Harry Lime, the charismatic friend Martins hero-worshipped at school who had 'died' in a bizarre car accident on the streets of the Austrian capital. Lime invited Martins to Vienna with an offer of work and the chance to rekindle their old friendship.

The Vienna setting allowed Greene to paint the Russian menace as thick as he wished, likening Lime's racketeering to the operation of a 'totalitarian state'.[63]

After his car 'accident' Harry Lime disappeared by crossing over to the Russian sector, where he resurfaced to explain to Martins his new-found philosophy of economic expediency: 'How much do you earn a year with your Westerns, old man?'

'A thousand,' Martins replies.

'Taxed. I earn 30,000 free. It's the fashion. In these days, old man, nobody thinks in terms of human beings. Governments don't, so why should we? They talk of the people and the proletariat, and I talk of suckers and the mugs. It's the same thing. They have their Five-Year Plan and so have I.'[64]

When Martins enquires about his means of survival, Harry replies: 'I'm only safe in the Russian Zone . . . I'm safe as long as they can use me.'

*

In Greene's novella, Lime arranges for the terrified Anna Schmidt, the daughter of a Hungarian Nazi and Lime's innocent girlfriend who becomes the subject of Martins' unrequited affections, to be kidnapped by Russian soldiers.[65] The kidnapping is thwarted at the last minute by an American who accuses the British of 'never knowing when to make a stand'.[66]

It later emerges that Lime isn't concerned about getting Anna back, only providing intelligence to the Russians in return for help with his racketeering. When Martins challenges Lime about what would have happened to her if the Russians had caught her, Lime replies: 'Nothing very serious. She'd have been sent back to Hungary. There's nothing against her really. A year in a labour camp perhaps. She'd be infinitely better off in her own country than being pushed around by the British police.'[67]

In the final cut of the film, the Russian kidnapping scene was removed at a 'very late stage' because Greene (and Carol Reed) said it looked too much like political propaganda:

'We had no desire to move people's political emotions: we wanted to entertain them, to frighten them a little, to make them laugh.'[68] (Smolka also advised against the kidnap plot as it unnecessarily cast the Russians in a bad light).

However, when the film was released Anna is a refugee from Czechoslovakia, a democracy crushed by Stalin and visited by Greene in between filming.

Because Anna's kidnapping *is* political it tells the reader that Lime is working with the Russians for his own criminal profit, not any political ideal. Is this how Greene, after his visit to Prague, now regarded Philby – an opportunistic adventurer out only for his own gain?

Greene and Philby's relationship undercut political ideology and was much more complex and nuanced. Greene's instinct was not to make Lime a political figure. Even after being told of Lime's betrayal, Martins remembered how he was drawn to his old friend's sense of humour, one of the many human traits that Greene valued in Philby.[69] Back in Rome, away from the turmoil of Vienna and Prague, Greene settled down to write himself and Philby into the story.

In the famous scene set on the 65-metre-high Ferris wheel in the Prater, it is possible to imagine Greene seeing Philby for who he really is and trying to hold him to account for his personal betrayal as well as the harm he had done to countless others.

Harry Lime: 'I wouldn't have asked you to come if I'd known what was going to happen, but I didn't think the police were on to me.'

Martins: 'Were you going to cut me in on the spoils?'

Lime: 'I've never kept you out of anything, old man, yet.'

He stood with his back to the door as the car swiped upwards and smiled back at Rollo Martins, who remembered him in just such an attitude in a secluded corner of the school quad, saying, 'I've learned a way to get out at night, it's absolutely safe, you are the only one I'm letting in on it.'

For the first time, Rollo Martins looked back through the years without admiration, as he thought: 'He's never grown up. Marlow's devils were squibs attached to their tails: evil was like Peter Pan – it carried with it the horrifying and horrible gift of eternal youth.'

Harry chides: 'Old man – you never should have gone to the police. You know you ought to leave this thing alone.'

Martins finally comes to his senses and reproaches his old friend, who had always stood up for him: 'Have you ever visited the Children's Hospital? Have you seen any of your victims?'

Harry answers: '. . . Victims? Don't be melodramatic.'

Chapter 20

Secrets in the Sewer

When Graham Greene returned to Vienna from Rome in June 1948, he still hadn't figured out how he was going to credibly paint the roguish Harry Lime as evil rather than merely criminal. But this was the task he had set himself.

The discovery of the Nazi death camps and the virulent antisemitism that gave rise to the final solution were still fresh in people's minds. Lime's act of evil would have to at least match the Nazis if it was to register with the audience. Seeking inspiration for the finishing touches to his script, he once more sought out Harry Smolka. Elizabeth Montagu arranged a taxi to take Greene to Smolka's villa at Jagdschlossgasse 27 on the very edge of the British zone to the west of the city.[1] The well-proportioned white stucco-walled building is still standing today, all alone on the side of a wide, sandy road heading out towards the forests that fringe the west of the city.

Montagu remembers how well the two men got on, sipping afternoon tea and whiskey in Smolka's villa: 'He [Smolka] was wonderfully well informed about the city and had written some very unusual and gripping tales, concerning the shady aspects of post war Vienna, which he hoped to get published in London. Greene was very interested, this meeting was very successful and the two men talked for almost two hours – when we left I noticed Graham had Smollett's manuscript tucked under his arm. "Please don't lose it will you, I've only got one copy," pleaded Smollett, full of hope that Graham might help him find a publisher.'[2]

SECRETS IN THE SEWER

Armed with Smolka's stories, Greene, now joined by Carol Reed, began exploring the city in the hope of filling out his plot with suitable filmic locations. The sewers were just as Smolka had described them – half as wide as the Thames and crawling with rats.[3] Greene attributed the infestation to the Russians whom, without any evidence, he blamed for releasing the rodents from rat fur farms into the sewer network.[4]

Relying on Smolka's notes, they found the giant Ferris wheel in the Soviet sector, where they later filmed Lime, played by Orson Welles, making his infamous nihilistic speech while gazing down on the 'dots' of people below.

Turning to Martins, Lime asks:

'Look down there. Would you really feel any pity if one of those dots stop moving – forever? If I offered you twenty thousand for every dot that stops, would you really, old man, tell me to keep my money or would you calculate how many dots you could afford to spare? Free of income tax, old man. Free of income tax.'[5]

Although Greene and Reed were happy with the locations for the filming, Greene was still struggling with his plot.

'It had proved difficult to find my story,' Greene wrote.[6] 'Harry's phony funeral was the only scrap of plot I have to cling to.' All that came to him as the days too rapidly passed were 'glimpses of photogenic background; the shabby Oriental nightclub, the offices bar at Sachers, the little dressing rooms which form the kind of interior village in the old Josefstadt Theatre, the enormous cemetery where electric drills were needed to pierce the ground that February.'[7]

He told Catherine that he had promised Reed and Korda he would finish the story before he left Vienna, but he complained: '[the] story seems to get longer and longer. I do it straight on the typewriter usually about two and a half hours in the morning, then the first drink ... then lunch; then a couple more hours perhaps an hour on a bed with Hardy's poems: then the drinking starts again.'[8]

The cast was being assembled, and Korda was keen to begin shooting. Time was running out for Greene to finish his script: 'There were three days left [before he left for Italy to start writing] and I had no story, not even the storyteller, Colonel Calloway, whom I see now always in my mind with the features of Trevor Howard.'[9]

On the day before he was due to fly back to Rome, Greene claims he fortuitously ran into a young intelligence officer, Charles Beauclerk the Duke of St Albans, who provided him with the vital missing piece of his screenplay jigsaw – a real wickedness that transformed Lime's racketeering into something truly evil.[10] The officer told Greene how penicillin had become a very scarce drug and that Viennese racketeers were acquiring it from the military, watering it down and selling it on to Vienna hospitals where children were being treated for meningitis. The direct consequence of this practice was the painful deaths of hundreds of children while others 'went off their heads' and were transferred to 'the mental wards'.[11] Greene explains that this was how he was able to inject a sinister edge to Lime's profiteering – an illicit trade in a drug that caused the deaths of young children.

Yet this story about how Greene came by his penicillin plot line may be a smoke screen designed to hide its true origin.[12] A much more likely source of the story is Harry Smolka, whose own newspaper *The Times* had reported two years earlier about penicillin racketeering in Berlin, writing: 'There is great illicit demand for penicillin here for the treatment of venereal diseases. Supplies are strictly controlled by the British and American authorities, being reserved for the treatment of their soldiers, and secondarily for the treatment of German women likely to spread disease. Otherwise supplies are not available.'

Smolka, who suffered from debilitating MS, was being kept

alive by two drugs supplied by the Americans and so was acutely aware of the terrible effects of the trade in the life-saving penicillin.[13]

Elizabeth Montagu was convinced that Greene had borrowed the story from the manuscript Smolka had slipped into the author's hands when Montagu and Greene had visited Smolka at his villa days earlier.

Montagu explained in her memoir: 'Later I handed the stories safely back to their author. I had the impression that Graham had only glanced through them, for he made no comment to me and Peter's [Harry Smolka] longed-for introduction to a publisher was not forthcoming. However, there was one tale which I found particularly interesting, about a shadowy man who pedals diluted penicillin. Later I realised that this bore striking similarity to Greene's Vienna-based story which became *The Third Man*.'[14]

Greene makes no acknowledgement of Smolka's contribution to his original *Third Man* screenplay. Other than the single entry in his diary referring to a meeting with *The Times* correspondent in Vienna, Greene is silent about his profitable encounter with the mysterious Smolka. It begs the question why should he not wish to credit Smolka? Did he already know that Smolka was a Soviet agent working with Philby and that by keeping Smolka anonymous he was protecting Philby? Greene was only too aware that his former colleagues at MI6 and MI5 would be able to recognise his old boss Kim Philby in Harry Lime and publicly linking the film to Harry Smolka would further risk exposing both Philby and Smolka. It may not have been Greene's intention to have his old friend offered up as a public sacrifice. Perhaps all he intended was a warning shot across Philby's bows, a warning that there were people in the intelligence world who suspected him of working for the Russians.

Elizabeth Montagu believed there was another, more commercial, reason for writing Smolka out of *The Third Man*, which she decided to raise directly with Alexander Korda: 'I was still uneasy about the matter of Peter Smollett [Smolka] and his story. Surely sooner or later he would spot the similarity between his tale and *The Third Man*. Although I had spoken to Korda about the problem, I got no reaction but felt it was still not too late to warn the associate producer, Hugh Percival. I was relieved to find that he took me more seriously and delighted when a few days later he told me the matter had been settled.'[15]

When Montagu discovered how the matter was resolved her delight turned to 'horror'.

In a contract signed by Smolka, the suspected Russian agent agreed to give up his 'story' for a fee. Korda and Percival had simply bought off Smolka for 200 guineas for 'assisting with the script'. The 'horrifying' part of the contract was that Smolka had not yet read Greene's script so had no idea how closely it resembled his own. Percival had also insisted that Smolka agree to a condition in the contract that he could 'not make any claim against the company or its associates'.[16] When Montagu quizzically asked Percival, 'and he signed that?', the wily film executive merely answered with a knowing smile.

It was unlikely that such a demonstrably unfair contract would ever stand up in court. If Montagu was right about this episode, then Greene had betrayed Smolka, stealing his story and burying him in a dodgy contract that stripped him of any right of redress.

By the time the film reached the screen, and with Smolka suitably restrained by the terms of the contract, Greene found it impossible to resist a last-minute mischievous allusion to the contribution made by the Austrian journalist/Soviet agent. At the beginning of *The Third Man*, after Harry Lime's funeral, Major Calloway instructs his driver to take himself and Martins to 'Smolka's', a fictional drinking den in the city. 'Smolka's' could also be a reference to Harry Smolka's villa in the western suburbs of the city, where Greene and Montagu went to collect Smolka's manuscript.

Further light was thrown on the sourcing of the penicillin story when MI5 made a surprising discovery two years later. During MI5's 1951 investigation into the Cambridge spies, confidential Cabinet papers and briefings copied by Smolka were found in Guy Burgess's apartment in London after Burgess and Maclean had fled to Moscow. From these papers, the MI5 investigators were able to allege that an agent (the name is redacted in the MI5 files), possibly Smolka, had been selling penicillin to the Russians: 'In this connection he [the MI5 investigating officer] will bear in mind the suspicion that xxx when leaving government employment for business, may have played a part in assisting the Russians to obtain penicillin equipment from America, of which the Americans were at the time anxious to ban the export to the Soviet Union.'[17]

Penicillin was at the heart of the chemical cold war being waged by the West against the Soviets, whose laboratories were unable to produce the drug in sufficient quantities. In 1948, a Russian scientist called Borodin arrived in Vienna. He was an expert in penicillin production and had made contact with MI5 after travelling to London, then defected shortly afterwards.[18] Greene's penicillin twist to *The Third Man* plot was not only sinister, it was also very real.

Smolka's ties to Greene were further cemented by the Austrian's request that Greene's literary agents, Pearn, Pollinger & Higham, should represent him in selling his own work.[19]

If Greene had gleaned new insight into the character and motivation of Kim Philby from Smolka and Montagu, another of Greene's professional contacts held the key piece to solving the Philby puzzle. Greene's doomed relationship with Catherine Walston had severely aggravated his depression, forcing him to seek medical help. On Catherine's suggestion he became the patient of psychiatrist Eric Strauss, an Austrian doctor practising in London.[20] Strauss was a Jew who had converted to Catholicism and the two men hit it off, with Greene attending psychoanalysis sessions two to three times a week. It was Strauss who diagnosed Greene's manic depression for the first time, prescribing a therapy of cathartic writing about his childhood, a treatment that partially relieved the condition.

Strauss's lover was Flora Solomon, Philby's former mistress and a one-time Soviet agent in the 1930s.[21] Solomon was still in contact with Philby; she and Tomás Harris had been the only witnesses at his marriage to Aileen at the Chelsea Register Officer on 25 September 1946.[22] According to an MI5 report, she had confided in Strauss about Philby's Russian connections, including her belief he was still working for the Soviets and had been somehow caught up in the Volkov affair.[23]

After Maclean and Burgess defected in 1951, Aileen Philby's doctor warned MI5 that Strauss had been talking indiscreetly about Philby in terms of him being a Soviet spy who had tried to recruit Solomon.[24] Knowing that Greene worked for Philby during the war, had Strauss already shared his suspicions about Philby with Greene?

Happy with their screenplay, Graham Greene, Alexander Korda and Carol Reed sailed to New York on the *Queen Elizabeth* to meet the American producer David Selznick, who had agreed to co-promote *The Third Man*. Selznick was well known in Hollywood as the producer of *Gone with the Wind* (1939) and *Rebecca* (1940), both of which had earned him an Academy Award for Best Picture. He was an American Jew of Russian descent and a staunch Republican, but had been supportive of American Communists who stood against fascism before the war.

Selznick, like Greene an amphetamine user, was the Harvey Weinstein of his day – Shirley Temple had accused the overweight film producer of holding her captive in his office and attempting to rape her when she was 17 years old. Nevertheless, Selznick was one of the few Americans Greene said he liked, perhaps a character assessment meant to be taken in context with his own legal run-in with Temple before the war.[25]

Selznick was determined to Americanise *The Third Man* and engaged Reed and Greene in six-hour-long booze-fuelled meetings finishing at 4am, during which Selznick would press them both for material changes to the script. His first bone of contention was his belief that the script hinted at a homosexual relationship between Lime and Martins: 'It won't do boys . . . it's sheer buggery. It's what you learn in your English schools. This guy comes to Vienna looking for his friend. He finds his friend's dead. Right? Why doesn't he go home then . . . it's just buggery, boys.'[26] Greene and Korda could only humour the American in the hope he would forget his ridiculous protests once filming started.

Selznick then moved on to changing the title of the film: 'Listen boys, who the hell is going to a film called *The Third Man*? . . . a title like *A Night In Vienna* will bring them in.' Greene and Reed had little trouble seeing off this potentially disastrous suggestion but after a week's worth of late-night meetings Selznick produced 40 pages of notes containing numerous idiotic complaints, each of which had to be professionally and tactfully rebutted.

Not all the rebuttals were successful and not all Selznick's complaints turned out to be idiotic, leading to some key changes. Greene's original idea was for his film to be a very English one, played by English lead characters. But in the final de-anglicised version, Lime and Martins are Americans. Rollo Martins becomes Holly Martins because Joe Cotton, the American actor playing him, thought American audiences would find the name Rollo too effeminate. The replacement Holly sounds even more effeminate and so there must have been another reason Greene plumped for Holly. Colonel Calloway, the narrator, was the sole surviving strong British part.

The drama of the film, however, was left largely unchanged. The famous climax to *The Third Man* takes place in the Vienna sewer system where Martins has lured Harry for a final showdown.[27] In the ensuing subterranean chase, Lime is cornered by Martins and Colonel Calloway. One of Calloway's officers shines his torch along the edge of the lapping water and calls out to the others 'he's gone that way' and then to Martins: 'keep behind me sir, the bastard may shoot.' Greene's own visit to the sewers allowed him to describe the scene in vivid detail:

'For just as a deep stream when it shallows at the rim leaves an accumulation of debris so the sewer left in the quiet water against the wall a skunk of orange peel, old cigarette cartons, and the like and in this scum, Lime had left his trail as unmistakably as if he had walked in mud.'[28] In the final moments the British soldiers trap their man in the shadows against a cold brick sewer wall. Refusing to surrender, Lime fires first, killing one of Calloway's officers. Calloway returns fire, wounding Lime.

For a few seconds, Harry and Holly are locked in each other's gaze, before Harry succumbs to his end and submissively nods at Holly, giving him permission to deliver the coup de grâce. It is a suicide by shooting that allows the Catholic Lime to take his own life without facing eternal damnation. In this way, Greene has distinguished Lime's death from the suicide of Scobie, whose deliberate drug overdose in *The Heart of the Matter* is a mortal sin.

Chapter 21

The End of the Affair

Graham Greene's considerable writing output in Vienna, Rome and New York during 1948 and 1949, matched by his equally taxing late-night drinking sessions, had finally taken their toll.

In less than 18 months, Greene had written one third of *The Heart of the Matter*, three film scripts and a 30,000-word novella for *The Third Man*. On the morning before their return flight to London, Greene was with Carol Reed in his New York hotel room while Reed was talking to his wife on the telephone. The colour drained from Greene's cheeks and he tried to get Reed's attention: 'I suddenly felt wet, and I looked down and saw ... blood ... soaking out from my trousers. It came from my penis. And the trouble was that I couldn't draw Carol Reed away from his conversation with his wife. I kept on saying Carol I'm bleeding.'[1]

Greene was rushed to hospital where he was told there were three diagnoses for his haemorrhage, two of which were terminal while one was merely serious. 'When I came through the anaesthetic,' said Greene, 'he [the doctor] told me all was well, but I must be off the drink for a month.'[2] The medical bill was, as with all the American financing for *The Third Man*, picked up by David Selznick.

The Third Man was released to huge acclaim in September 1949, as much for its atmospheric cinematography as for the acting and story. It was the most widely viewed film of that year, winning best

British picture as well as an Oscar for cinematography and nominations in two further categories.

Even so, not everybody was happy with the final version. Despite Greene and Reed's efforts to strip the film of all overt political propaganda, the *Daily Worker* (later the *Morning Star*) complained that 'no effort is spared to make the Soviet authorities as sinister and unsympathetic as possible.' And in Vienna one Soviet-friendly newspaper wrote: 'Naturally the poison of Russian hatred is essential in such a cocktail. That a beautiful girl has had to fly to Czechoslovakia for some quite unknown reason. But it suffices that she is wanted by the Russians.'[3]

The Cold War was the new political reality, Soviet spies were suspected everywhere, and the launch of *The Third Man* coincided with a very hush-hush enquiry being undertaken at the heart of British intelligence. In January 1949, MI6 had received a report from a Russian official at the Soviet embassy in London that at least one Russian mole was active inside the Foreign Office, an investigation that was widened to include three possible suspects: a first, second and third man.[4]

This was exactly what Konstantin Volkov had told the British embassy in Istanbul four years earlier, just before Philby had arranged for the Russian's liquidation, before being conveniently forgotten. It built on the intelligence picture painted by the Soviet defector Gregori Tokaev, who had arrived in the UK in 1947 and had begun spilling beans before publishing his 1951 book *Stalin Means War*, in which he set out how Moscow had been waging a strategic war against the West ever since the Allies' successful landings on D-Day.

By the time *The Third Man* was being made, MI5 had opened four separate lines of enquiry relating to Russian penetration while two

THE END OF THE AFFAIR

counter-intelligence operations had collapsed because of suspected leakage.[5] The timing of the British mole hunts and the release of *The Third Man* may not have been merely coincidental. The Russian spy who would later become most associated with the film's central character, Harry Lime, was in Istanbul making the most of his foreign posting, out of sight of his SIS bosses.

Kim Philby had begun an affair with his secretary Esther Whitfield, and was enjoying hosting old chums, including Guy Burgess and Nicholas Elliott, at his Bosphorus retreat while all the time leading both the British and Turkish intelligence services on a merry dance.[6]

On a visit to Berne, where Elliot was station chief, Philby discussed his pressing personal troubles. His adulterous affairs and the stress of the move to Turkey with their four children had triggered Münchausen syndrome in his wife Aileen, resulting in several episodes of self-harm, including injecting herself with urine, which caused her skin to erupt in boils.[7] The ever-loyal Elliott said he knew a Swiss doctor who he was sure could help Aileen. A grateful Philby confessed to Elliott that he always 'regarded loyalty to friends as more important than loyalty to country'.[8] Shortly afterwards, Philby's time in Istanbul came to an abrupt end. In 1949, days after the release of *The Third Man*, Philby was recalled to London and offered the plum Cold War job as the SIS man in Washington working with the CIA and the FBI at the highest level. Philby was being tipped as a possible leader of MI6 and a stint working closely with the Americans was an unofficial precondition of his appointment to the top job.

'It took me all of half an hour to decide to accept the offer,' Philby wrote in *My Silent War*. 'It would be a wrench to leave Istanbul, both because of its beauty and because it would mean leaving a job considerably less than half accomplished.' Philby does not say whether 'the job' he was thinking of was in the service of his Soviet or his British spymasters.

He explained: 'But the lure of the American post was irresistible for two reasons. At one stroke, it would take me right back into the middle of intelligence policy making and it would give me a close-up view of the American intelligence organisations. These, I was beginning to suspect, were already of greater importance from my point of view than their British opposite numbers. I did not even think it was worth waiting for confirmation from Soviet colleagues.'[9]

A few weeks later, *The Third Man* opened at the Plaza Piccadilly on 2 September 1949.[10] A few days later Elizabeth Montagu, the former SIS agent who had introduced Greene to Harry Smolka in Vienna, was approached by two of Philby's longest-standing colleagues. Montagu was invited to a London dinner party hosted by Nicholas Elliott and introduced to Elliott's old Etonian school friend Richard Brooman-White, who had transferred to MI6 and had been stationed in Istanbul with Philby.[11]

It was Brooman-White who, six years earlier, had been tasked by MI5 to make enquiries about Philby regarding his association with Harry Smolka and the Continental News Agency. According to Montagu, Brooman-White was now sounding her out for a very sensitive assignment. She explained how a clandestine meeting was set up in central London: 'He gave me careful instructions which were both terse and to the point. I was to meet him on a specified date at a specified place in Hyde Park, and he urged me to make a careful mental note of this. Accordingly, I turned up in the right place at the right time. At first, we seemed to walk aimlessly around the park, saying little. Then suddenly he seized two park chairs, placing them on the grass well out of earshot of any strollers.'[12]

Most of the details about the mission Montagu had been offered remain secret to this day. All Montagu was prepared to say was that she would be working for a Mr 'X' of MI5.

One of the reasons Montagu was unable, or unwilling, to disclose anything more about the secret mission was that she had decided to reject the offer on the advice of her friend and now known Soviet spy, Moura Budberg. Montagu later admitted in her autobiography *Honourable Rebel*: 'In retrospect it seems extremely odd that of all the friends I could have turned to, I chose Moura Budberg as Roland [Richard] had always claimed that she was a Soviet agent.'

Moura was not only a Soviet agent but also close to Alexander Korda, who had appointed her Russian adviser on the set of his film *Anna Karenina*.[13] She was at the heart of a Soviet spy matrix and was also well known to Graham Greene, who she had advised during his pre-war visit to Tallinn, and Harry Smolka, who she had helped secure a job as head of the Russian section at the Ministry of Information in the first years of the war. Crucially she was also close to Kim Philby, who knew all about her 'talent spotting' for Korda under the cover of the 'film crowd'.[14] Montagu was herself a member of the Anglo-Soviet Friendship Society, which explains her connection to Budberg. Montagu recounted in her autobiography:

'When I told her the nature of my problem, the strength of her reaction took me by surprise. She became quite vehement in her rejection of the whole idea. Moreover she urged me to refuse to have anything to do with these people and not to become embroiled in such matters either now or ever.' Montagu said she found Budberg's arguments so convincing that when Mr X telephoned again, 'I told him firmly that my decision not to accept his offer stood. The conversation was short but polite and I was never to hear from him or his department again.'

So, what was the 'problem' that prevented a seasoned agent like Montagu, who had worked for SIS and the OSS in Switzerland, from accepting the job? And who was MI5's Mr X and who was the intended target of her assignment? Could it have been that the release of *The Third Man* that year had shone a bright light on the relationship between Harry Smolka and Kim Philby? Had the public screening of *The Third Man* made it impossible for the intelligence and security services to ignore the mounting evidence that Kim Philby might be a double agent working for the Russians? And had Montagu's closeness to Smolka and Greene made her the obvious choice to be the agent to flush out Philby? Was Mr X Roger Hollis?

The answers to these questions wholly depend on whether at this stage of the early days of the Cold War any case or suspicions had been raised against Philby. Philby certainly thought there had, and shortly before his appointment to Washington, he had taken to bouts of heavy drinking having become consumed by a 'grave anxiety'.[15]

Upon the film's release, one of his Soviet handlers in Istanbul had warned Philby that the British were investigating leaks from the British embassy in Washington, an investigation that Philby said was being led by the 'formidable Maurice Oldfield'.[16] At the same time, a British agent working in the Russian embassy in London had tipped off MI5 about a leak in the Foreign Office that had triggered a new mole hunt for the three British traitors.[17]

There were also whispers about Philby in other countries' intelligence services. Teddy Kollek, who was with Philby in Vienna in 1934, and was now a senior member of the precursor agency to the Israeli security service, Mossad, suspected that the British intelligence officer was still a communist and passed on his suspicions to James Jesus Angleton at the CIA. Angleton brushed off Kollek's concerns, saying: 'Kim is a good friend of ours.'[18] Kollek had spent the war working closely with MI6 in the Middle East where he had an office in Cairo next door to Maurice Oldfield and in 1946 he arrived in London where he made contact with Oldfield.[19]

In January 1948, Maurice Oldfield decided to review the Volkov affair after reports that the Russian officer may be alive in Moscow. Philby had done his best to bury the file by making sure it never found its way into the MI6 Registry, but someone had discovered the error and Philby was forced to apologise.[20]

Someone as institutionally suspicious as Oldfield surely recognised a malign hand at work.

THE END OF THE AFFAIR

At the same time, the CIA had also picked up intelligence of a Soviet agent working in the British embassy in Washington. He would turn out to be another scientist – Wilfrid Mann, known as 'Atomic man'.[21] These twin investigations, coupled with the cracking of the Venona codes, would culminate in the defections of Burgess and Maclean. The American-run Venona programme decrypted secret messages transmitted by the Soviets from 1943 onwards, and it had identified a number of Russian agents, including a British mole codenamed 'Homer'. This was Donald Maclean, although he only found himself in the MI6/CIA crosshairs at the beginning of 1951.

While all these investigations were circling, the speculation and gossip about a traitor in the heart of the British establishment became the talk of the 'office'. One MI6 officer who debriefed Tokaev about NKVD agents operating abroad concluded: 'The Soviets penetrate everywhere.'[22] In the spring of 1948, a young ex-army officer, Philip Hay, came to Buckingham Palace to be interviewed for the post of private secretary to the widowed princess Marina, Duchess of Kent, mother of the present Duke. As he walked down a red carpeted corridor with Sir Alan Lascelles, the King's private secretary, they passed Anthony Blunt examining a picture in silence. When he thought they were out of earshot, Sir Alan whispered to Hay: 'that's our Russian spy.'[23]

Dick White, soon to become the Director General of MI5 and later chief of MI6, had also considered the possibility that Philby may be a Russian spy.[24] White had been one of the MI5 officers who had interviewed Walter Krivitsky in 1940 and remembered the agent's description of the mole at the heart of British intelligence.

By the summer of 1948 the gossip, speculation and suspicion had unnerved Guy Burgess and he decided to embark on an emergency visit to Istanbul to consult with Philby over the growing threat to their security.[25] When Burgess told his friends he was leaving immediately after purchasing a £250 (£8,000 today) plane ticket they were 'staggered.'[26] The expense suggests Burgess's Russian handlers thought the visit was important.

Burgess was now Philby's main link with the Centre, and his unchecked paranoia and sense of impending doom became a self-fulfilling prophecy.[27] His fears were not groundless; the Soviets had found out about Venona and put Philby and Burgess in the picture. The two Cambridge spies now knew that it was a fair assumption that the Americans were working on transcripts of secret messages that referred to their new Soviet codenames respectively 'Stanley' and 'Hicks'.[28] How soon would the American cryptographers break the Soviet code?

To Burgess's controller Yuri Modin, it seemed: 'that his [Burgess's] nerve was going, and that he could no longer take the strain of his double life.'[29] Sometime that summer Philby and Burgess boarded a pleasure cruiser at Istanbul sailing to Cyprus and Haifa in what appears to have been an aborted defection operation. But they were both spotted by a friend of Philby, who described them as being 'drunk and very badly behaved', and they returned to port.[30]

The increasingly unhinged Burgess was fast becoming a dangerous liability who had hit the self-destruct button. By now Graham Greene may have secured from his former MI6 colleagues, including Rodney Dennys and Desmond Pakenham, sufficient evidence to deduce that Burgess, who Greene had met but never liked, was a Soviet asset. That year Burgess had confessed to Greene's friend Claud Cockburn in the bar of the House of Commons that he was 'a Soviet agent as I expect you already know'. Justifying his treachery, Burgess explained to Cockburn, a fellow communist: 'An English Catholic in the days of Elizabeth I would certainly have seen nothing disgraceful in spying against the English in the interest of the Vatican.'[31]

Greene's knowledge of all this subterfuge is buried in his many drafts and redrafts to the script of *The Third Man*. As a writer with an exceptionally low boredom threshold, Greene could not resist dangling morsels of real life in the text to entertain readers, critics and his old spook colleagues. In *The Third Man,* Greene dangerously mixed fact with fiction in order to lay clues, score points and uncover secrets. In the following telling scene, beefed up by Greene from the original script, he uses Holly Martins to inform the audience that the film they are watching is concealing important facts in the fiction.

Holly Martins agrees to give a lecture on the contemporary novel at the British Cultural Centre at the Salesianer Annenkirche, Rennweg, in Vienna.

Popescu, the mysterious Romanian who falsely claimed to have seen Harry Lime die in a car accident, asks Martins a question about his writing.

Popescu: Can I ask, is Mr. Martins engaged on a new book?
Martins: Yes. It's called '*The Third Man*'.
Popescu: A novel, Mr. Martins?
Martins: It's a murder story. I've just started it. It's based on fact.
Popescu: I'd say you were doing something pretty dangerous this time.
Martins: Yeah?
Popescu: Mixing fact and fiction.
Martins: Should I make it all fact?
Popescu: Why, no, Mr. Martins. I'd say stick to fiction. Straight fiction.
Martins: I'm too far along with the book, Mr. Popescu.
Popescu: Haven't you ever scrapped a book Mr. Martins?
Martins: Never.
Popescu: Pity.

None of the names used in *The Third Man* are there by accident. The British Chief of Police, Colonel (Major in the film) Calloway, derives from the head of the British Military Police in Vienna at that time, Lt Colonel Alexander Galloway. The very real blunt-speaking Galloway, who was in charge of all British forces in Austria, fully recognised the Russian threat and advocated a strong British presence as a deterrent to Soviet aggression.[32]

Greene had used a very similar name corruption to conjure up his other famous police chief Henry Scobie from the real one, Patrick Brodie. Greene's deliberate reference to the Western novelist Zane Grey as one of the subjects of Holly Martins' lecture was Greene's nod to Zane Grey Todd, the FBI officer who had been investigating a penicillin scandal in Vienna run by American GIs and embroiling a beautiful Miss Austria.[33]

The kidnapping of the Estonian Anna Schmidt in Greene's original script is based on an Estonian woman called Sinaida Kao, who had fled from the Red Army to Vienna with her only child in 1947.[34] The Soviets decided to repatriate Kao, but she was able to elude them in Vienna's International (First) District and make an emergency plea for help to the US Provost Marshal.

No name in the film is wasted. This is particularly so of Baron Kurtz, the Austrian racketeer agent working with Harry Lime who gives false testimony to Colonel Calloway about Lime's death. Kurtz was also the name of the corrupt MI5 officer who falsely gave evidence about the pro-Nazi sympathies of Greene's cousin Ben Greene and whose testimony was the basis of Ben's internment at the beginning of the war. The injustice of the case had long rankled with Greene and was the original source of his distrust of MI5.

There is ample evidence to suppose the leading protagonist, Harry Lime, was based on a real person and that the Lime character is laden with clues as to whom Greene had in mind.

Harry was of course Philby's first name and Harry and Holly were old friends, just like Greene and Philby. ('Harry' was also the codename the NKVD had given to Kim Philby's new Russian handler Valeri Makayev at this time, but it's very unlikely Greene knew this.[35])

THE END OF THE AFFAIR

Harry's girlfriend Anna Schmidt is helped by Lime, who provides her with documentation to evade the authorities. Kim Philby's girlfriend Lizy was only able to escape from fascist Vienna in 1934 because Philby married her.

Schmidt was the surname of an agent who spied for the Russians against the British who Philby tried to hide from British and American intelligence after the war. It has been alleged that it was this discovery that first raised suspicions about Philby with OSS/CIA officer James Jesus Angleton.[36] Schmidt is also the name of the Abwehr agent Ernst Schmidt who headed a spy ring in Lisbon successfully broken up by Greene and Philby in 1943.[37]

There is no doubt the menacing threat posed by Soviet Russia in Europe had a profound influence on Greene. If he suspected Philby was working for the NKVD, his film would have been the perfect vehicle to expose the double agent to those who mattered without telling the whole world. Few MI6 officers, especially the more intuitive ones like Malcolm Muggeridge, could have failed to recognise the likeness between Lime and Philby. Right from the outset comparisons between the Philby/Greene and Lime/Martins relationships are in plain sight. Lime's offer of a dubious job in his racketeering business is neatly analogous to Philby offering Greene a upgraded position in Section V, in effect a job working for the Russians. Lime's job when he first arrived in Vienna was working for the International Refugee Office, very close to Philby's role on the Committee for Aiding Refugees from Fascism when he first arrived in Vienna in 1933.[38]

When Martins discovers that Lime has betrayed him, he elects to do his duty to justice and humanity by entrapping his 'best friend' and then takes it upon himself to deliver the coup de grâce, a bullet to his head.

In real life, Greene's residual loyalties to Philby may have prevented him from playing out his revenge beyond the scenes in the film. Greene's prime duty was always to his art and so the character of Harry Lime is an amalgam of many duplicitous figures the writer had encountered in real life, including Harry Smolka, his school days tormentor Lionel Carter and even partly Greene himself (Lime-Green) who possessed his own cold streak, the 'icicle in the heart of the writer'.[39]

There may also be something of Harry Walston in the Lime psychology. Walston was a central figure in Greene's world at this time, the cuckolded husband of the woman with whom Greene remained utterly besotted. Greene could not help his antipathy towards her husband to whom she was ultimately loyal, refusing to divorce him. But did Greene know that MI5 had a file on the wealthy socialist Walston?[40] An MI5 document released to the National Archives concerning the Guy Burgess affair identifies Walston as a subject of interest (PF 1550059) along with suspected high profile communist figures Christopher Isherwood, Stephen Spender, and W.H Auden.[41]

Just before his haemorrhage in the New York hotel and after the completion of *The Third Man* script, Greene wrote to Harry Walston with a cryptic message on a postcard declaring: 'People are no damn good.'[42]

The central charge against Harry Lime is his nihilistic amorality, immortalised by Orson Welles in the Ferris wheel scene. Whatever one thinks of Philby's ruthless betrayal of the many brave agents who worked for Britain as well as handing over the invasion plans for D-Day, he did nevertheless subscribe to a set of communist ideals. He did not commit his treachery for money and his outlook couldn't be described as nihilistic. In this one respect, Philby is not Greene's Lime.

Greene was not conventionally political. He only ever voted once (probably for Margaret Thatcher), was never bound by a political line and was suspicious of most forms of government.[43] Nevertheless, he told the literary critic Marie-Francoise Allain that he was more attracted to the Communist Party than the far right, saying that 'in 1923 one could still believe in the October Revolution' whereas after the war that was no longer possible.[44]

Greene continued to be drawn to issues concerning social injustice, always more interested in people than political parties. The betrayal of a political system was too abstract a notion to get worked up about. Greene later said that he couldn't have betrayed Kim Philby because he could never be 100 per cent against anybody in the same way that he could never be 100 per cent in favour of anybody.[45] Yet Greene put these qualms to one side when he betrayed his old friend Commissioner Patrick Brodie in Freetown when he felt such a betrayal was justified in the national interest of the war.

Greene's wartime experience at the heart of British intelligence and the secrets he kept continued to find expression in his early post-war writing. He simply could not shake off the dirty business of espionage. His first writing endeavour after *The Third Man* was a little-known short story called *No Man's Land*, a hostile attack on communist rule. It contains all Greene's by now familiar themes: betrayal, competing political ideologies, a dangerous love affair and the struggle with existential Catholicism. The central character is a British agent named Brown who employs a German spy called Kramer. Brown is of course Greene and Kramer was a private joke between Greene and Philby when they worked together in the Iberian section of MI6. The Abwehr were running three, possibly four, agents in Portugal all named Kramer and Greene and Philby had to get to grips with each of them. Indeed, Philby candidly admitted: 'In default of reliable descriptions or photographs it seems to me that we are bound to get confused between them sooner or later.'[46]

Greene steadfastly denied that Harry Lime was his charismatic friend from his SIS days, just as he denied any of his characters bore a resemblance to reality even though he was repeatedly sued for exactly this.[47] Over the years, he deployed evasion and disingenuity to defend himself, admitting in 1981:

'I am the last person who can say what the truth is about me ... During a brief period of my life, I had for personal reasons, to train myself to lie. Falsehood became a protection – it afforded me several "covers". And with journalists I certainly do cheat.'[48]

When it came to unlocking the clues to his books, this was always his standard negotiating position. He liked the game. He once claimed that if anyone tried to write his biography, they would find that they had been 'misled'.[49]

This was also true about the real identities hidden in his characters – the reader would be misled. There were good legal reasons for this: potential defamation claims and potential breaches of the Official Secrets Act. But Greene was certainly capable of betrayal of a friend such as Brodie. He had also betrayed Harry Smolka by acquiring from him the vital penicillin plotline for *The Third Man* without crediting him. To a lesser extent, he had betrayed the American OSS men when he exposed their sloppy security methods while working at Ryder Street.

It seems quite possible that Greene picked up from his friends and family still working in MI6, including his brother-in-law Rodney Dennys, intelligence about the on-going investigation into suspected Russian moles. Smolka's personal knowledge of Philby, which he shared with Greene, combined with his own misgivings, may have forced Greene to posit the question: could Philby be one of the three agents being hunted by MI5? Volkov had described one of them as MI6's head of counter-intelligence and the suspicions were stoked by a further leak from the Russian embassy in London. Some of the other senior MI6 officers may have already had Philby in their sights.

John Reed, the diplomat stationed in Istanbul when Volkov tried to defect, had come to the conclusion that Philby was either 'incompetent or a Soviet agent'. Was this the story that breathed such treacherous life into the character of Harry Lime? As we have seen, *The Third Man* was loaded with coded messaging relating to Greene's private and professional lives – a fiction that was blended into Cold War reality.

The two MI5 investigators closing in on the Soviet moles at the time of release of *The Third Man* were Roger Hollis, who had been keeping a 'restricted access' file on Philby, and Arthur S Martin, a former major in the Radio Security Service who joined MI5 in 1946.[50] Was 'Holly Martins' the biggest clue of all that Greene knew about Philby and the officers who were on to him. If one removes the 's' from Martins and attaches it to Holly you have 'Hollys Martin', the surnames of these two MI5 officers. It might explain why Rollo was changed to Holly in the film script. Hollis is an English surname derived from a Middle English holis '(dwelling by) holly trees'; it was also used as a masculine given name. Greene told readers that he chose Holly because he wanted it to sound 'absurd'.[51]

Like Wheeler and Carter from his schooldays, Philby had become an important influence on Greene's writing. Greene had long ago made peace with his schoolboy tormentors and the treachery perpetuated against him. But had Greene, a professional spy deeply proud of his war record with British intelligence when so much more was at stake, really forgiven Philby for the sins of his 'great betrayal'?

In 1972 Greene admitted that ever since his school days 'the subject of disloyalty has obsessed me', comparing it to a 'tiresome and persistent weed'[52] infecting almost all his books; adding 'my friend Philby accurately' identified this running theme of treachery when he had written about Greene in his autobiography, *My Silent War*.

The question that remains is whether Greene intended *The Third Man* as a warning to his friend Philby or a clue for Greene's colleagues at MI6. Or perhaps both. Had Greene lit the touchpaper of an incendiary investigation and then stepped back to watch how it blew up?

It begs this intriguing question. In 1949, had Greene's film done its job and alerted British intelligence chiefs to the idea that Philby might be a prime candidate for one of the Russian moles about whom Volkov had warned them? And was Philby handed the American job with a view to using him as a penetration agent against the Russians?

A conspiracy theory suggesting Philby was a willing or even an unsuspecting treble agent working for MI6 from this point onwards seems far-fetched (although once he is in Moscow the idea has more merit). Given all the subsequent damage Philby did to American-British relations, it does not seem possible that Philby was working for British intelligence at this time. Much more likely was his loyal friends at MI6 and their unwillingness to countenance a traitor in their midst, either missed Greene's clues or decided to willfully ignore them.

None of this was true of the one confirmed Soviet agent who was working on Greene's film and whose bulging and increasingly incriminating case file must have been something of an embarrassment to both MI5 and MI6. It is much more likely that *The Third Man* triggered a doubling of British intelligence efforts against Peter 'Harry' Smolka. It would also explain why Moura Budberg, who knew Smolka, was so vehemently opposed to Montagu taking on the MI5 assignment.

Smolka's vital assistance during the filming of *The Third Man* proved just how easily he slipped between the zones of occupation and revealed how he wielded considerable influence in Vienna, London and Moscow. Smolka held positions of trust that made him the perfect double agent. But his double dealing was about to enter a new dimension. MI5 documents released by the National Archives show he was planning to turn

THE END OF THE AFFAIR

traitor to the Soviet cause, but not necessarily to defect to the British.

MI5 fears that Smolka might elude them were confirmed in 1951 when officers made the alarming discovery that he had been working for 'American intelligence sources' in Vienna since early 1948, a suspicion that was confirmed at the time by SIS agents in Czechoslovakia who passed on to London reports from the local communists claiming to know where Smolka's true loyalties lay.[53] Smolka's work with the UK government during the war made him valuable to both the Russians and the Americans. MI5 and MI6 decided to set in play an audacious operation to approach Smolka in Vienna and bring about his defection to the British. Vienna station chief Peter Lunn, who was guiding the operation, believed Smolka was 'too intelligent to swallow the Soviet line and was of a liberal outlook' and so might be willing to 'come over'.[54]

While Greene and Smolka were working together in Vienna on *The Third Man*, the British were trying to coax Smolka away from his Russian and American handlers.

In which case, were Graham Greene, Alexander Korda and Elizabeth Montagu all part of the British counter-intelligence operation? And was this why Smolka had so meekly accepted Korda's unfair contract clause that so fraudulently exploited his contribution to the film?

There is some reason to believe that 'operation Smolka' may have been successful. Philby and Smolka were both awarded OBEs for services to the war effort. After Philby's treachery was exposed in 1963, he was stripped of his honour. Harry Smolka, a well-known Soviet agent, was allowed to keep his OBE, awarded in June 1944 four days after D-Day[55], even though he had relocated to communist Europe. It is hard to think of a more official stamp of approval.

As we have seen, Graham Greene never really left SIS, and throughout his later relationship with Kim Philby he was taking instructions from Maurice Oldfield, the head of MI6. Oldfield had first suspected Philby was 'up to no good' in 1949,[56] but not because of anything he recognised of Harry Lime in *The Third Man*. Oldfield's suspicions were based on the disastrous results of two covert operations in which Philby was involved. In 1946 MI6 began the clandestine support of Ukrainian nationals, some of whom were former Nazis, engaged in an insurgency in Ukraine against Soviet occupation. Nearly all the British-trained agents were eliminated by Soviet patrols or ambushed at border crossings. Later, when the Americans sent in their own operatives the result was exactly the same.

Operation Valuable was another joint CIA and SIS mission, this time to secretly land Albanian agents in their home country with the object of bringing about a coup that would overturn the newly established pro-Soviet regime. Dozens of these agents, some trained by Rodney Dennys,[57] were captured shortly after landing and summarily executed.

Oldfield suspected a leak but couldn't identify where it had come from. He quickly connected the Volkov, Vermehren and Rado cases with the deaths of the Ukrainian and Albanian agents. In each case, Philby had a direct hand.[58] Oldfield's nephew Martin Pearce claims that Oldfield had only been prevented from naming Philby by the absence of anything other than circumstantial suspicion. One retired SAS officer told him: 'had Maurice made allegations of that kind against Kim on that basis, at that time he'd been laughed out of the service.'[59]

When the Burgess and Maclean story broke in 1951 Graham Greene was in Malaya where he was confronted by Augustus Wheeler, the traitor from his school days. Greene always believed that the best policy for dealing with known Russian agents working in the UK was to let them run so that they would lead MI6 to bigger fish. After Philby fell under suspicion when Burgess and Maclean defected, several intelligence sources believe this is exactly what happened. Harold Macmillan's high-risk public exoneration of Philby in 1955 may have been in compliance with MI6 policy to let Philby and the Russians believe that the KGB spy suspect was in the clear.[60] However, a criminal prosecution in Britain along the lines of the successful conviction of George Blake was favoured by MI5 and most of the senior politicians who had been selectively briefed on the intelligence against Philby.

In his marathon showdown with MI5's interrogator-in-chief Helenus Milmo, a barrister and later a High Court judge, Philby was denied permission to smoke and subjected to a series of probing questions about his links to known communists. Philby was a cornered animal and had no hesitation throwing Burgess and Maclean under the bus, one time suggesting the two spies were in a gay relationship, even pointing to Maclean's 'pansyish tiny white gasmask' he carried to meetings during the war.[61] All MI5 had against Philby was his association with Peter Harry Smolka, his marriage to the communist Lizy Friedmann and lingering suspicions connecting him to the disappearance of Volkov.

Despite many more interviews with MI5 no direct evidence against Philby emerged but the circumstantial case against him, mostly his personal ties to Burgess, remained strong and he had little choice but to tender his resignation.

Roger Hollis and Arthur Martin were convinced of Philby's guilt and ordered round-the-clock surveillance of his country home in Rickmansworth and tails wherever he went.

What they found was a man very much enjoying his newfound freedom out of government employment. He returned to his old drinking holes in Piccadilly and gathered around him a band of loyal friends from the service who were convinced of his innocence and his shoddy treatment by the Foreign Office.

MI5's B5 surveillance teams were soon writing down the familiar names of Philby's Piccadilly drinking companions,

Tommy Harris, Richard Brooman-White and Erich Vermehren who routinely met in the Three Crowns before going on to the Ritz and the Goring hotels where they were joined by wives and girlfriends.

One lunchtime, an MI5 report recorded, Philby was so plastered he was observed walking out of the pub and then 'vomiting in the Piccadilly Underground station lavatory.'[62]

On other occasions he was spotted shopping in Knightsbridge at Harvey Nichols and Peter Jones and walking down Piccadilly carrying a ladies' fur coat, a present for Aileen.

If MI5 thought Philby was having fun at their expense his next purchase must have seemed a deliberate provocation. In September 1951 he splashed out on a decommissioned London black taxi which he drove around town with 'a big grin on his face'.[63]

The watchers noted the vehicle had an illegal broken mirror so he couldn't even see whether he was being followed. One surveillance officer wrote admiringly of Philby's sangfroid and the increasingly bizarre tradecraft performed in his signature belted fawn-coloured raincoat and cabbie's flat cap: 'He gives no outward sign of being either nervous or on alert,' bemoaned the officer.[64]

Philby, financed by his pay-off from the Foreign Office, drove his taxi crammed with drinking pals, to various county cricket grounds and to Highbury in north London to watch his beloved Arsenal. He also used it to ferry his children to various boarding schools in Oxfordshire and Hampshire.

But by the close of the year, a reckless air of complacency had crept into Philby's taxi jaunts.

At 6pm on 11 November 1951, an MI5 surveillance team who had tailed Philby's cab from Tommy Harris's home at Garden Lodge, Logan Place, Kensington, noticed a much taller and much thinner man perched on the driver's box. The uncomfortable looking passenger was Anthony Blunt, recently appointed Surveyor of the King's Pictures, and as the two men got out of the cab

THE END OF THE AFFAIR

the MI5 team was able to overhear Blunt tell Philby 'leave it as arranged' before walking to 19 Upper Phillimore Gardens where he rang the bell and was let in.[65]

Knowing that MI5 wasn't able to lay a glove on him had considerably raised Philby's morale.[66] The following year he sought medical help for his stammer and began an affair with a younger woman called Constance Ashley-Jones, who he spent weekdays with at her Highgate flat and the weekends with his family in Rickmansworth and Crowborough after the move to Sussex.

Encouraged by Tommy Harris, who had contacts in the publishing world (and presumably agreement from his KGB handlers), Philby decided the time was right for him to write his autobiography which he said promised to put the record straight as to what happened in Washington at the time of the defections of Burgess and Maclean. Spurred on by a £600 advance (£16,000 today), from publishers Andre Deutsch, Philby knocked off the first three chapters covering his time in Austria, Spain and Washington.[67]

MI5, who had bugged both his family home and Ashley-Jones' flat, were so horrified at the prospect of a damaging, one-sided report of the Burgess and Maclean affair that they secretly arranged for an informant to send them copies of his manuscript.[68]

What they discovered was an insightful and crafted memoir that skilfully navigated the Official Secrets Act, typified by this account of the working behaviour of Spanish journalists during the Spanish Civil War: 'Given a typewriter and a few sheets of foolscap, he would expand on an official communique of two words Sin novedad – Nothing to report – into pages of exalted breathless prose, as tempestuous and as empty as the wind.'[69] This is pure Graham Greene and begs the question whether Philby consulted his best qualified author friend about the mechanics of writing his first book.

However, the passages on Burgess's close relationship with Churchill's shadow foreign secretary Anthony Eden were seriously damaging to the British government now that Eden was Prime

Minister. Philby revealed that Burgess had been Eden's personal assistant during a visit to the US in 1950/51 and that Eden had told Burgess: 'We have become firm friends. Now, Guy is there is anything I can ever do for you . . .'[70]

Then in June 1955, just as MI5 were about to take action against publication, Philby decided to pull the whole project and informed Deutsch he no longer wished them to publish. It was a tough decision that had financial implications.

Philby, who had now separated from the mentally fragile Aileen and was about to break up with Connie, had run out of money leaving Tommy Harris to repay the £600 advance in full.[71]

Harris told friends he was concerned Philby was on the 'edge of a nervous breakdown.'[72]

On 25 October 1955, following a report in the *New York Times*, MP Marcus Lipton used parliamentary privilege to ask Prime Minister Eden to confirm to the House that Philby was the third man who had tipped off Burgess and Maclean. Suddenly, thrust into the limelight, Philby was forced to tough it out until the government finally exonerated him in July when he hastily arranged a press conference at his mother's flat where he beguiled Fleet Street hacks with 'no comment' answers accompanied by mischievous rolls of his tongue.

Meanwhile Roger Hollis, still desperate to nail his man, arranged to meet the editor of the *Spectator* who claimed to possess incriminating information concerning Philby's links to another suspect being watched by MI5, Goronwy Rees.[73] But the new information merely added to the circumstantial case; it didn't help reach the threshold for a criminal prosecution.

On 6 September 1956, Philby was finally able to slip the attentions of MI5 when he took a plane from London Airport to Beirut where he was installed as Middle East correspondent for the *Observer* and the *Economist*, just in time to report on the Suez Crisis. He was also given a new KGB handler, Alexei Petrukhov, who ordered

THE END OF THE AFFAIR

him to write pro-Egypt articles praising president Gamal Abdel Nasser who had nationalised the Suez Canal earlier in the year.[74]

Defection to a hostile state outside a time of war was not a crime under UK law so Hollis, now Director General of MI5, and Martin were forced to sit on their hands in the hope that a smoking gun would turn up.

In October 1961 Hollis's hopes appeared to be realised when an MI5 agent reported that the Austrian spy and Philby's associate, Harry Smolka, was leaving Vienna on a business trip to London. Arthur Martin tracked him down to a central London hotel where he persuaded him to be interviewed at MI5's offices.[75]

Smolka's MS was advanced, leaving him permanently confined to his wheelchair. He was chain-smoking and every time Martin wanted to show him a document he had to hold it up close to Smolka's face so he could read it. He happily admitted supplying Guy Burgess with copies of top-secret government papers, which were traced to him because of a wonky letter M on his typewriter,[76] but only because he said he thought Burgess was working for MI5. He also admitted knowing Philby through Lizy but said that after the couple had separated he hadn't seen him since 1942. When Martin finally cut to the chase and asked whether he and Philby had been working for the Russians, Smolka said he was a capitalist now and always thought Philby was a fascist and an anti-semite.[77]

In a 33-page verbatim report[78] of Smolka's interrogation there was not a scrap of testimony that could help Hollis and Martin. Whatever secrets Smolka knew about Philby he was only prepared to share them with people he could trust. For MI5 it was a case of going back to the drawing board.

Then the following year, 1962, Victor Rothschild contacted his former colleagues at MI5 to say that he had spoken to a Russian woman, who had known Philby before the war and who was ready to spill her secrets.[79]

Rothschild's witness was Philby's former lover, Flora Solomon, who had kept quiet about Philby's communist past all this time, but after reading his anti-Israel articles in the *Observer* she could keep quiet no longer. Solomon was prepared to tell everything she knew about Philby. In an interview with Arthur Martin, she laid out in detail how Philby had tried to recruit her in the 1930s. Martin reported: 'In a Spanish restaurant [in London] . . . Kim confessed to her he was working as an agent for Soviet Russia. He said that he was carrying burdens and that he was in danger. He asked her to work "for us".'[80]

This was the critical breakthrough that MI5 had been waiting for, the final nail in Philby's coffin. It was decided that Philby's old friend and MI6 colleague Nicholas Elliott should be sent to Beirut to try to use the new intelligence, which included additional testimony from a recent KGB defector Antoliy Golitsyn, to coax a confession out of Philby.[81] In January 1963, Elliott reported to Peter Lunn, the MI6 bureau chief in Beirut who had previously been in charge of intelligence matters in Vienna when Greene was researching and filming *The Third Man*.

When Elliott knocked on Philby's apartment door, Philby is reported to have said: 'I thought it would be you.' Elliott quickly came to the point and told him there was new evidence that showed Philby was working for the Russians. The game was up. Philby appeared to be resigned to his fate, almost relieved, and told Elliott his spying days were like suffering from a form of 'controlled schizophrenia'.[82]

Armed with a list of questions prepared by Roger Hollis, Elliott tried to get his old friend to confess. Question 7 concerned Philby's communist associate Peter 'Harry' Smolka who Golitsyn said was part of the 'ring of five' and was close to Philby:[83] 'Could he try to remember anything definite about Smolka who was in the Ministry of Information at the same time as Burgess during the war and who visited the USSR on behalf of the MOI in February 1944?'[84]

THE END OF THE AFFAIR

Philby must have known from his previous grillings by MI5 in 1951 that he would not be able to deny his association to Smolka, so he tried to diminish Smolka's importance to the Russians.

In Philby's 1951 interrogation with Helenus Milmo, he was forced to admit that Smolka, then a known communist agent of great interest to British intelligence, had been a regular guest at the London home he shared with Lizy when she was part of the Vienna Circle.[85] Now twelve years later, Elliott reported: 'Peach [MI5's codename for Philby] thought that he [Smolka] was a communist and would not be at all surprised if he had worked for the Russians. He considered him, however, to be a most undesirable figure and of no great stature.'[86]

Philby decided to cut his losses and confessed to working for Russian intelligence during the war but convinced Elliott that he had ended all ties with the NKVD in 1946 after the creation of the National Health Service and other socialist reforms brought in by the Labour government of Clement Attlee.[87]

Philby agreed to write a typed confession setting out his involvement with the Russians between 1934 and 1946. Elliott reported back to London that Philby was able to say 'he could now tell us everything he knew within the dictates of his conscience'. But 'the dictates of his conscience' meant of course Philby's partial confession was littered with lies, half-truths and obfuscations.

Yet one truth could not be avoided. A transcription of the secretly recorded conversation between Philby and Elliott in Philby's apartment shows that Elliott had reminded Philby of their meeting in Berne in 1948, when Philby had told him how he always 'regarded loyalty to friends as more important than loyalty to country'.[88]

Elliott told Hollis: 'It was clear in the light of what K [Philby] had said, that in practice, idealism could bitch the friends.'

Philby confided in Elliott that 'if he had his whole life to lead again, he would probably have behaved in the same way'.[89] He had placed his loyalty to communism and Russia above his loyalty to all his friends. There is something strikingly familiar about the way Philby chose to frame his betrayal of Britain and his MI6 colleagues who he described as 'really marvellous friends'. He told Elliott that he knew what it must have felt to be a Catholic confessing his sins.[90]

Elliott gave Philby 24 hours to complete his written confession. It was just enough time for Philby to plan his escape and exactly what Graham Greene said he might have done if he had been placed in the same position as Elliott. On the evening of 23 January, Philby hopped aboard a Russian freighter bound for Odessa in the Soviet Union.[91] There could now be no denying that Kim Philby was 'The Third Man'. Almost as soon as Philby received the keys to his new Moscow flat he began an affair with Donald Maclean's wife, Melinda – a bitter betrayal of his friend and fellow Cambridge spy.

In the aftermath of Philby's defection, all his former colleagues were contacted by MI5 and interviewed about what they knew about the traitor. The interviews were conducted under a presumption of suspicion by association. Graham Greene took his turn and was quizzed by Peter Wright, of *Spycatcher* fame. Greene's hostility to MI5 always meant he was never going to say any more than he felt absolutely necessary about his personal dealings with his old friend, and in any case he must have already passed on any useful intelligence via his own family channels to MI6 directly. Wright concluded that Greene knew more than he had told him but cleared him of any 'complicity' in the case.[92]

In Washington, where Philby had arguably caused greatest damage, the FBI diggers had turned up a piece of evidence that did implicate Greene. Its source was another celebrated writer, Christopher Isherwood, a distant member of the Greene family through his mother, a third cousin to Graham. Isherwood, a suspected communist, had already been named by Anthony Blunt as a friend of himself and Guy Burgess. MI5 had also quizzed Philby in 1951 about his knowledge of Isherwood who had since settled in America.[93] In the dragnet that followed the defection of Burgess and Maclean, Isherwood was pulled in by the FBI for questioning about what he knew of the Cambridge spies and any of their associates. He volunteered the name of Graham Greene who he said had tried to get him to travel to Spain to fight for the communists in the Civil War.[94] On Greene's FBI file, released to the author under the terms of the US FOIA, it was already stated that he had been a member of the Oxford University Communist Party.[95] Pieced together this wasn't enough to link Greene to the Soviets but it caused him considerable disruption whenever he travelled to the US.

The Philby case went cold for several months until the *Sunday Times* published on 14 July 1963 a sensational article about Philby's treachery. The article suggested that the real enemy facing Britain may not be the Russians but the Americans, arguing Philby had been one of the first to appreciate the threat posed by the OSS, the predecessor to the CIA, during the war.

The author of the piece was Graham Greene. 'I sometimes wonder,' he wrote, 'what treachery may yet be disclosed under a different regime. Which of us then were betraying secrets to our American allies. Which of us in the far past at Oxford and Cambridge have become corrupted by the capitalist way of life.'[96]

Recalling his time working with Philby in Room 51, 14 Ryder Street, Greene said he remembered his 'chief with great affection' and hoped Philby would read the article and accept it as a 'salute of genuine affection.'

He closed the article with this elliptical comment: 'As for The Third Man with whom the Press has made us so familiar, there was no danger from him in those days for I hadn't yet invented him.'[97]

The article was guaranteed to anger the British government and MI5 as much as it would curry favour in Moscow. A copy of it is retained in MI5's file on Philby at the National Archives.[98]

*

Four months later, on 22 November 1963, Lee Harvey Oswald assassinated US president John F Kennedy in Dallas. It was the height of the Cold War, and only a year after the Cuban Missile Crisis, when it quickly emerged that Oswald was a former US marine and security-cleared radar operator who had defected to the Soviet Union. There was no evidence to support a Soviet assassination plot but that didn't prevent conspiracy speculation that inevitably drew in the last high-profile Russian traitor to defect. Evidence of a possible Philby/Oswald connection was provided the following year by the Warren Commission which found Oswald had travelled to Southampton on his way to defecting to Russia and had visited Soviet embassies in the US and Mexico days before he carried out the Kennedy killing.

Five years later in March 1968, Jim Garrison, a New Orleans District Attorney investigating the Kennedy assassination, took sworn testimony from two key witnesses claiming Kim Philby, working for the Russians, played a part in a neo-Nazi conspiracy to murder the president and bring down the government.[99] Parts of this evidence was published in the American media but was not followed up in Garrison's final report, although it demonstrated the continued depth of worldwide interest in the notorious Cambridge spy and what people thought he was capable of even after he had defected to Moscow.

Kim Philby chose this moment to announce his intention to publish his own memoirs which he called *My Silent War*. There was so much interest that when the rights were offered to American publishers it triggered a bidding war.[100] British intelligence recognised it for what it was: well-written, self-serving propaganda and a Cold War card expertly played by the Soviets. The timing was interesting as it came as the Russians were threatening to put on trial for a second time a British teacher named Gerald Brooke who was accused of spying in Moscow. The star prosecution witness was to be Kim Philby himself.[101] Before the start of the trial

THE END OF THE AFFAIR

the Russians offered to exchange Brooke for two Russian spies imprisoned in the UK. Philby had tried to blackmail the British government the year before, offering to cancel plans to publish his book (as well as a television interview with David Frost)[102] which threatened to identify serving MI6 and CIA officers, in return for the release of the same two Soviet spies.[103] That offer was rejected out of hand,[104] but the Gerald Brooke spy swap eventually went ahead in 1969 after *My Silent War* was published. Brooke, characterised as an innocent abroad, was championed by his North Finchley constituency MP, Margaret Thatcher, who lobbied the Labour Prime Minister Harold Wilson for his release.

There is some evidence that Graham Greene helped to facilitate publication of *My Silent War* in the UK by collecting Philby's finished manuscript from Paris and safely conveying it to MacGibbon & Kee, Greene's publishers in London.[105] Greene had contact with the publishers through his friend Rupert Hart-Davis. Did he know that the founder of MacGibbon & Kee was another Soviet spy, James MacGibbon, a former military intelligence officer who on his death bed admitted passing the secrets of D-Day to the Russian military attaché in London? Certainly, the Foreign Office was sufficiently worried to have managed to obtain a copy of the manuscript by 'covert means'.[106]

Those 'covert means' may have been Greene. Knowing that there was nothing the British government could do to prevent publication it made sense, as it had with Philby's aborted memoirs, to have someone trusted by MI6 working with the British publishers.

My Silent War was the first indication that the Cambridge spy had been reactivated by the Russian leader Leonid Brezhnev to coincide with the Soviets' brutal repression of the people of Czechoslovakia who in 1968 began mounting mass protests against Moscow. Philby's 'honest' tale of a gentleman spy who had seen through the incompetence and class hierarchies of the Western spy agencies appeared on British and American bookshelves at the same time as Western media was carrying sickening images of T-55 tanks crushing the embryonic democracy movement. Forty years earlier Graham Greene had witnessed first-hand how the communists had violently seized power in Prague. In 1968 he had friends in Prague, mostly fellow writers, who were being persecuted by the Soviets and he had publicly protested against the occupation.[107] The idea that Greene would want to support Soviet propaganda seems barely credible.

Philby's memoirs painted post-war British intelligence as inept and still suffering from classism while those working for the people's KGB were portrayed as serving a worthy cause. But it was also obvious Philby was having some fun playing with the truth, opening his memoirs: 'I will therefore content myself with a few hints at the truth, adjuring the reader only not to fall flat on his face into traps of his own making.' Which was almost exactly how he had introduced his 'confession' to Nicholas Elliott in Beirut in January 1963 when he talked in terms of the 'dictates of his conscience'. At the end of the work, Philby adds to his literary subterfuge: 'the first duty of an underground worker is to perfect not only his cover story but also his cover personality.'

Despite all this, Greene agreed to write a foreword in which he appeared to accept Philby at face value as well as to defend Philby's treachery, comparing his actions to the Catholic resistance of 16th-century Protestant England. This was identical to the justification Guy Burgess had proffered to Greene's friend Claud Cockburn about his own treachery: 'As an English Catholic in the days of Elizabeth I would certainly have seen nothing disgraceful in spying against the English in the interest of the Vatican.'[108] And this was the same principled act of conscience to which Philby had alluded when he was being quizzed by Nicholas Elliott in Beirut. It had the hallmark of a concocted line of defence agreed by the Cambridge spies.

Greene, now out on a perilous limb, boldly told Philby's readers that he valued loyalty to a friend over loyalty to a country. 'He "betrayed his country" – Yes, perhaps he did, but who among us has not committed treason to something or someone more important than a country? In Philby's own eyes he was working for the shape of things to come from which his country would benefit.'[109]

The Catholic defence and the case for putting friends before country were to be the twin arguments guaranteed to endear him to the Cambridge traitor. It raises the possibility that Greene had been played the secret Philby/Elliott tapes from Beirut in which Philby compared his guilt to that of a Catholic and when Elliott had reminded him how he had once betrothed his loyalty to his friends above his country.

Philby greatly valued Greene's brave and independent-minded, if rather perverse, show of support that had made Greene very unpopular among his literary peers, including the spy writer John Le Carre, most of his SIS colleagues and the British media. Many found particularly galling that there could be any moral equivalence between Greene's personal loyalty to his friend Philby and a duty of patriotic loyalty owed to his country. *The Times*, Greene's former employer, declared: 'Mr Greene's foreword is a melancholy act of misplaced loyalty . . . There is no faith that can excuse treachery of this order.' While Malcolm Muggeridge wrote in the *Sunday Times*: 'Greene's introduction reads like an elegy for a fallen comrade. It would be touching if it were not so indecent.'

Against a storm of protest, Greene continued to justify his defence of Philby, telling Marie-Francoise Allain in 1983 that 'the one great danger of treachery was the defection of secret agents' like Philby: 'I myself would not be capable of such courage, of such a force of conviction.'[110] What had gone unsaid was that Greene owed Philby a further professional debt of loyalty after Philby had intervened at risk to himself, not once but three times, to protect Greene from his own misadventures and save his friend's career. Philby's actions directly spared Greene from humiliation and in the case of Freetown, an embarrassing resignation from SIS.

Privately, however, Greene was also wise to Philby, a thoroughbred secret agent, perhaps the best the world had ever seen.

In 1981, Greene confided in the playwright and Second World War conscientious objector Michael Meyer that he believed Philby was behind a Soviet disinformation operation to convince MI5 that Philby's long-time foe Roger Hollis was a Russian double agent. Philby had met the journalist Chapman Pincher in Moscow, where he sowed the seeds of suspicion about Hollis's supposed treachery. The story caught fire and for a long time Hollis had to defend himself against unfounded accusations that he was a Russian double agent, doing great personal damage to the man and the reputation of the security service. The leading proponent of the Hollis mole conspiracy was his MI5 colleague Arthur Martin, a twist of the knife that must have delighted Philby.

Greene told Meyer: 'I have great doubts about the Roger Hollis story and Mr Chapman Pincher. It looks to me like a classical piece of disinformation and destabilisation perhaps engineered, who knows, by Kim.'[111]

Pincher was not the only writer Philby was speaking to. Amid the perestroika of the late 1980s, the Russian journalist Genrikh Borovik persuaded the Kremlin to open its archives and grant him exclusive access to Philby, who guaranteed him that no lines of enquiry would be out of bounds.

Borovik began by exploring the idea promulgated by the Centre in the first years of the war that Philby may have been an SIS plant, but after several hours of conversation he quickly dismissed this notion.[112] (Yuri Modin, the Cambridge spies' Soviet handler after the war, even thought it was possible that Philby could have been

THE END OF THE AFFAIR

working for MI6 and NKVD at the same time without betraying either.[113])

What struck Borovik as particularly strange was how Philby repeatedly brought up the case of Harry Smolka, someone of whom Borovik was hitherto unaware. Philby insisted on explaining his relationship with Smolka, confirming for the first time that he had met Smolka in Vienna in 1933, not London where he had told MI5 they had been introduced.[114]

Borovik recounted: 'I had the impression that Kim did not like Smolka very much. The stimulus for bringing up the memories of Smolka in our conversation was also insignificant and random – it could have reminded him of Smolka, it could have not. At the end of his story about Smolka, Kim felt it necessary to stress one thing. Smolka knew a lot about him and about Guy Burgess, and maybe he had known about the other members of the group. However, he had never told anyone about them, even though the business with Slansky[115] took place in the late 40s, while Kim continued to work for another 13 years for the Soviets – in America, then in England, and then in the near East.'[116]

Philby was smearing Smolka, who had died in Vienna 1980, in the same way he had smeared Hollis, suggesting he knew exactly to which foreign power Smolka had finally betrothed his loyalty.

The summer of 1951 was the most worrying period in Philby's career as he not only had to defend his close friendship with Burgess and Maclean but also his association with Smolka. In his interview with Borovik, Philby tried to play down his fears of being exposed. 'Of course,' said Borovik, 'Kim felt that even if Smolka had wanted to, he would not have been able to prove Kim's ties to the KGB. But his testimony would have provided another link in the chain of indirect evidence against Philby and the longer the chain, the heavier it is and the harder it is to escape.'[117]

*

Kim Philby never recovered from the defections of Burgess and Maclean and, combined with his ties to Smolka and Lizy, remained a suspected double agent until his own defection in 1963.

Throughout all Philby's professional turmoil, Graham Greene doubled down on their friendship, even when he too was questioned by the MI5 spy catchers about his own relationship with Philby.

Greene's cosying up to Moscow during visits to the Soviet Union in the 1950s in which he made pro-Soviet statements must have helped to fan the flames of suspicion in MI5. But of course Greene's loyalties lay with SIS, not MI5. His public sentiments in support of Soviet Russia concealed his true feelings towards Stalin's form of totalitarian government, which had not changed from the views he expressed while writing *The Third Man* and the first-hand impression he had of the communist coup in Czechoslovakia in 1948. His tilt towards Moscow may have been a smoke screen to cover the freelance spying missions he was now undertaking for SIS. This could have included a long-term operation to coax Philby in from the cold, a final reckoning with the traitor he had allowed to get away. Although of course the wily Soviet agent may have suspected and expected as much.

Maurice Oldfield had never given up on the chance of catching his man. Bringing Philby back would have been a huge propaganda coup for SIS, and in this venture he enrolled the services of Graham Greene, who he hoped remained more loyal to his country than to his friend.[118] Such an operation, if successful, would force the Soviets to question everything Philby had told them and potentially undermine much of the intelligence generated by Soviet penetration of British intelligence.

Greene had risked his reputation by openly backing Philby. Was this then part of the game, a ruse to win Philby's confidence?

Greene always believed that SIS and the West 'suffered more from his [Philby's] flight than his espionage', writing in 1968: 'how right SIS were to defend Philby and how wrong MI5 were to force him into the open.'[119] He had already concluded that the damage done by the atomic spies Klaus Fuchs and Allan Nunn May was not caused by the scientific secrets they passed to the Soviets (who would have achieved parity in nuclear weaponry anyway) but their public capture and the ensuing breakdown of intelligence relations between Britain and America.[120] Curiously, these critical caveats that undercut Greene's unconditional support for Philby were removed from the original draft of the foreword to *My Silent War*.[121]

Greene even ventured that it would have been better to have left Philby in his post:

'I sometimes like to imagine what would have occurred if Kim Philby had in fact, as many foretold, become "C", the chief of the Secret Service. The kind of information he would have had at his disposal as "C" could hardly have increased greatly in interest, and it might even have diminished: no nuts and bolts, only the minutes of great vacuous high level conferences. The moment would certainly have arrived sooner or later when the KGB thought it time to arrange a tip off to MI5, followed by "C"'s successful flight and the world's laughter.' In tacit acknowledgement of his own role in the subterfuge, Greene added: 'Since espionage has taken to psychological warfare, it has taken, too, to literature, so that it is just as well to examine carefully any spy memoirs.'[122]

If Greene believed Philby's book was pure propaganda, then his own foreword was a carefully choreographed 'chicken feed' designed to lower Moscow's guard.[123] Yet at the heart of Graham Greene's relationship with Kim Philby there was a complex dichotomy. Greene genuinely admired Philby's conviction and loyalty to the communist cause as well as owing him a debt of comradeship and friendship. He owed him something else too. Greene's moment of true international success can be pinpointed to 1949 just after the publication of *The Heart of the Matter* and the release of *The Third Man*. Both works were inspired by his close friendships with two big characters:

the psychologically flawed Captain Patrick Brodie and the morally certain Kim Philby.

Did Greene feel he partly owed Philby his success? None of this emotional attachment necessarily negated or trumped Greene's fealty to his own country, democracy and former employers, SIS.

While working on *The Third Man*, Greene had taken time out to write to V.S. Pritchett and Elizabeth Bowen, setting out in allegorical form the writer's obligation to the state: 'I met a farmer at lunch the other day who was employing two lunatics; what fine workers they were, he said; and how loyal. But of course they were loyal; they were like the conditional beings of the brave new world. Disloyalty is our privilege.'[124]

Philby's disloyalty was a privilege conferred on him by a free and open society. A communist state like Soviet Russia harshly punished all forms of disloyalty.

Greene's reference to E.M. Forster's quotation about valuing loyalty to a friend above one's country was deliberately taken out of context. Forster was speaking about the importance of friendship in society, but not at the expense of one's love for one's country. He was complaining about the modish trend of friendships being jettisoned in favour of 'causes'; he was not endorsing the idea of letting traitors off the hook just because they were friends.[125] And Greene must have known this. Forster was another of the Cambridge Apostles who toyed with betrayal and had signed the Reform Club nomination papers for both Guy Burgess and Anthony Blunt.[126]

If Greene had really agreed to pen the foreword purely out of loyalty to Philby, why did he demand such a hefty payment for doing so? He told his agent he wanted 150 guineas (£2,500 in today's money) for 800 words, later placating one complaining reader that his foreword was not meant to be taken so seriously, saying: 'I disclaim approval of doing any evil that good may come.'[127]

Here was a glimpse of the 'splinter of ice' in the heart of agent Greene's dealings with commissar Philby, not the altruistic act of friendship it pretended to be. He was, as he said, 'very fond' of him, but he couldn't stop treating Philby as a player in the game, a game that had moved into the Cold War.

Greene's fraternisation with Philby did not fool his old friend Evelyn Waugh, who remarked in 1960: 'I think also he is a secret agent on our side and all his buttering up of Russians is "cover".'[128] Greene and Philby were both professionally trained spies who even in semi-retirement hadn't, or couldn't, quit their trade. Graham Greene remained on the SIS unofficial payroll until his death.[129] In Greene's blue-chipped eyes, Philby was both a friend from the old days and a member of the opposing side in the game. As one of Greene's characters says in *The Human Factor:* 'The player is as important as the game. I wouldn't enjoy the game with a bad player across the table.'[130]

Greene had been drawn to the 'dangerous edge of things' all his life which was why he found the idea of a loyal friendship with a traitor so irresistibly appealing.

After Philby had slipped behind the Iron Curtain, MI6 and MI5 had not forgotten about the traitor.

Throughout all Philby's time in Moscow, MI5 had been carefully monitoring the Philby family correspondence and could see that the defector was struggling with his exile.

Writing to explain his treachery to his sisters Philby said: 'When I took my decision more than 30 years ago you [Patricia] and Hel [Helena] were under teens and therefore could have had only the haziest idea of the early background. Anyway, the answer is quite simple. If only people were not afraid to look at the questions straight. What I was then I still am, and always have been. So there! . . . You will probably have seen various items in the press to the effect that I was being kept under wraps by the authorities. All rubbish: many visits to the Bolshoi, today's trip to Leningrad and our impending December holiday in the Caucuses.'[131]

His sister Helena, who in the early days of MI5's investigation into Philby was being investigated herself as a possible Soviet agent,[132] wrote back bitterly complaining: 'You simply have no idea how shattering events were to all the rest of us emotionally and practically and quite what repercussions there have been in our lives. The children have suffered cruel remarks and so has John [Philby's son] from his workmates . . . I am putting the shutter down and signing off for good.'[133]

Philby's bravado hid a melancholy truth that deep down he missed England, constantly badgering his Moscow handlers for English marmalade, copies of *The Times* and up-to-date cricket scores. Greene also knew that Philby, who despite his claims, was never rewarded with an official military rank with the KGB, had been sidelined because the Russians did not wholly trust him. There was residual speculation in Moscow that he was a treble agent who had never left the employ of the British secret service. Yuri Modin, Philby's KGB handler after the war, didn't believe anyone (British intelligence, the Soviets nor the women he loved) had 'ever managed to pierce the armour' that protected Philby's innermost self.

Greene knew that he, Greene, was Philby's only living trusted link to the old days. Over the years as Greene reviewed the wartime conversations he had shared with Philby during their daily battles with German intelligence, how vivid they must have seemed. Greene replayed them, searching for clues to Philby's political and personal betrayal.

Towards the end of 1975 Graham Greene was in Budapest working with the Hungarian communist filmmaker Laszlo Robert who wanted to interview him about Greene's time in Vietnam.[134] Robert, like Harry Smolka, was a slippery character who had double dealings with the West and Moscow. As soon as Greene reached Budapest he sent a telegram to the Soviet embassy with a message for Kim Philby announcing his presence in the city and suggesting a meeting so the two spies could catch up on old times. Greene appears to have known, perhaps informed by Robert, that Philby was visiting Hungary with his Russian wife Rufina.[135] What exactly transpired next is unclear and Robert later claimed that it was not possible for the two former MI6 officers to meet at such short notice. There is no doubt Philby would have welcomed a reunion with the one Western writer who had loyally supported him during his exile.

The following year, Graham Greene's nephew, the publisher Graham C Greene, son of Hugh, was in Moscow for a book fair where he wrote a letter to Philby asking him to meet for drinks.[136] Philby received the letter but didn't reply until three months later, by which time Graham C Greene was back in Britain. In his reply to G.C.G., Philby expressed an interest in a meeting with his 'respected uncle', adding: 'Incidentally, if you should come here again. I shall always be able to locate you wherever you are.'[137]

A few weeks later Laszlo Robert turned up at Greene's flat in Antibes, south of France, where he lived since the 1960s, with a message from Philby saying the KGB agent wished to pass on his best wishes.[138]

This in turn resulted in Greene sending a draft of his new novel, *The Human Factor*, requesting Philby's views of his portrayal of the motivations of a reluctant double agent who defects to Moscow. There was much characterisation in the book for Philby to enjoy, including this candid self-assessment by one of the British spies: 'Thirty years ago when I was a student I rather fancied myself as a kind of communist. Now..? Who is the traitor . . .? I really believed in internationalism and now I'm fighting an underground war for nationalism.'[139] Thus began a decade-long correspondence between the two men.[140]

Every meticulous detail and coded implication of all these tentative communications was reported, via Rodney Dennys, to Maurice Oldfield who must have had high hopes that it might still be possible to lure Philby from the clutches of the KGB.[141]

In their deepening correspondence there are hints that the two veteran spies, Greene and Philby, were still playing the old game.

In 1985, Philby wrote this letter to Greene, acknowledging for the first time the significance of *The Third Man*:

'My dear Graham, Many belated thanks for *The Tenth Man*. As you suggested it amused me – and a bit more. It occurred to me that if *The Tenth Man* had been filmed and *The Third Man* forgotten, I might have been spared some personal notoriety. I hope there are some more men in your head struggling to get created. They say that the seventh and the 13th are cabalistically significant, but I cannot remember why. If I were a punster (which I am not) I would say that you seem to prefer ordinals to Cardinals.'[142]

The '13th man' is a reference to Saint Anthony, born in Lisbon (a city Greene and Philby knew very well when they worked at MI6) under the name Fernando Martins. He is the patron saint of lost souls, particularly those who have committed mortal sin or lost their faith. He died on 13 June and he is worshiped in the Tredicina, a 13-day novena.[143] Saint Anthony was well known to Greene who refers to a statue of Saint Anthony standing over the altar at his church in Freetown during the war in his 1968 essay Soupsweet Land.[144] Were Philby and Greene secretly communicating about Anthony Blunt (actually the fourth man)?

Philby's hope that Greene would name 'more men' might well have been his wish for Greene's next story to be about Anthony Blunt or even a coded message meant for Blunt himself.

During Philby's Moscow years, following the defections of Burgess and Maclean, Anthony Blunt remained Philby's Soviet contact in London. It was Blunt who sent Philby an engraving shortly after Philby's arrival in Moscow in 1963 with the inscription 'Piranesi's Antonine Column'.[145]

Philby's suggestion that Greene preferred ordinal numbers to cardinal numbers meant he thought the order of the 'men' was

THE END OF THE AFFAIR

more important than how many men there were. In the context of the Cambridge spies, this code is hard to decipher as the sequence in the exposure of the British Soviet agents is a media construct. But in strict chronological terms, Philby was the first of the Cambridge men to be recruited by the Soviets and therefore in Philby's eyes the most important ordinal number.

Rodney Dennys suspected that buried in Philby's complaints about modes of modern living and rants about East/West politics there were hidden messages.[146]

In early 1980, Dennys wrote to Maurice Oldfield's successor Dickie Franks, telling him that there was a chance Philby's letters were 'gambits in the game' of espionage given that they were sanctioned by the KGB. Dennys arranged to meet Franks for lunch at the Garrick Club as he thought it possible Philby was letting MI6 know that the 'KGB doves' were unhappy with the war in Afghanistan and were looking for a solution to the conflict. He told Franks: 'As you know during the war I worked pretty closely with him [Philby] from time to time and got to know him about as well as most people. He had a remarkable flair for strategic deception combining imagination with audacity.'[147]

MI6, however, believed Philby's talk of an Afghan entente was part of a KGB trap that Philby was trying to set with Greene as the bait.[148]

By the early 1980s, the spectre of Philby toying with Greene from behind the Iron Curtain had crept into Greene's dreams.

In January 1980, a few months after Philby's Havana postcard had turned up out of the blue, Greene wrote down one of these dreams: 'Kim Philby came to see me secretly in London. He was not as I remembered him – he was furtive and sharp featured, and I was disappointed. He brought me an essay which he had written for *The Spectator* and I could honestly praise it. He had come from Havana by an English boat and I asked him whether he wasn't afraid of being arrested on the boat – but he gave me vaguely to understand that he was safe now. All the same, when he came to leave he readily accepted my offer to walk in front of him.'[149]

Greene's subconscious also wrestled with betrayal. In the same year he had dreamt of meeting Philby in London, he awoke one morning from a vivid dream in which he had handed over a secret MI6 dossier to the Russian ambassador. He wrote: 'I had no sense of being a traitor – it seemed to me a good thing for both sides that he should read it.'[150]

He didn't know it then, but Philby was about to step out of Greene's dreams into a final reunion between the author and his old friend turned Russian traitor.

Epilogue

Final Curtain

On a late September evening in 1986, just before the Russian winter closed in, a dark brown Chaika Limousine stopped at a nondescript side street close to Pushkin Square in the centre of Moscow.[1] Inside sat a silent Englishman, his head lowered to avoid bumping it on the roof of the car.[2] It was getting late and the car's headlamps half-blinded the one-woman reception committee anxiously waiting to welcome the famed English guest.

Graham Greene climbed out of the limousine and was immediately confronted by Rufina Philby, Kim Philby's fourth and last wife. She led Greene into the dark hallway of the rundown apartment block and they took the lift to the second floor. There, standing in the doorway excitedly waiting to greet them, was Greene's old friend, former boss and latterly Soviet agent living out his quiet retirement in the communist heartlands. The two men hadn't seen each other for 35 years.

'Just don't ask me any questions,' said Philby.[3]

'How's your Russian?' replied Greene.

They hugged, clapping each other on the back.[4]

It was only a few months earlier, in the thawing political climate of Glasnost and the opening up of the Soviet Union, that Greene had finally been given permission to meet Kim Philby in Moscow. He repeated the visit in February the following year, spending hours in long, private conversation about the old days, the Second

World War, the Cold War and the dawning of a new political climate that promised to bring Russia back in from the cold.

Neither Greene nor Philby ever disclosed exactly what the two spies talked about during these secret discussions, nor whether there was an ulterior motive to their meetings after such a long period of silence between them. Afterwards Kim Philby told Rufina: 'He is burdened with doubt as well.'[5] Perhaps Greene's disarming expression of doubt was his way of tempting Philby into indiscretions and ultimately a return journey to the West.

Philby wrote to Greene a few days later: 'While the memory of your visit is still fresh in our minds, I am writing to tell you how much we appreciated it. Rufa said, without any prompting from me, that the three days we spent on and off together were among the happiest in her life. As for myself, I find myself suffering from an acute attack of the esprit d'escalier: so many questions I want you to ask but I didn't, so many things I want to say but I didn't. Well you can't bridge a gap of 35 years in a few hours. Zut Alors!'[6]

There were three further Moscow meetings and much correspondence, but Philby remained loyal to his Russian home, although what he really thought of his political masters we will never know.

Six weeks after their final meeting in 1988 and 25 years after he had defected to the Soviet Union, Philby was dead at 76, the Russians announcing that their most successful and celebrated double agent, a true hero of the Comintern, had died from a heart attack. There were rumours on both sides of the Iron Curtain that Philby had been poisoned, but Rufina Philby said her husband had drunk himself to death.[7]

Kim Philby and Graham Greene became friends while working as intelligence officers for MI6 during the Second World War. The spycraft they had acquired was instinctive and deeply embedded. Greene had used it to significant effect to keep biographers off his scent, while Philby had deployed it in the service of the KGB at the

EPILOGUE

height of the Cold War and well into the Glasnost era. The lifelong adult friendship between the writer Graham Greene and the traitor Kim Philby is one of the most enigmatic relationships of the 20th century. Both men were drawn to communism before the Second World War and it is easy to see how Greene might have become the stand-out figure in an Oxford University 'spy ring' (and there is plenty of evidence that one existed) – after all, Soviet illegals were recruiting from both Cambridge and Oxford.

In his books, Greene continuously wrestled with the twin themes of loyalty and betrayal. He came to see espionage as a moral and psychological condition rather than merely cloak-and-dagger work.[8] Whether he was writing about religion, relationships or espionage, it was always possible to sense the presence of Kim Philby in his novels' characters. In turn Philby, throughout his exile in Russia, wrote to Greene, his only contact with his MI6 days and the modern West, seeking an understanding of the old country he had been forced to leave.

It seems the two men were never able to escape the past. They were fascinated by the inscrutable nature of the other. In their attempts to protect, preserve and enhance their legacies, the past became ever more secret. Greene's last lover, Yvonne Cloetta, said his real secret was 'his passion for secrecy'.[9] Only now, through the discovery of the correspondence and files from the cases they worked on, is it possible to shine a light on the spying lives of these two MI6 officers waging war against the Nazis and making peace with the politics of the Cold War.

Greene was defensive and proud of his service to his country as an MI6 officer but rarely spoke or wrote about it. He strictly observed the holiest tenet of the Secret Intelligence Service, enforced by the Official Secrets Act: an intelligence officer must never talk about their work. He warned one of his biographers to restrict coverage of his wartime record to 'just a few lines' or they would both face prosecution.[10]

*

During those final years, had Graham Greene maintained a pretence of loyalty to Philby in the hope of unlocking his secrets, as Maurice Oldfield's nephew believes? Or was Philby still deceiving his old friend and trying to lure MI6 into one last espionage catastrophe?

Greene may have deserted England and moved to France, but he had never given up on his country. He had little time for Britain's pretensions, its snobbish sense of Imperial destiny or its rigid class system, but he recognised and valued its democracy and sense of justice. In weighing up whether to place Philby's friendship above his loyalty to his country he would have had to calibrate the greater love and duty to his family. Elisabeth Greene and her husband Rodney Dennys, who was more aggrieved[11] by Philby's treachery than Greene was, remained his closest family throughout his life.[12] But he was also close to his brothers Hugh and Raymond who both worked for the security and intelligence agencies protecting Britain during the war.[13] They were all, just like him, life-long 'friends of the firm', sharing an unwritten oath of allegiance to the nation's security. And Greene believed the trade they practised was an 'honourable one.'

A betrayal of his country would have amounted to a betrayal of his sister, to whom he dedicated his best book about Britain's intelligence services, *The Human Factor*, and his much-loved brother-in-law, as well as all the agents he had worked so desperately hard to protect during the war. He dedicated much of his post-war life to standing up for victims of political oppression of all forms.

In the novel *The Quiet American*, Vietminh organiser Mr. Heng tells British journalist Thomas Fowler: 'Sooner or later one has to take sides.'[14] When Holly Martins faces the dilemma of choosing between betraying his friend Harry Lime's malign view of the world or making a stand for democratic values of the West he emphatically chooses the latter.

In April 1978, Kim Philby wrote to Greene thanking him for sending an early manuscript of *The Human Factor*, about an MI5

EPILOGUE

officer who defects to Moscow. The book had been delayed by a decade because Greene did not want readers to automatically think his principal character, Maurice Castle, was Philby. Nevertheless, there were aspects of life in Moscow that Greene wished Philby to check for accuracy. Philby took umbrage at Greene's description of the chilly reception and spartan living conditions that confronted Castle, arguing that this was 'very un-Russian' as he himself enjoyed excellent hospitality and comfort, to the point that for the first time in his life he told Greene that he had acquired a shoehorn. 'Oh, everyone is very kind. They have given me a sort of job. They are grateful to me.'[15]

It would have been of great service to Philby and his KGB overseers if Greene had agreed to alter his text, softening the Soviet treatment of a valued defector from the West. Such a revision would have deepened Philby's trust and respect for the writer. It would also have curried favour with the KGB and promoted Greene's position of influence as a friend of SIS with hooks into Moscow.

Always the writer first and spy second, Greene remained loyal to his text, conceding only, at Philby's request, that Maurice Castle's Moscow apartment was heated by modern radiators rather than coal fires.

As Greene approached the last days of his life, he was besieged by three biographers: Norman Sherry, with whom he was closely cooperating, and Anthony Mockler and Michael Shelden, both of whom he had kept at arm's length. In the case of Mockler, Greene was so incensed by his intrusive attempts to contact his family that his personal address book refers to him as the 'bastard' Mockler.[16] Greene was also facing increasingly desperate requests from Sherry, who sensed his window for his research was rapidly closing. Sherry, who was told he couldn't visit Greene in Switzerland because the author was too ill, wrote to Greene saying he believed Greene had more to tell about his time in Vienna, when he had been busy conducting his research for *The Third Man*, and what actually lay behind the story of 'a man raised from the dead'.[17]

Acknowledging the urgency of Sherry's eleventh-hour enquiries, Greene wrote back saying: 'I regret more and more putting you off coming here.'[18]

In his final correspondence with Sherry, Greene was still troubled by his service history with MI6, including his time as a station head in Sierra Leone: 'there are all sorts of explanations to give you of the situation in Sierra Leone and also anecdotes that spring to mind.'[19] Greene was particularly worried that Sherry had failed to understand the strategic importance of Freetown during 1942/43 when the Mediterranean was cut off and Vichy forces threatened to invade Sierra Leone.[20] Sherry was more concerned that Greene should have a final chance to correct Kim Philby's three-page, deeply personal opinion of Greene during their time together working as MI6 spies and Philby's claim that the results of Greene's work in Sierra Leone were 'meagre.'[21]

Greene embraced the opportunity of putting the record straight while also remaining loyal to Philby: 'Philby's assessment of my work in Freetown is not a bit bleak to my mind. He's defending me rather than criticising. I didn't at that time know that he was my boss in London. One interrogation I had to make of a prisoner disgusted me so much I never made another . . . It was a relief to join Kim and his outfit when I returned.'[22]

Sherry had also recently been granted access to the letters Greene had written to his lover Catherine Walston, which contained new material about how Greene had come up with the idea of *The Third Man*. It gave Sherry the chance to question Greene one final time about why he had stubbornly stood by a traitor who had been responsible for the deaths of many brave agents.

Sherry later recalled that, during the thousands of hours of questioning Greene about his life, loves and misdemeanours, the writer had only ever once lost his temper.

Greene's loss of composure was prompted by Sherry's final question: 'You'd think that despite the loyalties we bear to friends and

EPILOGUE

lovers, there would come a time when the act committed is too great to be forgiven or forgotten?'

Greene, red with rage, interrupted Sherry in mid-flow: 'You do not know him. And cannot judge.'[23]

On 26 January 1991, John Cairncross wrote a final letter to his old friend. There was something he had to get off his chest. He told Greene he had reluctantly come to the conclusion there was indeed a 'fifth man' but it wasn't him. He wrote that it was very likely that the 'fifth man' was Roger Hollis.[24] This too must have deeply troubled Greene who believed Hollis to be a loyal intelligence officer who had been deliberately smeared by Philby.

Amanda Saunders, Greene's niece who was caring for the author in Switzerland during his last days, had spoken to her uncle about Sherry's enquiries. She has left a prominent note in the Greene archive in Boston: 'These two letters worried Graham a lot. He said, "Norman had it all wrong". He asked me to bring them to him in Switzerland. The day before he died he tried to tell me what it was but he was unable to speak. I asked him if he would like to talk about them the next day – he answered a very definite yes. When I returned the next day he was in a coma.'[25]

Sherry believed he knew what was troubling Greene, and wondered, as had Moscow, whether Philby had been working for SIS all along and therefore played the ultimate betrayal on Greene, secretly working for British intelligence while setting up Greene as the innocent dupe one more time.[26]

Greene is reported to have been so disturbed by this notion that he spent his last days re-reading all his correspondence with Philby.[27] On his bedside table lay Sherry's last letter to Greene setting out Philby's personal and professional views of Greene.[28]

Graham Greene died on 3 April 1991 at La Providence Hospital in Vevey, near Lake Geneva in Switzerland. He was 86 years old, and his cause of death was given as leukaemia. His final act: searching for clues as to where his friend's true loyalties lay.

Appendix

The Numbered Men

Graham Greene's *The Third Man* spawned the mythology of a tight-knit group of five Cambridge University friends[1] who all spied for the Soviet Union. It would turn out to be a rather superficial classification that helpfully served the needs of both British intelligence and the Kremlin as it gave the impression there were only ever five traitors.

MI6 and MI5 wanted the world, and particularly the USA, to believe the penetration of the British secret service was contained and limited. Conversely it mattered to the KGB that the British would be so obsessed with the five members of the 'Cambridge group' that they stopped looking for any more of their spies. Yet there were many more Cambridge agents working for the Russians and many more Soviet spies who had not attended Cambridge University.

The Third Man was released in 1949 and referred to a mysterious missing third witness to the death of a dangerous Cold War racketeer living in Vienna called Harry Lime. 1949 also marks the year from which MI6 decided to stop disclosing secrets about its official history.[2] It had always seemed an arbitrary date, but seen in the context of *The Third Man*, it makes perfect sense. Everything after 1949 is simply too difficult and damaging to explain.[3] Two years later, British intelligence had begun the hunt for a real spy, dubbed 'the third man' by the media and suspected of being the key accomplice who had tipped off the two Cambridge spies Guy Burgess and Donald Maclean, prompting their flight from London to Moscow.

Greene's Harry Lime and MI6's hunted spy were the same man – the most famous Cold War warrior of them all, Harry 'Kim' Philby. Without Philby there would have been no *Tinker Tailor Soldier Spy*,

APPENDIX

no Smiley, no Bill Hayden and no Karla. And perhaps no Harry Palmer, the cockney antidote to the public school Cambridge spy.

Before the film's release, there had been no attempt to number Soviet agents spying against Britain. Greene's popular film noir, which premiered in 1949 in the UK and 1950 in America, gifted the world's media an irresistible shorthand for numbering and naming spies who they knew extraordinarily little about.

In 1955, Harold Macmillan, then Foreign Secretary, was forced to deny the very existence of a 'Third Man', telling Parliament: 'I have no reason to conclude that Mr. Philby has at any time betrayed the interests of this country, or to identify him with the so-called "third man", if, indeed, there was one.'[4] It was a dangerous misjudgement that temporarily damaged Macmillan's political career, while serving as testimony to the steely spycraft of one of the world's most successful traitors.

What Macmillan does not appear to have been told is that MI6 had been hunting three British Soviet agents at least two years before Burgess and Maclean broke cover. An MI6 spy inside the Soviet embassy had tipped off MI6 about a leak from the Foreign Office that triggered an investigation culminating in a hunt for a first, second and third man.

After Philby was dubbed the Third Man it was inevitable that the next outed spies would follow in numerical sequence. The journalist Andrew Boyle proudly wrote to Graham Greene in 1979, telling him he was about to name the fourth and fifth spies: 'I wouldn't have persevered with the book if I'd failed to discover new evidence. I was lucky. I know now who the fourth and fifth men were in the case.'[5] Greene wrote back on 6 March 1979, ignoring Boyle's fantastic revelation and testily declaring, 'frankly I'd rather you left me out of your book entirely.'

The fourth man was Anthony Blunt, who Greene knew as a family friend of Catherine Walston, the woman with whom he became destructively involved after the war.[6] Boyle's fifth man was the nuclear scientist Wilfrid Mann,[7] who didn't attend Cambridge and so had no academic connection to the Cambridge spies, although he was close to Philby and Burgess in Washington.[8]

The real fifth man would turn out to be John Cairncross, although he was only the fifth man in the sense he was the fifth spy to study at Cambridge. Cairncross, the only non-public school member, maintained until the day he died that he had never been part of the Cambridge Group.

Yet Britain's security and intelligence services insisted he was an integral part of the homogeneous collection of spies of whom they now had the measure. Greene was a loyal friend to both Philby and Cairncross from their time working together as MI6 officers in the Second World War and throughout their lives as outed traitors.

Graham Greene thought the numbering of the Cambridge spies unhelpful, warning Cairncross that it would be only a matter of time before the media produced a Sixth Man. But the intelligence establishment ensured they never did, although of course there were plenty of candidates: Peter Astbury, Michael Straight and Leo Long all worked for the Russians and were members of Cambridge University's Apostles. In 1989 Robert Cecil, a close assistant to the head of MI6 during the war, wrote to Greene with evidence that the Cambridge Five was a myth as there were many other 'sleeper agents' at Cambridge who became agents of influence.[9]

Kim Philby was never comfortable with his designated number. For one thing he knew he was really The First Man: the first of the Cambridge recruits who had been head-hunted and schooled by the Soviet agents Arnold Deutsch and Teodor Maly. It was Philby who, after his return from Vienna in 1934, brought into the fold Guy Burgess and Donald Maclean.

In 1963, he followed Burgess and Maclean to Moscow. Twenty-two years after his defection, Philby decided to write to Graham Greene to complain, partly out of vanity, that the sequencing did not do him justice and had brought him unwanted media attention, stating that he hoped there were 'more men in your head struggling to get created'. The coded suggestion in Philby's letter was clear – the numbering system had served its purpose by distracting everybody from the many other Russian agents who had worked against Britain during and after the Second World War.

In 1987, Philby appeared on Soviet television as part of a tribute to Graham Greene. Midway through his appearance he intriguingly and mischievously suggested that there was more to Greene's *The Third Man* than the press had appreciated.[10] The next year Philby was dead, given a state funeral in Moscow. Greene was to follow fewer than three years later. During his final years, the author was assailed by questions about Kim Philby and *The Third Man*.

Just weeks before Greene died, Cairncross had written to him supporting the claim that the real fifth man was Roger Hollis, the head of MI5 who was educated at Oxford with Graham Greene and therefore excluded from membership of 'the Group'.[11] Another former SIS man, Ronnie Challoner, the consul at the British embassy in Nice, became close to both Greene (he ended up buying Greene's apartment in Antibes) and Cairncross. Challoner strongly believed that Cairncross had been fitted up as the fifth man and that Philby could not be 'the third man' because he was a treble agent who had switched sides and was really working for the British.[12] The truth was Greene knew much more about Philby than he let on and took issue with the error-strewn media coverage around the mythology of the Cambridge Five he had helped to create, remarking in 1990: 'I was amused by the exchanges of authors of various books about the secret service who had no experience of the secret service.'[13] Greene faithfully obeyed the MI6 omerta of never disclosing the secrets of the service to the outside world. He took everything he knew to the grave, leaving behind a body of work woven with clues.

Acknowledgements

I owe a huge debt of gratitude to Richard Greene, Graham Greene's brilliant biographer, for his time, support and sage advice. It takes a special kind of academic to be so generous to another writer trespassing on their specialist field. Charlotte Philby offered invaluable encouragement, and Michael Shelden pointed me in the direction of sources. Piers Blofeld was the first to see the literary potential in the 'odd couple', the enigmatic relationship between Greene and Philby and without Piers this book could not have been written. With special thanks to Patrick Insole who designed the book's cover. The editorial guiding hand of Martin Redfern at Headline helped shape the book and kept the project on track. Martin was assisted by Raiyah Butt and Oliver Holden-Rea. Special thanks to the Graham Greene Estate for permission to quote from Greene's titles.

Along the way, I have benefited from the extraordinary professional help of experts working in the Greene and Philby archives in the UK and the US. Among the best were Faye McLeod, Archivist and Records Manager Balliol College Library; and Benjamin Gross (John Merritt Associate Director for Research Services), Meghan Hoefling and Courtney Welu, all of the Harry Ransom Center, The University of Texas at Austin.

I wish to acknowledge the generous cooperation of the Reform Club where Graham Greene and two of the Cambridge spies were members. Special thanks to Morris Lockwood (Chair of Cryptos),

ACKNOWLEDGEMENTS

Peter Hill, editor of the Reform magazine, and club librarian Simon Blundell.

Equally helpful were Ted Jackson, the Manuscripts Archivist at Georgetown University and Andrew Isidoro of the John J. Burns Library at Boston College.

I also wish to acknowledge early assistance from Mark Dunton of the National Archives, Kew, and Amanda Landis and Ashley Bryan from the Special Access and FOIA Program (RF) of the US National Archives and Records Administration.

Finally, special thanks for the contributions and support of Linda King, Jonathan Ames, Paul Ferris, Marisa Galiza Filipe, Anthony Glees, Richard Kerbaj, Montasser AlDe'emeh, Rob Colson, Lee Wright and Doc Kirby.

Bibliography

Aldrich, Richard J. & Cormac, Rory, *The Black Door*, William Collins (2016)
Allain, Marie-Francoise, *The Other Man*, The Bodley Head (1983)
Andrew, Christopher, *The Spy Who Came in from the Circus*, Biteback (2024)
Andrew, Christopher, *Secret Service: The Making of the British Intelligence Community*, Viking (1986)
Andrew, Christopher, *The Defence of the Realm: The Authorized History of MI5*, Penguin (2009)
Andrew, C, Gordievsky, Oleg, *K.G.B: The Inside Story*, Hodder & Stoughton (1990)
Andrew, C, Mitrokhin, Vasili, *The Mitrokhin Archive: The KGB in Europe and the West*, Penguin (2000)
Arnold-Baker, Charles, *For He is an Englishman*, Jeremy Mills (2007)
Bauer, Kurt, *Der Februar-Aufstand 1934: Fakten und Mythen* [*The February Uprising 1934: Facts and Myths*] (in German), Vienna: Böhlau Verlag (2018)
Beer, Siegfried, 'Film in context: The Third Man', *History Today*, May 2001
Beevor, Antony, *D-Day: The Battle for Normandy*, Viking (2009)
Benton, Kenneth, The IOS years Madrid 1941–43, *Contemporary Journal of History*, July 1995
Birstein, Vadim J. Smersh, *Stalin's Secret Weapon*, Biteback (2013)
Bower, Tom, *The Perfect English Spy*, William Heinemann (1995)
Boyle, A., *The Climate of Treason: Five Who Spied For Russia*, Hutchinson (1979)
Borovik, Genrikh, *The Philby Files*, Little, Brown (1994)
Bristow, Desmond, *Game of Moles*, Little, Brown (1993)
Bulloch, John, *Akin to Treason*, Arthur Barker (1966)
Bullock, Alan, *Hitler and Stalin: Parallel Lives*, Harper Collins (1991)
Cairncross, John, *The Enigma Spy*, Century (1997)
Calder, Walton, *Spies: The epic intelligence war between East and West*, Abacus (2013)
Carter, Miranda, *Anthony Blunt: His Lives*, Macmillan (2001)

BIBLIOGRAPHY

Cave Brown, Anthony, *Treason in the Blood: H. St John Philby, Kim Philby and the Spy Case of the Century*, Houghton Mifflin (1994)
Cave Brown, A, *Bodyguard of Lies*, Fletcher & Son (1976)
Churchill, Winston S., *The Second World War* Vol VI, Cassell (1949)
Cloetta, Yvonne, *In Search of a Beginning: My Life with Graham Greene*, Bloomsbury (2004)
Cockburn, Claud, Britain's Spy Serial, *New York Times* (1979)
Cookridge, E. H., *Set Europe Ablaze*, Arthur Barker (1966)
Cookridge, E. H., *The Third Man: The Truth About Kim Philby Double Agent*, Arthur Barker (1968)
Corera, Gordon, *The Art of Betrayal: Life and Death in the British Secret Service*, Pegasus (2011)
Costello, John, *Mask of Treachery: Spies Lies Buggery & Betrayal* (The first documented dossier on Anthony Blunt's Cambridge Spy Ring), William Morrow (1988)
Costello, John, and Tsarev, Oleg, *Deadly Illusions: The KGB Orlov Dossier Reveals Stalin's Master Spy*, Century (1993)
Davenport-Hines, Richard, *Enemies Within*, William Collins (2018)
Davies, Philip, *MI6 and the Machinery of Spying*, Routledge (2004)
Day, Peter, *Bedbug: Klop Ustinov: Britain's Most Ingenious Spy*, Biteback (2015)
Drazin, Charles, *In Search of the Third Man*, Methuen Publishing (1999)
Elliott, Nicholas, *Never Judge a Man by His Umbrella*, Michael Russell Publishing (1991)
Farago, Ladislas, *The Game of Foxes*, Hodder and Stoughton (1971)
Folly, Martin, Roberts, Geoffrey, and Rzheshevsky, Oleg, *Churchill and Stalin: Comrades-in-Arms during the Second World War*, Pen and Sword (2019)
Foot, M.R.D., *SOE in the Low Countries*, St Ermin's (2001)
Foot, M.R.D., and Langley J.M., *MI9: Escape and Evasion 1939–1945*, The Bodley Head (1979)
Fry, Helen, *Women in Intelligence*, Yale University Press (2024)
Fry, Helen, *Spymaster: The Man Who Saved MI6*, Yale University Press (2021)
Garton Ash, Timothy, 'Orwell's List', New York Review of Books (2003)
Gerth, Mathew, British McCarthyism: The Anti-Communist Politics of Lord Vansittart and Sir Waldron Smithers, The Journal of the History Association, Volume 107, Issue 378, December 2022, pages 927–948
Gilbert, Martin, *The Second World War: A Complete History*, Weidenfeld & Nicolson (1989)
Gorodetsky, Gabriel, *The Maisky Diaries*, Yale University (2015)
Greene, Richard, *Graham Greene: A Life in Letters*, Little, Brown (2007)
Greene, Richard, *Russian Roulette*, Little, Brown (2020)

Hanning, James, *Love and Deception: Philby in Beirut*, Corsair (2021)
Harrison, Edward, *The Young Kim Philby*, Liverpool University Press (2012)
Hinsely, F.H., Simkins, CAG., *British Intelligence in the Second World War Vol 4*, HMSO Publications Centre (1990)
Holt, Thaddeus, *The Deceivers*, Scribner (2004)
Honigmann, Barbara, *Ein Kapitel aus meinem Leben*, Carl Hanser Verlag (2004)
Hull, Christopher, *Our Man in Havana: The Story behind Graham Greene's Cold War Spy Novel*, Pegasus (2019)
Jeffrey, Keith, *MI6: The History of the Secret Intelligence Service 1909–1949*, Bloomsbury (2010)
Kerbaj, Richard, *The Five Eyes: The Untold Story of the International Spy Network*, Blink (2022)
Knightley, Phillip, *Philby: KGB Masterspy*, Andre Deutsch (1988)
Le Carre, John, *The Pigeon Tunnel: Stories from My Life*, Penguin (2022)
Lewis, Jeremy, *Shades of Greene*, Jonathan Cape (2010)
Lownie, Andrew, *Stalin's Englishman: The Lives of Guy Burgess*, Hodder & Stoughton (2015)
Lunn, Bernard, *Memoirs of Peter Lunn*, privately published.
Modin, Yuri, *My Five Cambridge Friends*, Headline (1994)
Macintyre, Ben, *A Spy Among Friends*, Bloomsbury (2014)
Meyer, Michael, Sherman, William, and Deeds, Susan, *The Course of Mexican History*, 9th edition, Oxford University Press (2010)
Milne, Tim, *Kim Philby: A Story of Friendship and Betrayal*, Biteback (2014)
Mockler, Anthony, *Three Lives, Novelist! Explorer! Spy!*, Hunter Mackay (2003)
Montagu, Elizabeth, *Honourable Rebel: The Memoirs of Elizabeth Montagu*, Montagu Ventures (2003)
Montefiore, Simon Sebag, *Stalin: The Court of the Red Tsar*, Vintage (2003)
Muggeridge, Malcolm, *Chronicles of Wasted Time*, HarperCollins (1972)
Muggeridge, Malcolm, *Like It Was: The Diaries of Malcolm Muggeridge*, HarperCollins (1981)
O'Sullivan, Donal, *Dealing with the Devil: Anglo-Soviet Intelligence Cooperation During the Second World War*, Peter Lang (2010)
Payne Best, S., *The Venlo Incident*, Skyhorse (2016)
Pearce, Martin, *Spymaster: The Life of Britain's Most Decorated Cold War Spy and Head of MI6, Sir Maurice Oldfield*, Bantam (2016)
Penrose, Barrie, and Freeman, Simon, *Conspiracy of Silence: The Secret Life of Anthony Blunt*, Grafton Books (1986)
Philby, Charlotte, *Edith and Kim*, The Borough Press (2022)
Philby, Kim, *My Silent War*, MacGibbon and Kee (1968)
Philby, Rufina, *The Private Life of Kim Philby: The Moscow Years*, St Ermin's Press (2003)

BIBLIOGRAPHY

Pincher, Chapman, *Their Trade is Treachery*, Sidgwick & Jackson (1981)
Pincher, Chapman, *Too Secret, Too Long*, Sidgwick & Jackson (1984)
Poretsky, Elisabeth K, *Our Own People: A Memoir of Ignace Reiss and His Friends*, Michigan Press (1970)
Purvis, Stewart, Hulbert, Jeff, *Guy Burgess: The Spy Who Knew Everyone*, Biteback (2016)
Rose, Kenneth, *Who Loses, Who Wins: The Journals Of Kenneth Rose, Vol II 1979–2014* by Kenneth Rose and edited by D R Thorpe, Weidenfeld & Nicolson (2019)
Shelden, Michael, *The Enemy Within: The Biography of Graham Greene*, Random House (1995)
Sherry, Norman, *The Life of Graham Greene Vols 1, 2 and 3* (1989, 1994, 2004)
Solomon, Flora, *Baku to Baker Street*, HarperCollins (1984)
Stafford, David, *Spies Beneath Berlin*, John Murray (2002)
Stafford, David, *Britain and the European Resistance, 1940–1945: A Survey of the Special Operations Executive*, Macmillan (1980)
Stanton Evans, M & Romerstein, Herbert, *Stalin's Secret Agents: The Subversion of the Roosevelt Government*, Threshold (2012)
Sudoplatov, Pavel and Sudoplatov, Anatoli, with Schechter, Jerrold L, and Schechter, Leona, *Special Tasks*, Little, Brown (1994)
Tarrant, V.E., *The Orchestra: Arms and Armour* (1995)
Tokaev, Gregory A, *Stalin Means War*, Weidenfeld & Nicholson (1951)
Trepper, Leopold, *The Great Game*, Michael Joseph (1997)
Trevor-Roper, Hugh, *The Philby Affair*, William Kimber (1968)
Trevor-Roper, Hugh, edited by Edward Harrison, *The Secret World: Behind the Curtain of British Intelligence in World War II and the Cold War*, I.B. Tauris (2014)
Verkaik, Robert, *Posh Boys*, Oneworld (2018)
Walker, Shaun, *The Illegals: Russia's Most Audacious Spies and the Plot to Infiltrate the West*, Profile (2025)
Wapshott, Nicholas, *The Man Between: A Biography of Carol Reed*, Chatto and Windus (1990)
West, Nigel, *Cold War Spymaster: The Legacy of Guy Liddell, Deputy Director of MI5*, Pen and Sword (2018)
West, Nigel, *The Circus: MI5 Operations 1945–1972*, Stein and Day (1984)
West, N, *The Friends: Britain's Post-War Secret Service Intelligence Operations*, Weidenfeld & Nicholson (1988)
West, N, *Churchill's Spy Files. MI5's Top-Secret Wartime Reports*, The History Press (2018)
West, N, Tsarev, Oleg, *Triplex: Secrets from the Cambridge Spies*, Yale (2009)
West, N, Tsarev, O, *The Crown Jewels: The British Secrets at the Heart of the KGB Archives*, HarperCollins (1998)

West, W.J., *The Quest for Graham Greene*, Weidenfeld & Nicholson (1997)
West, Nigel, *The Guy Liddell Diaries Vol II: 1942–45*, Routledge (2005)
Wright, Peter, *Spycatcher*, William Heinemann (1987)

Various works of Greene, Graham:
The Man Within, Heinemann (1929)
Stamboul Train, Heinemann (1932)
It's a Battlefield, Heinemann (1934)
England Made Me (also published as *The Shipwrecked*), Heinemann (1935)
A Gun for Sale (also published as *This Gun for Hire*), Heinemann, (1936)
Brighton Rock, Heinemann, (1938)
The Confidential Agent, Heinemann (1939)
The Power and the Glory (also published as *The Labyrinthine Ways*), Heinemann, (1940)
The Ministry of Fear, Heinemann (1943)
The Heart of the Matter, Heinemann (1948)
The Third Man (novella, as a basis for the screenplay), Heinemann (1949)
The End of the Affair, Heinemann (1951)
The Quiet American, Heinemann (1955)
Loser Takes All, Heinemann (1955)
Our Man in Havana, Heinemann (1958)
A Burnt-Out Case, Heinemann (1960)
The Comedians, The Bodley Head (1966)
Travels with My Aunt, The Bodley Head (1969)
The Honorary Consul, The Bodley Head (1973)
The Human Factor, The Bodley Head (1978)
Doctor Fischer of Geneva or The Bomb Party, The Bodley Head (1980)
Monsignor Quixote, The Bodley Head (1982)
The Tenth Man, The Bodley Head and Anthony Blond (1985)
The Captain and the Enemy, Reindhart Books (1988)

Short stories by Greene, Graham:
'Alas, Poor Maling' (1940)
'Men at Work' (1940)
'The Basement Room' (1936), film adaptation named *The Fallen Idol* (1948)
'Nobody to Blame' (1944)
'The Hint of an Explanation' (1948)
No Man's Land (1949), published as a paperback by Hesperus Press (2005)
'The Stranger's Hand' (1950), (Verdant SA 1993)

Poetry by Greene, Graham:
Babbling April, Basil Blackwell (1925)

BIBLIOGRAPHY

Memoirs by Greene, Graham:
A Sort of Life, The Bodley Head (1971)
Ways of Escape, The Bodley Head (1980)
A World of My Own: A Dream Diary, Reindhart Books (1992)
Greene, G., and John R. MacArthur, *Graham Greene: The Last Interview: And Other Conversations*, Melville House Publishing (2019)

Travel books by Greene, Graham:
Journey Without Maps, Heinemann (1936)
The Lawless Roads (published as *Another Mexico* in the United States), Longmans (1939)
In Search of a Character: Two African Journals, The Bodley Head (1961)
'The Soupsweet Land', *Vintage Greene: Collected Essays*, Vintage Classics (1999)

Essays and non-fiction by Greene, Graham:
Why Do I Write? An Exchange of Views between Elizabeth Bowen, Graham Greene and V.S. Pritchett, Percival Marhsall (1948)
The Lost Childhood and Other Essays, Eyre & Spottiswoode (1951)
The Spy's Bedside Book (ed. with Hugh Greene) Rupert Hart-Davis (1957)
The Virtue of Disloyalty, The Bodley Head (1972)
Yours, etc.: Letters to the Press, Reinhardt Books (1989)
Reflections (ed. by Judith Adamson), Reinhardt Books (1990)

Articles
Stage And Screen: The Cinema, *Spectator*, 3 January 1936
In Room 51, A Third Man entertainment on security, *Sunday Times*, (1967)
The Spy's Role, *Collected Essays* (1969) first published in the *Sunday Times* (1967)
Graham Greene Birthplace Trust
McKay, C.G., Intelligence and National Security, The Krämer Case: A Study in Three Dimensions, 1989.
Riegler, Thomas, 'The Spy Story Behind The Third Man', Journal of Austrian-American History (2020), Volume 4, Issue 1–2.
Reynolds, David, & Pechatnov, Vladimir, The Kremlin Letters, Yale University, 2018.
Rosenbaum, Ron, Kim Philby and the Age of Paranoia, *New York Times* Magazine, 10 July 1994
Sheehan, Edward (US Press Attaché in Beirut), The Rise and Fall of a Soviet Agent, *Saturday Evening Post*, 15 February 1964

Notes

Epigraph
1. Sherry, Norman, *The Life of Graham Greene, Vol 2 1939–1955*. Front epigraph.
2. Philby, Kim, *My Silent War*, xxix.

Introduction
1. Sherry, Norman, *The Life of Graham Greene: Vol 2 1939–1955*, p.182; Milne, Tim, *Kim Philby: The Unknown Story of the KGB's Masterspy*, Biteback (2014), p.139; https://www.24land.pt/uncategorized/graham-greene-contra-espionagem-e-portugal/
2. A remark made by Maria Milne, wife of Tim Milne, after Burgess and Maclean's defection in 1951, KV-2-4733, p.24.
3. Philby, Kim, *My Silent War*, p.79; Graham Greene Papers, Burns Library, Boston College, Box 71 23–25, p.23.
4. Milne, pp.63, 75, 83.
5. Philby, K, *My Silent War*, p.xiix–xx (Graham Greene's foreword)
6. Milne, pp.63, 75, 83.
7. Milne, p.139; The Graham Greene Papers, Burns Library, Boston College, Box 72 1–6, pp.41–42.
8. Sherry, N, Vol 2, p.182; Philby letter to Sherry 1978, The Graham Greene Papers, Burns Library, Boston College, Box 72, Folders 1–6, pp.41–42.
9. Greene's letter to the *Sunday Times* 1967, The Graham Greene Papers, Burns Library, Boston College, Box 71 23–25, p.6.
10. Philby, K, *My Silent War*, p.xiix–xx; Greene, G, *Collected Essays*, Vintage Greene, p.313; Greene's letter clarifying name of pub after a reader's enquiry, The Graham Greene Papers, Burns Library, Boston College, Box 71 23–25.
11. The Graham Greene Papers, Burns Library, Boston College, Box 71, Folders 23–25, p.23.
12. Milne, p.139.
13. Milne, p.139.
14. The Graham Greene Papers, Burns Library, Boston College, Box 71 23–25, p.23; Box 72 1–6, pp.41–42.
15. Greene, Richard, *Russian Roulette*, Little Brown (2020), p.155.
16. Sherry, N, Vol 2, p.182; Philby letter to Sherry 1978, The Graham Greene Papers, Burns Library, Boston College, Box 72 1–6, pp.41–42.
17. Sherry, N, Vol 2, p.183.
18. Philby's statement to Nicholas Elliott (1963), KV-2-4737(2), pp.61,164.

NOTES

19. West, Nigel, *The Crown Jewels*, pp.329–331.
20. Penrose and Freeman, *Conspiracy of Silence,* Trevor-Roper interview 1985 with Barrie Penrose, Simon Freeman, p.286.
21. Allain, Marie-Francoise, *The Other Man*, p.46.
22. Sherry, N, Vol 2, p.184.
23. Inner Temple Library Newsletter, Issue 17 July 2009; *The Times* Obituary 10.6.2009.
24. Sherry, N, Vol 2, p.177.
25. Philby said of his time with Greene at Section V: 'Of course I couldn't talk to him as a Communist but I did talk to him as a man with left-wing views and he was a Catholic, but at once there was human contact between us.' Philby, Rufina, *The Private Life of Kim Philby*, p.174.
26. West, N, *The Crown Jewels*, p.219.
27. Greene, R, *Russian Roulette*, p.155; Tim Milne's name is redacted in Philby's confession to Nicholas Elliott January 1963, KV-2-4737 pp.155–175.
28. Greene, G, Foreword to *My Silent War* by Kim Philby.

Chapter 1

1. Greene, G, *A Sort of Life*, p.7.
2. Greene, G, *A Sort of Life*, p.5.
3. Greene, G, *A Sort of Life*, p.48.
4. Ibid.
5. Lewis, Jeremy, *Shades of Greene*, p.41.
6. Greene, G, *A Sort of Life* pp.36–37.
7. Allain, Marie-Francoise, p.37, and Greene's *Collected Essays*.
8. Greene, R. *Russian Roulette*, p.8.
9. Greene, G, *A Sort of Life*, p.11.
10. Greene, G, *A Sort of Life*, p.19.
11. Greene, G, *A Sort of Life*, p.65.
12. Greene, G, *A Sort of Life*, pp.83–84.
13. Greene, G, *A Sort of Life*, p.34.
14. Reynolds, E H, *The impact of epilepsy on Graham Greene*.
15. Greene, G, *A Sort of Life*, p.32; Greene, R, p.11.
16. Allain, Marie-Francoise, p.33.
17. Greene, G, *A Sort of Life*, p.55.
18. Greene, G, *The Lost Childhood*, p.19.
19. In his adult years Greene was still affected by the book and when it was republished in 1960, he wrote the foreword.
20. Greene, G, *A Sort of Life*, p.61.
21. Greene, R, *Russian Roulette*, p.14.
22. Greene, G, *A Sort of Life*, p.61.
23. Greene, G, *A Sort of Life*, p.60.
24. Greene, G, *A Sort of Life*, p.62.
25. Greene, R, *Russian Roulette*, p.14.
26. Greene, G, *A Sort of Life*, p.61.
27. https://evelynwaughsociety.org/2024/waugh-greene-the-odd-couple/
28. Greene, G, *A Sort of Life*, p.31.
29. Greene, G, *A Sort of Life*, p.31.
30. Sherry, N, Vol 1, p.155.
31. Greene, G, *A Sort of Life*, p.31.
32. Ibid.

33 Greene, G, *A Sort of Life*, p.103.
34 Sherry, Norman, *Vol 2, The Life of Graham Greene*; Shelden, Michael, *The Enemy Within: The Biography of Graham Greene*; Greene, R, *Russian Roulette*, p.32.
35 Ibid.
36 Greene's next effort, *The Name of Action* (1930), a political novel drawing on Greene's time in Germany featuring a wealthy Englishman involved in a communist plot to overthrow the German government, was a flop. *Rumour at Nightfall* (1932), a historical novel set in 19th-century Spain that also concerned betrayal, sold even fewer copies.
37 https://erenow.org/biographies/a-preface-to-greene/2.php
38 Greene, R, *Russian Roulette*, p.67.
39 Greene, G, *A Sort of Life*, p.62.
40 Greene, G, *A Sort of Life*, p.63.
41 Greene, G, *The Lost Childhood*, p.19.

Chapter 2

1 https://dangerousminds.net/comments/the_forgotten_mole_men_of_viennas_sewers
2 West, Nigel, *The Friends: Britain's Post-War Secret Service Intelligence Operations*; Davenport-Hines, Richard, *Enemies Within*, p.206; Milne, Tim, *Kim Philby*, p.14; Harrison, Edward, *The Young Philby*, p.15.
3 MI5 interview with Philby 14.6.51, KV-2-4723 (2), p.14.
4 KV-2-4737, p.143.
5 KV-2-4742 (2), p.3; Sheehan, E.
6 Milne, Tim, *Kim Philby: A Story of Friendship and Betrayal*, p.182.
7 Harrison, Edward, *The Young Kim Philby*. p.21.
8 Her Austrian name was Litzi but after marrying Philby she used Lizy. Milne, T, p.38.
9 KV-2-4723 (1)
10 https://www.theguardian.com/uk/2004/nov/07/books.world
11 Rimington, Stella, foreword to *A Spy's Bedside Book*, by Graham Greene and Hugh Greene, p.13.
12 Harrison, Edward, *The Young Kim Philby*, p.10.
13 Harrison, p.27.
14 Philby graduated with a second class degree in History and Economics.
15 Andrew, Christopher; Mitrokhin, Vasili, *The Mitrokhin Archive*, p.764.
16 KV-2-4667 (2)
17 Ibid.
18 KV-2-4667 (2)
19 KV-2-4667, p.24; Knightley, Phillip, *Philby: KGB Masterspy* (1988), pp. 40–41.
20 Yuri Modin says Maly made contact with Philby and Lizy in Vienna. Modin, Yuri, *My Five Cambridge Friends*, p.62.
21 Philby's interview with MI5, 23.6.51, KV-2-4723(1), pp.21–22.
22 Cookridge knew Philby in Vienna and later in London when Cookridge escaped to the UK and was recruited as an MI5 agent. Cookridge, EH, *The Third Man*, p.34.
23 Cookridge, EH, *The Third Man*, p.36.
24 Honigmann, Barbara, *Ein Kapitel aus meinem Leben*, Munich: Hanser (2004), pp.48, 49.

NOTES

25 Honigmann, Barbara, *Ein Kapitel aus meinem Leben*, pp.48, 49; Cookridge, EH, *The Third Man*, p.21.
26 Bauer, Kurt, *Der Februar-Aufstand* 1934. *Fakten und Mythen* [The February Uprising 1934. *Facts and Myths*] (in German), Vienna: Böhlau Verlag (2019), p.29.
27 Borovik, G, *The Philby Files*, p.21.
28 https://scholarlypublishingcollective.org/psup/austrian-american-history/article/4/1-2/1/273245/The-Spy-Story-Behind-The-Third-Man
29 Cookridge, EH, *The Third Man*, p.24.
30 Ibid.
31 KV-2-4667 pp.29–30; "My Spy", Lapham's Quarterly, 14 January 2016. Retrieved 13 February 2016.
32 Davenport-Hines, R, p.233. Gedye may have also been working for MI6's head of station Thomas Kendrick; Ellison, Kevin, *Special Counter Intelligence in WW2 Europe*, p.24.
33 Harrison, Edward, *The Young Philby*, p.30.
34 Fry, Helen, *Spymaster, The Man Who Saved MI6*, pp.53, 67.
35 To Come
36 1972 MI5 report on Lizi Philby, KV-2-4667, p.30.
37 Harrison, Edward, p.28.
38 Knightley, Phillip, *The Master Spy: The Story of Kim Philby*, p.49
39 KV-2/4091.
40 KV-2-1603 (1,2,3).
41 KV-2-1012 (2).
42 Liddell's letter to Valentine Vivian in 1930 to find out about Edith Suschitsky after taking part in demos, KV-2-1012 (2), p.75.
43 Valentine Vivian to Captain Liddell of Scotland Yard re SIS rep in Vienna, 11.12.1930, KV-2-1012 (2), p.46.
44 Harrison, Edward, p.23.
45 KV-2-1012 (2)
46 Andrew, C, Mitrokhin, V, *The Mitrokhin Archive*, p.73.
47 Mitrokhin, p.73.
48 KV-4667, p.41; *The Mitrokhin Archive* p.75.
49 https://www.historytoday.com/history-matters/end-british-communism
50 https://www.marxists.org/history/international/comintern/sections/britain/congresses/XIII/soviet_britain.htm
51 KV 2/416, p.3.
52 KV 2/4167.
53 KV 2/416.
54 Ibid.
55 Ibid.
56 Ibid.
57 Mitrokhin, p.74.
58 Mitrokhin, p.74.
59 KV 2/416.
60 Philby interview 23.6.51, KV-2-4723 (1).
61 Harrison, Edward, p.31.
62 KV 2/4725.
63 Kim Philby admitted in 1951 that he and Lizy 'saw the Smolkas fairly regularly' when they came back from Vienna. KV-2-4723 (3) p.48.
64 KV 2/4428, pp.17, 84, 99.

65 KV 2/4428, p.111.
66 KV-2-1013, p.78.
67 https://www.tate.org.uk/tate-etc/issue-46-summer-2019/lives-artists-edith-tudor-hart-great-aunt-spy-peter-stephan-jungk
68 KV-2-4705 (2), p.49; https://charlottephilby.com/features/edith-tudor-hart-the-grandmother-of-the-cambridge-spies/
69 Andrew, C, Mitrokhin, V, p.764; Verkaik, R, *Posh Boys*, p.133.

Chapter 3

1 Graham Greene, *The Last Interview*, pp.119–20; Greene, Richard, *Russian Roulette*, p.29.
2 Sherry, N, Vol 1, p.137.
3 Greene, G, *A Sort of Life*, pp.110–116.
4 Greene, G, *A Sort of Life*, p.114.
5 Greene, G, *The Last Interview*, pp.119–20.
6 Sherry, N, Vol 1, p.161.
7 KV 2/1553.
8 https://www.theguardian.com/books/2024/oct/13/a-street-boy-throwing-stones-at-pompous-windows-claud-cockburn-and-the-birth-of-guerrilla-journalism
9 Philby's interview with MI5, 23.6.51, KV-2-4723(1), p.72.
10 KV-2-4667, p.74.
11 Greene, R, *Russian Roulette*, p.29.
12 Greene, R, p.29.
13 Greene, R, p.76.
14 Ibid.
15 Day, Peter, *Bedbug*, pp.240–44.
16 http://www.ianthomson.info/blog/996/2/https://link.springer.com/chapter/10.1057/9781137343963_2
17 Greene, G, *Ways of Escape*, p.70.
18 Greene, R, p.82.
19 Greene, R, p.96.
20 https://grahamgreenebt.org/new-research-into-graham-greene/
21 KV-2-635 (1), p.11.
22 KV-2-635 (1), pp.24–25, Special Branch Report, and p.36, Letter to Greene signed by Takata.
23 KV-2-635 (1), p.28.
24 KV-2-635 (1).
25 KV-2-635 (3), p.41.
26 Sherry, N, Vol 1. pp.493–500, relationship with 'bounder and charming drunk' Herbert Greene.
27 Drazin, Charles, *In Search of the Third Man*, pp.1–4.
28 Gerth, Mathew, "British McCarthyism: The Anti-Communist Politics of Lord Vansittart and Sir Waldron Smithers", History: The Journal of the History Association, Volume 107, Issue 378 (December, 2022), pp. 927–948.
29 Jeffrey, K, *MI6*, p.314; Foot, MRD, *SOE in the Low Countries*, Little Brown (2001), pp.14, 36.
30 Greene, R, p.99.
31 Drazin, C, p.212.

NOTES

Chapter 4
1. Valentine Vivian to Captain Guy Liddell of Scotland Yard re SIS, 11.12.1930, KV-2-1012 (2), p.46.
2. KV-2-4737.
3. KV 2/4428, pp.24, 25.
4. Costello, John, Tsarev, Oleg, *Deadly Illusions, The KGB Orlov Dossier Reveals Stalin's Master Spy*, Century (1993), p.114.
5. Borovik, Genrikh, p.39.
6. Ibid.
7. Borovik, Genrikh, pp.39, 40.
8. Harrison, Edward, p.36.
9. Borovik, Genrikh, p.52.
10. KV 2/4428, pp.24–25.
11. Ibid.
12. KV-2-4737.
13. KV 2/4428, pp.24–25.
14. Andrew, C, Mitrokhin, V, p.81.
15. KV 2/4428, pp.24–25, Extract par 13.
16. Ibid.
17. West, Nigel, *The Crown Jewels*, Philby's reports to the Centre about potential recruits.
18. Andrew, C, Mitrokhin, V, p.78.
19. Andrew, C, Mitrokhin, V, p.81.
20. 17 Russian agents in the UK according to Neil Costello, *Deadly Illusions*, p.138.
21. Andrew, C, Mitrokhin, V, p.75.
22. KV 2/4167.
23. Andrew, C, Mitrokhin, V, p.81.
24. Poretsky, Elisabeth K, *Our Own People: A Memoir of Ignace Reiss and His Friends* (1969).
25. Kv-2-4633, p.29.
26. Kv-2-4633, pp.73–75.
27. Borovik, G, pp.86–93; Andrew, C, Mitrokhin, V, p.87.
28. Borovik, G, p.89.
29. Harrison, E, p.51.
30. Harrison, E, p.55.
31. Harrison, E, p.58.
32. Borovik, G, p.103.
33. The reason Gallacher failed to recall Philby's application may have been that he thought he was called Philpot. https://hansard.parliament.uk/commons/1938-04-05/debates/8f235d97-20b9-46f0-aa8e-dff83ee03ead/CommonsChamber
34. Borovik, G, p.103.
35. Borovik, G, p.121.
36. Borovik, G, p.119.
37. Borovik, G, pp.117–118.
38. Borovik, G, p.113.
39. Borovik, G, p.114.
40. Borovik, G, p.115.
41. Borovik, G, pp.119, 126.
42. Ibid.
43. Borovik, G, pp.126, 131.

44 Andrew, C, Mitrokhin, V, p.102.
45 Ibid.
46 Borovik, G, p.13.
47 Stella Rimmington, a case officer and future head of MI5, tried to follow up this lead in 1973 but was unable to make any progress, KV-2-4667, p.23.
48 KV-2-802
49 KV 2/4428.
50 KV 2/4428, Deutsch file, pp.25, 26, New extract par 13, dated 11.1.63.
51 KV 2/4428, pp.24, 25.
52 Wright, Peter, *Spycatcher;* Ali, Tariq, *The Guardian* Sat 20 Feb 1999.
53 Andrew, C, Mitrokhin, V, p.103.
54 Harrison, E, p.65.
55 Andrew, C, *Defence of the Realm*, p.185.

Chapter 5

1 Meyer, Michael, Sherman, William, and Deeds, Susan, *The Course of Mexican History*, 9th edition, Oxford University Press (2010).
2 Greene, R, p.123.
3 Greene, R, p.103.
4 Greene, G, *Ways of Escape*, pp. 69–71.
5 Sherry, Norman, Vol 1, p.723.
6 Greene began *The Power and the Glory* in March 1939 and finished the first draft on 13 September the same year. Sherry, N, Vol 1 p.700; Greene, R, *Russian Roulette*, p.129.
7 Muggeridge, M, *Chronicles of Wasted Time*, p.82.
8 In *The New Yorker*, Greene tells about a meeting of the Book Committee of the Ministry of Information: 'The committee meeting usually lasted about an hour. It was always agreeable talking with men from other divisions. Sometimes the committee coopted some other man they thought nice. It gave an opportunity for all sorts of interesting discussions on books and authors and artists and plays and films. The agenda didn't really matter; it was quite easy to invent one at the last minute.' *The New Yorker*, 25 October 1941, p.63.
9 Sherry, N, Vol 2, p.38.
10 Greene, R, p.134.
11 Sherry, N, Vol 2, p.16.
12 Greene, R, p.133.
13 Letter to Greene's mother, Sherry, N, Vol 2, p.58; Greene, G, *Ways of Escape*, p.113.
14 Sherry, N, Vol 2, p.49.
15 Sherry, N, Vol 2, p.53.
16 Sherry, N, Vol 2, pp.71, 79.
17 Sherry, N, Vol 3.
18 Sir Hugh Walpole's review of *The Power and the Glory*, Sherry, N, Vol 2, p.42.
19 Vivian letter to MI5; Greene, R, p.159.

Chapter 6

1 Harrison, E, p.67.
2 Borovik, G, p.135.
3 Harrison, E, p.82.
4 Harrison, E, Illustrations, pp. 82–83.
5 Harrison, E, p.77.

NOTES

6   Ibid.
7   KV 3/140 The Henry Robinson Papers.
8   KV-2-4633, p.32.
9   Solomon, Flora, *Baku to Baker Street* (1984) p.172.
10 KV-2-4633, p.32.
11 https://www.mkheritage.org.uk/archive/jt/tw/docs/158.html
12 KV-2-4633, p.32.
13 Harrison, E, p.87.
14 Borovik, G, p.157; Private papers of Basil F Marsden-Smedley https://www.iwm.org.uk/collections/item/object/1030014281 The Chelsea Society papers of Basil F Marsden-Smedley https://chelseasociety.org.uk/basil-marsden-smedley-obe-1945-56-and-1959-64/
15 Borovik, G, p.163.
16 Borovik, G, pp.158,163.
17 Borovik, G, p.159.
18 KV-2-4727, p.20.
19 KV-2-4633, p.32.
20 Card, Tim, *Eton Renewed, A History from 1860 to the Present Day*, p.186.
21 KV 2/1118 MI5 reports on St John Philby
22 Borovik, G, p.164.
23 Harrison, E, p.96.
24 Helenus Milmo interrogation of Philby, 12.12.51, KV-2-472, p.24.
25 Harrison, E, p.82.
26 Letter to the Foreign Office, KV-2118 (1), p.29.
27 Ibid.
28 Letter to Liddell, KV-2118 (1), p.22.
29 KV-2118 (2), p.29.
30 Correspondence between Vivian and Liddell, KV-2118, p.34.
31 KV-2118 (2), p.28.
32 Andrew, C, *Defence of the Realm*, pp.284, 285.
33 Harrison, E, p.108.
34 KV-2-4723 (3) p.86.
35 KV-2-4725 (1), pp.55, 56.
36 KV-2118 (1), pp.3, 4; FCO 158/28, p.242.
37 Harrison, E, p.111.

Chapter 7

1   The Reform Club nomination papers for Graham Greene, 17.10.40, Accessed 15.8.2024.
2   Ibid.
3   Ibid.
4   Ibid.
5   Ibid.
6   Eric Kessler said Peter Smollett/Smolka introduced him to Burgess/Blunt when he was at the Reform Club in the later 1930s. 14.9.1965, KV-2-4708 (1), pp.32, 33.
7   Reform Club Ballot Book, Accessed 15.8.2024.
8   MI5 interview with Anthony Blunt, 28.8.64, KV-4706 (1), p.20.
9   Author's interview with Cryptos members of the Reform Club, August 2024.
10 Greene, G, *The Third Man*, Preface.
11 Author's interview with Cryptos members of the Reform Club, August 2024.

12 Richard Leven's interview with MI5 at Room 055, 14.8.1972, KV-2- 4720 (3), p.16.
13 Ibid.
14 The Philby Conspiracy. Insight.*The Sunday Times*, 8 October 1967.
15 Davenport-Hines, R, p.292.
16 Sherry, N, Vol 1, p.165.
17 Wright, Peter, *Spycatcher*, p.242.
18 Verkaik, Robert, *The Traitor of Arnhem*, pp.117–19.
19 Greene, R. *Russian Roulette*, p.127.
20 Sherry, N, Vol 2, pp.29, 30.
21 Lewis, Jeremy, *Shades of Greene*, p.234.
22 Sherry, N, Vol 2, p.30.
23 Verschoyle was recruited to MI6 during the war. Greene, R, p.134; Lewis, J, p.236.
24 Lewis, J, p.247.
25 Lewis, J, pp.248–49.
26 https://www.theguardian.com/news/1999/feb/10/guardianobituaries
27 Greene, R, p.137.
28 Greene, G, *Ways of Escape*.
29 Sherry, N, Vol 2, p.182; Philby letter to Sherry 1978, Burns Box 72, Folders 1–6, pp.41–42.
30 Lewis, J, p.318.
31 Muggeridge, M, *Chronicles of Wasted Time*, p.127.
32 Vivian's letter to Sir Arthur Jelf, 13.12.41, KV4/310.
33 Allain, Marie-Francoise, *The Other Man*, p.39.
34 Shelden, M, *Graham Greene: The Enemy Within*, p.246.
35 Jeffrey, Keith, *MI6: The History of the Secret Intelligence Service*, pp.480–81.
36 Greene, R, p.138.
37 Sherry, N, Vol 2, p.85.
38 Greene's letter to Philby 17.5.1978. Burns Library, Boston College, Box 71, Folders 23–25
39 Greene, R, p.138.
40 Box 72, Folders 1–6, pp.41, 42; Sherry, N, Vol 2, p.130.
41 Davies, Philip, *MI6 and the Machinery of Spying. Case Series: Studies in Intelligence*, Series Editors: Christopher Andrew and Richard J. Aldrich, ISSN: 1368-9916.
42 Harrison, E, p.163.
43 Greene, G, *In Search of a Character*, p.97.

Chapter 8
1 Greene, G, *In Search of a Character*, pp.97, 98.
2 Greene, G, *In Search of a Character*, p.102.
3 Greene, G, *In Search of a Character*, p.112.
4 Gibbs B1b report on Freetown, 24.7.42, KV4-310.
5 Greene, G, 'The Soupsweet Land', *Vintage Greene: Collected Essays*, p.339.
6 Gibbs B1b report on Freetown, 24.7.42, KV4-310.
7 In 1942, the term was officially adopted in the Declaration by United Nations, a document signed by 26 nations fighting against the Axis powers.
8 Jeffrey, Keith, pp.236, 487; Harrison, E, p.116; Philby, K, *My Silent War*, p.43.
9 14th of July 1942 'Wagon' Telegram M.A. Haigh-Wood to Sir David Petrie, KV4-310.

NOTES

10 Office of Swinton resident minister: Notes on reorganisation of security in West Africa. Written by Arthur Jelf, head of Overseas Control MI5, 3.8.42, KV4/310.
11 KV4/311, p.100a.
12 Ibid.
13 KV4/311, p.104a.
14 Sherry, N, Vol 2, p.98.
15 Taken from GG's Journal, Sherry, N, Vol 2, p.102.
16 Greene, G, 'The Soupsweet Land', *Vintage Greene: Collected Essays*, p.339.
17 Sherry, N, Vol 2, p.182; Philby letter to Sherry 1978, The Graham Greene Papers, Burns Library, Boston College, Box 72, Folders 1–6, pp.41–42.
18 West African Intelligence and central security, KV4/310.
19 Greene, G, *Essays*, p.341.
20 Greene, G, *Ways of Escape*, p.95.
21 KV4/310.
22 Greene, G, *The Soupsweet Land, Collected Essays*, p.342
23 Greene, G, 'The Soupsweet Land', *Vintage Greene: Collected Essays*, p.341.
24 Greene letter to Norman Sherry 11 March 1991, Burns Library. Box 72 Folders 1–6.
25 Greene G, *Ways of Escape*, p.99.
26 Ibid.
27 KV4/310, 19.8.42.
28 Greene G, *Ways of Escape*, p.99.
29 Ibid.
30 Greene, G, *Ways of Escape*, p.98.
31 Greene G, *Ways of Escape*, p.99.
32 Sherry, Vol 2, p.123.
33 Greene, G, *A Sort of Life*, p.109.
34 Greene's correspondence with Sherry, February to March 1991, Burns Library, Box 72, Folders 1–6.
35 Sherry, N, Vol 2, p.138.
36 Greene letter to Sherry, February 1991, Burns Library, Boston College, Box 72, Folders 1–6.
37 Ibid.
38 Greene, G, 'The Soupsweet Land', *Vintage Greene: Collected Essays*, p.342.
39 Ibid.
40 Greene letter to Sherry, February 1991, Burns Library, Boston College, Box 72, Folders 1–6.
41 Greene letter to Sherry, April, Burns Library, Boston College, Box 72, Folders 1–6.
42 Greene letter to Sherry, February 1991, Burns Library, Boston College, Box 72, Folders 1–6.
43 https://www.ukwhoswho.com/display/10.1093/ww/9780199540891.001.0001/ww-9780199540884-e-244881
44 KV4-311 p.213b.
45 Greene's Brodie report, 9.11.42, KV4/311.
46 1942 'wagon' telegram, MA Haigh-Wood to Sir David Petrie (Sherry says boss in Lagos was Alexis Forter but he was too young, born 1925), KV4/310. https://www.google.co.uk/books/edition/The_Diplomatic_Service_List/2SvwAAAAMAAJ?hl=en&gbpv=1&dq=alexis+FORTER+Nigeria&pg=PA257&printsec=frontcover)

47 West African Intelligence and central security, KV4/311; Greene's Brodie report, 9.11.42, KV4/310.
48 Greene, G, *In Search of a Character*, Congo Journal, p.81.
49 Greene, G, *Ways of Escape*, p.121.
50 MI5 report, KV3, p.425.
51 KV 3/424.
52 KV 3/424, 25.7.41.
53 KV 3/424.
54 KV3/425.
55 Sherry, N, Vol 2, p.117.
56 Greene, G, *Ways of Escape*, p.119.
57 Greene, G, 'The Soupsweet Land', *Vintage Greene: Collected Essays*, p.345.
58 Greene, G, *Ways of Escape*, p.118.
59 Sherry, N, Vol 2, p.126.
60 Haigh-Wood to Sir David Petrie, 10.07.42, KV4/310.
61 Greene, G, *Ways of Escape*, p.121.
62 Greene, G, 'The Soupsweet Land', *Vintage Greene: Collected Essays*, p.345.

Chapter 9

1 Macintrye, Ben, *A Spy Among Friends*, p.29.
2 Extract from SIS letter, KV3/269.
3 Under Abwehr security procedures the KO substations in neutral countries acted as undercover attachments of the diplomatic missions, and the field stations reproduced the functions of the headquarters divisions in recruiting, training and dispatching espionage agents and informants. Extract from SIS letter, KV3/269, p.41.
4 https://uboat.net/allies/warships/ship/6967.html
5 Liddell, G, *Diaries 1942*, Edited by Nigel West, p.217.
6 Letter to Cecil Liddell, 20.7.42, KV3/269, p.39b.
7 Philby to Robertson about Pohlmann, 7.2.42, KV3/269.
8 KV3/269, p.31b, 3.4.42.
9 KV3/269, p.30b.
10 Philby, K, *My Silent War*, p.43.
11 Philby, K, *My Silent War*, p.46.
12 Entries in Liddell diary, July 1943, KV-4/192.
13 Philby, K, *My Silent War*, p.63.
14 Ibid.
15 Philby, K, *My Silent War*, pp.66–67.
16 KV3/270 Philby Letter to Hart re Iberian enquiries. There are many examples of Philby using Hart as a back channel when he needed MI5 help. Hart's wife was a communist and the couple fell under suspicion after the war.
17 Philby, K, *My Silent War*, p.70.
18 KV3-270.
19 KV3-270, p.69b, 3.7.43.
20 Milne, Tim, p.95.
21 Milne, Tim, p.96.
22 https://scalar.usc.edu/works/the-space-between-literature-and-culture-1914-1945/vol13_2017_kimsey
23 Greene, G, 'A Third Man Entertainment on Security in Room 51', *The Sunday Times*, 14 July 1963.
24 Ibid.

NOTES

25 Ibid.
26 SS HQ in Portugal and Spain, KV3/269.
27 KV3/269, p.18a.
28 KV3/269, pp.9a,10a.
29 KV3/269, p.9a.
30 KV3/269, pp.7z, 1x.
31 Lt Col Robin Stephens, head of Camp 020, to Dick White, deputy head of B Division, 3.8.41, KV3/269.
32 KV3/270, p.53b.
33 Philby, K, *My Silent War*, p.64.
34 Ibid.
35 Philby, K, *My Silent War*, p.64.
36 Major Blunt internal memo, 29.5.43, KV3/270, p.68a.
37 Philby, K. *My Silent War*, p.xxxii.
38 Borovik, G, p.137.
39 Borovik, G, p.138.
40 Bristow, Desmond, *Game of Moles*, p.33.
41 Macintyre, Ben, *Double Cross*.
42 Bristow, Desmond, *Game of Moles*, p.34.
43 Ibid.
44 Bristow, D, p.35.
45 Bristow, D, p.36.
46 Ibid.

Chapter 10

1 'Security in West Africa', KV4/309, p.54a.
2 'Report on the Operation of Overseas Control', Appendix C.21, KV 4/18; KV 4/310.
3 Greene, R, *Graham Greene: A Life in Letters*, p.129.
4 Sherry, N, Vol 2, p.128.
5 Sherry, N, Vol 2, p.129.
6 Intelligence from Philby about Manuel Dos Santos, KV-2-2108 (1), p.4; KV-2-2108 (3).
7 Telegram from police headquarters Freetown to David Petrie, 21.10.42, KV-2-2108 (3), p.32.
8 KV-2-2108 (3), p.18.
9 MI5 report February 1945, KV-2-2108 (1), p.40.
10 Telegram from police headquarters Freetown to David Petrie, 21.10.42, KV-2-2108 (3), p.32.
11 Ibid.
12 Ibid.
13 Ibid.
14 KV-2-3000 (1), p.93.
15 KV-2-3000 (1), p.94.
16 MI5 note on Philby's intelligence, KV-2-3000 (1), p.8; https://www.navalhistory.net/xDKWD-WAfrica1942.htm
17 Blunt's memo to B1B, 26.10.42, KV-2-3000 (1), p.9.
18 KV-2-3000 (2), p. 42.
19 Brodie's report to Sir David Petrie, 7.11.42, KV-2-3000 (1), p.96.
20 Philby's correspondence with Herbert Hart about how to handle Avila, KV-2-3000 (2), pp.71, 77.

21 Brodie's report to Sir David Petrie, 7.11.42, KV-2-3000 (1), p.96.
22 Ibid.
23 Philby memo to Hart, KV-2-3000 (2), p.5.
24 Santos names 344 suspects and acquaintances in alphabetic order, KV-2-2108 (2), pp.20–48; Kim Philby's telegram to MI5 re Santos, KV3/175, p.6a.
25 Philby memo to JLS Hale (MI5), 12.10.42, KV3/175, p.1a.
26 Liddell, Guy, *Diaries Vol 2*, p.21.
27 Resident Minister's office Accra Swinton to Gibbs (care of His Excellency, The Governor / The Secretary at Lagos, Nigeria), 17.11.42, KV4/311.
28 Mockler, Anthony, *Three Lives, Novelist! Explorer! Spy!*, p.182.
29 Ibid.
30 Cowgill to White, 5.12.42, KV4/311.
31 West African Intelligence and Central Security. Greene's Brodie report, 9.11.42, KV4/311, p.231b.
32 Philby's letter to Norman Sherry, Burns Library, Boston College, The Graham Greene Collection, Box 72, Folders 1–6.
33 DG White to DGSS, 9.12.42, KV4/311.
34 Memo MI5 Overseas Control, 2.12.42, KV4/311.
35 https://slptrainingschool.wordpress.com/about/
36 Greene, R, p.145.
37 Supplement to the *London Gazette*, 8 June 1944. https://slptrainingschool.wordpress.com/about/; Sherry, N, Vol 2, p.129.
38 Harrison, Edward, *The Young Philby*, p.141.
39 Harrison, Edward, *The Young Philby*, p.141.
40 Figures from The National Archives, Admiralty Records, ADM 223/485; Harrison, E, p.142.
41 Harrison, E, p.142.
42 ADM 223/485.
43 Harrison, E, p.145.
44 Edwards, Bernard, *Dönitz and the Wolf Packs*, Brockhampton Press (1999), p.115.
45 Arnold Hague Convoy Database.
46 Hague, Arnold, *The Allied Convoy System 1939–1945*, Naval Institute Press (2000).
47 https://veteransbreakfastclub.org/a-curious-case-from-the-battle-of-the-atlantic-was-convoy-sl-125-sacrificed-on-purpose/
48 Greene, G, *Ways of Escape*, p.100.
49 Letter from Philby to Sherry, June 1978, Sherry, Norman, Vol 2, p.154; see also Burns Library, Box 72, Folders 1–6.

Chapter 11
1 Fry, Helen, *Women in Intelligence*, Kindle, location no 1957.
2 KV-2-1008 (2), p.19. KV-2-1008 (1), p.9.
3 Andrew, Christopher, *The Defence of the Realm*, p.131.
4 Ibid.
5 West, N. *The Circus, MI5 Operations 1945–1972*, p.62.
6 KV-2-1013, p.62.
7 KV-2-1013, p.82.
8 Leopold and Anna Hornik, KV 2/3938.
9 KV-2 4169.
10 Ibid.

NOTES

11 Anthony Blunt files, KV-2-4702 (2).
12 H Shillito, KV 2/4169.
13 Internal memo, R Fulford to R Brooman-White, 10.9.42, KV 2/4169.
14 Internal memo from R Brooman-White to R Fulford, 12.9.42, KV 2/4169.
15 Borovik, G, p.216.
16 Borovik, G, p.212.
17 Ibid.
18 Borovik, G, p.xiv.
19 Andrew, Christopher, *The Defence of the Realm*, p280.
20 Borovik, G, p.219.
21 Philby's report to Moscow, West, Nigel and Tsarev, Oleg, *Triplex: Secrets from the Cambridge Spies*, pp.106–07.
22 Philby's report to Moscow, West, N, *Triplex*, p106.
23 West, N, *Triplex*, p.106.
24 Ibid.
25 Ibid.
26 Andrew, C, *Defence of the Realm*, p281.
27 Andrew, C, *Defence of the Realm*, p.281.
28 Walton, Calder, *Empire of Secrets*, p.68.
29 Andrew, C, *Defence of The Realm*, p.282; Walton, Calder, *Empire of Secrets*, p.68.
30 KV-2/4723 (1), p.65.
31 Andrew, C, *Defence of the Realm*, p.282.
32 Philby, K, *My Silent War*, p.107.
33 Jeffrey, Keith, *MI6*, p.561.
34 West, Nigel, *Triplex*, p.105.
35 West, N, *Triplex*, p.107.
36 KV-2/4723 (1), p.63.

Chapter 12

1 KV4/310.
2 Sherry, N, Vol 2, p.155.
3 Sherry, N, Vol 2, p.154.
4 Sherry, N, Vol 2, p.162.
5 West, Nigel, *The Crown Jewels*, p.313.
6 Borovik, G, p.207; Burns Library, Box 71, Folders 23–24.
7 Helena Engelbach nee Philby letter to Graham Greene in 1963. Burns Library, Box 71, Folders 23–25.
8 Greene, G, Foreword to *My Silent War*, p.xix.
9 Macintyre, B, *A Spy Among Friends*, p.56.
10 Greene, G, Foreword to *My Silent War* by Kim Philby, p.13.
11 Burns Library, Box 72, Folders 1–6, pp.41, 42.
12 Greene, G, Foreword to *My Silent War*, p.xx.
13 Philby, K, *My Silent War*, p.78; Burns Library, Box 72, Folder 16.
14 Philby, K, *My Silent War*, pp.40, 78.
15 Milne, Tim, p.119.
16 Greene, G, Foreword to *My Silent War*.
17 Harrison, E, p.151.
18 Harrison, E, p.150.
19 Sherry, N, Vol 2, p.154.
20 Philby, K, *My Silent War*, p.71.
21 Milne, T, p.136.

22 Milne, T, p.126.
23 Sherry, N, Vol 2, p.180.
24 Ibid.
25 Tsarev, Oleg, West, Nigel, *The Crown Jewels*, p.309.
26 Tsarev, Oleg, West, Nigel, *The Crown Jewels*, p.310.
27 Tsarev, Oleg, West, Nigel, *The Crown Jewels*, p.312.
28 Ibid.
29 Tsarev, Oleg, West, Nigel, *The Crown Jewels*, p.309.
30 Ibid.
31 Tsarev, Oleg, West, Nigel, *The Crown Jewels*, p.219.
32 Cairncross, John, *The Enigma Spy*, pp.146–48.
33 Ibid.
34 Tsarev, Oleg, West, Nigel, *The Crown Jewels*, p.218.
35 Tsarev, Oleg, West, Nigel, *The Crown Jewels*, p.219.
36 Tsarev, Oleg, West, Nigel, *The Crown Jewels*, p.220.
37 Harrison, E, p.84.

Chapter 13
1 KV 3/424; KV-2-2267 (3), pp.46–50.
2 Ibid.
3 KV 3/424; KV-2-2267 (3), pp.46–50.
4 KV-2-2267 (4).
5 KV3 425 BIC, 27.8.1941.
6 KV3 425 BIC, 27.8.1941.
7 KV3 425 BIC, 27.8.1941.
8 KV-2-2267 (2), pp.1–7, 17.7.42.
9 KV-2 4347.
10 KV-2-2267 (3), p.20.
11 Philby's memo to Major T.A. Robertson, 14.7.42, KV-2-2267 (2), p.14.
12 Josef may have been run by the NKVD separately without Philby's knowledge and that may be why Philby denounced him as a rabid communist, KV-2-2267 (3), p.40; Also, Philby gave away Maclean when he knew it was too late and would do him good, see Bower, Tom, *The Perfect English Spy*, p.103.
13 https://www.iwm.org.uk/collections/item/object/80009385.bhsportugal.org%2Fuploads%2Ffotos_artigos%2Ffiles%2F16_OperationLifebuoy_Hesketh%255B1%255D.pdf
14 KV-2-2271 (4), p.16.
15 KV-2-2271 (4), p.16.
16 KV-2-2271 (4), p.2.
17 Ibid.
18 KV-2-2270 (2), p.29.
19 Ibid.
20 KV-2-2274 (1), p.16.
21 KV-2-2271 (4), pp.24, 26.
22 KV-2-2272 (3), p.37.
23 Robertson's memo to Hooper: Portuguese Stevedore told SIS in Lisbon that a 'fireman' in Josef's vessel brought a packet of quinine to Lisbon for the Portuguese. He was a German agent. Germans wanted to use the quinine to get someone drunk and interrogate him. When the fireman left he was given four canaries by the Portuguese. 'If you (Hooper) could shed any light on this by interviewing Plato.' 13.1.44, KV-2-2272 (3), p.37.

NOTES

24 KV-2-2272 (4), p.36, 29.12.43.
25 Stopford letter to Greene, 14.2.44, KV-2-2272 (3), pp.29–31.
26 KV-2-2272 (3), p.3, 29.1.44.
27 Stopford and Greene correspondence, 14.2.44, KV-2-2272 (3), pp.29–31.
28 Harrison, E, p.12.
29 Philby, K, *My Silent War*, p.60.
30 Harrison, E, p.127.

Chapter 14

1 Benton, Kenneth, *The IOS years Madrid 1941–43*, Contemporary Journal of History; Macintyre, Ben, *Double Cross*, p.165.
2 Ibid.
3 KV-2-856 (4), p.12.
4 KV 2/3568, KV 2/858(1)
5 Ibid.
6 Ibid.
7 KV-2- 858(1), p.51.
8 XX Committee Meeting on 9.5.44, KV-2-858 (1), p.60.
9 A Sydney Albert memo to Ian Wilson, KV-2-857 (2), p.49.
10 Philby memo to Hart telling him that SIS agent has found an address book in Madrid belonging to Roberto Zinkel or Moldenhauer with two addresses in UK: Sophia Biberfeld, Golders Green and 'Doris' 17 Linden Gardens W.2, 17.4.44, KV3/270, Headquarters of the SS in Spain, p.89a.
11 Kv-2-857 (2), pp.17, 77.
12 KV-2-857 (2), p.49.
13 KV-2-857 (1), p.31, 21.4.44.
14 Frank Foley memo to T.A. Robertson, KV-2-856(1), p.14.
15 KV-2-857 (1), pp.33–35, 20.4.44; Berlin suspects Artist working for the British, KV-2-856 (1), p.64; KV-2-410 (1), p.32.
16 KV-2-960.
17 KV-2-859 (3), p.18.
18 KV-2-857 (1), pp.31–32, 21.4.44.
19 KV-2-857 (1), p.38.
20 Foley asks Robertston to give him a full report on the background to the warning, KV-2-859 (3), p.18. Charles de Salis, the Lisbon station chief, had dutifully passed on the guarded warning to Jebsen. But it was not enough to alert Jebsen to the dangers he faced. He counted Brandes as a close friend and had even suggested approaching him to spy for MI6. But Brandes, becoming increasingly nervous, feared Jebsen would reveal to Berlin that his own spy network was demonstrably fake. To protect himself he had decided to betray Jebsen.
21 Greene to Gwyer for Philby about Brandes Mexican passports, 7.8.43, KV-2-3295 (3), p.44.
22 KV-2-859 (3), p.18.
23 KV-2-859 (3), p.15.
24 Macintyre, Ben, *A Spy Among Friends*, pp.77–89 https://warfarehistorynetwork.com/article/the-vermehren-betrayal/
25 KV-2-3295 (3), p.27; Macintrye, Ben, *Double Cross*, p.248.
26 Milne, Tim, p.124.
27 KV-2-856 (1), p.71.
28 KV-2-856/7
29 Ibid.

30   Greene, G, *The Tenth Man*, pp.9, 10.
31   Greene, G, *The Tenth Man*, p.11.
32   KV-2-199 (2), pp.24–25.
33   Paul Georg FIDRMUC, alias FIDERMUTZ, RANTZAU, codename OSTRO: a freelance Abwehr agent in Lisbon, whose prolific reporting was based on gossip, speculation and press reports, KV 2/197.
34   KV 856 (3), p.67; KV 856 (4), p.3.
35   KV-2-857(1), p.29.
36   KV-2-3568, p.33.
37   There is evidence that Philby tried to recruit Ostro in the summer of 1944 using the pseudonym Carter in Portugal, KV-2-197 (3), p.49; Ostro could have been working for the Russians – he was linked to Kremlin spy chief Beria, KV-2-199 (2), p.31.
38   Ian Wilson: 'On receipt of the second most secret reference to Brandes reporting on Artist about the latter's enquiries into Ostro, I discussed with Colonel Robertson, Major Masterman and Mr Marriott and subsequently Major Foley whether a most immediate telegram should be sent to Lisbon before their contact on the 17th to instruct them that if Artist should mention that he was being accused of noticeable curiosity about Ostro, he might, if he agreed, be encouraged to take a bold line indicating that his curiosity about Ostro arose from his desire to expose Ostro if he could find proof of his existing suspicions that Ostro was a fraud.' KV-2-857(1), p.38.
39   KV 2/958 MI5 file on Erich Vermehren.
40   Ibid and Ben Macintyre's *A Spy Among Friends*, p.87.
41   Philby, K, *My Silent War*, p.42.
42   Liddell diaries, 28 April 1944, p.187.
43   https://warfarehistorynetwork.com/article/german-chief-spy-admiral-wilhelm-canaris/
44   Philby, Rufina, *The Private Life of Kim Philby*, p.397.
45   Trevor-Roper, Hugh, *The Philby Affair* (1968).
46   Greene, G interview with Sherry 13 Dec 1983, Sherry, N, Vol 2, p.177.
47   Trevor-Roper, Hugh, *The Philby Affair*.
48   Ibid.
49   Ibid.
50   KV 2/3295
51   Ibid.

Chapter 15

1   https://appledorehistory.org.uk/charles-de-salis-the-appledore-spy/#:~:text=Charles%20de%20Salis%20?orked%20in,and%20remembers%20de%20Salis%20well.
2   Greene, G, *Ways of Escape*, p.297.
3   Ibid.
4   KV-2-4737.
5   Offensive Against German Espionage in Portugal, KV-2-2416 (2), p.32.
6   KV 2/2454, p.84.
7   KV 2/2454, p.96.
8   The Azores Series of photostats, KV-2-2416 (3), p.36.
9   The Azores Series of photostats, KV-2-2416 (3), p.38.
10   Offensive Against German Espionage in Portugal, KV-2-2416 (2), p.2.
11   Hans Grimm confession, KV-2-2416 (2), p.4.

NOTES

12 Memo to Herbert Hart, 11.2.43, KV-2-2416 (2), p.18.
13 KV 3/175.
14 Ibid.
15 Milne, Tim, p.114.
16 Philby, K, *My Silent War*, p.40.
17 Ibid.
18 Muggeridge, M, *Like It Was: The Diaries of Malcolm Muggeridge* (1981), p.249.
19 Sherry, N, Vol 2, p.168.
20 Philby, K, *My Silent War*, p.41.
21 Muggeridge, M, *Chronicles of Wasted Time*.
22 Philby letter to Sherry 1978, Burns Library, Box 72, Folders 1–6, pp.41–42.
23 KV3/270 p83a.
24 KV3/270 p83a.
25 . . .https://digitarq.arquivos.pt/viewer?id=4295988
26 KV3/270.
27 KV-2-399 (2).
28 Letter to Alewyn Birch, Granada Publishing, 30.4.1968, Burns Library, Box 65, Folder 58, p1.
29 Ibid.
30 Burns Library, Box 71, Folders 23–25.
31 Milne's 1977 letter to Greene, Burns Library, Box 71, Folders 23–25, p.23.
32 Greene, G, *Ways of Escape*, p.297.
33 Greene, G, *The Human Factor*, p.47.

Chapter 16

1 Greene, G, 'A Third Man Entertainment on Security in Room 51', *The Sunday Times*, 14 July 1963.
2 Shelden, Michael, pp.254–55; Greene, Graham, 'A Third Man Entertainment on Security in Room 51', *The Sunday Times*, 14 July 1963.
3 Greene letter to his friend the bookseller David Low, Sherry, N, Vol 2, p.167.
4 Greene, G, Letter October 24 1987, Balliol College Archives & Manuscripts: The Cherry Record Collection of Josephine Reid's Papers and Books Relating to Graham Greene.
5 Greene, G, *Ways of Escape*, p.207.
6 Burns Library, Box 65, Folder 62.
7 Allain, Marie-Francoise, *The Other Man*, p.184.
8 Greene, G, *Vintage Greene*, p.310.
9 Ibid.
10 Allain, Marie-Francoise, p.183.
11 Allain, Marie-Francoise, p.20.
12 Greene, G, The Spy's Role, *Collected Essays* (1969) first published in the *Sunday Times* (1967).
13 Sherry, N. Vol 2, p.183.
14 Burns Library, Box 12, Folder 44.
15 KV-2-4702 (3), p.9, 17.11.1955.
16 Ibid.
17 Greene, G, Foreword to *My Silent War*.
18 Greene, G, *Ways of Escape*, p.99.
19 Walton, Calder, *Empire of Secrets*, p.198.
20 Sherry, N, Vol 2, p.187.
21 Sherry interview with Greene, 23.4.81, Sherry, N, Vol 2, p.187.

22 KV-2-4169.
23 Greene letter to Mrs Parvin, 20.8.1975, Burns Library, Boston College, Box 71, Folders 23–25.
24 Philby letter to Sherry, Burns Library, Box 72, Folders 1–6.
25 Ibid.
26 KV 2/4743 p.32.
27 Philby letter to Sherry, Burns Library, Box 72, Folders 1–6.
28 KV-2-4737 (1) p.79
29 Greene, G, Harry Ransom Center, University of Texas, MS01723, pp.20–26.
30 Ibid.
31 Ibid.
32 Sherry, N, Vol 2, pp.185, 187.
33 Burns Library, Box 70, Folder 22.
34 Sherry, N, Vol 2, p.185.
35 Sherry, N, Vol 2, p.192.
36 Sherry, N, Vol 2, p.193.
37 Letters to Sherry from Philby and Douglas Jerrold, Sherry, N, Vol 2, p.192.
38 Sherry, N, p.213.
39 Greene, G, *Ways of Escape*, p.239.
40 Greene, G, *The Tenth Man*, p.19.
41 KV-2-200 (2), p.13; KV-2-200 (3), p.6.
42 Greene, G, *Nobody to Blame, The Tenth Man*, p.21.
43 Greene, G, *Nobody to Blame, The Tenth Man*, Introduction, p.17.
44 Greene, G, *Nobody to Blame, The Tenth Man*, Introduction, p.16.
45 Greene, G, *Collected Essays, Soupsweet Land*, p.341.
46 https://www.newstatesman.com/culture/2019/06/from-cuba-to-greeneland-graham-greenes-long-relationship-with-the-island-republic
47 Leo Long (D1) interview about MI14, KV-2-4705 (1), pp.20–23. Long said George had good knowledge of London bus routes like Karl Marx and spoke very good English
48 KV-2-199 (2), p.31.
49 Greene, G, *The Tenth Man*, p.17.
50 Greene, G, *The Tenth Man*, p.83.
51 Greene, G, *The Tenth Man*, p.94.
52 Greene, R, *Russian Roulette*, p.162.
53 Greene, G, *The Tenth Man*, p.10.
54 Greene, R, *Graham Greene: A Life In Letters*, p.146.
55 Greene, R, *Graham Greene: A Life In Letters*, p.159.
56 Sherry, N, Vol 3, p.14.
57 Allain, Marie-Francoise, pp.109, 117.
58 The *Evening Standard*, 22 June 1945.

Chapter 17
1 Borovik, Genrikh, *The Philby Files*, pp.178, 239.
2 Modin, Yuri, *My Five Cambridge Friends*, p.113.
3 Borovik, G, p.177.
4 Philby was also a lifelong fan of Surrey County Cricket Club. He said Surrey and Arsenal 'were to give me crumbs of comfort in difficult times, Arsenal during their great period in the 30s, the years of triumphant fascism, Surrey during theirs in the 50s when I was in deep trouble.' Philby, Rufina, *The Private Life of Kim Philby*, p.215.

NOTES

5   Borovik, G, p.178.
6   Borovik, G, p.231.
7   Borovik, G, p.232.
8   KV-24737 (2) p.56.
9   Borovik, G, p.233.
10 Borovik, G, p.234.
11 Philby, K, *My Silent War,* p.93.
12 Philby, K, *My Silent War,* p.92.
13 Philby, K, *My Silent War,* p.94.
14 Harrison, E, p.162.
15 KV-2-1009, p.37.
16 KV-2-1009, p.7.
17 KV-2-1009, p.36.
18 Ibid.
19 Costello and Tsarev, *Deadly Illusions,* pp.331–39.
20 Macintyre, Ben, *A Spy Among Friends* (2014), pp.47–48.
21 KV 2/1008 (2).
22 MI5's 23rd Interview with Anthony Blunt 26.5.65; Martin and Wright, KV-2-4708 (2), p.45.
23 Milne, Tim, p.117.
24 Milne, Tim, p.118.
25 Borovik, G, p.13.
26 KV-2-4667, pp.50, 74.
27 KV 2/4665
28 MI5's 23rd Interview with Anthony Blunt 26.5.65, KV-2-4708 (2); Martin and Wright, pp.34–38.
29 Ibid.
30 Arthur Martin says in 1961 that Gillitsin was adamant that the 'ring of five' existed before the war. Blunt is suggesting that John Cairncross was not an integral member of the 'ring of five' but Lizy Philby was. MI5's 23rd Interview with Anthony Blunt, 26.5.65, KV-2-4708 (2); Martin and Wright pp. 34–38.
31 Danks, Catherine, 'The Anglo-Soviet Alliance: What does Manchester think?' Article published online by Manchester Metropolitan University.
32 Gordievsky, Oleg, Andrew, Christopher, *KGB: The Inside Story of its Foreign Operations from Lenin to Gorbachev.*
33 Borovik, G, p.216.
34 Borovik, G, p.137.
35 Philby, Rufina, *The Private Life of Kim Philby,* p.244; Philby's lecture to KGB's First Chief Directorate, Yasenevo, near Moscow, July 1977, Philby, K. pp. 93–100.
36 Philby, K, *My Silent War,* p.95.
37 Ibid.
38 Philby, K, *My Silent War,* p.96.
39 Philby, K, *My Silent War,* p.100.
40 Ibid.
41 Yuri Modin, Hugh Trevor-Roper and Keith Jeffrey all attest to Philby's achievement.
42 Philby, K, *My Silent War,* p.101.
43 Borovik, G, p.236.
44 Borovik, G, p.237.

45 Jeffrey, Keith, *MI6*, p.596.
46 Harrison, E, p.116.
47 Liddell's diary entries September–November 1944, KV-4-195 (1) (2).
48 Ibid.
49 KV-4-195 (1), p.87.
50 Stuart Menzies said 'Present state of affairs was unacceptable', KV-4-195 (1), p3; and KV-4-196(1), 6 Feb 1945.
51 Liddell Diaries 22 September 1944, KV-4-195 (1), pp.91, 174.
52 Liddell Diaries 3 November 1944, KV-4-195 (2), p.217.
53 Philby, K, *My Silent War*, p.105.
54 Dickinson, PL, *Independent* obituary of R Dennys, 16 August 1993.
55 Jeffrey, K, *MI6*, p.386.
56 Jeffrey, K, p.432.
57 https://www.independent.co.uk/news/people/obituary-rodney-dennys-1461667.html
58 March 1946 Philby reports on Dennys and Menzies, West, N, *Triplex*, pp.183–84.
59 Bower, Tom, *The Perfect English Spy*, p.306; West, Nigel, *Cold War Spymaster*, p.147.
60 7 March 1945 Liddell Diaries, 'Kim was anxious Victor should work for Section 9 in Paris', West, N, *Triplex*, pp.116–17; and KV-4-196(1), p.174.
61 KV-2-4737, p.148.
62 Philby, K, *My Silent War*, p.105.
63 Philby, K, p.106.
64 Philby, K, p.105.
65 KV-4-196(1) Did a double agent in MI5 sack this woman for uncovering the Cambridge spy ring? *Mail on Sunday*, 27 April 2003.
66 Ibid.
67 KV-4-196 (1), 5 January 1945.
68 Jeffrey, Keith, p.599.
69 Liddell diary October 24, KV-4-195 (1).
70 Liddell diary 21 October and 24 October, KV-4-195 (2), p.187.
71 KV-4-195 (2), 9 Nov.
72 Jeffrey, Keith, p.619. Liddell warned the Foreign Office's Peter Loxley: 'We have a pride in our show and none of us wish to find ourselves serving under Sir Claude Dansey, Lousy Paine, Moses Beddington, Col V or anyone else. We took the lowest possible view of them and of the organisation.' KV-4-196 (1), p.18, 5 Jan 1945. This appears to have prompted another visit from Philby to MI5 headquarters, as recorded in Liddell's diary: 'I talked to Kim Philby who came to see me about the Amalgamation Project. I told him quite frankly that what really worried us more than anything was the prospect of being placed under the extremely unsatisfactory people who held directing positions in SIS. We felt that this would be a positive disaster.' KV-4-196 (1), p.155, 27 Feb.
73 Andrew, Christopher, *Secret Service: The Making of the British Intelligence Community*, p.462.

Chapter 18
1 Sherry, N, Vol 2, p.287.
2 Cairncross, J, *The Enigma Spy*, p.155.
3 Cairncross, J, *The Enigma Spy*, p.148.
4 Carter, M, *Anthony Blunt*, p.184.

NOTES

5 Andrew Revai invited Blunt to dinner with Graham Greene, but he turned it down on the excuse he had to see some students, 10.12.1956, KV-2-4704 (2), p.74.
6 Greene, Richard, *Graham Greene: A Life in Letters*, letter to Elisabeth Greene, 15 October 1942.
7 Kim Philby's letter to Graham Greene 2 January 1980, Georgetown University, Box 1, Folder 38, Graham Greene Papers part 2.
8 Philby letter to Sherry, Burns Library, Box 72, Folders 1–6, pp.41,42.
9 West, N, *Triplex*, p.139.
10 West, N, *Triplex*, p.144.
11 Philby said the politics of intelligence 'took up much of my time', Philby, K, *My Silent War*, p.115.
12 West, N, *Triplex*, p.137.
13 West, N, *Triplex*, pp.134–135.
14 West, N, *Triplex*, p.135.
15 West, N, *Triplex*, p.136.
16 West, N, *Triplex*, p.212.
17 West, N, *Triplex*, p.116.
18 Jeffrey, K, pp.476, 486; Philby, K, *My Silent War*, p.117.
19 Davenport-Hines, Richard, pp.371–73.
20 KV-2-4674 (1), p.60; Philby, K, *My Silent War*, p.119.
21 Seale, Patrick & Maureen McConville, *Philby: The Long Road to Moscow*.
22 KV-2-4674 (1), p.60; Philby, *My Silent War*, p.119.
23 Knox Helm in Ankara to William Codrington in London, 5.9.45, KV-2-4674 (2), p.36.
24 Philby, K, *My Silent War*, p.120.
25 Philby, K, *My Silent War*, p.127.
26 CSS had asked Philby to report to the Foreign Office on the Volkov affair. The report was based on Philby's longer account given directly to MI6. 18.10.1945, KV-2-4724 (2), p.18; KV-2-4674, p.17.
27 Knightley, P, *Philby: The Life and Views of the KGB Master Spy*, pp.135–36.
28 Ibid.
29 Tom Bromley Foreign Office. Keith Jeffrey says the Tom Bromley memo was sent to Sir Stewart Menzies. But by 19 September, Menzies knew all about it and the tone of Bromley's memo was far too informal to be reporting to the head of his organsiation. 19.9.45, KV-2-4674(2), p.26.
30 Philby, Rufina, p.263.
31 West, Nigel, *Cold War Spymaster*, pp.15, 16.
32 KV-2-4674 (2), p.25.
33 Macintyre, B, *A Spy Among Friends*, p.100.
34 KV-2-4674 (2), p.22.
35 West, Nigel, *Cold War Spymaster*, p.18.
36 Knightley, Phillip, *Philby: KGB Masterspy* (1988), p.133.
37 Borovik, G, p.178.
38 Philby's speech given to KGB in July 1977, Philby, R, *The Private Life of Kim Philby*, p.253.
39 Ibid.
40 Lewis, J, *Shades of Greene*, p.336.
41 Milne, T, p.37.
42 Dick White interview with Hugh Trevor-Roper who said Philby was 'of course another one of those ex-communists like Malcolm Muggeridge.' Trevor-Roper

said that on more than one occasion he had been specifically told by Philby's closest friend xxx [Tim Milne] that Philby had been a communist. 19.9.51, KV-2-4724 (1), p.18.
43 KV-3 301, 19.7.45.
44 Andrew, C, *Defence of the Realm*, p.281.
45 Andrew, C, p.282.
46 KV-2-4723 (3) p.35.
47 West, N, *The Circus – MI5 Operations 1945–1972*, Stein and Day, New York (1984), pp. 21, 62; Bower, Tom, *The Perfect Spy*, p.125; Ellison, Kevin, *Special Counter Intelligence In WW2 Europe*, pp.28–30.
48 Ibid.
49 29 March 1946, Dear Major Marriott (Mi5) with reference your PF39680/f2c/dm of 12th of March to Philby, KV-2-4169.
50 KV 2/2992, p.188a, PF 54073/f2a (b)/mbt.
51 Philby, K, *My Silent War*, p.129.
52 Pearce, Martin, *Spymaster*, p.68.
53 Pearce, Martin, *Spymaster*, p.67.
54 Trevor-Roper, Hugh, *The Canaris Affair*.
55 Pearce, M, *Spymaster*, p.68.
56 Macintyre, B, *A Spy Among Friends*, p.111.
57 KV-2-4723 (3) KV-2-4169.
58 KV-2-4169.
59 Ibid.
60 KV-2-4723 (3) p.88.
61 Special Branch report, KV-2-4169.
62 Philby, K, *My Silent War*, p.132.
63 Jeffrey, Keith, *MI6: The History of the Secret Intelligence Service 1909–1949*, p.709.
64 Philby, Rufina, *The Private Life of Kim Philby*, p.209.
65 Philby, K, *My Silent War*, p.139.
66 Philby, K, *My Silent War*, pp.143, 144.
67 MI5 file on Alexander Foote, KV-2-1613 (1), p.4.
68 MI5 file on Alexander Foote, MI5 interrogation report from Room 055, KV-2-1613 (1), p.17.
69 MI5 file on Alexander Foote, 22.9.1947, KV-2-1613 (1), p.6.
70 MI5 file on Alexander Foote, KV-2-1613 (1), p.13.
71 https://daily.jstor.org/the-spy-who-shared-my-foyer/
72 FO 1093549 (1).
73 Trevor-Roper, Hugh, *The Philby Affair*, p41.

Chapter 19
1 Shelden, M, *Graham Greene: The Man Within*, p.28.
2 Shelden M, p.31.
3 Shelden, M, pp.31, 33.
4 Greene, G, *Ways of Escape*, p.126.
5 Sherry, N, Vol 2, p.487.
6 Lewis, J, *Shades of Greene*, p.195.
7 Gerth, Mathew, *British McCarthyism: The Anti-Communist Politics of Lord Vansittart and Sir Waldron Smithers*, History: The Journal of the Historical Association.
8 KV 2/4169.

NOTES

9 KV-2-4169.
10 Sherry, N, Vol 2, p.239.
11 Greene, G, *Stage And Screen: The Cinema*, *The Spectator*, 3 January 1936, p.18.
12 Greene, R, p.175; Muggeridge, M, *Like It Was: The Diaries of Malcolm Muggeridge*, p.170–171.
13 Sherry, N, Vol 2, p.242.
14 Ibid.
15 Ibid.
16 Ibid.
17 Greene, G, Preface to *The Third Man* (the novella) 1949, p.7.
18 Sherry, N, Vol 2, pp.240, 242.
19 Greene, G. *Ways of Escape*, p.122.
20 Walston and Greene visited the Aran Islands after 28 September 1947, the date of the letter to Catherine, Sherry, Vol 2, p.242.
21 Drazin, C, *In Search of the Third Man*, p.4.
22 Drazin, C, *In Search of the Third Man*, p.45.
23 Montagu, Elizabeth, *Honourable Rebel: The Memoirs of Elizabeth Montagu*, pp.373–74. https://scholarlypublishingcollective.org/psup/austrian-american-history/article/4/1-2/1/273245/The-Spy-Story-Behind-The-Third-Man
24 https://www.archives.gov/publications/prologue/2002/spring/fritz-kolbe-1
25 Philby, K, *My Silent War*, p.86 (and in Jan 1944 had told the Russians about Ustinov's mission to contact Hitler opposition, Borovik, p.227).
26 Memorandum for the President from G. Edward Buxton, acting director, OSS, [Review of OSS intelligence operations in Switzerland], June 22, 1945, Folder 83, Box 18, Entry 99, RG 226, NACP.
27 Montagu, E, *Honourable Rebel: The Memoirs of Elizabeth Montagu*, p.411.
28 Philby, K, *My Silent War*, p.132.
29 Sherry, N, Vol 2, p.243.
30 Shelden, M, p.30. https://archives.kingscollections.org/index.php/codrington and Jean-Luc Fromenthal. Codrington Who's Who entry says that he was based on the Gold Coast from 1947 to 1958.
31 Stafford, David, *Spies Beneath Berlin*, p.16. https://www.militaryintelligencemuseum.org/smokey-joes
32 Lunn, Bernard, *Biography of Peter Lunn*. https://www.militaryintelligencemuseum.org/smokey-joes; Jeffrey, Keith, pp.670, 671.
33 Stafford, David, *Spies Beneath Berlin*, p.16.
34 Jeffrey, Keith, pp.670, 671.
35 https://botstiberbiaas.org/new-perspectives-on-the-spy-story-behind-the-third-man/
36 https://www.militaryintelligencemuseum.org/smokey-joes
37 Sherry, N, Vol 2, p.243.
38 Sherry, N, Vol 2, pp.243–44.
39 Greene, G, *The Third Man*, Vintage Classic, p.6.
40 Greene, G, *The Third Man*, p.11.
41 Greene, G, *A Sort of Life*, p.114.
42 Riegler, Thomas, 'The Spy Story Behind The Third Man', *Journal of Austrian-American History* (2020), Volume 4, Issue 1–2.
43 Sherry, N, Vol 2, p.244.
44 KV 2-4169.
45 KV 2-4169.

46 Montagu, Elizabeth, *Honourable Rebel,* pp.381–82.
47 Montagu, E, p.382.
48 Cloetta, Yvonne, *In Search of a Beginning – My Life With Graham Greene,* p.23.
49 Sherry, N, Vol 2, p.252.
50 Greene and Smolka had both worked at the Ministry of Information and had mutual friends including the communist Andrew Revai, who Greene remained close to after the war. KV-2-4169.
51 Garton Ash, Timothy, 'Orwell's List', *New York Review of Books,* 25.9.2003.
52 Ibid.
53 Walton, Calder, *Empire of Secrets,* p.198.
54 https://transdiffusion.org/2024/09/13/rebuilding-german-broadcasting/
55 An address given at Le Grand Conferences Catholiques in Brussels in January 1948. The translation is by Philip Stratford. Greene, Graham, The Pope, *Reflections,* p119 Penguin 1990.
56 Montagu, E, *Honourable Rebel,* p.382.
57 Sherry, N, Vol 2, p.245.
58 Greene, G, *Ways of Escape,* p.132.
59 Ibid.
60 Greene, G, *Ways of Escape,* p.133.
61 KV 2-4169.
62 Greene, G, *Ways of Escape,* pp.134, 135.
63 Greene, G, *The Third Man,* p.63.
64 Greene, G, *The Third Man,* pp.87, 88.
65 Greene, G, *The Third Man,* pp.77, 80.
66 Greene, G, *The Third Man,* p.76.
67 Greene, G, *The Third Man,* pp.86, 87.
68 Greene, G, *The Third Man,* Preface, p.5.
69 Greene, G, *The Third Man,* pp.16,17.

Chapter 20

1 Montagu, Elizabeth, *Honourable Rebel,* p.382.
2 Ibid.
3 Sherry, N, Vol 2, p.250.
4 Sherry, N, Vol 2, p.250.
5 Greene, G, *The Third Man,* p.86.
6 Greene, G, *Ways of Escape,* p.125.
7 Greene, G, *Ways of Escape,* pp.125–26.
8 Sherry, N, Vol 2, p.249.
9 Greene, G, *Ways of Escape,* p.126.
10 Greene, G, *Ways of Escape,* p.127.
11 Greene, G, *The Third Man,* p.64.
12 'Fake penicillin, *The Third Man,* and Operation Claptrap', BMJ 2016; 355 doi: https://doi.org/10.1136/bmj.i6494 (Published 13 December 2016).
13 KV-2-4170.
14 Montagu, E, *Honourable Rebel,* p.382.
15 Montagu, E, p.392.
16 Ibid.
17 Investigation into the Associates of Burgess and Maclean, 19.6.51, KV-2-4103(1), p.50.
18 CIA-RDP82-00457R002100040005-3.pdf and Richard Davenport-Hines.
19 Drazin, Charles, *In Search of the Third Man,* p.8.

20 Greene, R, *Russian Roulette*, p.195.
21 Aileen Furse's doctor, Dr Stephenson's (Stevenson) statement to MI5, Kv2-4737, p.20.
22 KV-2-4633, pp.158, 162.
23 KV-2-4730, p.7.
24 KV-2-4633, pp.158, 162. Dr Stephenson's interview with Arthur Martin naming Strauss KV-2-4736(1), p.21.
25 Sherry, N, Vol 2, p.253.
26 Sherry, N, Vol 2, p.254.
27 Greene, G, *The Third Man*, p.91.
28 Greene, G, *The Third Man*, p.95.

Chapter 21
1 Sherry, N, Vol 2, p.255.
2 Norman Sherry interview with Graham Greene, 25 April 1981; and Letter to Catherine Walston, 23 August 1948.
3 Drazin, C, p.134.
4 Washington Telegram no 2564, to Foreign Office. Guy Burgess and Donald Maclean: allegations that Kim Philby (PEACH) was the 'third man'. FCO 158–175, p.131, p.65.
5 'Evidence of penetration of British intelligence services as it could relate to the record of Mr H.A.R Philby.' KV-2-4724 (2), p.35.
6 KV-2-4735 1956, p.64 KV-2-4728 (2), p.38.
7 Macintyre, Ben, *A Spy Among Friends*, pp.116–17.
8 KV-2-4737, p.154.
9 Philby, K, *My Silent War*, p.145.
10 Drazin, C, p.131.
11 https://www.ukwhoswho.com/display/10.1093/ww/9780199540891.001.0001/ww-9780199540884-e-56416
12 Montagu, E, p.411.
13 Montagu, E, p.362.
14 Kim Philby interview with MI5 (Dick White), 23.6.1951, KV-2-4723 (1), p.73.
15 Modin, Yuri, *My Five Cambridge Friends*, pp.151, 231; Davenport-Hines, Richard, *Enemies Within*, pp. 376–7.
16 Philby, K, *My Silent War*, p.147.
17 Melman, Yossi, Raviv, Dan, *The Imperfect Spies*, p.82. https://api.parliament.uk/historic-hansard/lords/1955/nov/22/disappearance-of-burgess-and-maclean
18 KV-2-2263(1).
19 Philby minute, 9.4.46, KV-24674(2), pp.118–19.
20 KV-24723 (20), p.25–35; and Andrew Boyle, *Climate of Treason*. https://www.dailymail.co.uk/news/article-3223851/Unmasked-SIXTH-man-Cambridge-spy-ring-sent-nuclear-secrets-KGB-allowing-Russia-develop-atom-bomb.html
21 FO 1093 548 (1), p.36.
22 Rose, Kenneth, *Who Loses, Who Wins: The Journals of Kenneth Rose, Vol II 1979–2014*, Weidenfeld & Nicolson (2019).
23 Trevor-Roper, Hugh, *The Secret World, Behind the Curtain of British Intelligence in World War II and the Cold War*, Edited by Edward Harrison, p.157.
24 KV-2-4709 (1), pp.18–20. KV-2-4723 (2), p.34.

25 KV-2-4723 (3), p.29.
26 Andrew, C, Mitrokhin, V, *The Mitrokhin Archive*, p.202.
27 Venona_story.pdf
28 Modin, Yuri, *My Cambridge Friends*, pp.159, 161.
29 Wittkower said in early 1949 Kim Philby and 'friend' joined his ship at Cyprus on the way to Haifa and Philby and friend behaved very badly. KV2-4712, p.22.
30 'Burgess also stated that he was the illegitimate son of Lady Rothschild. Since the second claim was baseless and put down to Burgess's passion for boasting, people thought the other claim, which was true, should be treated in the same way. Sheltered for years behind his double bluff, he could speak with casual candor of why a person might turn to spying for the Comintern. "After all" he once said to me, as "an English Catholic in the days of Elizabeth I would certainly have seen nothing disgraceful in spying against the English in the interest of the Vatican."' Cockburn, Claud, *Britain's Spy Serial, New York Times*, 23.11.1979.
31 https://archivesearch.lib.cam.ac.uk/repositories/9/resources/1589
32 https://www.bmj.com/content/355/bmj.i6494
33 Williams, Warren Wellde, *British Policy and the Occupation of Austria, 1945–1955*, University of Wales, Swansea.
34 Andrew, C, *Defence of the Realm*, p.423.
35 Boyle, A, *The Climate of Treason*, p.289.
36 KV-2-3000 (1); Harrison, E, *The Young Philby*, p.24.
https://offscreen.com/view/the-trouble-with-harry-part-1
http://old.bfi.org.uk/sightandsound/feature/169
37 Drazin, C, p.146.
38 Allain, Marie-Francoise, pp.20, 21.
39 KV-2-2410(3), p.54; Sherry, N, Vol 2, pp.331, 253, 383.
40 KV-2-2410(3), p.54.
41 Sherry, N, Vol 2, p.253.
42 Allain, Marie-Francoise, pp.108, 109, 117.
43 Allain, Marie-Francoise, pp.20, 33.
44 Allain, Marie-Francoise, p.111.
45 Harrison, E, p.121.
46 Greene, G, *Ways of Escape*, p.298.
47 Allain, Marie-Francoise, p.23.
48 Sherry, N, Vol 2. Front epigraph.
49 Wright, Peter, *Spycatcher*, p.122. https://www.specialforcesroh.com/index.php?threads/martin-arthur-sydney.30672/
50 Greene said he had got the idea of Holly from the American poet Thomas Holley Chivers. Greene, G, *The Third Man*, p.4.
51 Greene, G, *The Virtue of Disloyalty*, Bodley Head (1972), Preparatory Note, p.1.
52 KV 2-4169.
53 KV-2-4170.
54 *The London Gazette*, 10 June 1944.
55 Pearce, Martin, *Spymaster: The Life of Britain's Most Decorated Cold War Spy and Head of MI6*, p.101.
56 Greene, Richard, *Graham Greene: A Life in Letters*, p.xxvi.
57 A CIA file concerning the Ukrainian affair released under the US FOIA concludes: 'All men were lost thanks to Soviet agent Kim Philby.' MykolaLebed_NAID139368008 p.286.

NOTES

Reports on Albanian Operations Fiend (US) and Valuable (UK) came to similar conclusions. Philby is identified as being responsible for betraying the mission when he was MI6 liaison officer in Washington. ShaqirKabashi_NAID139354976 p.176 and AhmetKabashi_NAID 139354870

58 Pearce, Martin, *Spymaster: The Life of Britain's Most Decorated Cold War Spy and Head of MI6*, p.101.
59 Sheehan, Edward (US Press Attache in Beirut) 15.2.64 'The Rise and Fall of a Soviet Agent', KV-2-4742 (1), p.4.
60 KV-2-4723 (2) p.74.
61 KV-2-4743 p.9.
62 Ibid.
63 Ibid.
64 KV-2-4743 p.25.
65 KV-2-4743 p.33.
66 KV-2-4735 p.90.
67 KV-2-4732 p.13.
68 KV-2-4732 p.12.
69 KV-2-4732 p.62.
70 KV-2-4732 p.31.
71 KV-2-4734 pp.45–50.
72 Ibid.
73 KV-2-4735 1956 p.86.
74 KV-2-4737 (1) p.32, Flora Solomon claimed the Russians told Philby to write pro-Arab articles. KV-2-4736 p.21.
75 Arthur Martin's interrogation of Harry Smolka 2.10.1962, KV-4736 pp.26–59.
76 KV-2-4169.
77 Ibid.
78 Ibid.
79 KV-2-4633, p.29.
80 Ibid.
81 Philby's confession statement to Nicholas Elliott, KV-2 4737, pp.164–71.
82 KV-2-4737(2) p.59.
83 KV-2-4736 p.7.
84 Questions to be put to Philby in Beirut, KV-2-4737, p.131.
85 Philby interview with MI5, 23.6.1951, KV-2-4723, pp.38, 39.
86 Philby's answers to questions put to him by Elliott in Beirut, January 1963, KV-2-4737, p.157.
87 KV-2-4737, p.149.
88 KV-2-4737, p.154.
89 KV-2-4737, p.154.
90 KV-2-4737, p.143.
91 KV-2-4737, p.106.
92 Shelden, Michael, p.35.
93 KV-2-4723 (1) p.38.
94 US FOIA 100-HQ-65643 Access request granted to the author in August 2025. Greene had also asked to see his FBI file in 1984 but complained that 16 pages of the 45 were redacted. Forty one years later (in 2025) the redaction amounts to just four pages. Greene, Graham, the *Spectator*, 7 April 1984.
95 Ibid.

96 Greene, Graham, *The Sunday Times*, 14 July 1963; Balliol College Archives & Manuscripts: The Cherry Record Collection of Josephine Reid's Papers and Books Relating to Graham Greene.
97 Ibid.
98 KV-2-4739(1) p.18.
99 44-page report authored by Jack Martin and David Lewis, US National Archives MartinLewisReport_NAID7564915
100 Grove Press won the right to publish in the US. *New York Times*, 30 January 1968.
101 US National Archives CIA report on Portland Spy Ring case C0206264 released on 2021/12/15.
102 Ellicott, Claire, *Daily Mail*, 30 December 2020.
103 US FOIA Case Number: F-2020-01404 Publication Date: September 1, 1968. Release date August 15, 2022. Philby, Rufina, *The Private Life of Kim Philby*, p.423.
104 *New York Times*, 30 January 1968.
105 West, Nigel. Talk given to the Graham Greene Birthplace Trust, 2004. Greene's personal contacts book has the address and telephone number for Laszlo Robert, the Hungarian communist writer who claimed Greene had conveyed the Philby manuscript from Budapest to London; Greene, Graham, *The Sunday Times*, 14 July 1963, Balliol College Archives & Manuscripts: The Cherry Record Collection of Josephine Reid's Papers and Books Relating to Graham Greene; Carlos Villar Flo, 'Graham Greene and the MI6: The Iberian Connection', Brno Studies in English Volume 47, No. 2, 2021.
106 Davies, Caroline, the *Guardian*, 30 December 2020.
107 Greene, R, *A Life in Letters*, pp.295–96, 298.
108 Cockburn, Claud, Britain's Spy Serial, *New York Times*, 23.11.1979.
109 Greene, G, Foreword to *My Silent War*.
110 Allain, Marie-Francoise, *The Other Man: Conversations with Graham Greene*, p.183.
111 Greene, R, *Graham Greene: A Life in Letters*, p.372. https://www.nytimes.com/1981/04/06/world/graham-greene-doubts-hollis-was-soviet-agent.html
112 Borovik, G, *The Philby Files*, p.219.
113 Borovik, G, p.368.
114 Borovik, G, p.139.
115 Slansky was a reference to the show trials in Czechoslovakia conducted by the CPC General Secretary Rudolf Slansky against communists who were suspected of working for the West. It was during the interrogation of one of the alleged communist double agents that Smolka was accused of being an American plant, leading to his arrest in February 1951.
116 Borovik, G, p.139.
117 Borovik, G, p.138.
118 Marie-Francoise Allain interview of Cloetta, Yvonne, pp.119, 144.
119 Graham Greene Papers, Burns Library, Boston College, *Observer* article, 18.2.68, Box 71, 23–25.
120 Greene, G, *The Spy, Collected Essays*, Vintage (1968), p.310.
121 Ibid.
122 Ibid.
123 Ibid.
124 Greene, R, *A Life in Letters*, p.151.
125 Davenport-Hines, Richard, *Enemies Within*, p.137.

NOTES

126 The Reform Club ballot papers for Guy Burgess and Anthony Blunt, 17.10.40 – accessed 15.8.2024.
127 Graham Greene Papers, Burns Library, Boston College, Box 71, Folders, 23–25.
128 Shelden, M, p.32.
129 Cloetta, Yvonne, p.144.
130 Greene, G, *The Human Factor*, p.163.
131 Kim Philby letter to sister Pat, 7.11.63, KV-2-4742 (2), p.41.
132 In 1951 Helena, who was recruited to MI6 by Philby, married Patrick Engelbach, who worked for British intelligence in Germany, KV-2-4724 (1), p.60; Investigations of Philby's three sisters ruled out Helena who was out of the country when the incriminating 'statement' was made at a party in Dec 1945. Diana and Patricia were still in the frame, 5.5.52, KV-2-4728, p.25.
133 Letter from Helena, 14.2.1964, KV-2-4742 (2), p.15.
134 Greene, R. *Russian Roulette*, pp.225, 225.
135 Philby, Rufina, p.157.
136 Graham Greene's letter to Kim Philby. 17.5.1978. Burns Library, Boston College, Box 71, Folders 23–25.
137 Ibid.
138 Greene, Richard, *Russian Roulette*, p.425 Burns Library, Boston College, Box 71, Folders 23–25.
139 Greene, Graham, *The Human Factor*, p.162.
140 Ibid.
141 Graham Greene Papers, Burns Library, Boston College, Box 71, 23–25.
142 Kim Philby letter to Graham Greene, Graham Greene Papers, Georgetown University Library.
143 https://www.santantonio.org/en/content/tredicina-thirteen-day-novena
144 Greene, G, 'The Soupsweet Land', *Vintage Greene*, p.344.
145 Philby, Rufina, p.177.
146 Ibid.
147 Graham Greene Papers, Burns Library, Boston College, Box 71, 23–25, p.36.
148 https://www.nytimes.com/1981/04/06/world/graham-greene-doubts-hollis-was-soviet-agent.html
149 Greene, G, *A World of My Own*, p.23.
150 Greene, G, *A World of My Own*, p.17.

Epilogue
1 Borovik, G, p.371; Philby, Rufina, p.173.
2 Philby, Rufina, p.173. Cloetta, Yvonne, p.133.
3 Ibid.
4 Ibid.
5 Philby, Rufina, p.175.
6 Philby, Rufina, p.176.
7 https://www.theguardian.com/world/2011/mar/31/spy-kim-philby-disillusioned-communism
8 Greene, G, The Spy's Role, *Collected Essays*
9 Cloetta, Yvonne and Allain, Marie-Francoise, *In Search of a Beginning*, p.118.
10 Greene letter to Anthony Mockler 1988, Balliol College Archives & Manuscripts: The Cherry Record Collection of Josephine Reid's Papers and Books Relating to Graham Greene.
11 Greene, R, *Graham Greene: A Life in Letters*, p.xxvi.
12 Allain, Marie-Francoise, *The Other Man*, p.35.

13 Hugh Carleton Greene set up the emergency information services during the Malayan Emergency in the 1950s.
14 Greene, G, *The Quiet American*, p.172.
15 The Graham Greene Papers, Burns Library, Boston College, Box 71, Folders 23–25, p.34.
16 Balliol College Archives & Manuscripts: The Cherry Record Collection of Josephine Reid's Papers and Books Relating to Graham Greene.
17 The Graham Greene Papers, Burns Library, Boston College, Box 72, Folders 1–6, p.70.
18 Greene letter to Sherry, 11 March 1991.
19 Ibid.
20 Ibid.
21 Greene, R, *A Life in Letters*, p.420.
22 Ibid.
23 Sherry, Norman, Vol 3, p.752.
24 Burns Library, Boston College, Box 13, Folders, 31–35, p.49.
25 The Graham Greene Papers, Burns Library, Boston College, 25.3.91, Box 72, Folders 1–6, p.74.
26 Cloetta, Yvonne, pp.120,121.
27 Ibid. Rosenbaum, Ron, *The New York Times Magazine*, July 10, 1994.
28 Ibid. Yvonne Cloetta says Sherry tried to gain access to see Greene's bedroom after he died but was denied.

Appendix
1 The term 'Cambridge Five' began to be used in 1961 when KGB defector Anatoliy Golitsyn named Maclean and Burgess as part of a 'Ring of Five'. He also said Harry Smolka was part of the group.
2 Jeffrey, Keith, *MI6: The History of the Secret Intelligence Service 1909–1949*, Bloomsbury (2010).
3 https://www.theguardian.com/global/2010/sep/21/historian-explored-mi6-secrets
4 Sheehan, Edward (US Press Attaché in Beirut) 15.2.64, 'The Rise and Fall of a Soviet Agent' KV-2-4742 (1), p.4.
5 Andrew Boyle letter to Graham Greene. The Graham Greene Papers, Burns Library, Boston College, Box 12, Folder 44.
6 The Graham Greene Papers, Burns Library, Boston College, Box 13, Folders 31–35 and Box 18, Folder 30.
7 https://www.dailymail.co.uk/news/article-3223851/Unmasked-SIXTH-man-Cambridge-spy-ring-sent-nuclear-secrets-KGB-allowing-Russia-develop-atom-bomb.html
8 KV-2-4723 (2), pp.25–35; https://www.washingtonpost.com/archive/politics/1979/11/21/ex-spy-admits-an-appalling-mistake/76f3d053-9279-4719-97c9-8c1ce2a29db2/
9 The Graham Greene Papers, Burns Library, Boston College, Box 64, Folder 54.
10 The Graham Greene Papers, Burns Library, Boston College, Box 71, Folders 33–35.
11 Greene correspondence with Cairncross, 22.1.91, The Graham Greene Papers, Burns Library, Boston College, Box 13, Folders 31–35.
12 Coletta, Yvonne, p.119. https://www.rivierareporter.com/profiles-of-residents/194-colonel-ronald-challoner-obe-honorary-consul-in-nice
13 The Graham Greene Papers, Burns Library, Boston College, Box 13, Folders 31–35.

Index

Abwehr 67, 103, 107–8, 113, 116, 118, 153, 156, 158, 164
Afghanistan 305
Albania 282
Allain, Marie-Francoise 187, 276–77, 295
Allain, Yves 187
Andrew, Christopher 133
Angleton, James Jesus 106, 270, 275
Anglo-German fellowship 43
Anglo-Soviet Friendship Society 269
Anthony, St 304
Archer, Jane 211, 214–16, 229, 230
Arnold-Baker, Charles xvii
Arnold-Forster, Christopher 209–10, 216, 221, 228
Ashley-Jones, Constance 285, 286
Astbury, Peter 316
Athenaeum Club, London 73
Attlee, Clement 201
Auden, W.H 276
Austria 50, 241–42
Austrian circle, formation of 24
Authors' Club, London 191, 193
Avila, Armando Borges De 117–18
Azores xii, 167–75

Bagot, Milicent 127–28, 129, 205, 229, 230
Balliol College, Oxford University 5–6, 25–26
Barclay, Sir Colville 214, 215
Battle of the Atlantic 114
Beauclerk, Charles 258
Beaulieu Abbey, SOE training camp 64, 66
Benton, Kenneth 153

Berkhamsted School 1, 2–5, 79
Berlin 29, 163–64
Berlin, Isaiah 74
Bernstorff, Albrecht von 25–26, 29
Bevin, Ernest 228
Birch, Frank 62
Bissau 91
Blake, George 283
Bland, Sir Neville 216
Bletchley Park 62, 104, 111, 116, 132
Blunt, Anthony 15, 23–24, 41, 50, 61, 67, 68, 109–10, 188, 207, 213, 244, 271, 304–5, 315–16
  and Avila arrest 117
  exposure 74
  and Greene 219–20
  kills Kessler report 110
  and Kusnecoff 147, 188–89
  MI5 investigation 133
  and Philby 284–85
  Reform Club membership 71–72, 73, 74, 300
Borovik, Genrikh 18, 296–97
Boulogne 61
Bowen, Elizabeth 300
Bowen, Marjorie, *The Viper of Milan* 3–4
Bowlby, Captain Cuthbert 'Curly' 76
Boyle, Andrew 188, 315–16
Bracken, Brendan 208
Brandes, Hans 158, 159, 166
Bremen Eins Marine Organisation 169
Brezhnev, Leonid 293
Brickendonbury Manor 64
Bristow, Desmond 68, 111–13, 140
British Communist 28

Brodie, Patrick Ian 92–94, 96, 96–98, 98, 101, 116, 117–18
  and Avila arrest
  Greene's betrayal of 120–24, 186–87, 188, 277
Brodie family 74–75
Bromley, Tom 225
Brooke, Gerald 292–93
Brooman-White, Richard 68, 129–30, 233–34, 268, 284
Browder, Earl 205
Brown, Peter 134–35
Brussels 251
Buchan, John 2
Budapest 302–3
Budberg, Moura 30, 269, 280
Burgess, Guy 15, 28, 39–40, 40–41, 63, 64, 67, 68, 109, 248, 267, 293–96
  confession 272
  defection 64, 282–83, 285
  Istanbul defection attempt 271–72
  MI5 investigation 133
  Reform Club membership 71–72, 73, 74, 300
  relationship with Anthony Eden 285–86
  sexuality 73
  and Smolka 208
Burn, Micky 248

Cairncross, John 15, 41, 143–44, 218–19, 313, 316, 317
Cambridge Five, the 15, 24, 28
  numbering system 314–17
Cambridge University 13

357

INDEX

Cambridge University Socialist Society 13
Campbell, Sir Ronald 169–70
Canaris, Admiral Wilhelm xvii–xviii, 164–65, 166, 233, 244
Cárdenas, Lázaro 52–53
Carter, Lionel 4–5, 54
Cavalcanti, Alberto 81, 137
Cecil, Robert 316
Challoner, Ronnie 317
Chodorov, Jerome 243
Christie, Agatha 22–23
Churchill, Winston 133, 174, 200, 208, 221, 238
CIA 270, 271
Cloetta, Yvonne 309
Cockburn, Claud 26–27, 28, 272
Codrington, Lt Colonel John 103, 124, 245
Cold War, the 239, 241, 266, 292
Comintern 27, 28, 49, 229
Communist Party of Austria (KPÖ) 16–17
Communist Party of Germany 27
Communist Party of Great Britain 20, 21, 37, 38, 45, 68, 129
Convoy SL (Sierra Leone) 125 125–26
Cookridge, E.H. 16
Coward, Noel 138
Cowgill, Felix 80–81, 91, 104–5, 112, 120, 141, 142–43, 204, 209, 210, 211, 212
Curry, John 204–5
Czechoslovakia 238, 293, 297

Daily Express 238
Daily Telegraph 29, 75
Daily Worker 266
Dalton, Hugh 73
Dansey, Claude 33–34, 78, 237
D-Day xi, 113, 191
de Salis, Charles 150, 154, 158–59, 167, 170, 214
Denham Film Studios 33
Dennys, Elisabeth (nee Greene) 76, 115, 138, 220–21, 310
Dennys, Rodney 213–14, 220–21, 221, 228, 232, 272, 278, 282, 305, 310
Deutsch, Arnold 20–24, 36–39, 41–42, 49–50, 206, 207, 236, 316

Deutsch, Josephine 21
Deutsch, Oscar 23
Dobb, Maurice 13, 14, 19–20
Doble, France 47
Dollfuss, Engelbert 16–17, 18
Dos Santos, Manuel Mesquita 115–17, 118, 152
Double Cross campaign xi
Double Cross Committee 72, 112–13, 149, 155, 163, 216

Eagle, HMS 169
Eden, Anthony 285–86
Egge, Mr and Mrs Gerhadt 68–69
Eliot, T.S. 85–86
Elliott, Nicholas 13, 33, 90–91, 143, 159, 188, 237, 267, 268
  Philby's confession 36–37, 39, 40–41, 49, 288–90
Estonia 30–31
Eyre and Spottiswoode 58, 191–92, 193

FBI 205, 206, 291
Fidrmuc, Paul Georg 162–63, 197
The First and the Last (film) 32
First World War 1–2
Foley, Frank 79–80, 134, 154, 157, 158, 160
Foote, Alexander Allan, defection 235–36
Forster, E.M. 72, 74, 300
France 55, 59–61
Franco, Francisco 44, 45, 65, 67, 124–25
Franks, Dickie 305
Freetown 83–84, 114, 115, 136
  accommodation 88–89
  Avila arrest 117–18
  brothels 91
  corruption 89
  counter-espionage breakthrough 115–19
  Dos Santos arrest 115–17
  German agents 85
  Greene's intelligence role 88
  importance 84–85, 86
  security situation 89, 94–96, 100–101, 121, 126
French Guinea 84, 88

Freud, Sigmund 20
Friedmann, Karl 14
Friends of India Society 22
Fuchs, Klaus 299
Fulford, Roger 127, 129
Furse, Aileen 61–62, 65, 142, 190, 227, 267

Gaitskell, Hugh 16–17
Gallacher, Willie 45
Garbo (Juan Pujol García) 111–13, 153, 155, 160
Garrison, Jim 292
Gedye, Eric 16–17
General Election, 1945 200–201
General Strike 29
Germany, Nazi 14, 50–51, 72
Germany, Weimar 25–27
Gibbs, Reggie 100–101, 116, 120, 185
Gibraltar 103, 124
Gisevius, Hans Bernd 243–44
Glading, Percy 42, 47–48
Glenalmond House, St Albans 102, 104, 106, 111, 137
Glover, Dorothy 54, 56, 137, 142, 191, 192, 199
Goetz, Ben 161
Golitsyn, Antoliy 288
Gollancz, Victor 92
Gordievsky, Oleg 208
Gorsky, Anatoly 59–61, 65, 131, 132
Gort, Lord 60
Gouzenko, Igor, defection 225–27
Great Depression, the 21
Greene, Ben 4, 29
Greene, Charles 1–2, 3
Greene, Graham 84–85, 147–48
  affair with Catherine Walston 199, 218, 249, 312
  affair with Dorothy Glover 54, 56, 137, 142, 191
  and Americans 106–7, 184
  analysis of childhood 11
  animus towards MI5 185
  appointment to Portuguese desk 136–37
  attitude to field agents 172–73
  and Avila arrest 118

358

INDEX

Azores spy ring operation 167–75
as bad husband 199–200
becomes novelist 8–9
betrayal of Brodie 120–24, 186–87, 188, 277
betrayal of Smolka 260, 278
biographers 311
bipolar depression 99, 261–62
birth 1
Blitz experience 56–58
break from USSR 201 in Budapest 302–3
Catholicism 8, 52–53, 218, 249
characters 277–78
Communist Party membership cancelled 28
comparison with Philby 138–41
contact with Philby in exile 302–4
contracted film plots 161–62, 194–95
creative process 31–32
death 313
debt to Philby 299–300
defence of Philby 293–96
desire to contribute to war effort 75–77
diabetes diagnosis 79
disenchantment 194
and Dos Santos arrest 116
on espionage 187
Estonia visit 30–31
exposure to Nazism 29
at Eyre and Spottiswoode 192, 193
family background 1–2, 9
family links to espionage 34–35
fascination for prostitutes 91
FBI file 291
film projects 238–39
financial situation 140–41
first book published 8
first dabbling in espionage 26–27
first dead body 57
first encounters Leslie 30–31
first great betrayal 4–5, 10–11
haemorrhage 265

infatuation for Gwen Howell 6
interest in women's rights 3–4
interest in writing sparked 3
introduced to Carol Reed 239
and Jebsen case 158, 159–62, 185
joins Communist Party 28
joins ILP 29
journalism 8
and Korda 32–34, 237, 238–39, 241
and Kusnecoff operation 145, 148, 148–49, 150–52, 188–89
last days 311–15
last year of the war 193–94
later spy work 237
left-wing views xviii
loyalty 185–89, 300
loyalty to Philby 185–86, 188, 189, 275–76, 295, 296, 298–99, 310, 312–13, 316
marriage strains 54
marriage to Vivien Dayrell-Browning 8
meetings with Smolka 248–51, 256–57
meets Cairncross 143–44
meets Philby 77–78
mental illness 4
MI6 recruitment xii, 76–79
MOI post 55–56
and Moldenhauer 156–57
Moscow meetings with Philby 307–8
My Silent War foreword xiii–xiv, 293–94, 299, 300
and Operation Torch 126
passion for secrecy 309
pathological fears 3
on Philby xiii–xiv, 189
Philby in dreams 305–6
Philby on 80, 173
and Philby's anti-peace intrigue 165
PID service xv, 189–90
poetry 8
political awakening 25–26
politics 276–77

post war contacts with Cambridge spies 218–21
psychoanalysis 261–62
pursuit of conflict 172
Reform Club membership 70–71, 73–74, 193
relationship with Philby 190–91, 221, 254–55, 299–301, 308–9
reputation 137–38
resignation from MI6 xi–xviii, 186, 221
return from Sierra Leona 136–37
return to civilian life 189–93
and Revai 128
Russian roulette incident 6–8
second great betrayal 11
and Selznick's complaints 262–63
senior education 2–5
sex drive 249
Sierra Leone posting 31–32, 78–79, 80, 83–96, 99–101, 114–24, 126, 186–87, 189, 312
silence 317
Soviet codename 142
spy training 79, 79–80
status as author 9–10
suicide threats 218
Sunday Times article 291
suspicion of Philby xvi–xviii
The Third Man earnings 243
The Third Man travel diversion 251–53
trip to Mexico 52–54
university education 5–6, 25–26
upbringing 1
values 187
in Vienna xviii–xix, 242–43, 245–51, 256–59
visit to Weimar Germany 25–27
visits Berlin 29
visits to Moscow 237, 297
voyage to Freetown 81, 82–83
Wee Willie Winkie defamation case 53–54
Wright interviews 290
on writer's obligation to the state 300

INDEX

Greene, Graham (works)
  A Sort of Life 4, 6–8
  Babbling April 8
  'The Basement Room' 239
  Brighton Rock 9, 52, 137, 138, 161
  The Confidential Agent 54, 55
  The End of the Affair 192
  England Made Me 143
  Gun for Sale 32, 137
  The Heart of the Matter 10, 89, 95, 96, 100, 120, 123, 162, 198, 200, 218, 240, 264, 299–300
  The Human Factor xvi, 58, 73, 175, 301, 303, 310–11
  Journey Without Maps 31–32, 52, 78
  The Lawless Roads 53
  The Lieutenant Died Last 81
  The Man Within 8, 9
  Men at Work 56
  The Ministry of Fear 57, 83
  Nineteen Stories 239
  No Man's Land 277
  Nobody to Blame 194–95
  Our Man in Havana 31, 73–74, 162, 195–97
  The Power and the Glory 9, 53, 54, 55, 58, 75, 81, 138, 143, 161
  The Quiet American 237, 310
  A Spy's Beside Book 15
  Stamboul Train 8–9, 32, 137
  The Tenth Man 197–98
  The Third Man 10, 72, 240–41, 253–55
  Ways of Escape 175
  see also *The Third Man* (film)
Greene, Graham C 303
Greene, Herbert, 1–2, 9, 34–35, 76, 78, 127
Greene, Hugh 9, 29, 75–76, 115, 190, 250, 310
Greene, Raymond 4, 9, 76, 310
Greene, Tooter 25–27
Greene, Vivien (nee Dayrell-Browning) 8, 56, 199, 218
Greene, Sir William Graham 34, 76–77
Greeneland 53
Grimm, Hans 169, 170, 170–71

Guest, David 39–40
GUGB 130–31
Gwyer, John 107–8

Haggard, H. Rider 2
Haigh-Wood, Maurice 85–86, 89, 93–94, 100–101, 120
Hamburg 27
Harker, Oswald 'Jasper' 22
Harris, Tomás 'Tommy' 67–68, 112, 262, 284, 285
Hart, Herbert 105–6, 117, 118, 173, 212
Hastings, Max 70
Hay, Philip 271
Heinemann 9
Hess, Rudolf 154
Hitler, Adolf 25, 72, 75, 162, 164, 165, 166
Hoare, Samuel 124–25
Hollis, Roger 71, 127, 132, 133–34, 205, 225, 226, 229, 233–34, 235, 279, 286–87, 296, 313, 317
Hooper, Bill 147, 148
Hornik, Leopold 128
Horthy, Miklós 32
Howell, Gwen 6
The Human Factor (Greene) xvi
Hungary, Soviet Republic 32

Independent Labour Party (ILP) 29
Information Research Department (IRD) 250
International Revolutionary Marxist Centre 29
Inter-Services Liaison Department 76
Isherwood, Christopher 276, 290–91
Istanbul 223, 224, 231–33, 234, 236, 245, 266, 267, 271–72

Japanese intelligence 34–35, 148–49, 149
Jebsen, Johannes-Nielsen 153–62, 163, 185
Jelf, Sir Arthur 86–87
Jerrold, Douglas 192, 193
John, Otto 165–66
Joint Committee for Spanish Relief 35

Kell, Major General Vernon 51
Kennedy, John F, assassination 292
Kerensky, Alexander 43
Kessler, Eric 71, 110

Kolbe, Fritz 243–44
Kollek, Teddy 18, 270
Korab, Clark 107
Korda, Alexander 32–34, 78, 237–39, 241, 241–43, 245, 247, 259–60, 262–63, 269, 281
Krivitsky, Walter 69, 127, 147, 215, 271
Krotenschield, Boris 202–4, 204, 222, 227
Krotkov, Yuri, defection 236
Kuala Lumpur 10–11
Kulekundis, Elias 151
Kusnecoff, Vladimir 96–98, 98, 100, 145–52, 188–89

Lagos 85–86, 88
Le Carre, John 295
Leigh, Vivienne 32
Leslie, Peter 30–31
Liberia 78
Liddell, Cecil 103
Liddell, Guy 19–20, 66, 68, 71, 104, 210, 212–13, 215–16, 217, 226
Lipton, Marcus 286
Lisbon 102–3, 111–12, 113, 147–50, 152, 155, 158, 162, 167, 169, 172
Livinov, Maxim 134
London 140–41
  Athenaeum Club 73
  Authors' Club 191, 193
  the Blitz 56–58
  Broadway Buildings 105, 109–10
  Oratory Central Schools 128
  Reform Club 70–75, 193, 300
  Section V return to 141
  wartime underbelly 57
  Windmill Theatre 57
London Continental News 41, 129, 233–34
London Film Company 33–34
London Film Productions 239, 243
Long, Leo 196, 316
Loxley, Peter 216
Lunn, Peter 245–46, 248, 281, 288

McCarthy, Joseph 238
MacGibbon, James 293
MacGibbon & Kee 293
Maclean, Donald 13, 15, 39–40, 40–41, 109, 271
  defection 64, 282–83, 285
Macmillan, Harold 283, 315

INDEX

Madrid 153, 156
Magnificent Five, the 41
Majewicz, Johann 169
Malaya emergency 10–11
Malta 125
Maly, Teodor 15–16, 42–44, 48, 144, 205, 316
Mann, Wilfrid 271, 316
Marsden-Smedley, Basil 63
Marsden-Smedley, Hester 62–63
Martin, Arthur S 279, 287, 288, 296
Martyn, Dr John 87
Masterman, John 72, 155, 158
Mathews, Paul 171, 175
May, Allan Nunn 226, 299
Menzies, Stuart 104, 165, 209–11, 212, 221, 223–24, 225, 227, 231
Mexico 52–54
Meyer, Michael 296
MGM 161–62, 194–95
MI5 xii, 51, 67–68, 68
  aftermath of Philby's defection 290–91
  amalgamation with MI6 plan 212–13, 216–17
  breakthrough in Philby case 288
  Cockburn files 28
  Dos Santos arrest 115–17
  evidence against Philby 283
  F Division 127, 212
  Greene's animus towards 185
  and Kusnecoff 145–51, 148
  on Lizy Philby 18
  and Moldenhauer 156–57
  mole hunt 127–35
  and *Our Man in Havana* 197
  penetration investigations 266–72
  Philby investigation 233–34
  Philby visits and contacts 105–6
  responsibilities xii
  and Sierra Leone 85, 89
  on Smolka 22
  Smolka enquiries 230–31
  tensions with MI6 86, 171–72, 173, 187, 207
MI6 68
  amalgamation with MI5 plan 212–13, 216–17

and Avila arrest 117–18
Azores spy ring operation 167–75
Greene's resignation from xi–xviii, 186, 221
intelligence successes 114
on Suschitzky 19
penetration investigations 266–72
penetration of USSR 221–22
recruits Greene 76–79
responsibilities xii
Section IX 203, 204–5, 209–12, 212, 213–16, 221–22
Section V 102, 136, 137, 139, 141
Section VD 140
and Sierra Leone 85
tensions with MI5 86, 171–72, 173, 187, 207
Venlo calamity 77
Vienna activity 245–46
Mid-Atlantic Gap 168
Milmo, Helenus 65, 283, 289
Milne, Anthony 214
Milne, Ian 'Tim' xii–xiii, xiv, 13, 68, 102–3, 142–43, 160, 175, 206–7, 214, 228
Minimax Fire Extinguisher Company 79
Ministry of Information (MOI) 55–56, 208
Mockler, Anthony 311
Modin, Yuri 272, 296–97, 302
Modrzchinskaya, Yelena 130–31, 204
Moldenhauer, Heinz 154–55, 155–57, 161
Molotov–Ribbentrop Pact 50–51
Montagu, Elizabeth 243–44, 245, 247, 249, 256, 259, 259–60, 268–70
Morrison, Herbert 66
Moscow
  Greene and Philby meetings 307–8
  Greene's visits 237, 297
Mossad 270
Muggeridge, Malcolm 30, 55–56, 57, 118, 172, 173, 240, 275, 295
My Silent War (Philby) 36, 139, 164, 267–68, 279, 292–95
  foreword xiii–xiv, 293–94, 299, 300

Naryan, R.K. 192
National Archives 109, 139, 158, 224, 276, 280–81, 291
Naval Intelligence 34
Neu Freie Presse 21, 22
New York Times 286
Night and Day 30, 53–54
NKVD 38, 130, 131, 204, 208
North Atlantic Treaty Organisation (NATO) 252
Nottingham Journal 8

Odd Man Out (film) 239
Office of Strategic Services (OSS) 106–7, 184, 206, 209, 233, 243, 244, 269, 275, 278, 291
Officer Training Corps (OTC) 3
Official History of British Intelligence in the Second World War 113
OGPU 20–21, 38
Oka, Orata 34–35
Oldfield, Maurice 232–33, 235, 270, 282, 298
Olivier, Laurence 32
Omerti, Arturo 170–71
Ondaatje, Michael 220
Operation Valuable 282
Oratory Central Schools, London 128
Organisation for Aid to Revolutionaries 14
Organisation Z 33–34
Orient Express (film) 8
Orlov, Alexander 40–41, 45–46
  defection 47, 48–49, 205–6
Orwell, George 56, 201, 249–50
Osten, Ulrich von der 46–47
Oswald, Lee Harvey 292
Oxford University, Balliol College 5–6, 25–26

Pakenham, Desmond 191, 194, 272
Paris 28, 60
Parklaan, SS 97–98, 145–46
Pateman, Fred 39–40
Peake, Mervyn 192
Pearce, Martin 282
Pearn, Pollinger & Higham 261
Pearson, Norman 106
Percival, Hugh 260

INDEX

Peter, Gabor 15
Petrie, David 86, 93–94, 100–101, 117–18, 119–20, 120, 122, 212, 216
Petrukhov, Alexei 286–87
Philby, Harry St John 14–15, 39, 65–67, 68–69, 213
Philby, Helena 138, 207, 301–2
Philby, Josephine 50, 65
Philby, Kim 163
  achievements 227–29
  affair with Constance Ashley-Jones 285, 286
  affair with Esther Whitfield 267
  aftermath of defection 290–91
  ambition to serve the communist cause 44
  American early warning system 206
  and Americans 106, 184
  anointed as a trusted man 69
  anti-peace intrigue xvii–xviii, 164–66, 244
  application to British intelligence 61, 62
  Athenaeum Club membership 73
  attempt to return 298
  attitude to field agents 172–73
  and Avila arrest 117, 118
  Azores spy ring operation 167–75
  birth 14
  and Blunt 284–85
  on Brodie 122
  Burgess and Maclean defection manuscript 285–86
  as "C" 299
  at Cambridge 13–14
  charm xii, xvii
  childhood 15
  and Cockburn 28
  codename 37
  communist ideals 18, 276
  comparison with Greene 138–41
  confession, 11.1.1963 36–37, 39, 40–41, 49, 288–90
  death 308
  defection 290
  denunciation of communism xviii
  divorce 227
  dominance over Soviet affairs 222
  and Dos Santos arrest 115–16
  drawn into the Kremlin's orbit 18
  dubbed the Third Man 315, 316–17
  education 15
  European tour 14
  exile in Russia 301–6, 307–8, 309, 310–11, 316
  fall of France 59–61
  family background 14–15
  father's arrest 65–67
  fear of exposure 227
  first child 50, 65
  Franco assassination plan 64
  Freetown counter-espionage breakthrough 115–19
  gives Russians D-Day plans xvi
  and Gouzenko's defection 225–27
  on Greene 80, 173
  Greene on xiii–xiv, 189
  Greene's debt to 299–300
  Greene's defence of 293–96
  in Greene's dreams 305–6
  Greene's loyalty to 185–86, 188, 189, 275–76, 295, 296, 298–99, 310, 312–13, 316
  Greene's post war contact 220–21
  and Greene's resignation from MI6 xii–xiii, xv–xvi
  and Greene's Sierra Leone posting 85, 88, 90–92, 114, 115
  and *The Human Factor* 310–11
  insinuation stratagem 16
  introduced to Deutsch 36–38
  investigation closing in on 278–79
  investigations 269–72
  Istanbul defection attempt 272
  Istanbul posting 231–33, 234, 236, 245, 267
  and Jebsen case 154, 159
  joins Anglo-German fellowship 43
  joins Cambridge University Socialist Society 13
  and Krotenschield 202–4, 204
  and Kusnecoff 147–48, 148–49
  lack of qualms 110
  left-wing views xviii
  likeness to Harry Lime 274–76
  Lipton names as third man 286
  Lizy's vetting 206–7
  Macmillan's exoneration of 283, 315
  maiden mission 39
  marriage to Lizy 18
  meets Flora Solomon 43
  meets Greene 77–78
  mental health 286, 288
  MI5 breakthrough 288
  MI5 evidence against 283
  MI5 investigation 127–30, 129–30, 132–33, 133–35, 233–34
  and MI6 penetration of USSR 221
  MI6 vetting 63–64
  Milmo interrogation 283, 289
  and Moldenhauer 156
  Moscow meetings with Greene 307–8
  Moscow's reassessment of loyalty 202–4
  My Silent War xiii–xiv, 36, 139, 164, 267–68, 279, 292–95, 299, 300
  names potential traitor candidates 39–41
  Nazi Germany visit 14
  OBE 217, 281
  Oldfield's suspicions 282
  and Operation Torch 124, 125, 126
  Order of the Red Banner 227
  and Orlov's defection 48–49
  penetration of the American secret services 206
  potential as a Soviet spy recognised 16
  promoted to head of Section IX 209–12
  and Pujol 112–13
  radical instincts 13
  recruitment to the Russian intelligence service 36–39

INDEX

Red Cross of Military
  Merit award 45
relationship with Aileen
  Furse 61–62, 65, 142,
  190, 227
relationship with Greene
  190–91, 221, 254–55,
  299–301, 308–9
relationship with MI5
  105–6, 209
relationship with Orlov
  45–46
reports to Soviet handlers
  142–43
reputation 138
return to Britain, 1934
  18–19, 23
on rise 227–28
schooling in spycraft 39
Section IX appointments
  213–16
Section V return to
  London 141
on significance of *The
  Third Man* (film) 304
SIS recruits 67–69
and Smolka 41–42,
  110–11, 129–30,
  207–9, 230–31,
  233–34, 297
Soviet distrust of
  130–32
Spanish Civil War 43–47
split loyalties 189
subversion of MI5/MI6
  amalgamation plan
  212–13, 217
Sunday Times article on
  291
supplies list of Catholics
  and democrats to
  Soviets 163–64
surveillance operation
  283–87
Suschitzky's portrait of
  23–24
suspicions of 228, 230
taxi 284
on *The Third Man* 317
on time with Lizy 18
treble agent conspiracy
  theory 280, 302, 313,
  317
VD section appointment
  80–81
and the Vermehrens
  163–64
in Vienna, 1933 12–18
Vivian interviews 132
Vivian's concerns about
  134–35
and Volkov affair
  223–25, 226

war service 102–13
Washington posting
  267–68
and Weltzein 152
Philby, Lizy (nee Kohlmann)
  14–16, 18–19, 36–37, 59,
  68–69, 206–7, 214, 227,
  238
Philby, Rufina 307–8,
  308
Pieck, Wilhelm 229–30
Pincher, Chapman 296
Pinney, Major-General Sir
  Reginald John 63
Playfair, Edward 72
Pohlmann, Lambrecht 103
Political Intelligence
  Department (PID) xv,
  189–90
Political Warfare Executive
  (PWE) xv
Popov, Dušan 'Duško 153,
  185
Portugal 102–3, 107–8,
  119, 136–37, 147–52, 167,
  174
Pound, Ezra 106
Powell, Anthony 240
Prae Wood House, St Albans
  102
Prague 251–52, 252–53
Priestley, J.B. 9, 138
Prince of Wales, HMS 82
Pritchett, V.S. 300
*The Private Life of Henry
  VIII* (film) 32
Proctor, Dennis 72
Pujol García, Juan (Garbo)
  111–13, 153, 155, 160
purple primers 167–68

Quanza, SS 115, 116

Rado, Alexander 232, 235
Read, Herbert 70
Reed, Carol 239, 254, 257,
  262–63, 265
Reed, John 223, 225,
  278–79
Rees, Goronwy 72, 286
Reform Club, London
  70–75, 193, 300
Reif, Ignatz 37–38, 41, 42,
  48
Repulse, HMS 82
Revai, Andrew 128, 220
Ribbentrop, Joachim von
  46
Richelieu (French battleship)
  88, 91
Rimington, Stella 15
Robert, Laszlo 302–3
Roberts, Douglas 232

Robertson, Thomas Argyle
  100, 103–4, 107–8,
  145–49, 158, 159, 160
Robinson, Henri 61
Rome 252
Rote Kapelle (Red
  Orchestra) 61
Rothschild, Victor 43, 61,
  68, 97–98, 106, 145–46,
  153, 214, 287–88
Russell, George 'AE' 11
Russell, Leonard 175
Russi, Felix 143
*Russia 1918, Anniversary of
  Red Army* (film) 208
Russian Civil War 21

St Albans xii
  Glenalmond House 102,
    104, 106, 111, 137
  Prae Wood House 102
Salazar, António de Oliveira
  67, 119, 152, 168, 169–70,
  174
Saunders, Amanda 313
Schreiber, Aloys 154–55,
  163
Schroeder, Erich 174
Scott-James, Rolfe Arnold
  70
SD (the Sicherheitsdienst)
  157
Second World War 11
  attack on Pearl Harbor
    47, 82
  the Azores 167–75
  Battle of the Atlantic
    114
  the Blitz 56–58, 74
  D-Day xi, 113, 191
  declaration of war 55, 59
  Double Cross pro-
    gramme xi, 72
  fall of France 59–61
  first weeks 55–56
  German invasion of
    Poland 55
  German occupation of
    Austria 50
  last year 193–94
  Operation Barbarossa 72
  Operation Fortitude 72,
    155
  Operation Overlord xi
  Operation Torch
    123–26, 132
  Philby's service 102–13
  Third Washington
    Conference 168
  U-boat threat 125–26,
    168
VE Day 222
V-weapons 191, 192–93

INDEX

Seghers, Anna 192
Selznick, David 262–63, 265
Senegal 88
Shelden, Michael xvi, 311
Sherry, Norman xv, xvi, 80, 115, 139, 165, 311–15
Sierra Leone xii, 31–32, 78–79, 80, 84–85
  apartheid rule 87–88
  breakdown of relations with Smith 90
  corruption 93
  German agents 85
  Greene's intelligence role 88
  Greene's posting 78–79, 83–96, 99–101, 114–24, 126, 186–87, 189, 312
  operation proposals 91–92
Sinclair, General John 231
Sissmore, Kathleen 'Jane' 127–28
Smith, Sidney 88, 89, 90, 93–94, 114
Smolka, Harry xix, 16–17, 64, 69, 258–61, 280
  background 21–22
  and Burgess 208
  contacts 128
  death 297
  defection operation 280–81
  establishes self in Britain 22–23
  Greene's betrayal of 260, 278
  and Greene's travel diversion 252
  interrogation 287
  loyalties 208–9
  meetings with Greene 248–51, 256–57
  MI5 investigation 128
  OBE 281
  Orwell on 250
  and Philby 41–42, 110–11, 207–9, 230–31, 233–34, 297
  Reform Club membership 71
  return to Britain 22
  The Third Man contract 260
  The Third Man
    contribution 248–51, 256–57, 258–61, 280
  Vansittart's support for 238
  wife 190
Smolka, Lotte 23, 190

Solomon, Flora 43, 262, 288
Spain 102, 107–8, 108–9
Spanish Civil War 35, 43–47, 67, 112, 235
Spectator 32, 75, 239, 286
Spender, Stephen 276
Spiro, Edward (later E.H. Cookridge) 16
Stalin, Joseph xvi, 16, 38, 46, 48–50, 51, 53, 201, 236, 238, 251, 254
Stauffenberg, Claus von 165–66
Stephens, Lt Col Robin 108, 116, 118
Stephenson, William 226
Stevens, Wilfred Leslie 39–40
Stevenson, Sir Hubert 117–18
Stevenson, Robert Louis 9, 138
Stewart, Sir Findlater 216
Stopford, Richman 148, 148–49, 150–52, 172, 173
Stott, Denis 39–40
Straight, Michael 219–20, 316
Strauss, Eric 261–62
Suez Crisis 286–87
Sun Studios 23
Sunday Telegraph 188
Sunday Times 174, 175, 291, 295
Suschitzky, Edith 18–19, 19–20, 23–24, 37, 128
Syers, Kenneth 134

Temple, Doris 115
Temple, Shirley 53–54, 262
Thatcher, Margaret 293
The Fallen Idol (film) 239
The Third Man (film)
  xviii–xix, 34, 198
  American financing 265
  cast 258
  central characters 253
  climax 263–64
  coded messaging 272–74, 279
  drafts 272–74
  Ferris wheel scene 255, 257, 276
  final cut 254
  genesis 240–41
  Greene offers idea to Korda 241
  Greene's earnings 243
  Greene's travel diversion 251–53

Greene's visit to Vienna 242–43, 245–51, 256–59
Harry Lime 251, 254–55, 256–57, 258, 263–64, 274–76, 277–78, 279, 314
  impact 314–15
  inspiration 240
  locations 257
  and MI6 activity 246
  names 273–74, 279
  origins 239
  penicillin plot line 258–61, 278
  Philby on 317
  plotting 257–58
  reception 265–66
  release 265, 267, 268, 269–70, 299–300
  Selznick's complaints 262–63
  significance 304
  Smolka's contribution 248–51, 256–57, 258–61, 280
  Vienna location 241–43
  as warning 279–80
The Times 8, 18, 22, 29, 43–45, 60, 68, 73, 234, 248, 249–50, 258, 295
Tokaev, Gregori 236, 266, 271
Trevor-Roper, Hugh xvi, 165, 165–66, 228
Trevor-Wilson, Geoffrey 143
Tudor-Hart, Alex 19, 20, 23
Turnbull, Peter 123
21 Days (film) 32

Ukraine 282
Ultra messages 157–58, 159, 160, 167–68
USSR
  break from 201
  German invasion of 72
  Great Terror 48–50
  intelligence 109–10
  interests aligned with Britain 109–10
  MI6 penetration 221–22
  Molotov–Ribbentrop Pact 50–51
  paranoia 65

Valentine, Vivian 62
Valli, Alida 249
Vansittart, Sir Robert 33, 238
VE Day 222
Venlo debacle 33–34, 216

INDEX

Venona programme 271, 272
Vermehren, Erich 157–58, 159, 163–64, 164, 232–33, 284
Vermehren, Petra 160–61, 163–64
Versailles, Treaty of 25
Verschoyle, Derek 75
Vienna xviii–xix, 241–43
    Allied occupation 242
    Central Cemetery 246
    communist evacuation 16–17
    Greene in 242–43, 245–51, 256–59
    Hotel Sacher 245, 247–48
    MI6 activity 245–46
    Philby in, 1933 14
    sewers 12, 248, 257, 263–64
    tensions 247
Vienna Circle 25–27, 28, 36–39
Vivian, Valentine 66, 68–69, 78, 86–87, 132, 134–35, 209, 210, 214–15
Volkov, Konstantin 222–25, 226, 266, 270

Wall Street Crash, 1929 13
Walston, Catherine 199, 218, 219–20, 240, 249, 261, 312, 315–16
Walston, Harry 276
Washington DC 267–68
Watson, Alister 71
Waugh, Evelyn 6, 138, 301
Wee Willie Winkie (film) 53–54
Weltzein, Kuno 152
Went the Day Well (film) 81
Wheeler, Augustus (Watson) 5, 10–11, 54
White, Dick 170–71, 271
Whitfield, Esther 267
Wilson, Edward 123
Wilson, Ian 154, 157, 157–58, 159, 160, 162
Wilson, Peter 68
Wormald, Francis 73–74
Wright, Peter 74, 290

Young, Courtenay 188–89

Robert Verkaik is a historian and award-winning journalist. He was the home affairs editor of the *Independent* and the security editor of the *Mail on Sunday*. He is the author of *Defiant: The Untold Story of the Battle of Britain*, *The Traitor of Colditz* (a *Sunday Times* bestseller) and *The Traitor of Arnhem*. He is a non-practising barrister and lives in Surrey.